the RISING STARS of MANGA™
United Kingdom and Ireland

Vol. 2

HAMBURG // LONDON // LOS ANGELES // TOKYO

Design and Layout - James Lee and Lucas Rivera
Cover Design - Christopher Tjalsma

Editor - Hope Donovan
Digital Imaging Manager - Chris Buford
Pre-Production Supervisor - Erika Terriquez
Art Director - Anne Marie Horne
Production Manager - Elisabeth Brizzi
Managing Editor - Vy Nguyen
VP of Production - Ron Klamert
Editor-in-Chief - Rob Tokar
Publisher - Mike Kiley
President and C.O.O. - John Parker
C.E.O. and Chief Creative Officer - Stuart Levy

A ☯ TOKYOPOP® Manga

TOKYOPOP and ☯ are trademarks or registered trademarks of TOKYOPOP Inc.

TOKYOPOP Inc.
5900 Wilshire Blvd. Suite 2000
Los Angeles, CA 90036

E-mail: info@TOKYOPOP.com
Come visit us online at www.TOKYOPOP.com

ISBN: 978-1-4278-0191-3

First TOKYOPOP printing: April 2007
10 9 8 7 6 5 4 3 2 1
Printed in the USA

the
RISING STARS of
manga
United Kingdom and Ireland

:TABLE OF CONTENTS

Welcome to the second *Rising Stars of Manga: United Kingdom and Ireland*!

One year ago, the very first *Rising Stars* anthology composed entirely of the work of artists and writers from the UK and Ireland came into being. We are pleased to be able to bring you a second installment of UK & Ireland *Rising Stars*, and continue a beloved tradition.

This year saw an unusual number of entries concerned with rather serious subject matter. It is apparent in reading such entries as "Knives" that events in the world today are bleeding into our creative endeavors. This is a very good sign for the medium—manga has the tools to tackle sobering topics. Fear, anxiety and apprehension weave the fabric of our lives, but when we can address these issues in story, we gain a little sense of control, order and peace.

But while it's clear that manga simply isn't child's entertainment, some of these entries are pretty funny. Entries like "Redeemon" and "Experiment 1817295#7205" have got a few belly laughs tucked inside. Even the more traditional stories like the riveting potboiler "Poison," the dark fantasy "Beyond," the dramatic "Promise Me" or the sci-fi tale "The Homecoming" contrast dark, chaotic worlds with moments of bright humor. And then there's "Happily Ever After," which may seem to be typically light-hearted shojo, but has got its own serious twist.

These manga-ka make it look easy. Manga creation is a long road, at the end of which may be no reward other than the journey. Congratulations to all the aspiring manga-ka who dedicated themselves to creating manga for this contest, because it would not be possible without your efforts and the belief that you have something to contribute. Thank you, and keep drawing!

—*Hope Donovan*
Editor

the **RISING STARS** of
manga
United Kingdom and Ireland

When I was 15 years old, I had the chance to become an exchange student to Japan. It changed my life. I had been a lifelong comic fan and hoped to one day become a cartoonist, but the time I spent there opened up possibilities, techniques and horizons I never could have imagined. The manga titles I discovered back then shaped so much of how I look at storytelling, and in a very large way, how I look at the world itself. I wanted to tell stories...and I wanted to believe it was possible to tell those kinds of stories, in that kind of way...even if I did not happen to have been born in Japan. Why not?

I want to thank TOKYOPOP, not only for the opportunity they gave me to present my characters and story to the world, but also for the honor of keeping those horizons expanding and helping introduce the next arriving class of storytellers!

—*Wes Abbott*
Rising Stars of Manga 2: "Dogby Walks Alone"
Creator of Original Manga series
Dogby Walks Alone

ABOUT THE INDEPENDENT JUDGE:

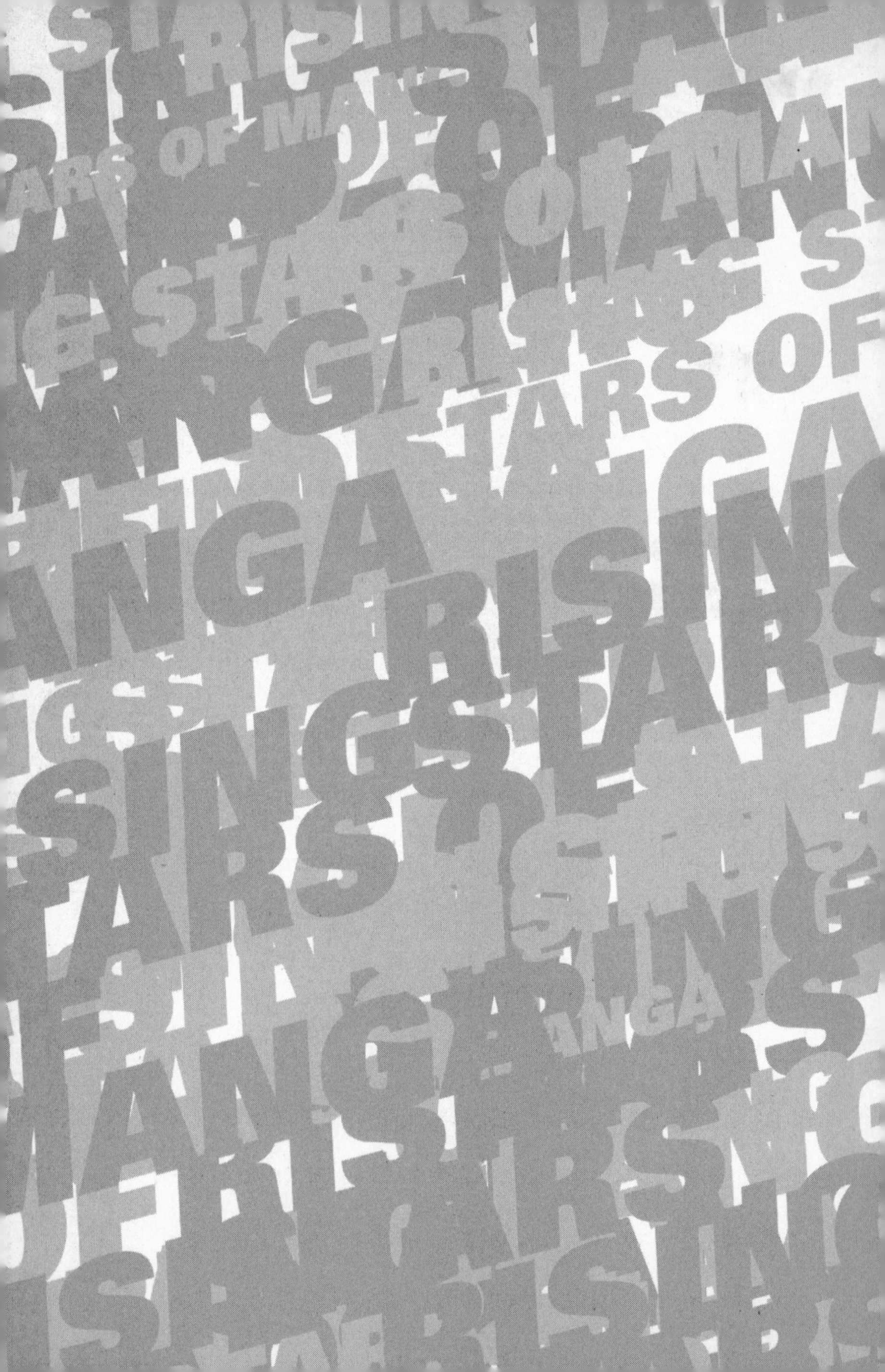
STARS OF

::

KNIVES :: Grand Prize Winner ::

John Aggs was born in 1984 in West Sussex, England. He studied illustration at University College Falmouth and currently works as an illustrator from his home near Brighton.
http://www.johnaggs.co.uk

Favorite manga:
Battlefield

Favorite manga artists:
Reiji Matsumoto, Katsuhiro Otomo

Author's Comments:
"Knives" is a short story about three kids playing marbles in the street, brought on by a sudden and overwhelming urge to draw someone in a newsboy cap.
—John Aggs

::

KNIVES

GRAND PRIZE WINNER

KNIVES
GRAND PRIZE WINNER

::

KNIVES :: Grand Prize Winner ::

....

Judge's Comments:
It was in reading "Knives" that I realized why the UK and Ireland edition of the *Rising Stars of Manga* contest is so valuable. As diverse and far-reaching as some of the entries in the American edition of *Rising Stars* have been, I've never seen an entry with "Knives'" particular subject matter in that contest, and I don't expect I ever will. Unfortunately, to go any further into the subject of "Knives" would damage your enjoyment of John Aggs' excellent manga, and as our Grand Prize Winner, there's a lot here to enjoy.

"Knives" struck me as an obvious choice for this year's Grand Prize for a variety of reasons. It's a well-structured, well-paced story that manages to pack quite a lot into its 16 pages without coming across as too dense or muddled. Artistically, it's top notch. One glance at the first two pages and it becomes clear that "Knives" is in a class by itself in this year's contest. The level of detail in the backgrounds and the dramatic use of perspective is unparalleled, and it effectively draws you into the story from the get go. Slightly less effective, but not inappropriate, is the retro look given to the characters. At times, it reminded us of the work of Katsuhiro Otomo, but to an audience weaned on *Naruto* and *Fruits Basket*, I'd imagine it could come off as unappealing—an effect that will surely be amplified by "Knives'" undeniably Western panel layouts.

"Knives" is an entry that begs to be read more than once, and I think my appreciation of it has only grown the more that I've read it. Rough spots and all, it's still a stellar short comic on all fronts, one that I believe will be a seminal entry in this contest.
—*Tim Beedle*

Judge's Comments:
"Knives" is one of those few *Rising Stars* entries that stands alone as a work of consequence, regardless of the bright future awaiting its creator. It's hard not to be caught up, and the judges were immediately stunned.

What strikes me most is that Aggs is telling someone else's story. This isn't a rehash of something Aggs experienced, nor an extension of who he wants to be or adventures he wants to have. Instead, "Knives" reminds us that the purpose of storytelling is to remember as well as whisk away in fantasy, to teach as well as entertain. To see a Rising Star entrust such valuable lessons to manga, well, it makes me darn proud of him and the genre.

Extremely talented when it comes to finishes and orchestrating scenes, we felt the backgrounds alone qualified this entry a place in the book. Aggs' weakest point is actually the characters. He doesn't have mastery over rotating his faces, and often views other than straight-on come off as warped. It is the backgrounds that take center stage, realistically rendered and often dramatic in their own right.
—*Hope Donovan*

::

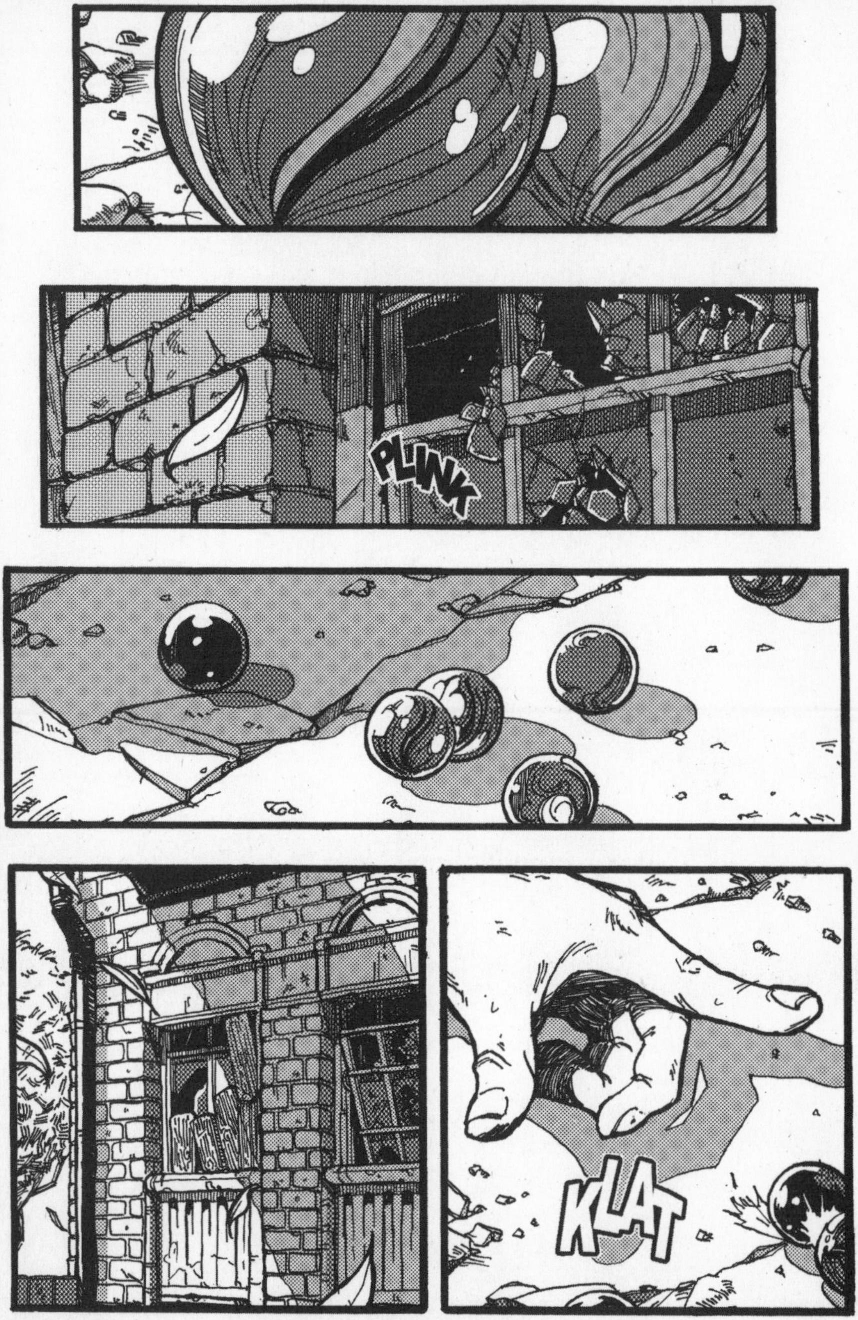
PLINK
KLAT

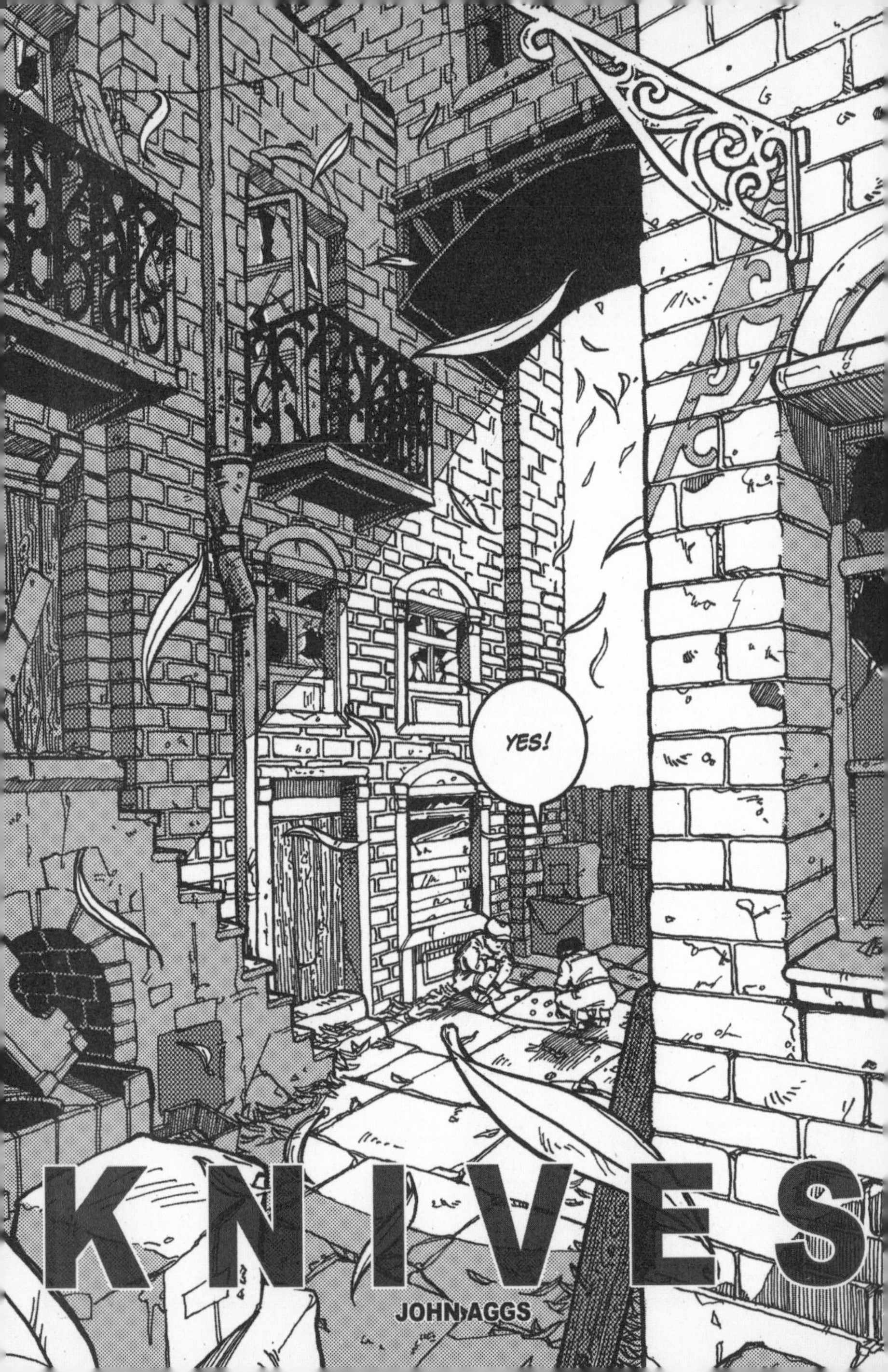
YES!

KNIVES

JOHN AGGS

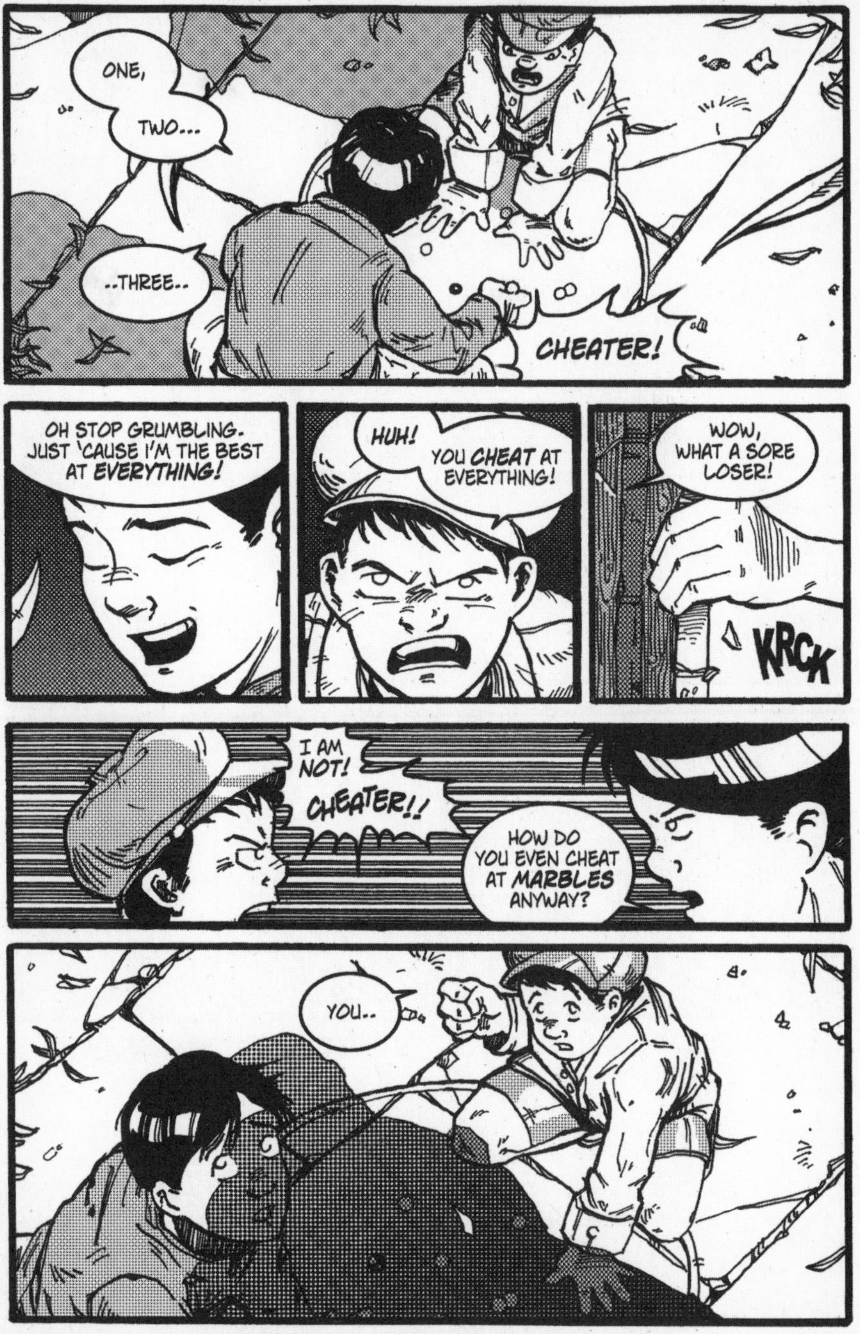
ONE,
TWO...
..THREE..
CHEATER!
OH STOP GRUMBLING. JUST 'CAUSE I'M THE BEST AT EVERYTHING!
HUH!
YOU CHEAT AT EVERYTHING!
WOW, WHAT A SORE LOSER!
KRCK
I AM NOT!
CHEATER!!
HOW DO YOU EVEN CHEAT AT MARBLES ANYWAY?
YOU..

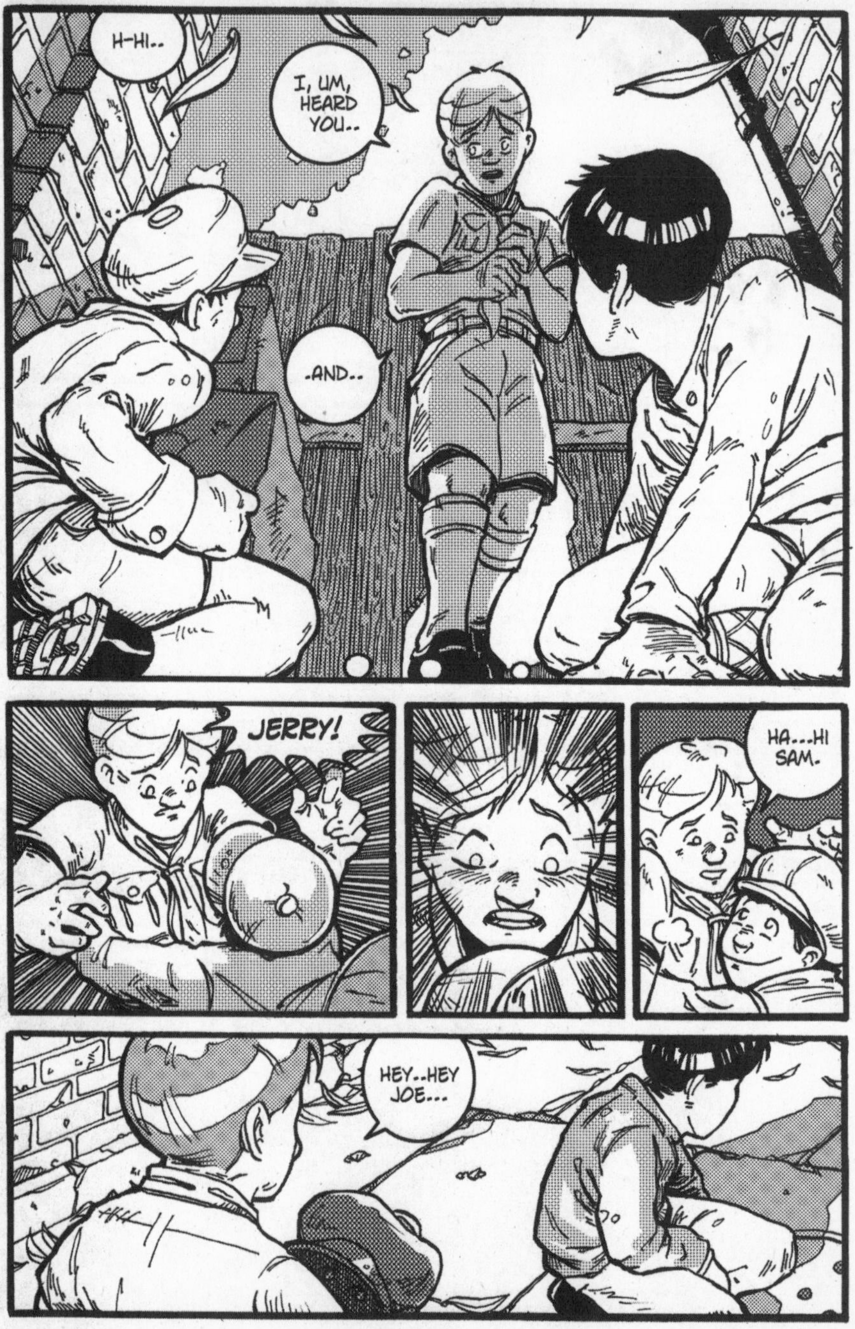
H-HI..
I, UM, HEARD YOU..
.AND..
JERRY!
HA...HI SAM.
HEY..HEY JOE...

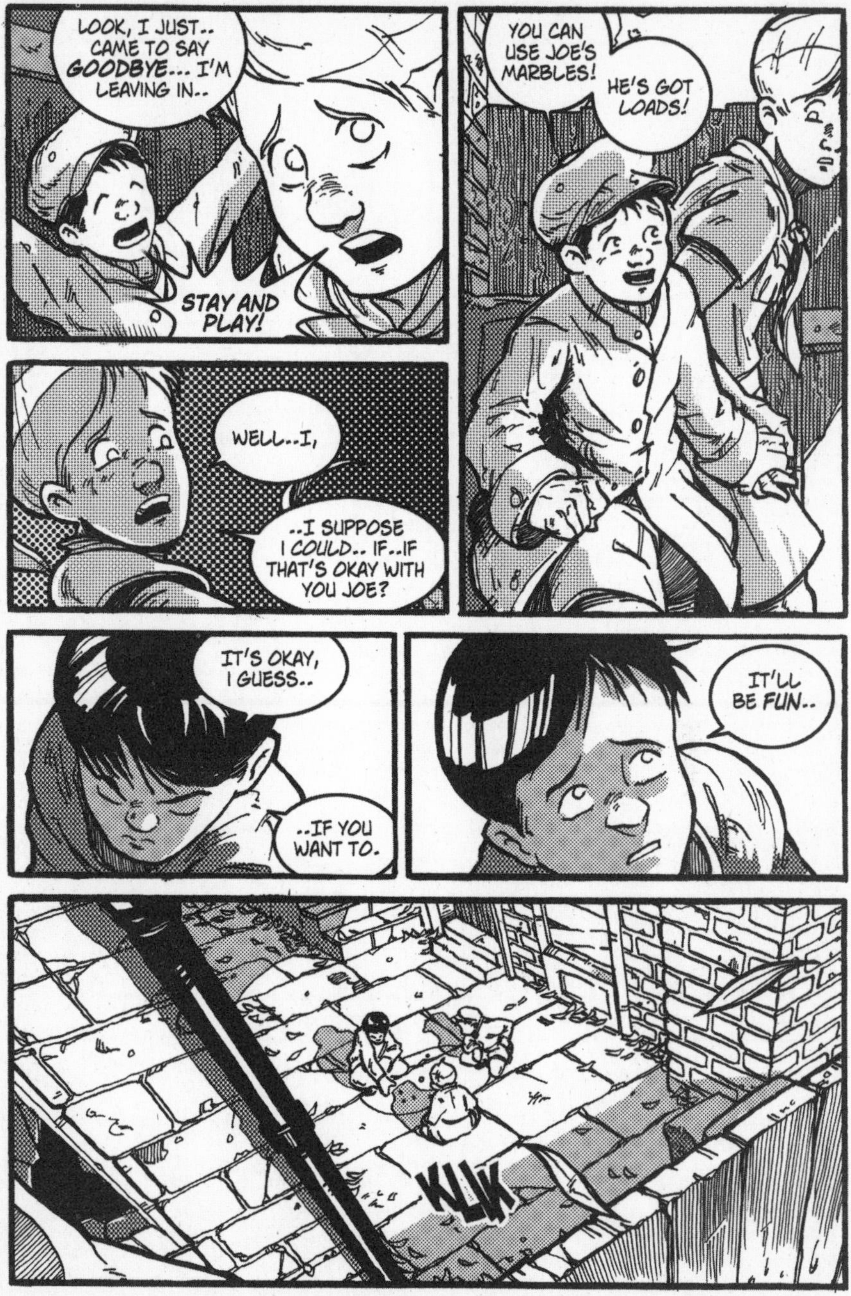
LOOK, I JUST.. CAME TO SAY GOODBYE... I'M LEAVING IN..
STAY AND PLAY!
YOU CAN USE JOE'S MARBLES!
HE'S GOT LOADS!
WELL..I,
..I SUPPOSE I COULD.. IF..IF THAT'S OKAY WITH YOU JOE?
IT'S OKAY, I GUESS..
..IF YOU WANT TO.
IT'LL BE FUN..
KLIK

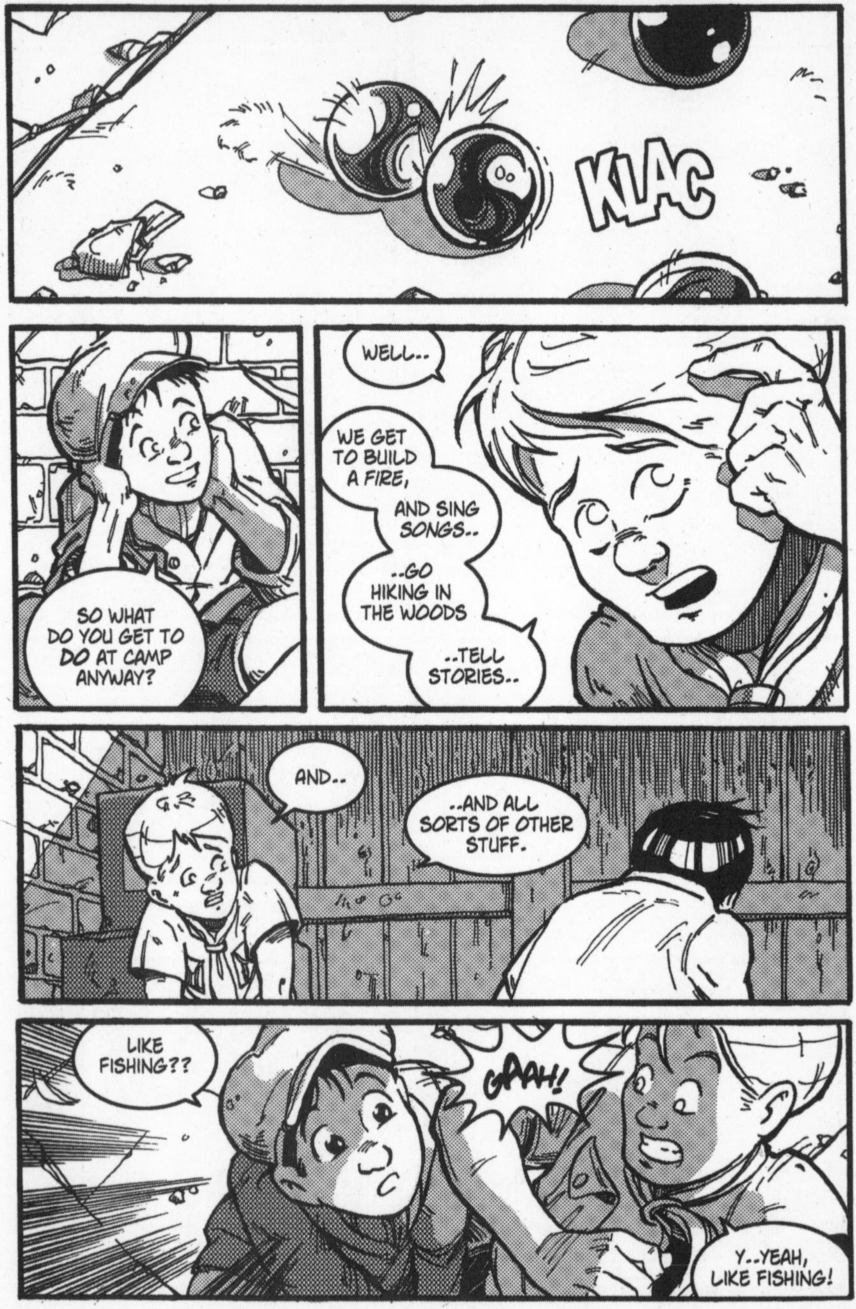
KLAC
SO WHAT DO YOU GET TO DO AT CAMP ANYWAY?
WELL..
WE GET TO BUILD A FIRE,
AND SING SONGS..
..GO HIKING IN THE WOODS
..TELL STORIES..
AND..
..AND ALL SORTS OF OTHER STUFF.
LIKE FISHING??
GRAAH!
Y..YEAH, LIKE FISHING!

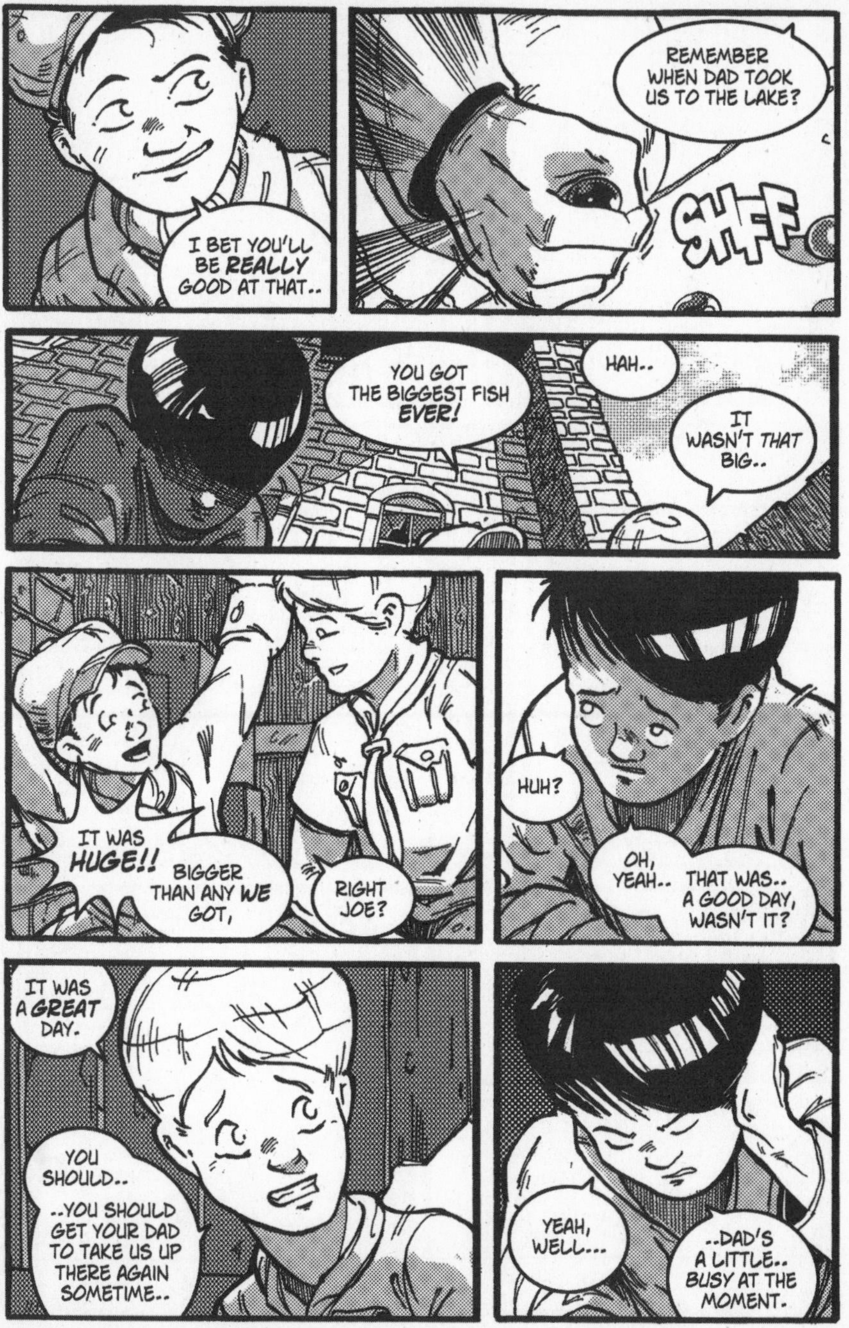
I BET YOU'LL BE **REALLY** GOOD AT THAT..
REMEMBER WHEN DAD TOOK US TO THE LAKE?
SHFF
YOU GOT THE BIGGEST FISH **EVER!**
HAH..
IT WASN'T THAT BIG..
IT WAS **HUGE!!**
BIGGER THAN ANY **WE** GOT,
RIGHT JOE?
HUH?
OH, YEAH..
THAT WAS.. A GOOD DAY, WASN'T IT?
IT WAS A **GREAT** DAY.
YOU SHOULD..
..YOU SHOULD GET YOUR DAD TO TAKE US UP THERE AGAIN SOMETIME..
YEAH, WELL...
..DAD'S A LITTLE.. BUSY AT THE MOMENT.

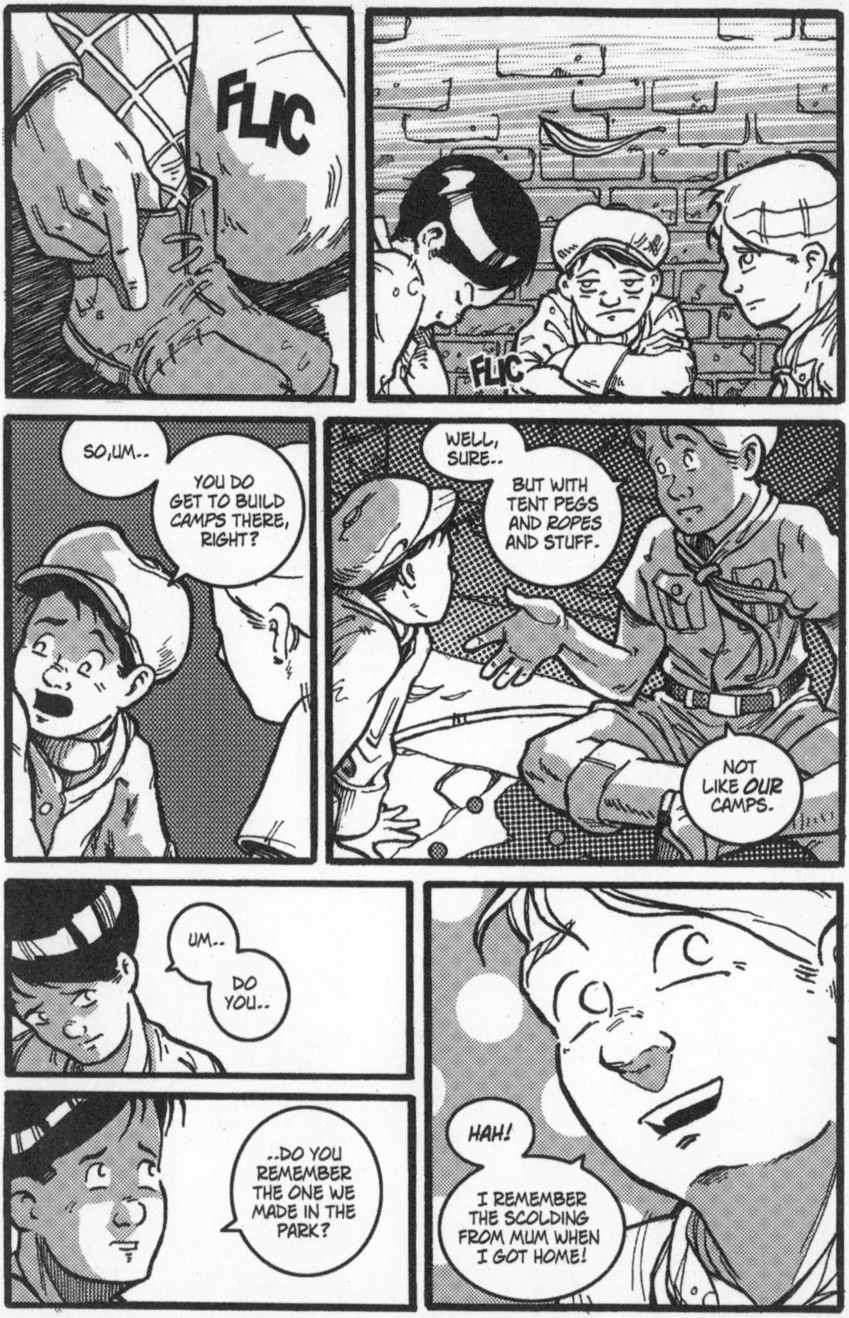
FLIC
FLIC
SO,UM..
YOU DO GET TO BUILD CAMPS THERE, RIGHT?
WELL, SURE..
BUT WITH TENT PEGS AND ROPES AND STUFF.
NOT LIKE OUR CAMPS.
UM..
DO YOU..
..DO YOU REMEMBER THE ONE WE MADE IN THE PARK?
HAH!
I REMEMBER THE SCOLDING FROM MUM WHEN I GOT HOME!

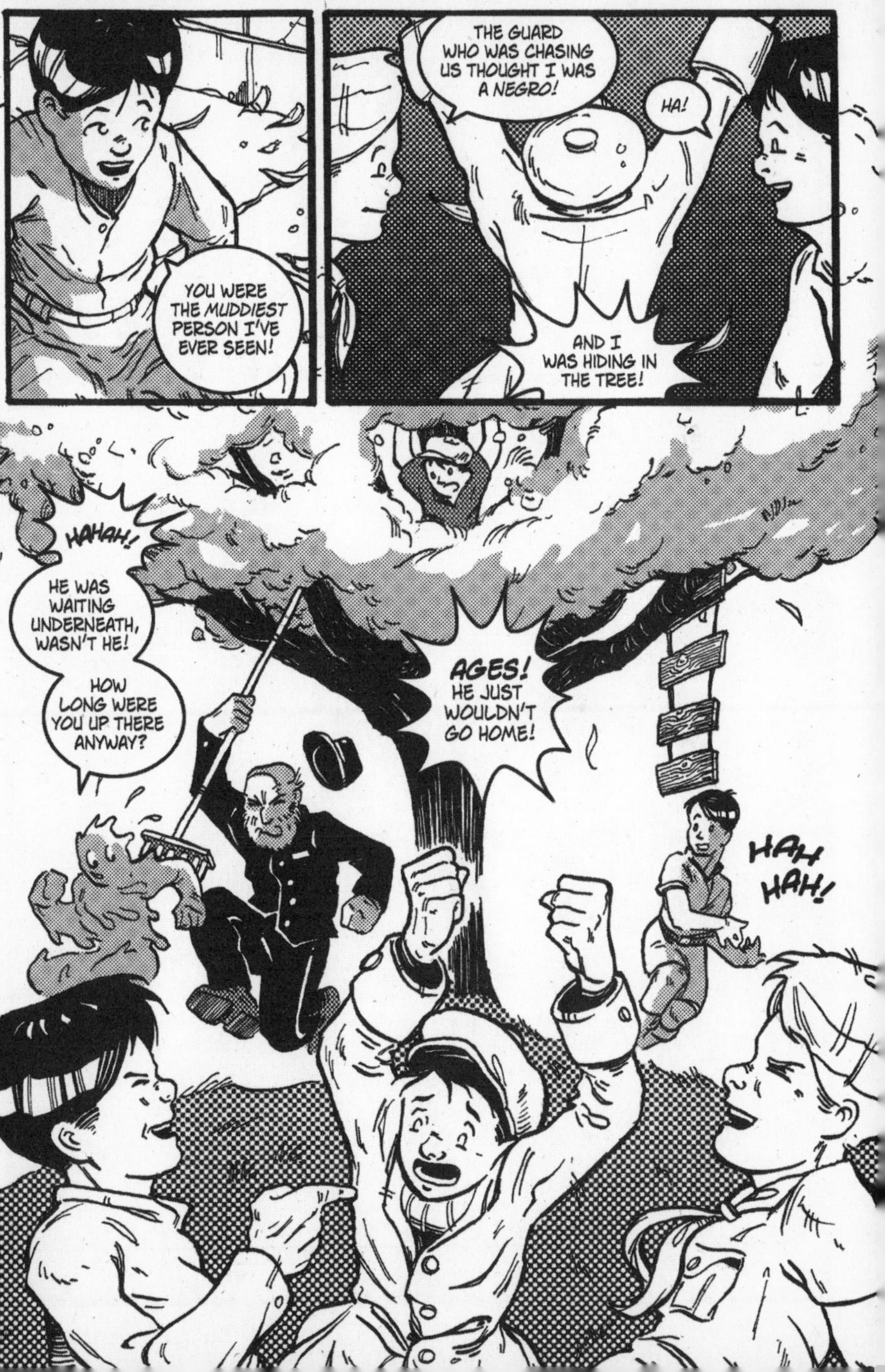
YOU WERE THE MUDDIEST PERSON I'VE EVER SEEN!
THE GUARD WHO WAS CHASING US THOUGHT I WAS A NEGRO!
HA!
AND I WAS HIDING IN THE TREE!
HAHAH!
HE WAS WAITING UNDERNEATH, WASN'T HE!
HOW LONG WERE YOU UP THERE ANYWAY?
AGES! HE JUST WOULDN'T GO HOME!
HAH HAH!

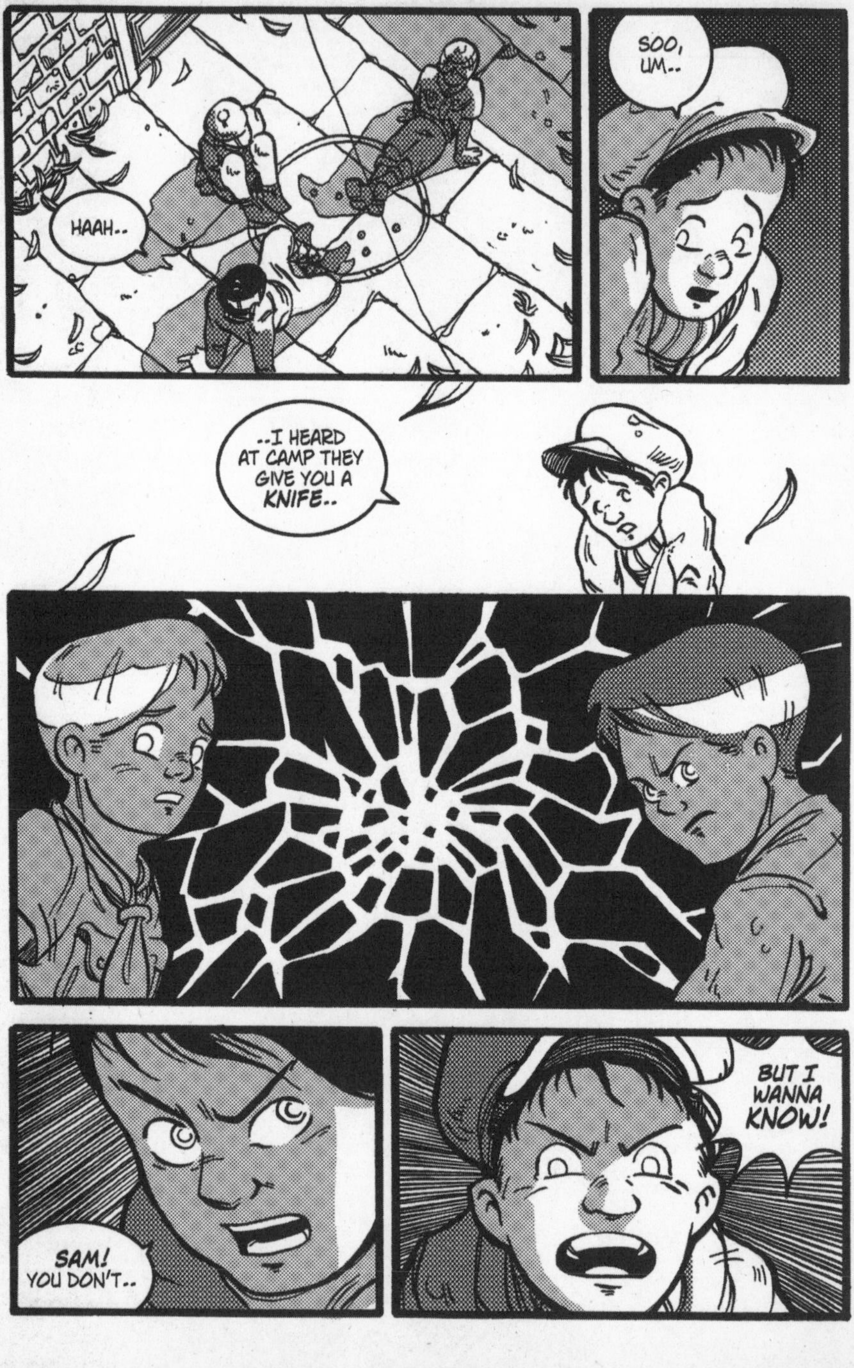
HAAH..
SOO, UM..
..I HEARD AT CAMP THEY GIVE YOU A KNIFE..
SAM! YOU DON'T..
BUT I WANNA KNOW!

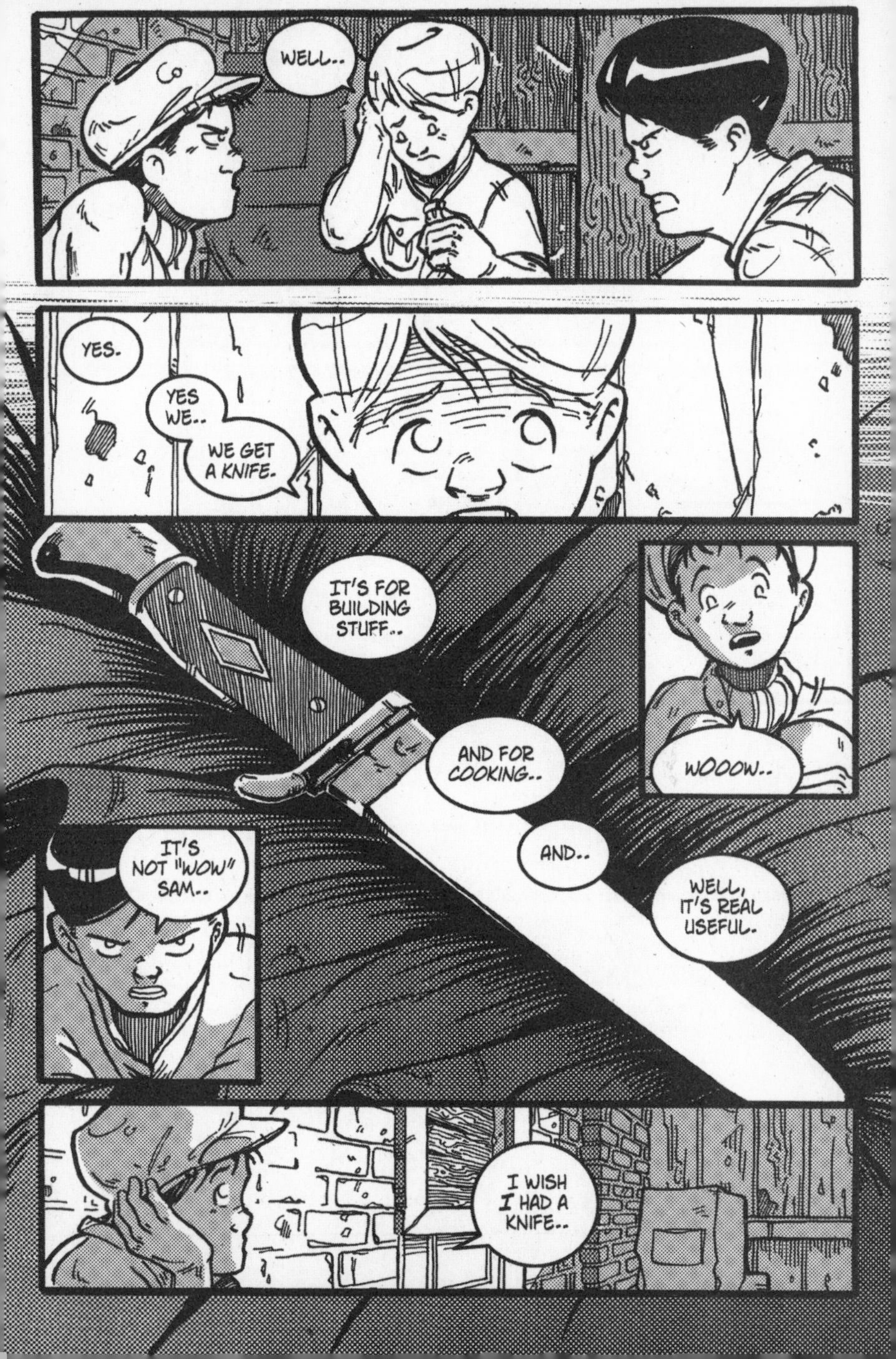
WELL..
YES.
YES WE..
WE GET A KNIFE.
IT'S FOR BUILDING STUFF..
WOOOW..
AND FOR COOKING..
IT'S NOT "WOW" SAM..
AND..
WELL, IT'S REAL USEFUL.
I WISH I HAD A KNIFE..

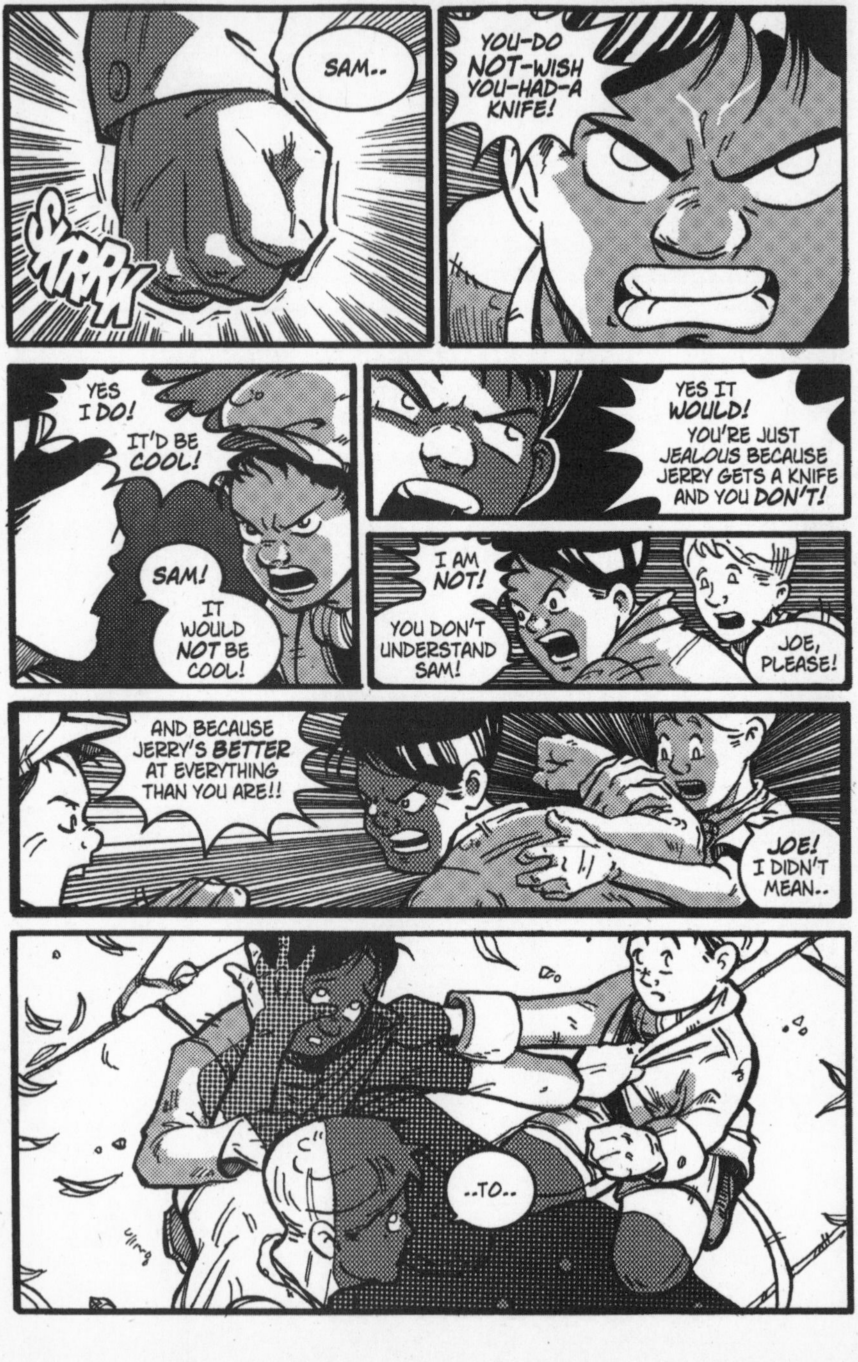
SAM..
SKRRK
YOU-DO NOT-WISH YOU-HAD-A KNIFE!
YES I DO!
IT'D BE COOL!
SAM!
IT WOULD NOT BE COOL!
YES IT WOULD! YOU'RE JUST JEALOUS BECAUSE JERRY GETS A KNIFE AND YOU DON'T!
I AM NOT!
YOU DON'T UNDERSTAND SAM!
JOE, PLEASE!
AND BECAUSE JERRY'S BETTER AT EVERYTHING THAN YOU ARE!!
JOE! I DIDN'T MEAN..
..TO..

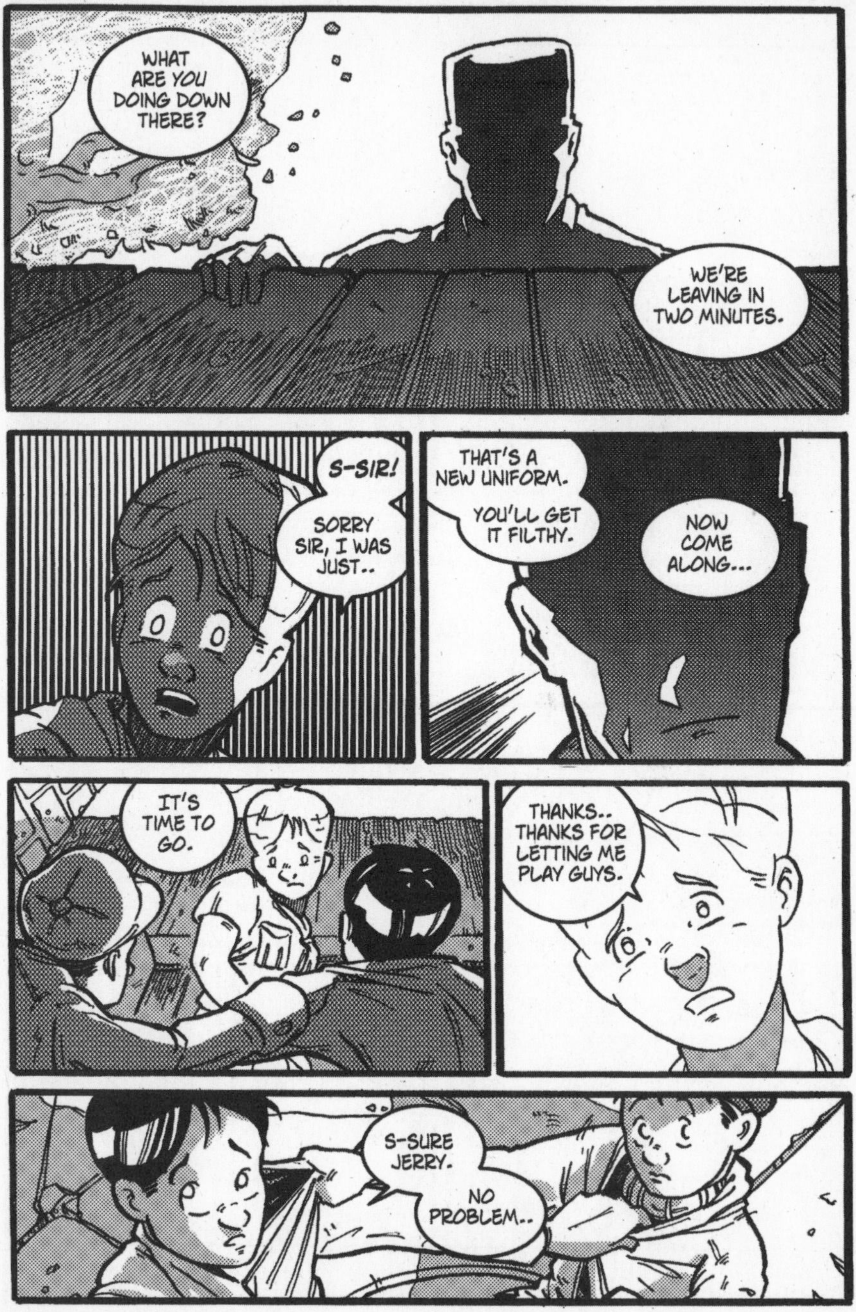
WHAT ARE YOU DOING DOWN THERE?
WE'RE LEAVING IN TWO MINUTES.
S-SIR!
SORRY SIR, I WAS JUST..
THAT'S A NEW UNIFORM.
YOU'LL GET IT FILTHY.
NOW COME ALONG...
IT'S TIME TO GO.
THANKS.. THANKS FOR LETTING ME PLAY GUYS.
S-SURE JERRY.
NO PROBLEM..

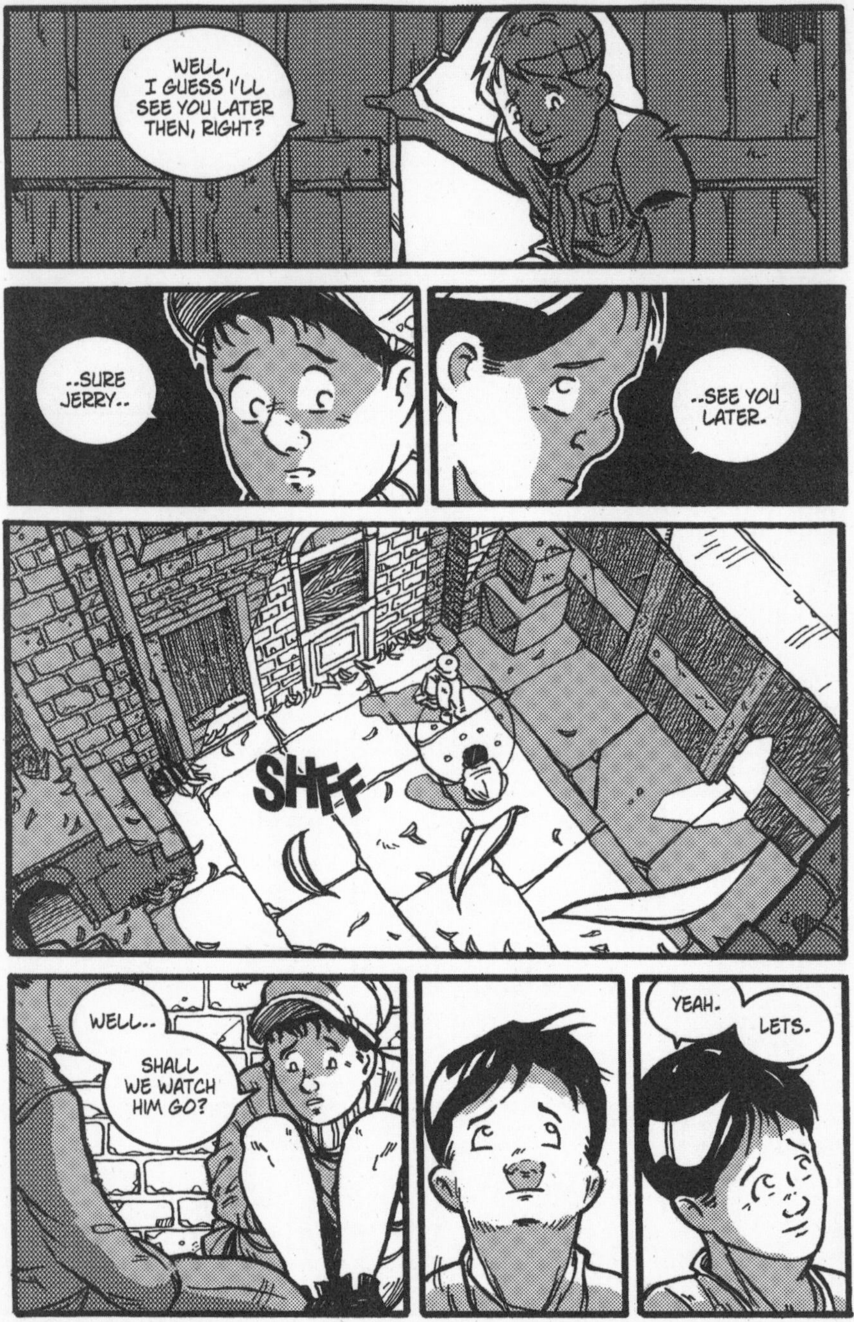
WELL, I GUESS I'LL SEE YOU LATER THEN, RIGHT?
..SURE JERRY..
..SEE YOU LATER.
SHFF
WELL..
SHALL WE WATCH HIM GO?
YEAH.
LETS.

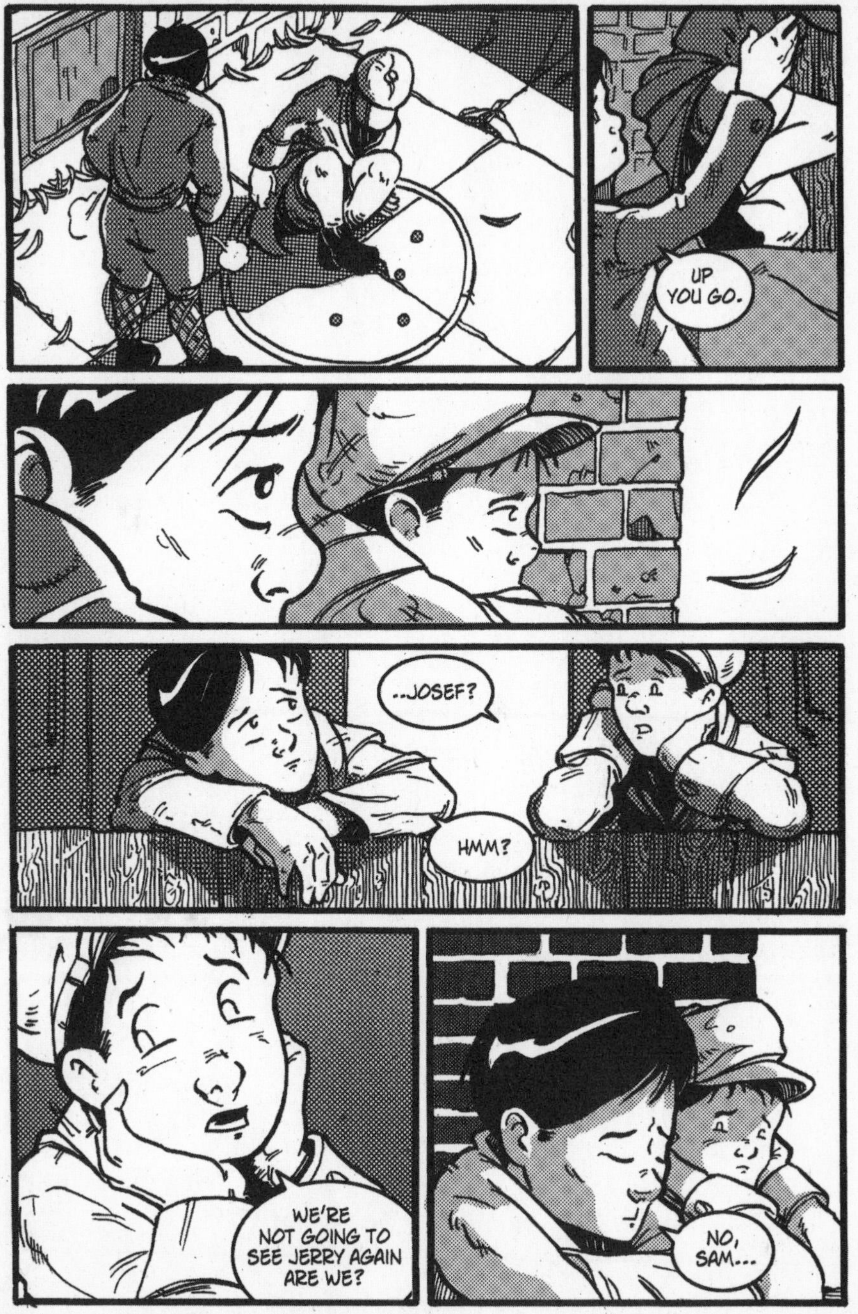
UP YOU GO.
..JOSEF?
HMM?
WE'RE NOT GOING TO SEE JERRY AGAIN ARE WE?
NO, SAM...

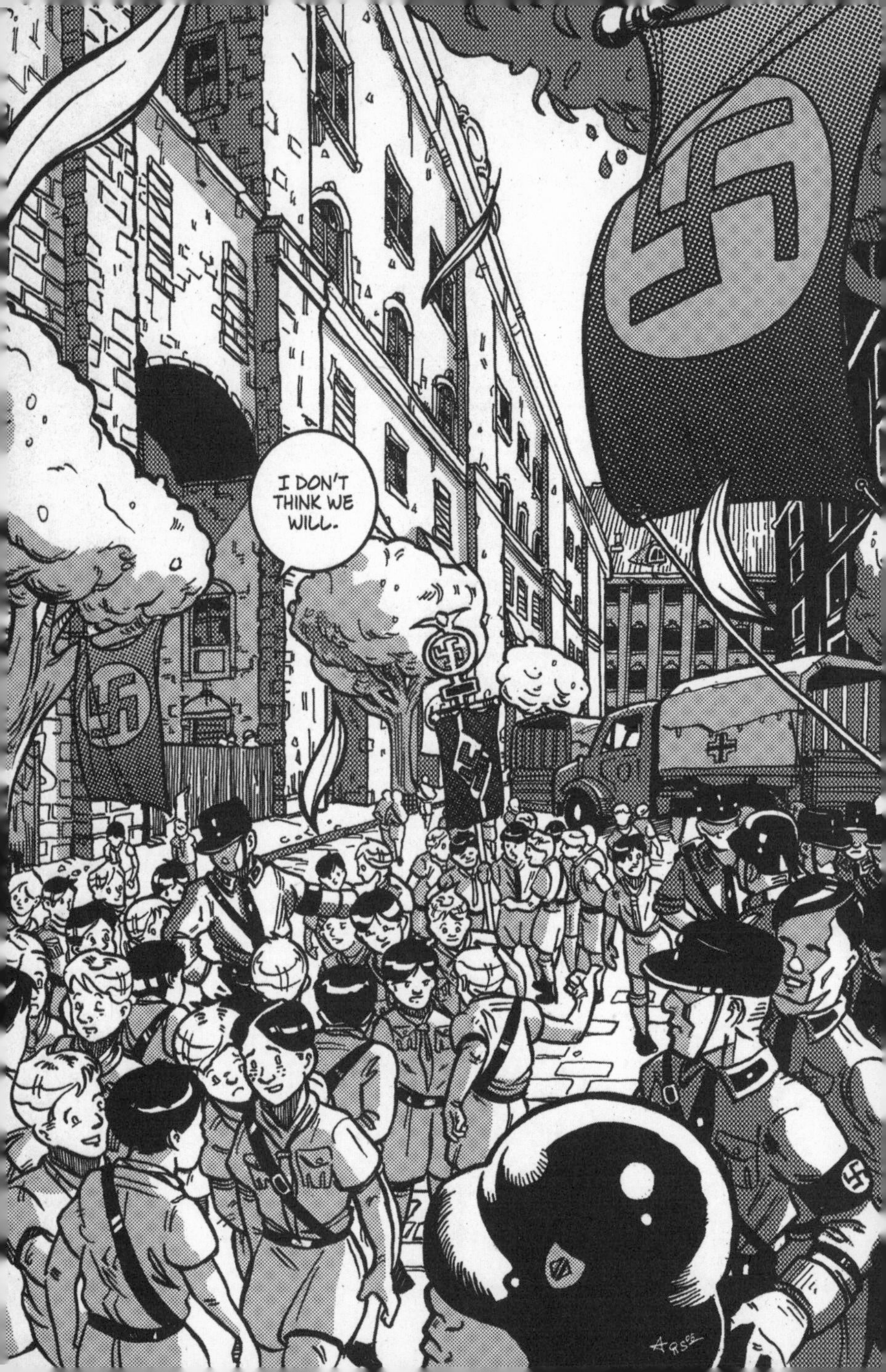
I DON'T THINK WE WILL.

POISON :: Second Place Winner ::

....

Selina Dean was born in Cambridge in 1982, and she still lives there today. She is a freelance artist and writer, and is a founding member of Sweatdrop Studios.
www.noddingcat.net
www.sweatdrop.com

Favorite manga:
Black and White, Banana Fish, Clover

Favorite manga artists:
Taiyo Matsumoto, Junko Mizuno, Ippei Gyoubu

....

Author's Comments:
I wanted to draw a comic where both the characters could be equally liked or hated, so I tried to be as balanced as possible. Also, this is the first time I've drawn a period drama! It was quite a challenge! I hope people enjoy my manga, and I'm always curious to know which of the characters people like best.
—Selina Dean

::

POISON :: Second Place Winner ::

....

Judge's Comments:

"Poison" was far and away my favorite of the entries. I also thought it was the most solid entry overall. Selina Dean has produced a work that is strong on all levels. She immediately creates an atmosphere that pulls us into the world of the characters. The character designs are rock solid...the head turns look perfect. Right on from every angle, they convey expression beautifully, and I love those hands! The storytelling is well-paced and clear. The tones add to the mood and lead focus without overpowering the drawings. The lettering and balloon placement is expertly handled, which is an area important to the flow of manga, but where some of the other *Rising Stars* entries fell short.

Aside from all that, what attracted me to Selina's piece is something that frequently gets overlooked and is often ridiculously under-appreciated: "Poison" is amazingly consistent in quality. Now I know "consistent" is not a word people normally associate with mind-blowing praise, but that's how I mean the word here. It really is one of the key areas that separates the "aspiring" from the "pro." It's the ability to remain consistent that makes whatever world you are creating feel real, and allows the readers to be pulled into it.

If there was one element of the piece I might be critical of, it would be in the execution of the flashback sequences. They worked fine as they were, but if you look back at manga from the '90s, the '80s, the '70s...you'll see a few of the same conventions used over and over. The reason is that they provide a visual shorthand that immediately conveys to the reader—subconsciously—that you have shifted the time frame. One of manga's biggest strengths, and one of the reasons they are so popular with all demographics in Japan, is that they are so intuitive. They put you right in the book with the characters. If a reader has to wonder for even a fraction of one second, "Wait, is this a flashback now...?" they are out of the book, and you have to pull them back in.

But this was a very minor gripe for an entry that was overwhelmingly strong. Things like that come as you discover new storytelling tools, and continue to find your voice. I can't wait to hear what Selina Dean's voice tells us next.
—Wes Abbott

Judge's Comments:

"Poison" tells a historical fiction vignette portraying the friction between social classes, hatred, betrayal...and murder—all with adorable chibified characters! Who'd have thought?!

Selina Dean does an excellent job with pacing and character development, so that even in these short 20 pages, we feel clearly for both of the main characters. First, there's Alice's frustrations with her abusive and unfair employer, as well as her work ethic and sense of loyalty (at first.) Likewise, Miss Ellen's high-class solitude and envy for her maid make the reader feel compassion for both characters' side of the story...and their motivations for killing in cold blood.

As for the art, to be honest, Selina's unique drawing style put me on edge the first time I scanned the panels. I feared the style might be limiting in the characters' expressions or movement, but Selina pulls off every unique show of emotion well within the scope of the style. Also, seeing the characters stay the same characters page after page, the strength and confidence in consistency made it legit in my book. Perhaps calling the style "chibified" isn't the right word. One could compare her unique and original "abstract" character design to Junko Mizuno, where the contrast between adorable style and gritty story makes you wonder...should I actually be laughing at this?

However, as it often goes with *RSoM* entries, the lack of backgrounds detracts from the richness (literally) of the setting. Some background choices in toning also left me confused. It may have been a good decision, for example, to clarify the subtle timeframe jumps between past and present. And while her ink work felt shaky at times, there is no doubt in my mind Selina is a Rising Star that can create an amazing next work of manga!
—Katherine Schilling

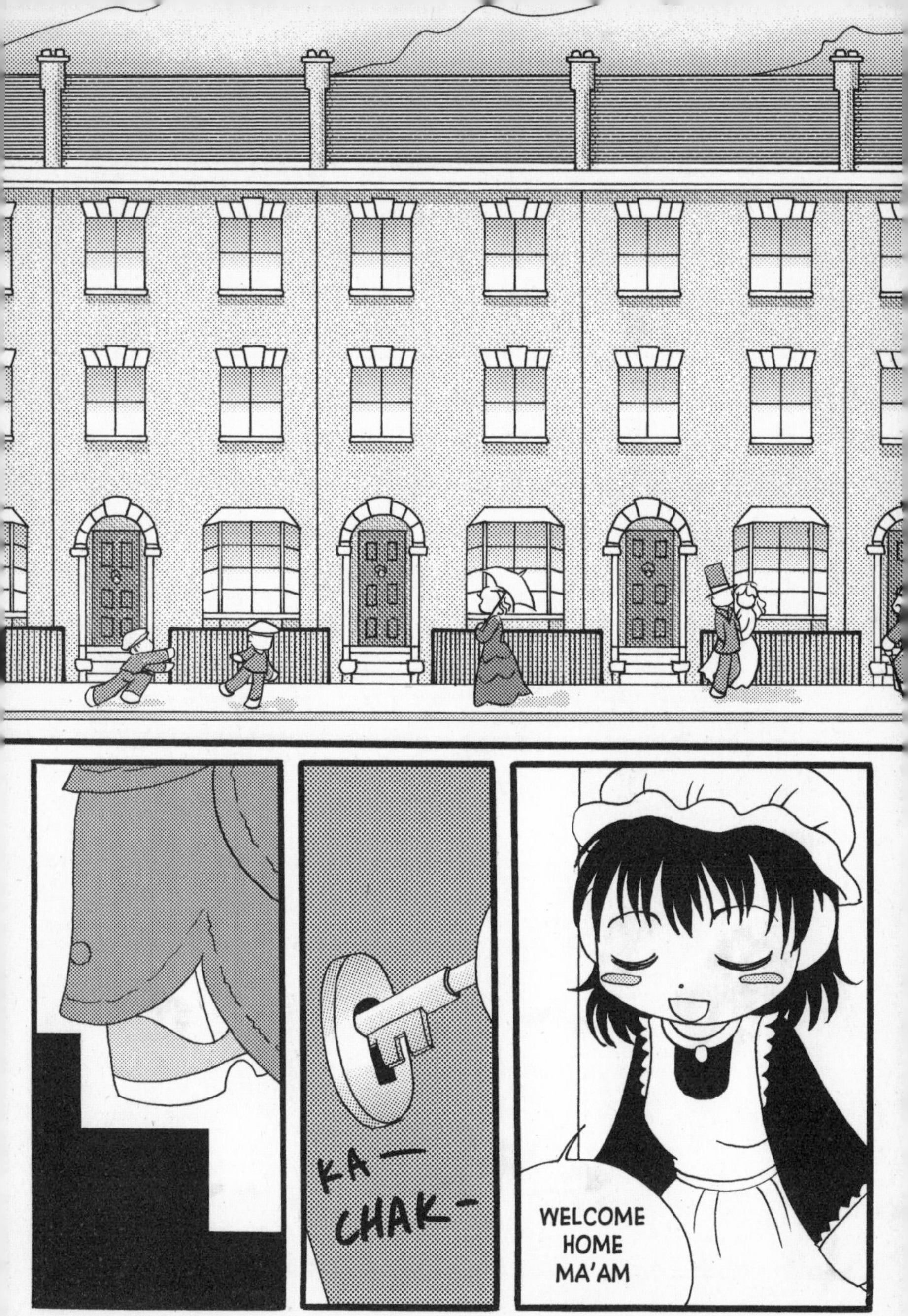
KA— CHAK—
WELCOME HOME MA'AM

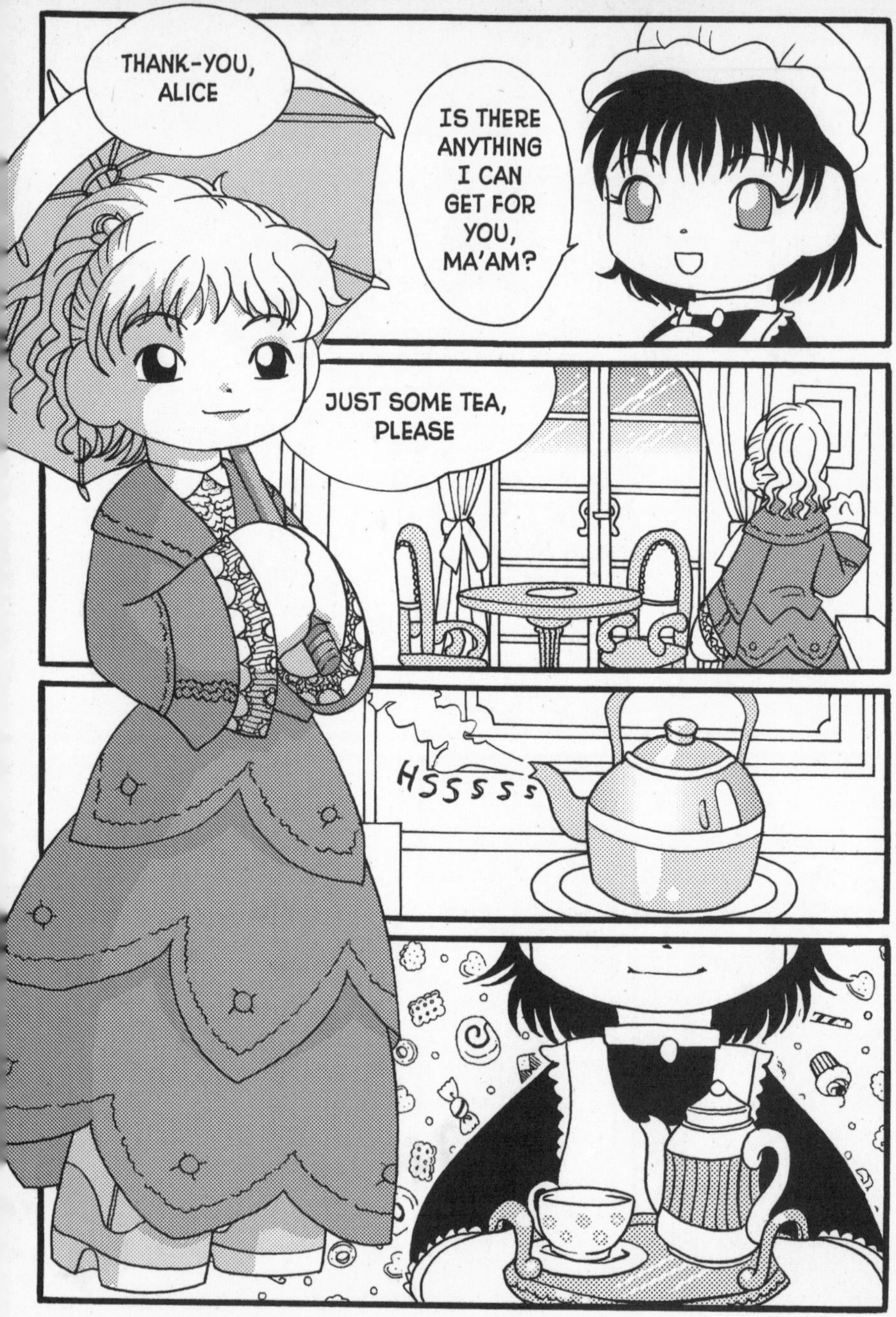
THANK-YOU, ALICE
IS THERE ANYTHING I CAN GET FOR YOU, MA'AM?
JUST SOME TEA, PLEASE
HSSSSS

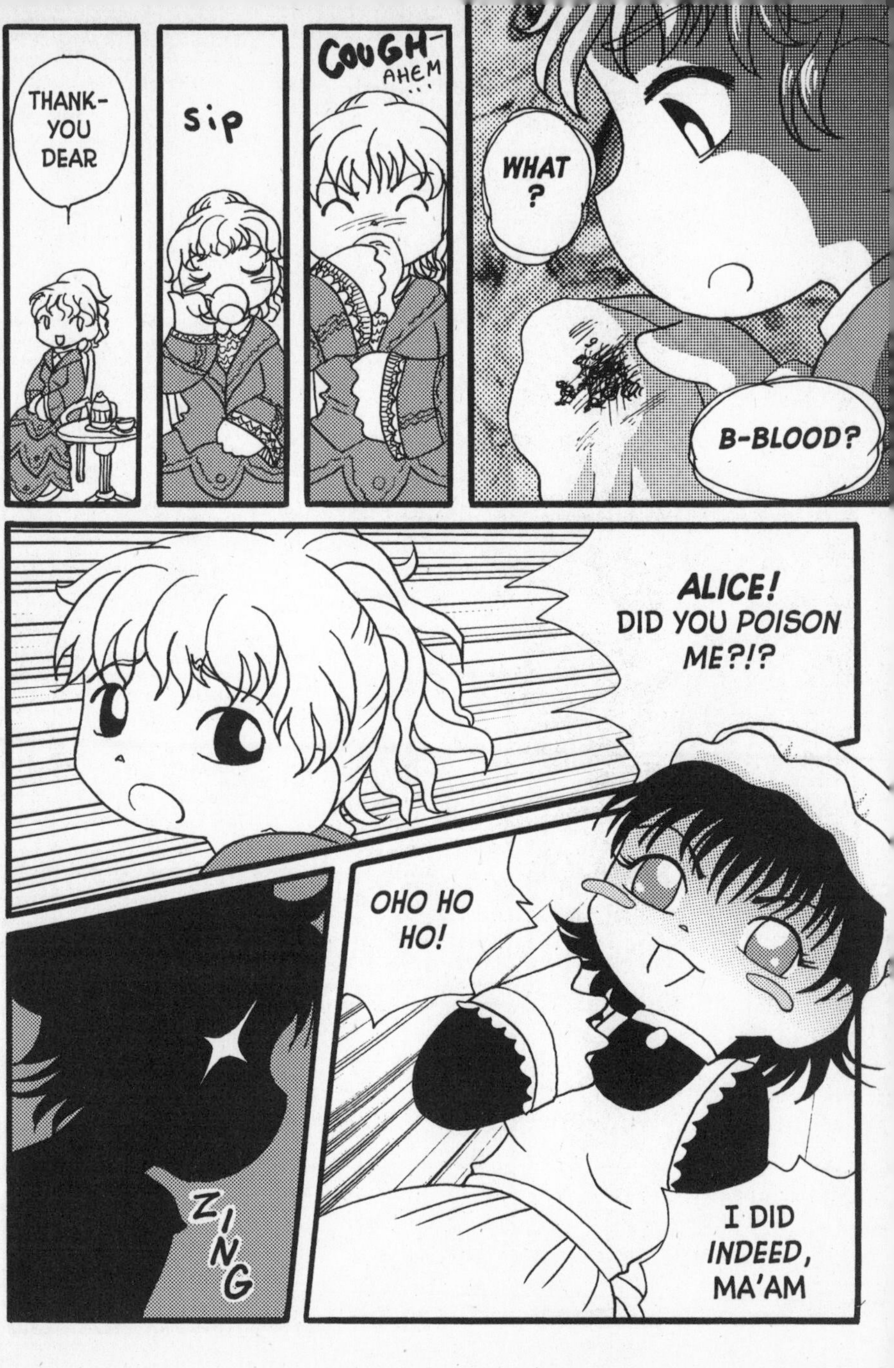
THANK-YOU DEAR
sip
COUGH-
AHEM...
WHAT?
B-BLOOD?
ALICE! DID YOU POISON ME?!?
ZING
OHO HO HO!
I DID INDEED, MA'AM

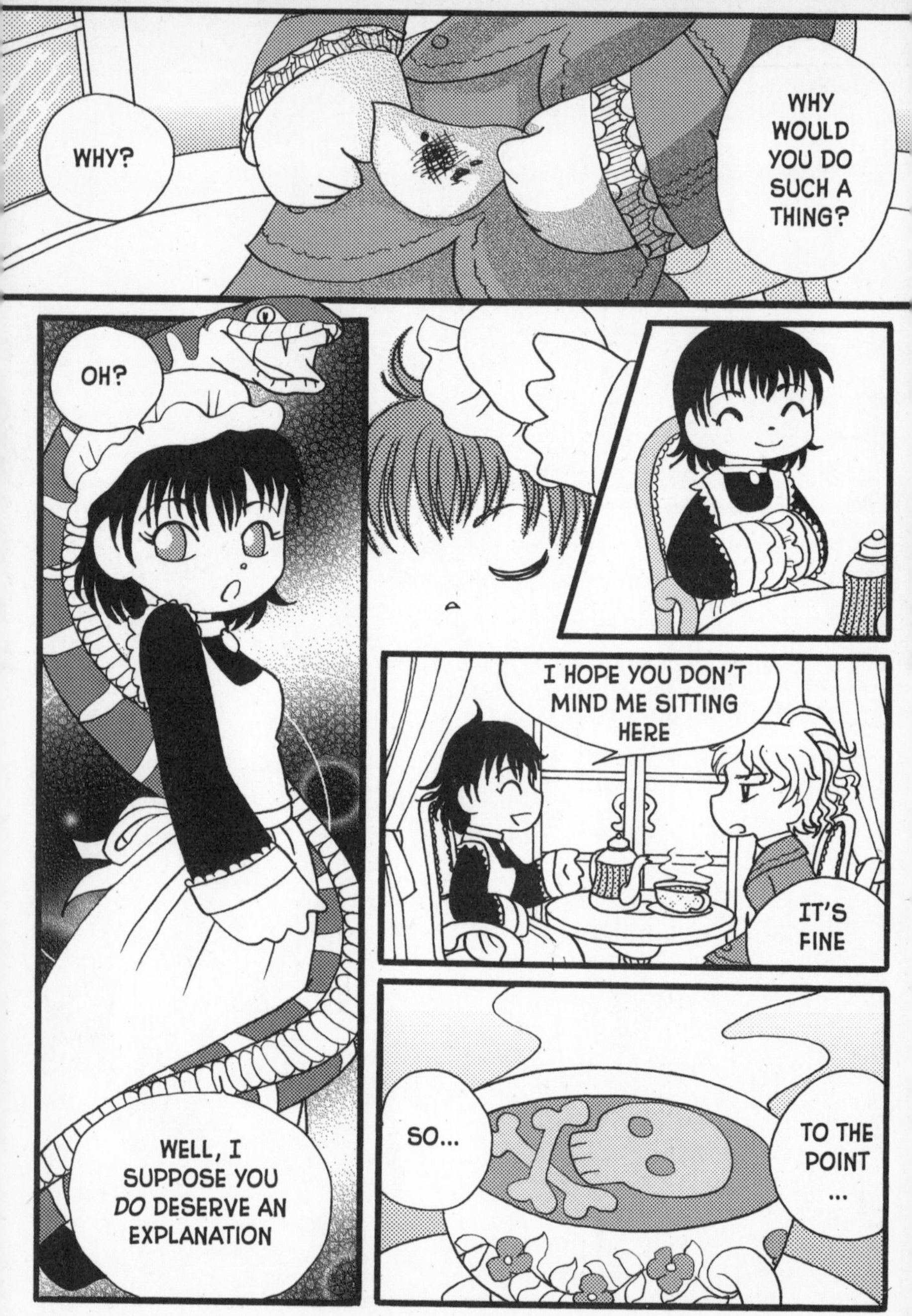
WHY?
WHY WOULD YOU DO SUCH A THING?
OH?
WELL, I SUPPOSE YOU *DO* DESERVE AN EXPLANATION
I HOPE YOU DON'T MIND ME SITTING HERE
IT'S FINE
SO...
TO THE POINT ...

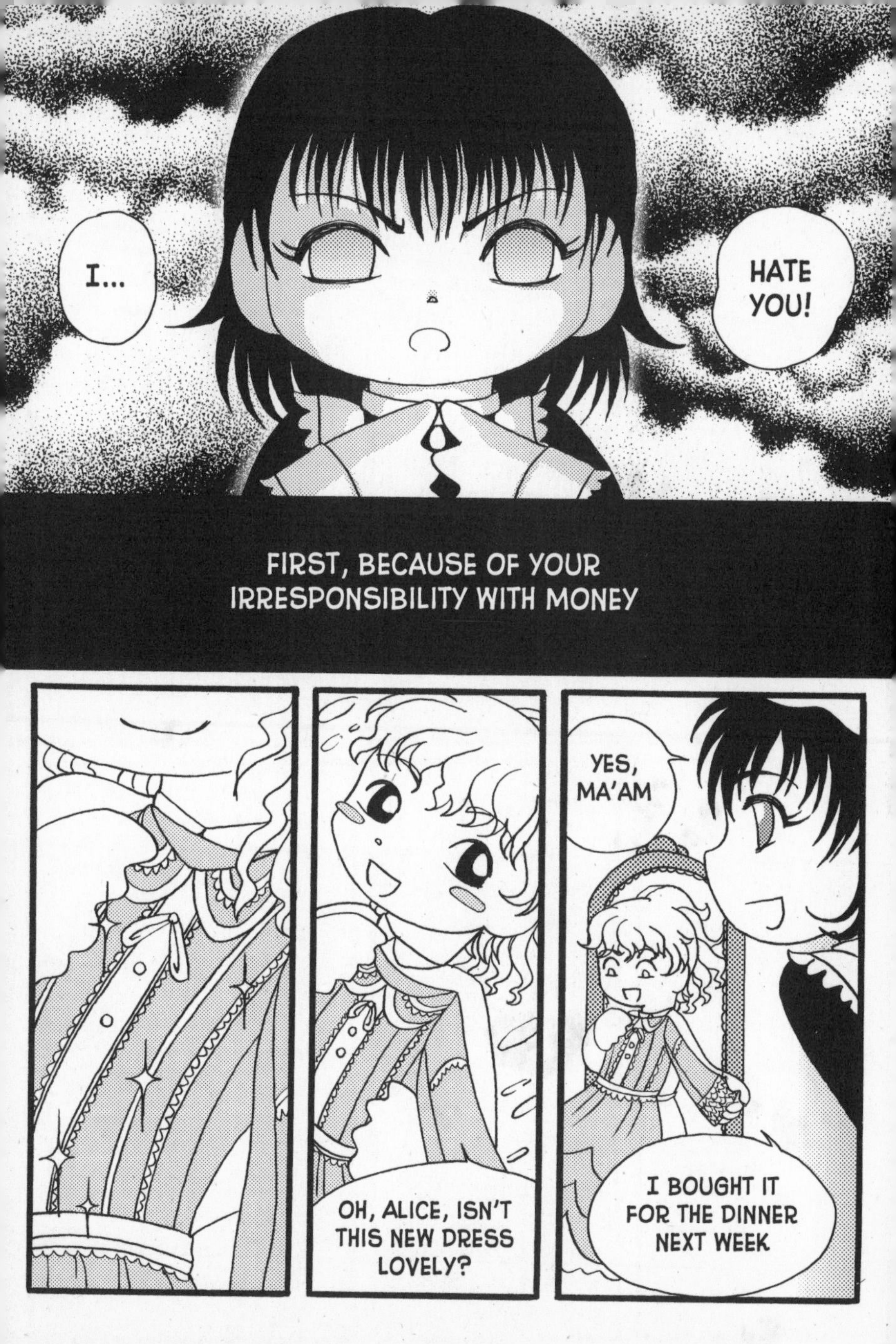

I...
HATE YOU!
FIRST, BECAUSE OF YOUR IRRESPONSIBILITY WITH MONEY
OH, ALICE, ISN'T THIS NEW DRESS LOVELY?
YES, MA'AM
I BOUGHT IT FOR THE DINNER NEXT WEEK

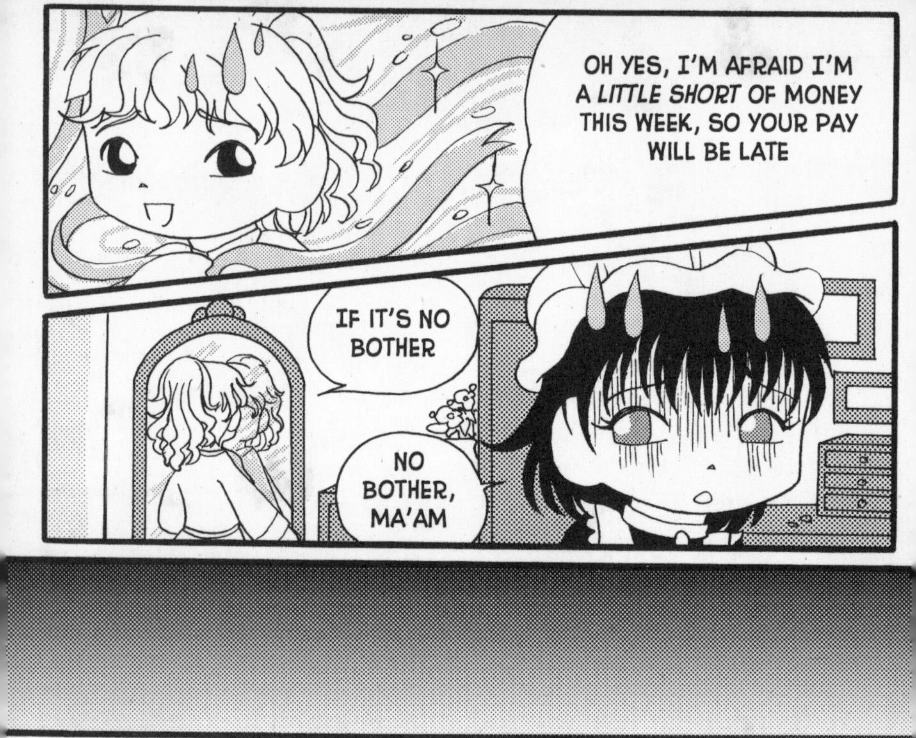
OH YES, I'M AFRAID I'M A *LITTLE SHORT* OF MONEY THIS WEEK, SO YOUR PAY WILL BE LATE
IF IT'S NO BOTHER
NO BOTHER, MA'AM

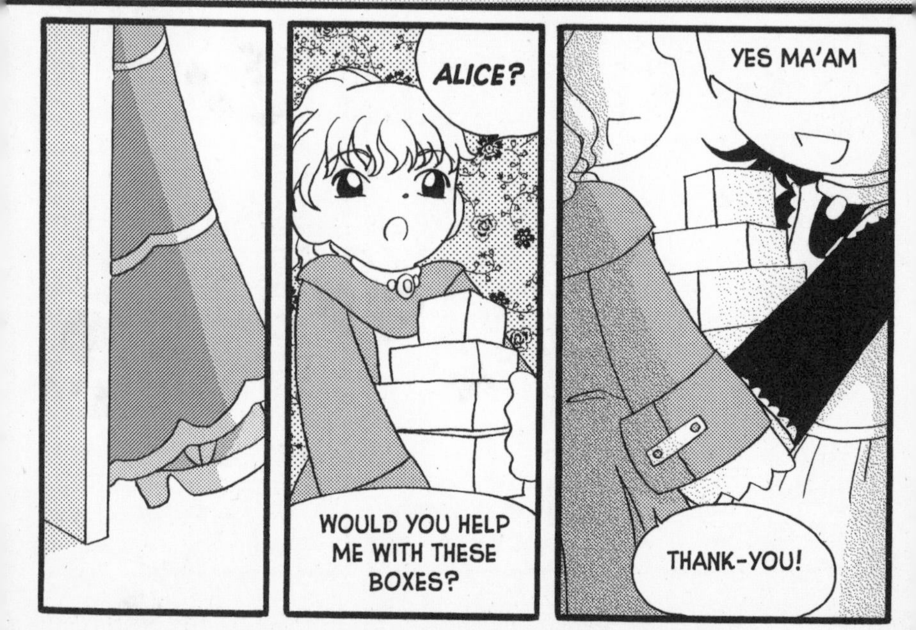
ALICE?
WOULD YOU HELP ME WITH THESE BOXES?
YES MA'AM
THANK-YOU!

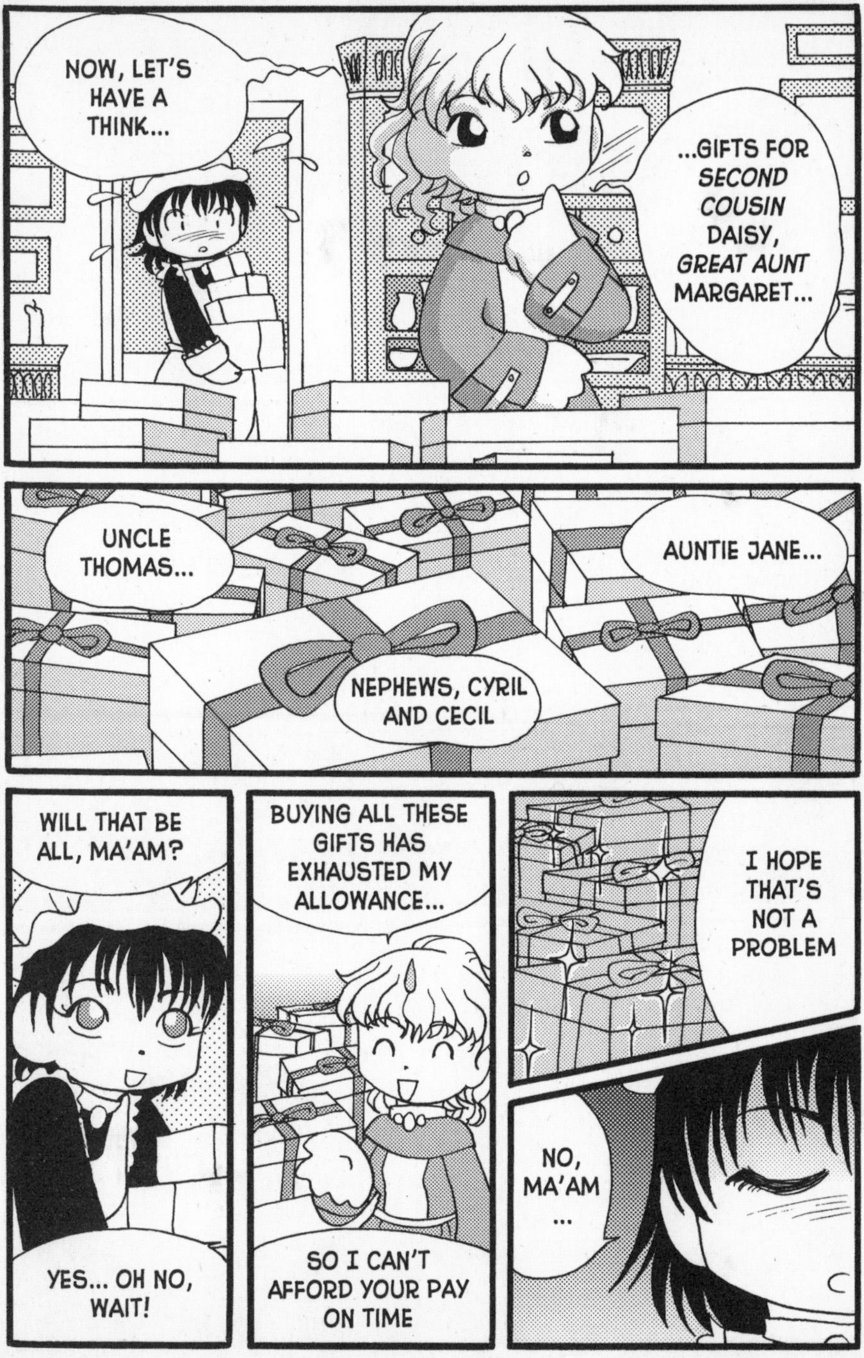
NOW, LET'S HAVE A THINK...
...GIFTS FOR *SECOND COUSIN* DAISY, *GREAT AUNT* MARGARET...
UNCLE THOMAS...
AUNTIE JANE...
NEPHEWS, CYRIL AND CECIL
WILL THAT BE ALL, MA'AM?
YES... OH NO, WAIT!
BUYING ALL THESE GIFTS HAS EXHAUSTED MY ALLOWANCE...
SO I CAN'T AFFORD YOUR PAY ON TIME
I HOPE THAT'S NOT A PROBLEM
NO, MA'AM ...

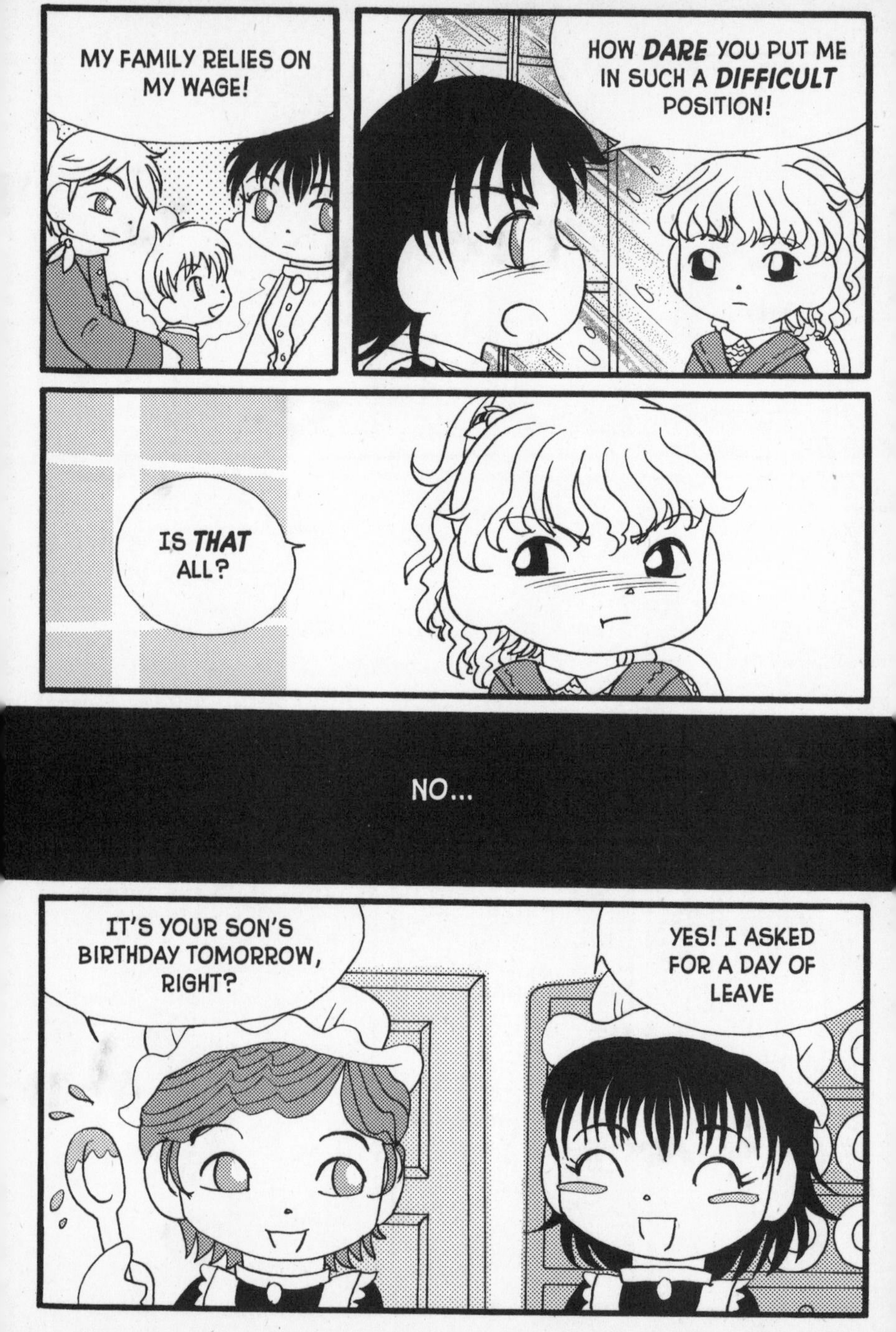
MY FAMILY RELIES ON MY WAGE!
HOW **DARE** YOU PUT ME IN SUCH A **DIFFICULT** POSITION!
IS **THAT** ALL?
NO...
IT'S YOUR SON'S BIRTHDAY TOMORROW, RIGHT?
YES! I ASKED FOR A DAY OF LEAVE

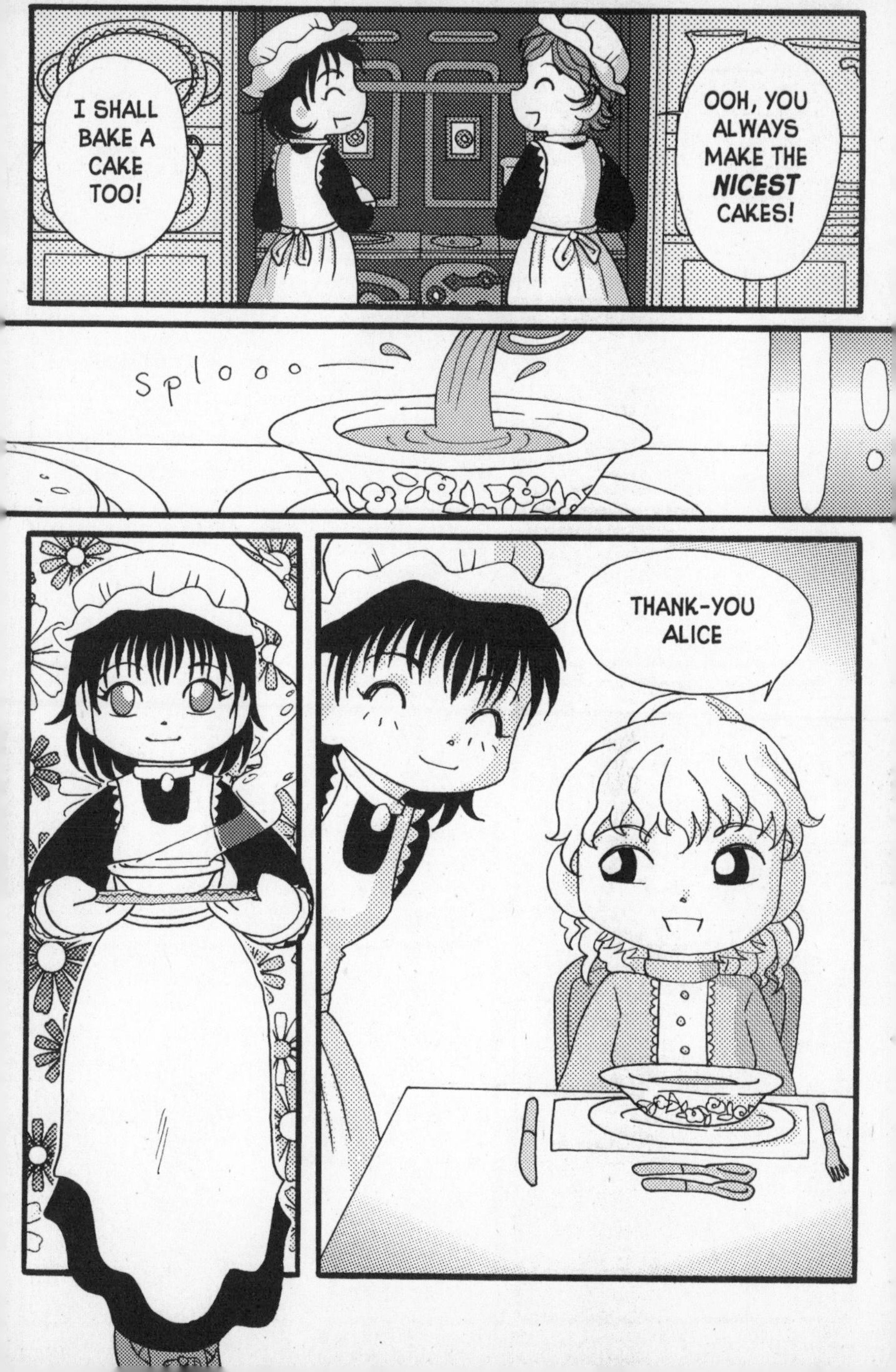
I SHALL BAKE A CAKE TOO!
OOH, YOU ALWAYS MAKE THE NICEST CAKES!
Splooo—
THANK-YOU ALICE

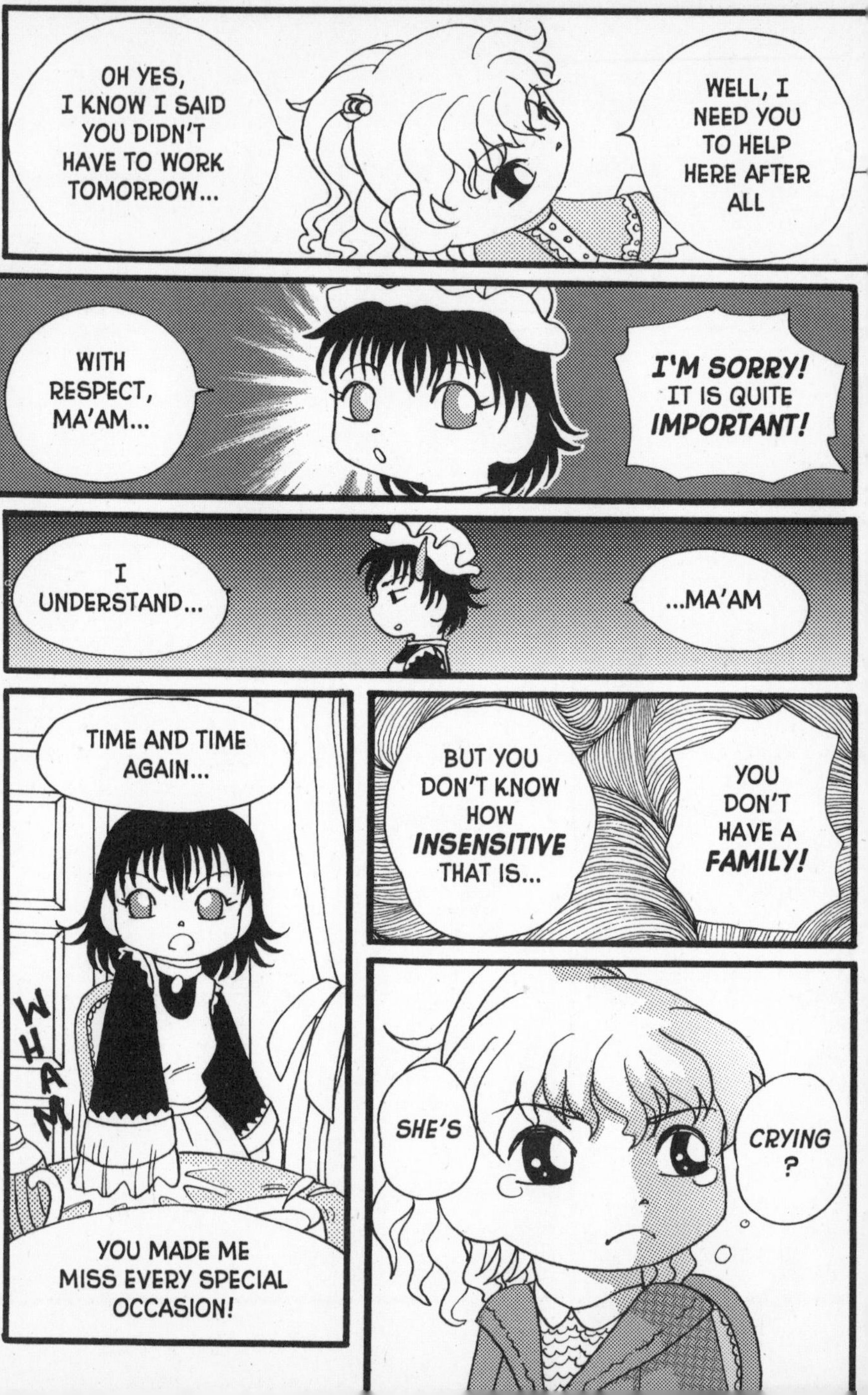
OH YES, I KNOW I SAID YOU DIDN'T HAVE TO WORK TOMORROW...
WELL, I NEED YOU TO HELP HERE AFTER ALL
WITH RESPECT, MA'AM...
I'M SORRY! IT IS QUITE IMPORTANT!
I UNDERSTAND...
...MA'AM
TIME AND TIME AGAIN...
WHAM
YOU MADE ME MISS EVERY SPECIAL OCCASION!
BUT YOU DON'T KNOW HOW INSENSITIVE THAT IS...
YOU DON'T HAVE A FAMILY!
SHE'S
CRYING ?

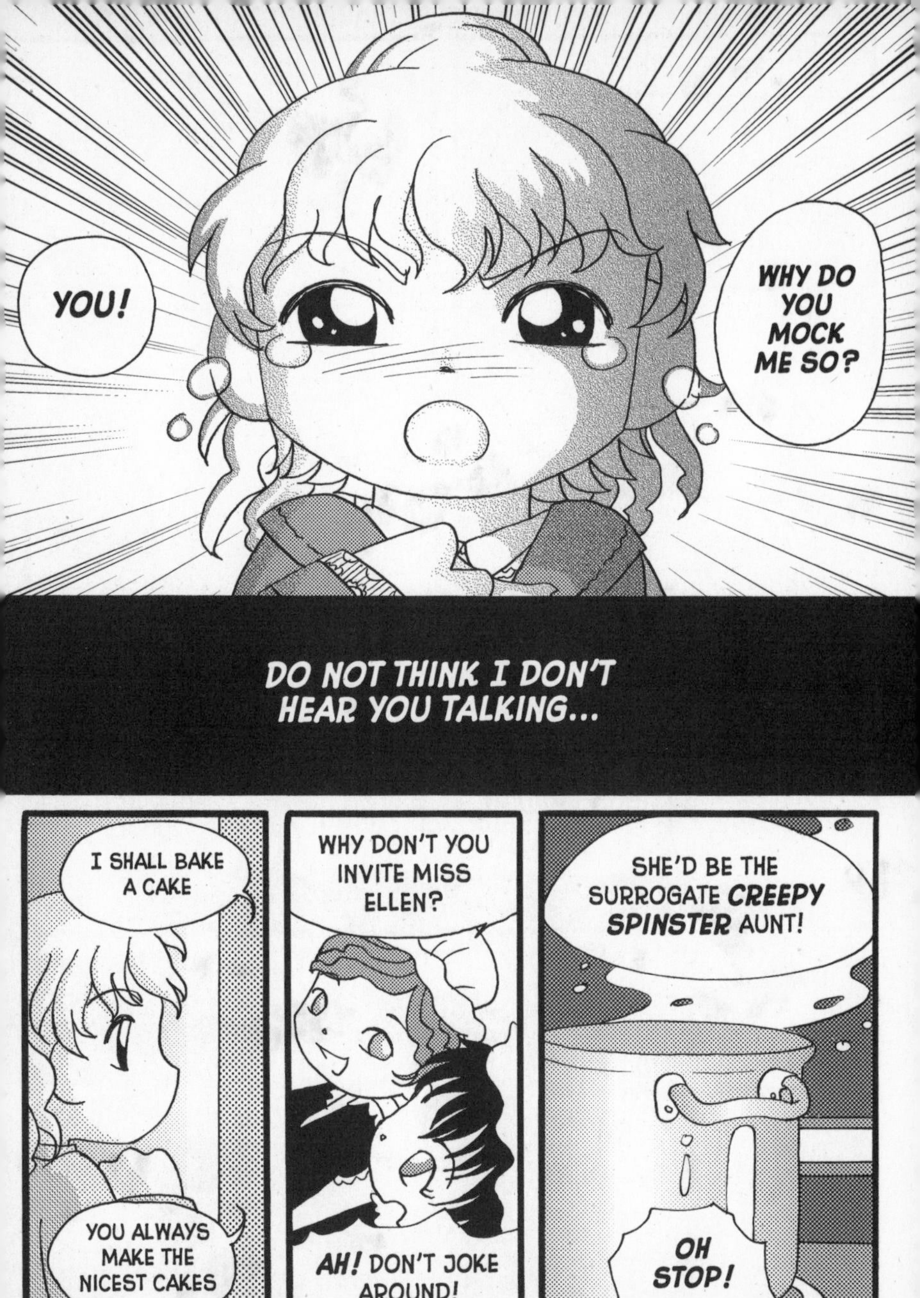
YOU!
WHY DO YOU MOCK ME SO?
DO NOT THINK I DON'T HEAR YOU TALKING...
I SHALL BAKE A CAKE
YOU ALWAYS MAKE THE NICEST CAKES
WHY DON'T YOU INVITE MISS ELLEN?
AH! DON'T JOKE AROUND!
SHE'D BE THE SURROGATE CREEPY SPINSTER AUNT!
OH STOP!

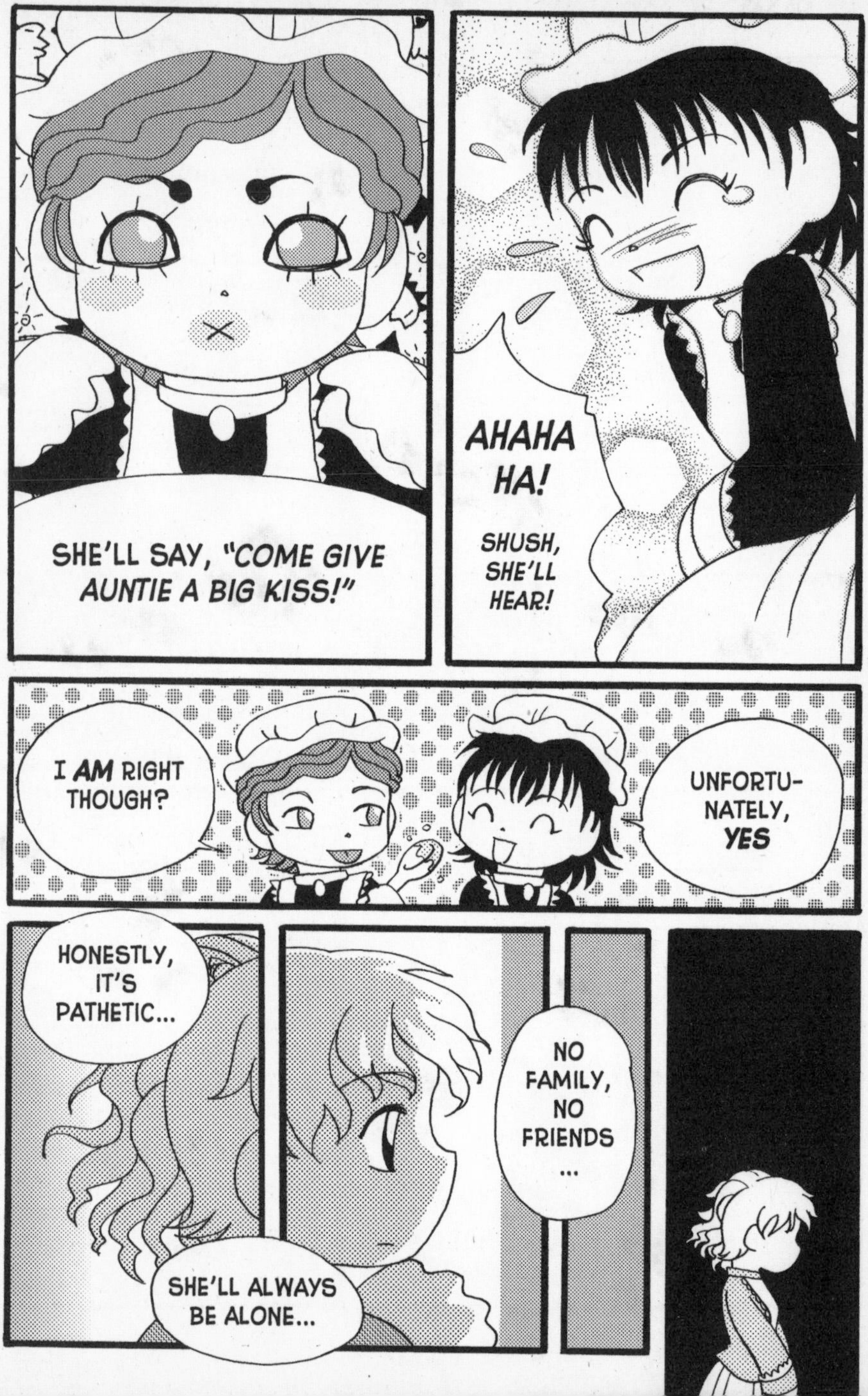
SHE'LL SAY, "COME GIVE AUNTIE A BIG KISS!"
AHAHA HA!
SHUSH, SHE'LL HEAR!
I AM RIGHT THOUGH?
UNFORTU-NATELY, YES
HONESTLY, IT'S PATHETIC...
NO FAMILY, NO FRIENDS ...
SHE'LL ALWAYS BE ALONE...

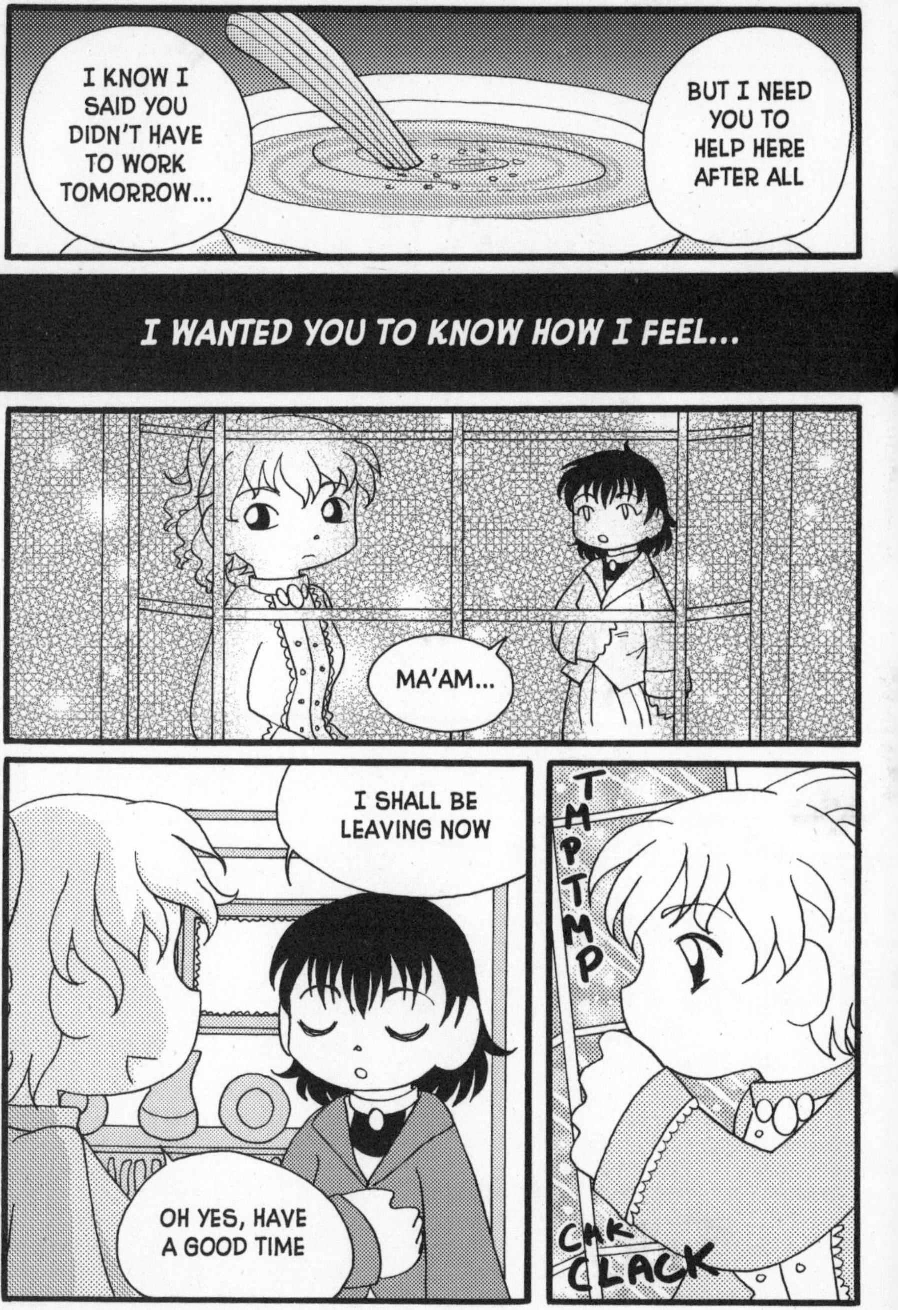
I KNOW I SAID YOU DIDN'T HAVE TO WORK TOMORROW...
BUT I NEED YOU TO HELP HERE AFTER ALL
I WANTED YOU TO KNOW HOW I FEEL...
MA'AM...
I SHALL BE LEAVING NOW
OH YES, HAVE A GOOD TIME
TMPTMP
CHK
CLACK

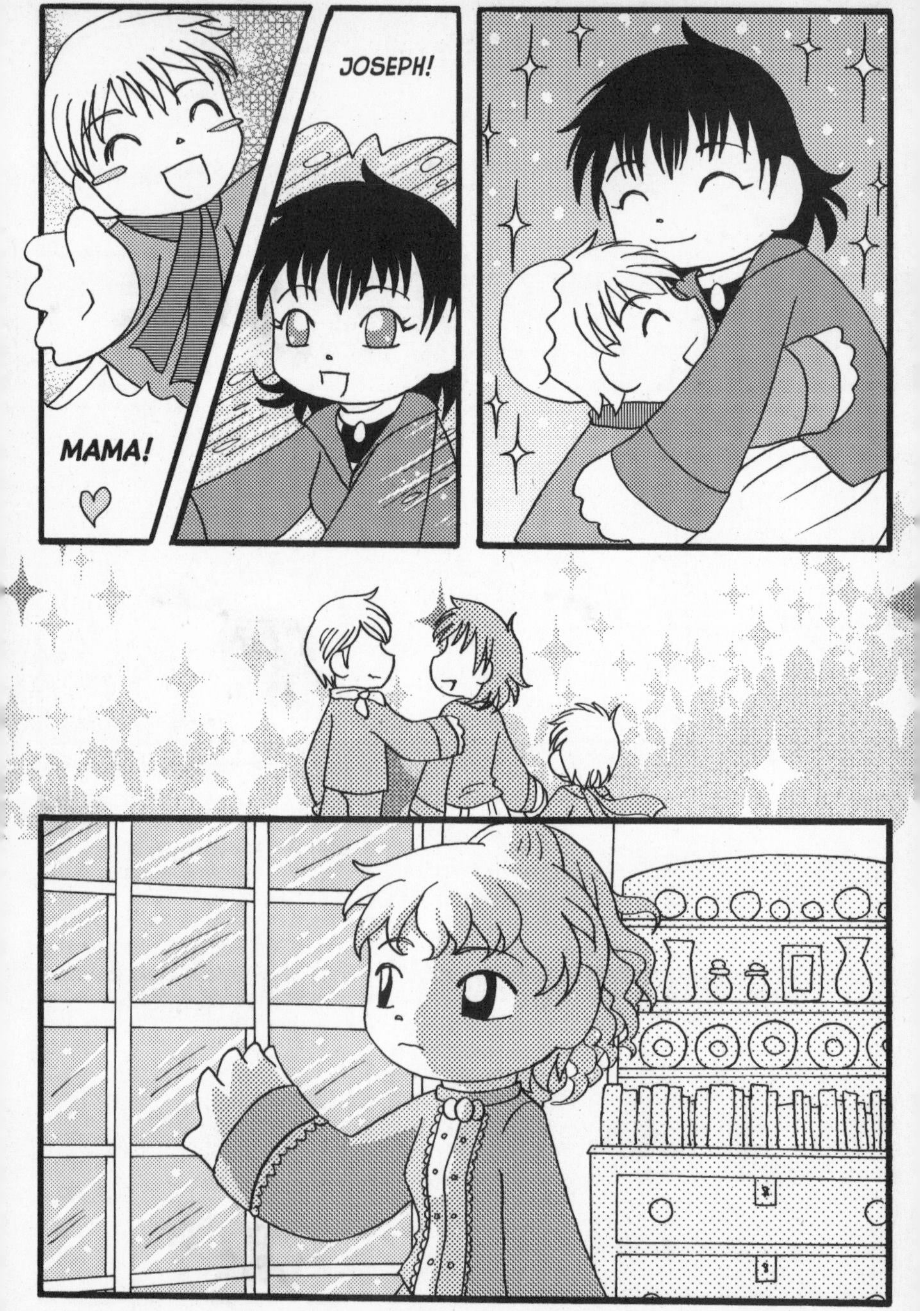
MAMA!
JOSEPH!

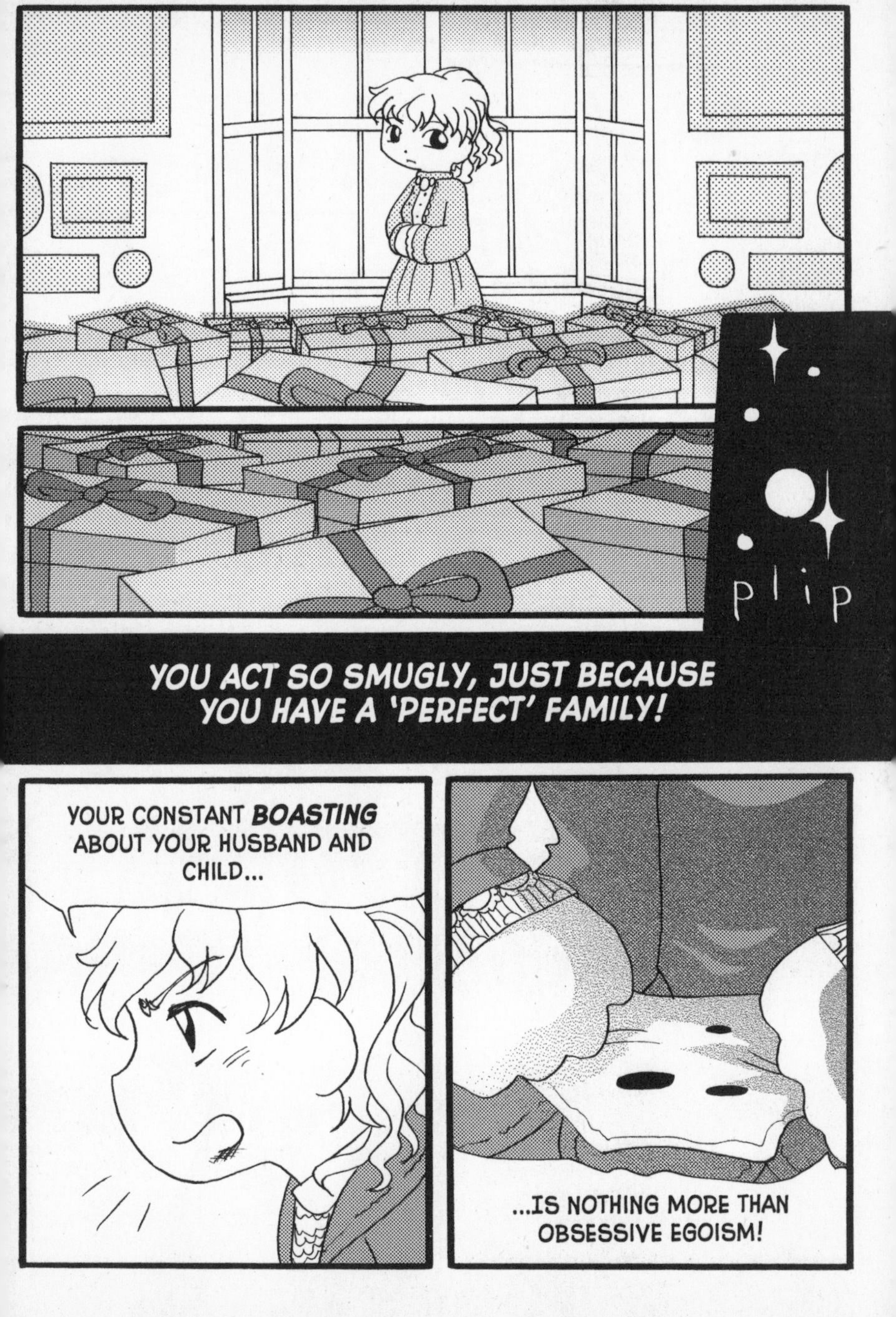
plip
YOU ACT SO SMUGLY, JUST BECAUSE YOU HAVE A 'PERFECT' FAMILY!
YOUR CONSTANT BOASTING ABOUT YOUR HUSBAND AND CHILD...
...IS NOTHING MORE THAN OBSESSIVE EGOISM!

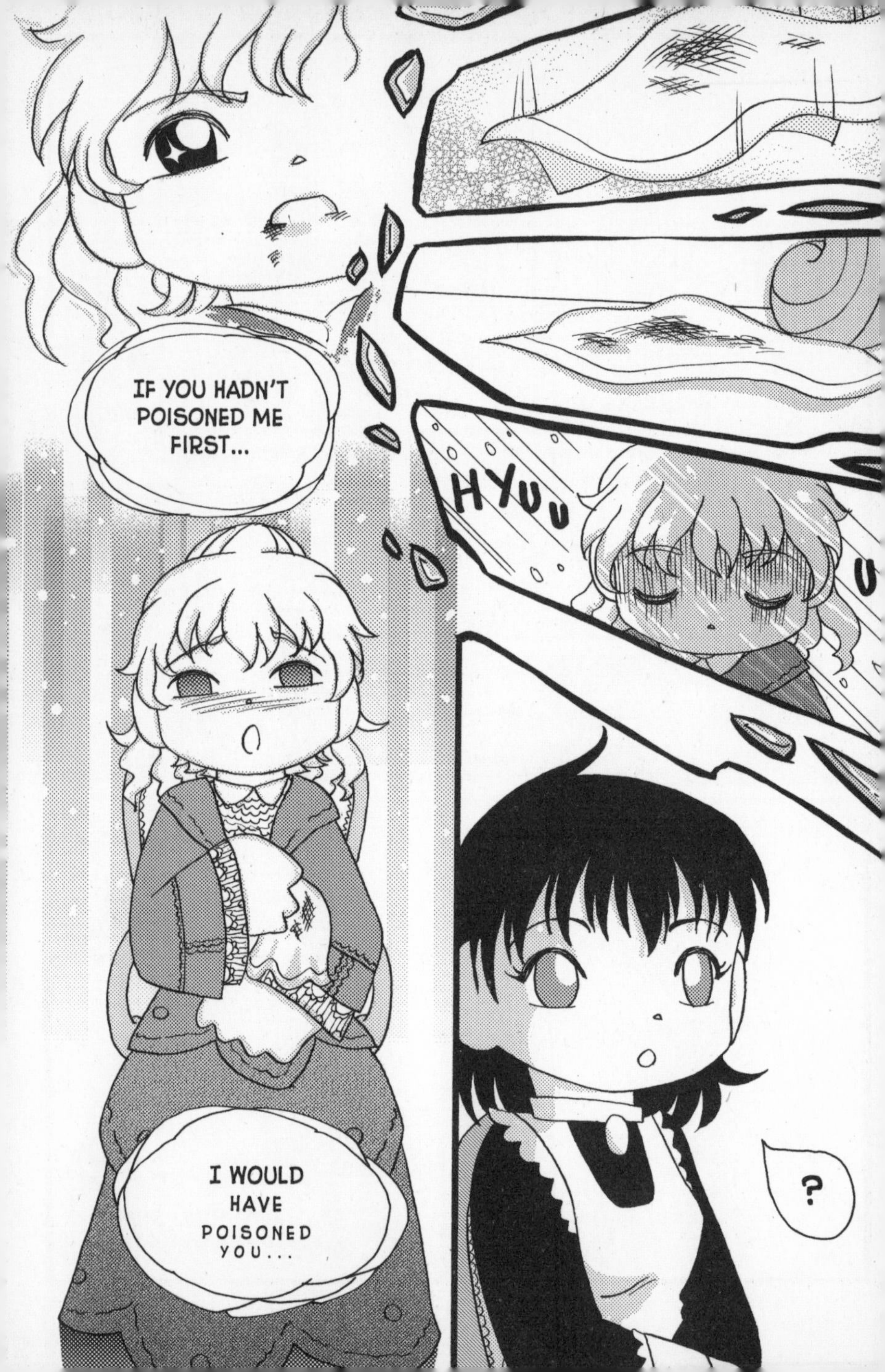
IF YOU HADN'T POISONED ME FIRST...
I WOULD HAVE POISONED YOU...
HYUU
?

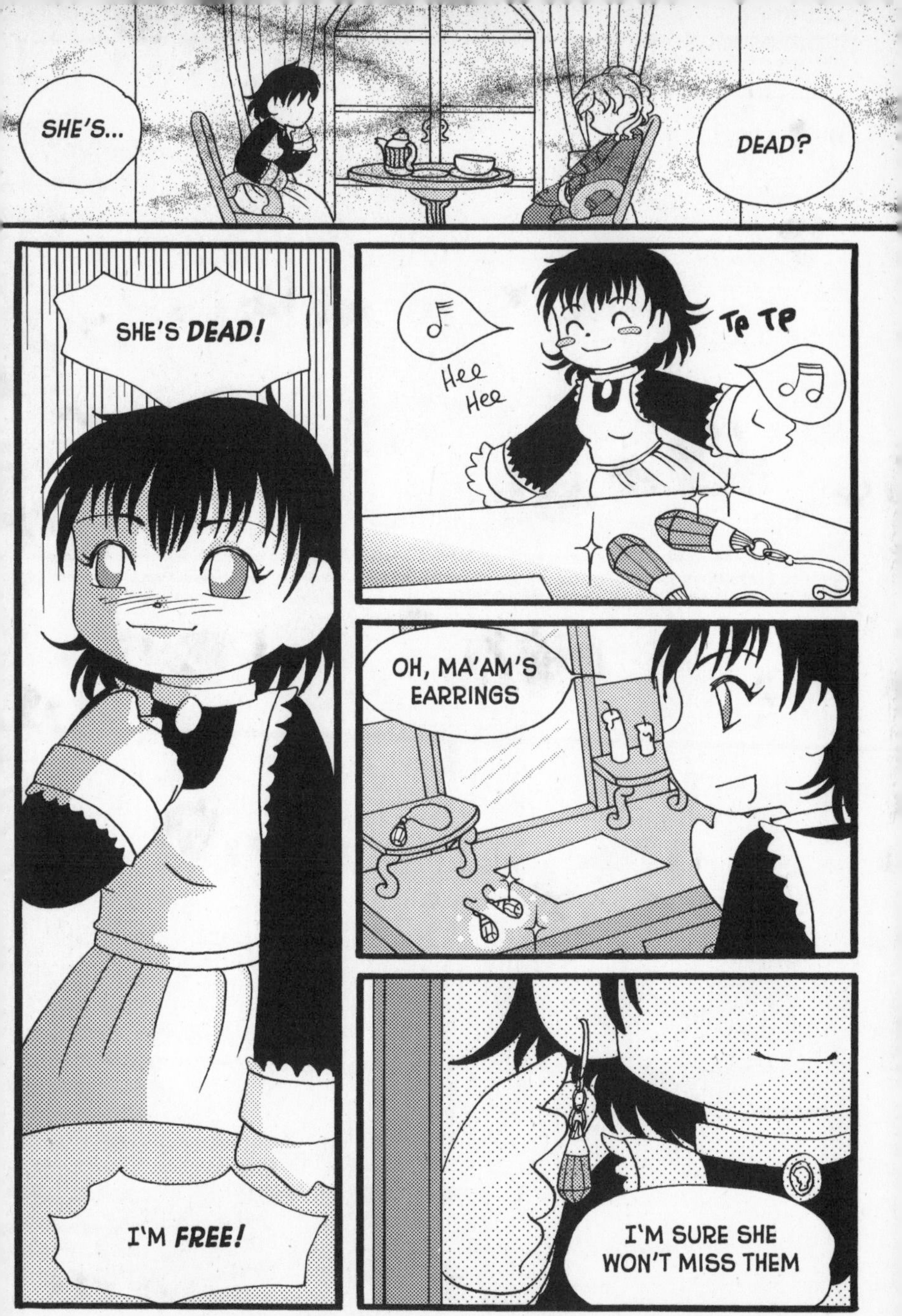
SHE'S...
DEAD?
SHE'S DEAD!
I'M FREE!
Hee Hee
Tp Tp
OH, MA'AM'S EARRINGS
I'M SURE SHE WON'T MISS THEM

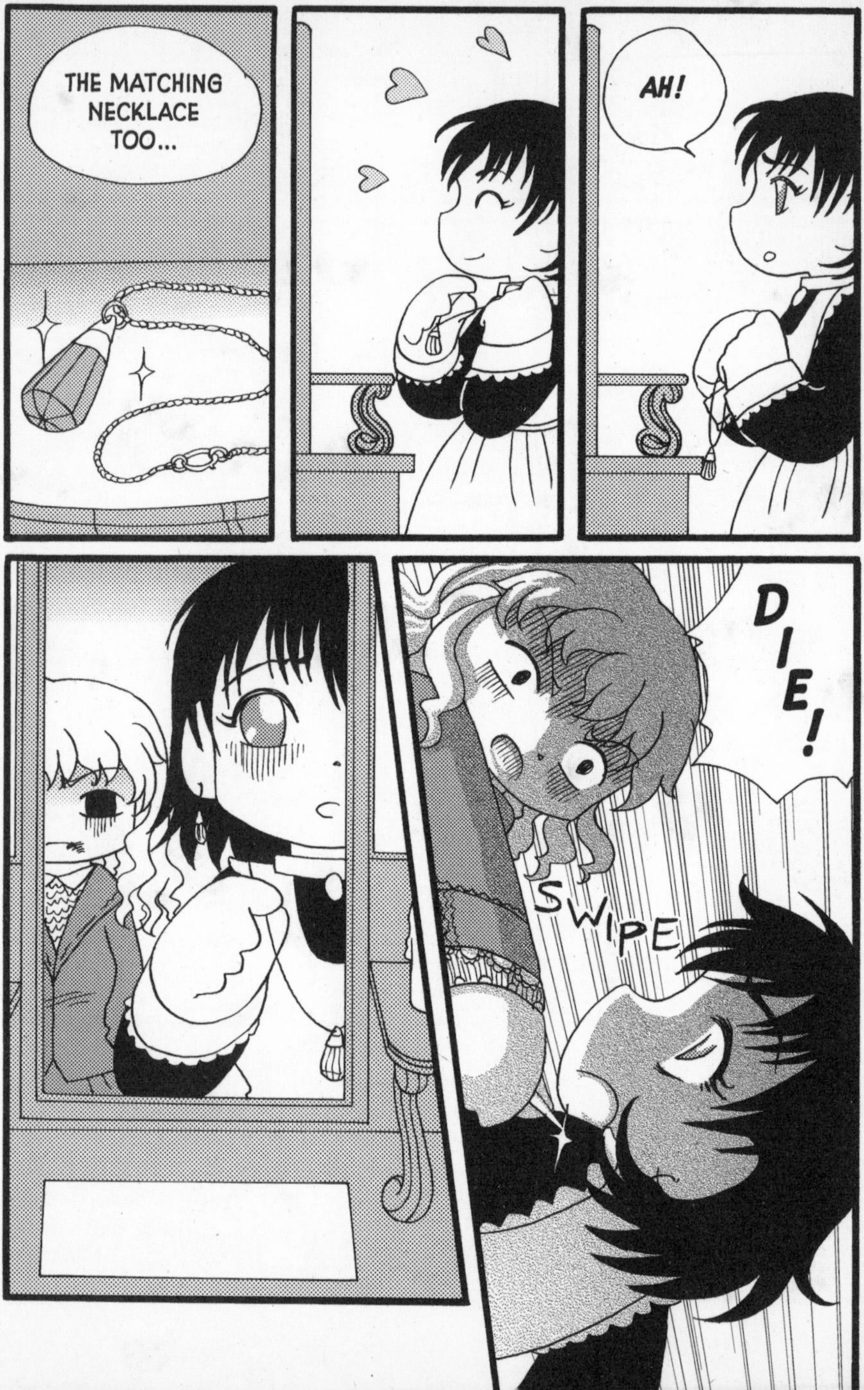
THE MATCHING NECKLACE TOO...
AH!
DIE!
SWIPE

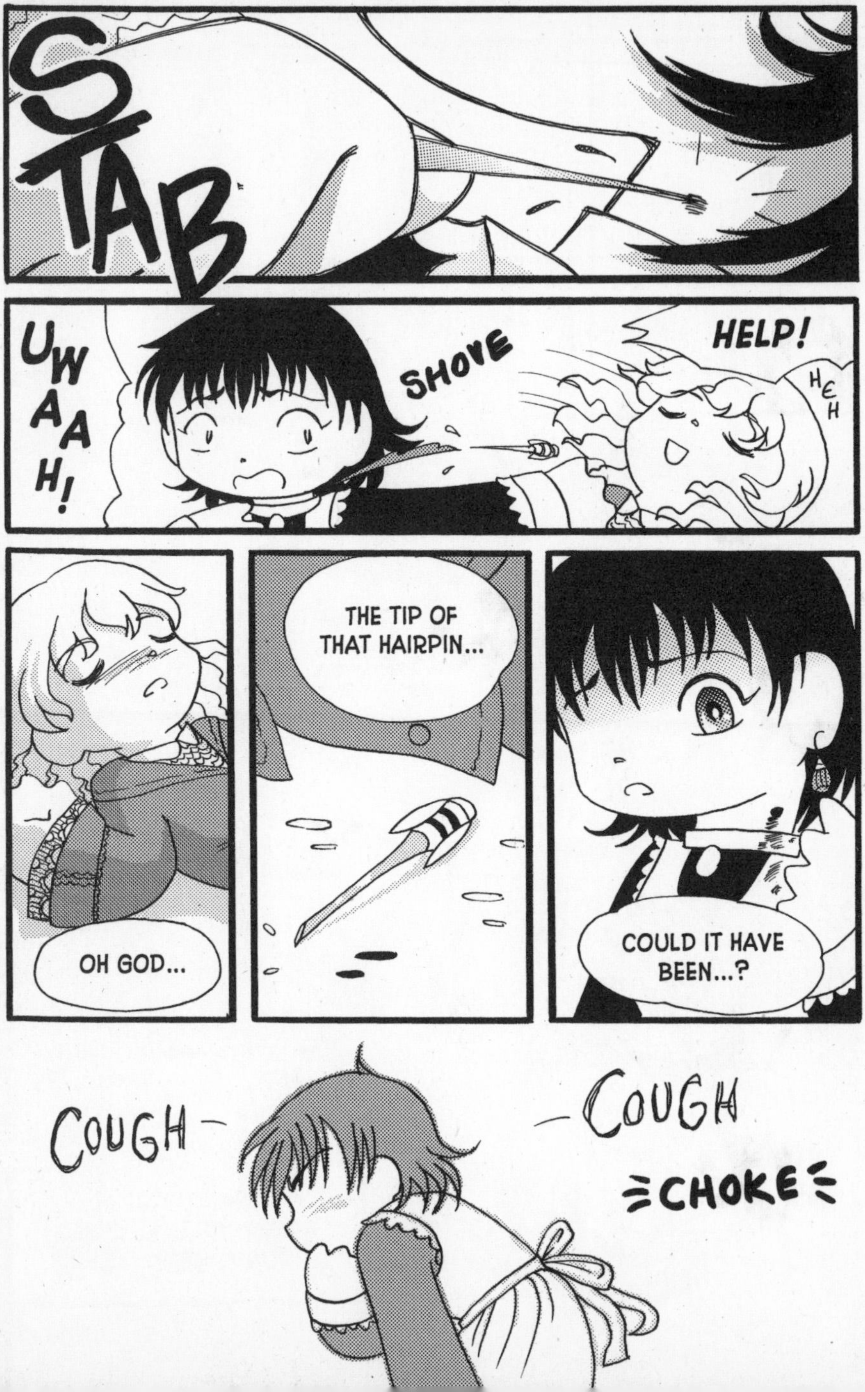
STAB
UWAAH!
SHOVE
HELP!
HEH
OH GOD...
THE TIP OF THAT HAIRPIN...
COULD IT HAVE BEEN...?
COUGH-
-COUGH
CHOKE

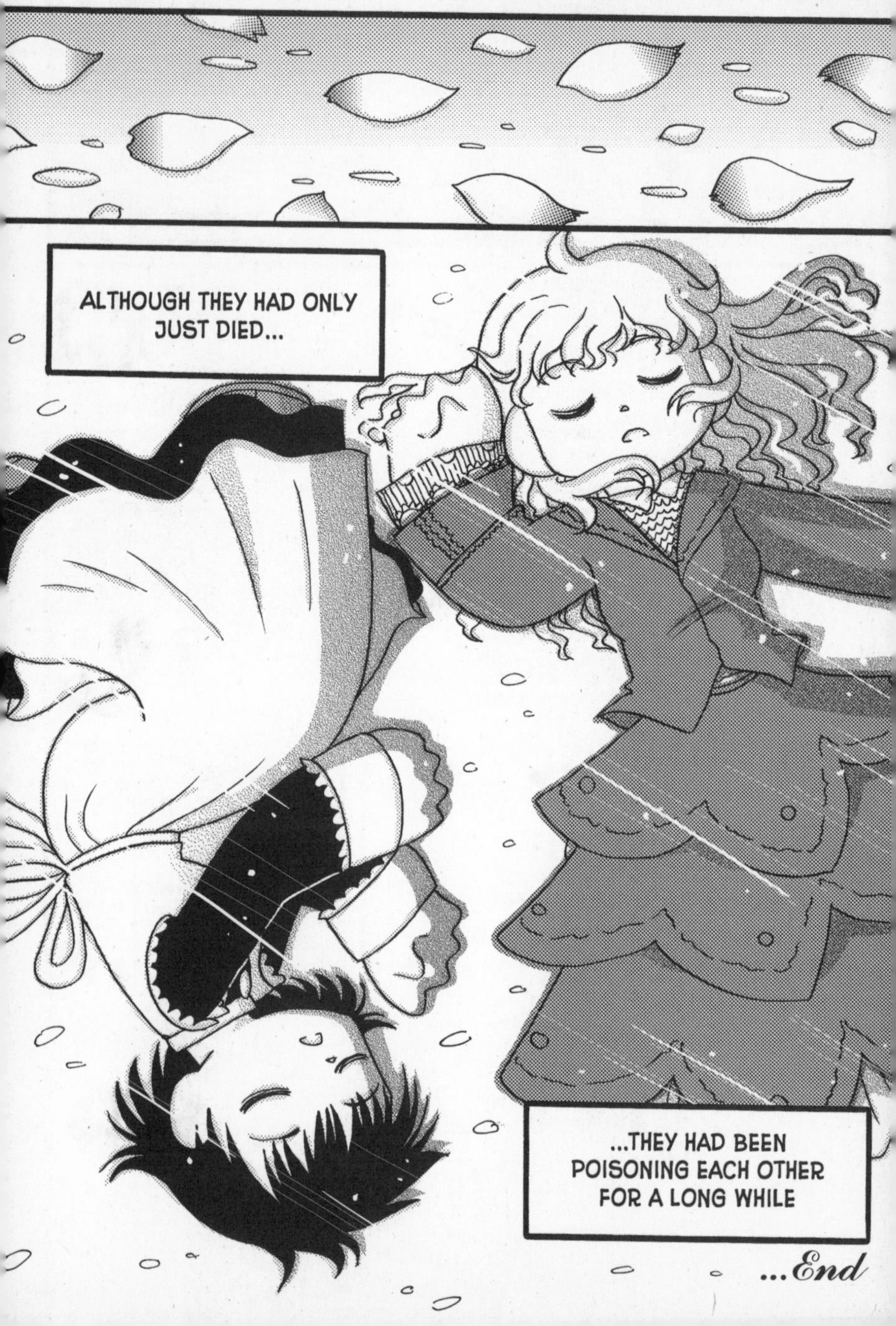
ALTHOUGH THEY HAD ONLY JUST DIED...
...THEY HAD BEEN POISONING EACH OTHER FOR A LONG WHILE
...End

::

BEYOND :: Third Place Winner ::

....

Hannah Saunders was born on the Isle of Wight in 1989. She is
currently studying Graphic Design at college.
www.wanderingmuse.com
www.musechan.deviantart.com

Favorite manga:
La Esperança, Cardcaptor Sakura, Kyo Kara Maoh!, ONE PIECE, Airgear

Favorite manga artists:
CLAMP, Ayami Kojima, THORES Shibamoto, Fumi Yoshinaga

....

Author's Comments:
"Beyond," the title of this story, came out of the blue. I lay in bed, racking
my brains, trying to think of something, anything, to call my nameless
manga before that looming deadline came and went. "Beyond" was all
I could think of. And "Beyond" stuck. And I thought afterwards, why did
I choose it? And I figured that this was what my manga was about—the
characters learn to look beyond the hate of those around them, and see
what lies beyond friendship, beyond love, beyond this life and into the next.

I hope you enjoy this manga as much as I enjoyed drawing and writing it
(although it was a grind at times!). And I also hope you feel like giving Shiro
a nice, big hug at the end. (laughs)
—*Hannah Saunders*

::

BEYOND :: Third Place Winner ::

....

Judge's Comments:
This entry stood out to me as being one of the most "manga" of the top 15. But that can be a detriment sometimes, mind you. An entry that blindly duplicates a "Japanese" aesthetic often winds up being too derivative, and lacking the originality and creativity that I look for as a judge. However, in spite of some less than subtle storytelling devices (naming your characters Kuro & Shiro, "black & white," is the literary equivalent of hitting the reader over the head with a hammer), the plot is rendered with skill, and by the end of the allotted twenty pages I cared about the characters and their tragic fate.

Hannah Saunders did a great job of using beautiful, cleanly-rendered figures and skilled toning to present a clear and comprehensible story, and I thought her designs were attractive and consistent (And the moon spirits were awfully cute!). The balance between more detailed designs and comedic chibi moments helped establish the initial tone of the story, which set up the sorrowful ending all the more solidly. Some anatomical elements could be stronger, backgrounds could be rendered in more detail in places, and there were a few pages where the reading order of the panels and balloons was a bit confusing, but overall I was impressed by how competent Ms. Saunders is as an artist and a writer. I look forward to seeing her go forward with her talent and create something even more original and compelling.
—*Lillian Diaz-Przybyl*

Judge's Comments:
This is a story of intimates at odds. One is committed to doing the right thing, whatever the cost—even if it means hurting the other, who wishes no harm to anyone, but can no longer hide what he truly is.

It is very touching...and very confusing.

The artist's most impressive strength is in the way she reveals emotion through the characters' expressions and body language. On page 14, when Kuro is leaving for battle, every look reveals volumes—from Aunty Yoko's stooped hopelessness to the way Kuro hides behind his glasses and uniform, unable to look into Shiro's eyes—so eager and loving, yet tinged with worry.

Unfortunately, not every page lives up to that standard. The artwork ranges from confident to hesitant, inspired to derivative, dense to sparse. One of the hallmarks of a professional is consistency, and while Saunders definitely shows promise, she isn't there yet. And some crucial story questions are left unanswered: Is Shiro a demon, or just supernatural? Are the characters alive or dead at the end? Does one friend kill the other, do both die, or are they the only two left standing in the rubble? Is the entire story a dream, or just one of the pair's many memories?

So many questions, but one thing is abundantly clear: these two characters love and need each other more than life itself. Communicating that in 20 pages is no easy feat, even for a professional, and to me it's worth volumes of story exposition. I may not always have been sure what was going on, but by the story's end I found myself wishing Shiro and Kuro many more adventures together—and, if invited, I would be honored to join them.
—*Carol Fox*

RISING.STARS.OF.MANGA.2007

BEYOND
THIRD PLACE WINNER

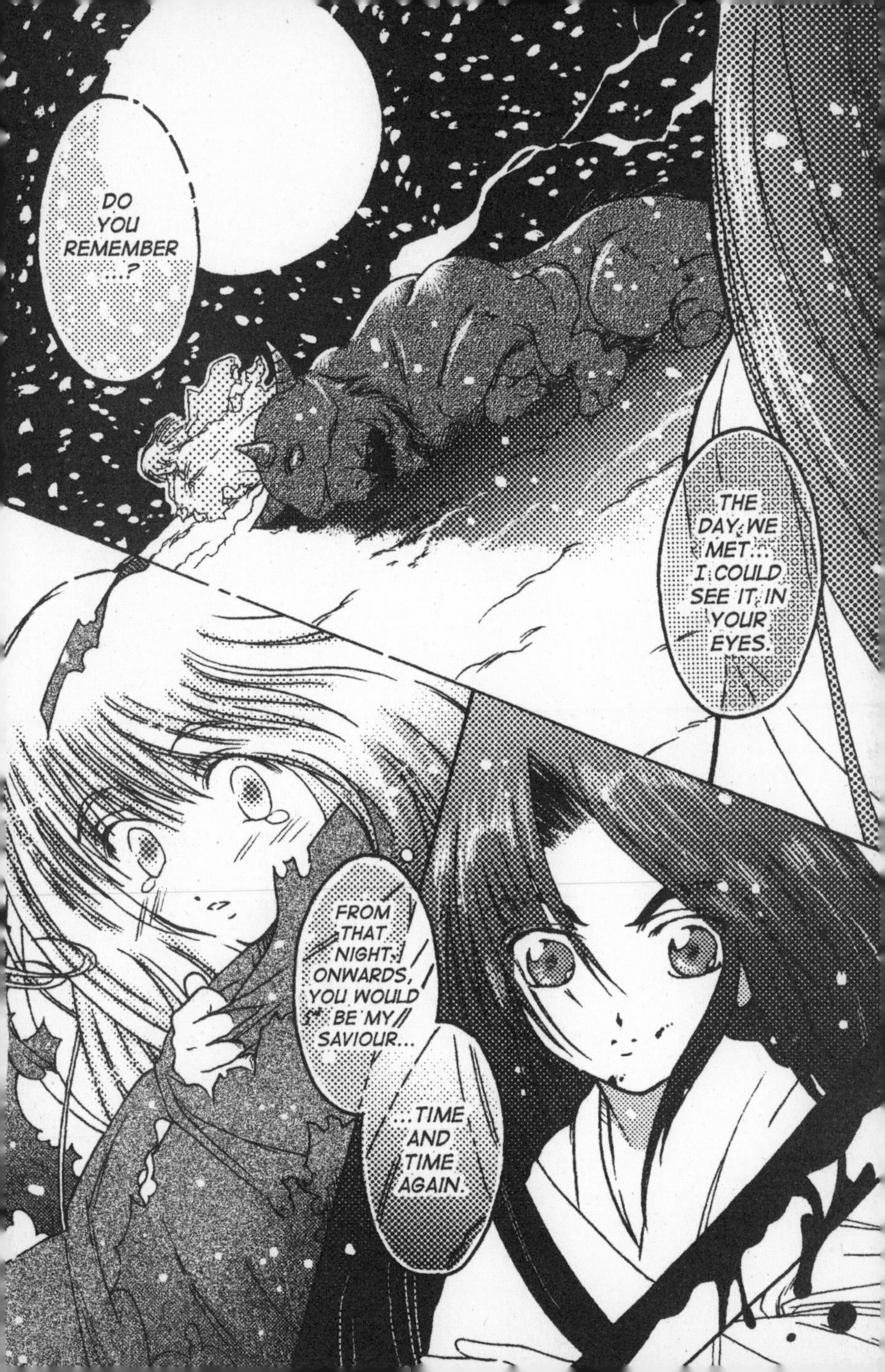
DO YOU REMEMBER ...?
THE DAY WE MET... I COULD SEE IT IN YOUR EYES.
FROM THAT NIGHT ONWARDS, YOU WOULD BE MY SAVIOUR...
...TIME AND TIME AGAIN.

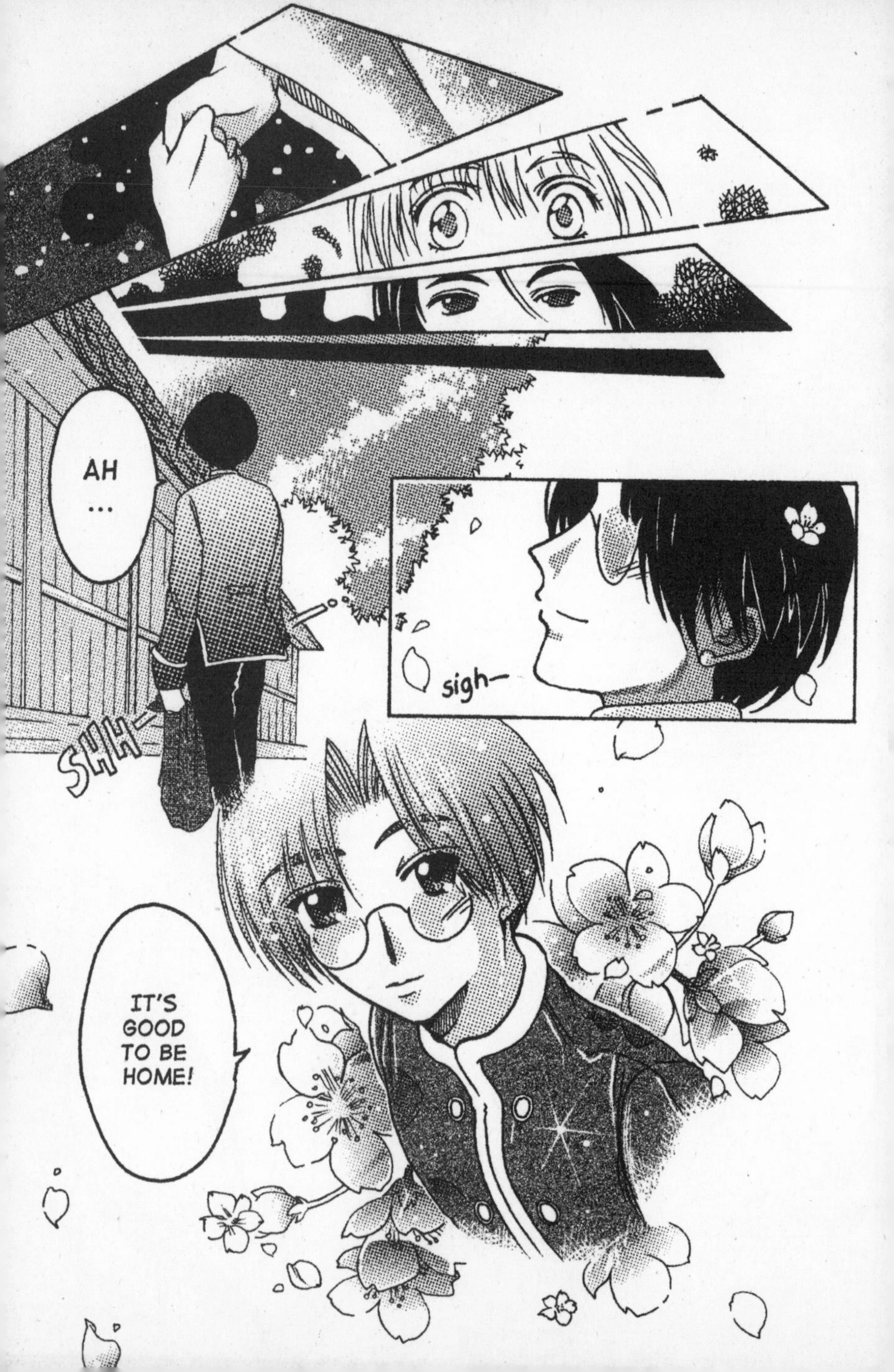
AH ...
SHH-
sigh-
IT'S GOOD TO BE HOME!

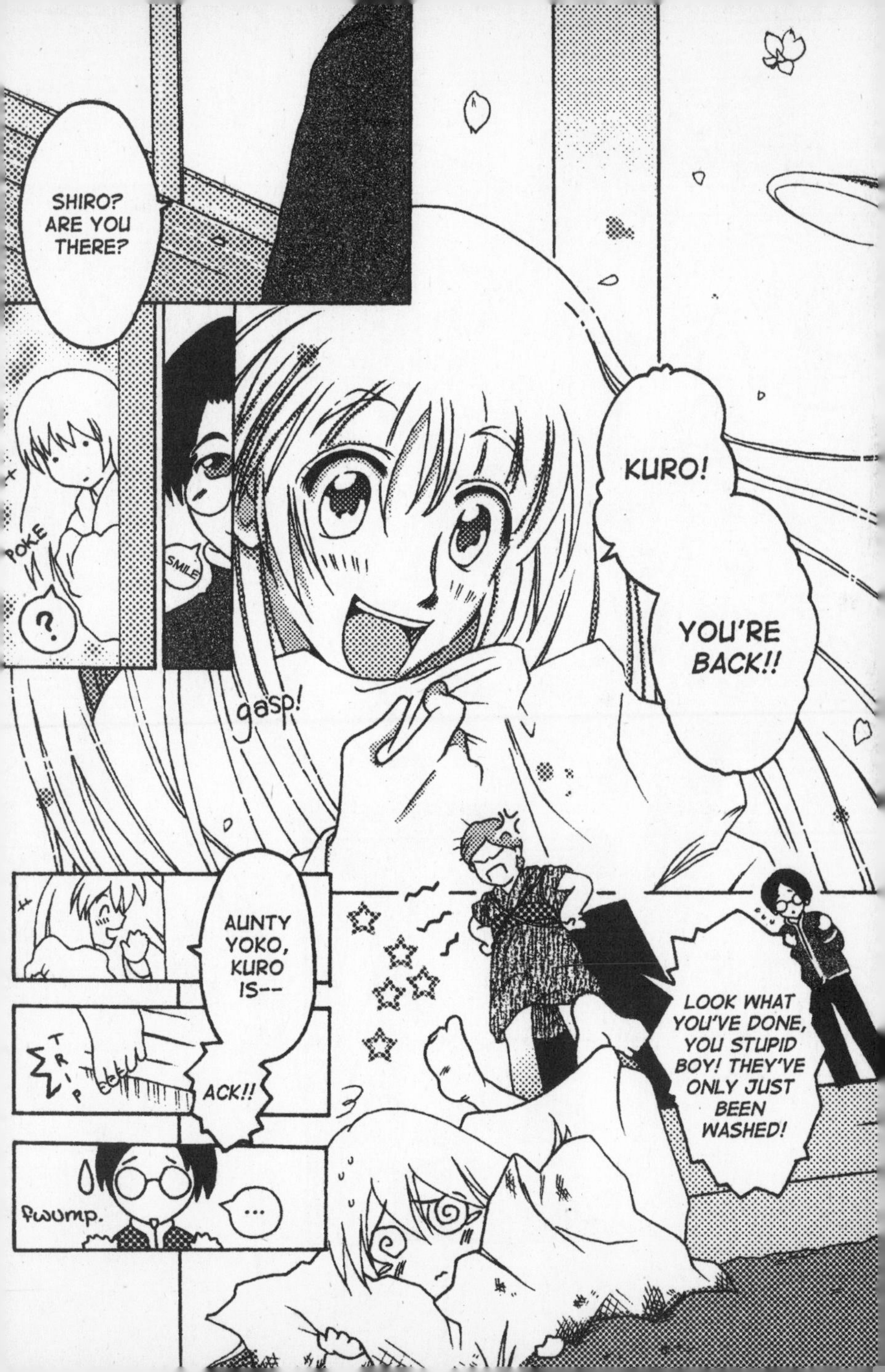
SHIRO? ARE YOU THERE?
POKE
?
SMILE
KURO!
YOU'RE BACK!!
gasp!
AUNTY YOKO, KURO IS--
TRIP
ACK!!
fwump.
...
LOOK WHAT YOU'VE DONE, YOU STUPID BOY! THEY'VE ONLY JUST BEEN WASHED!

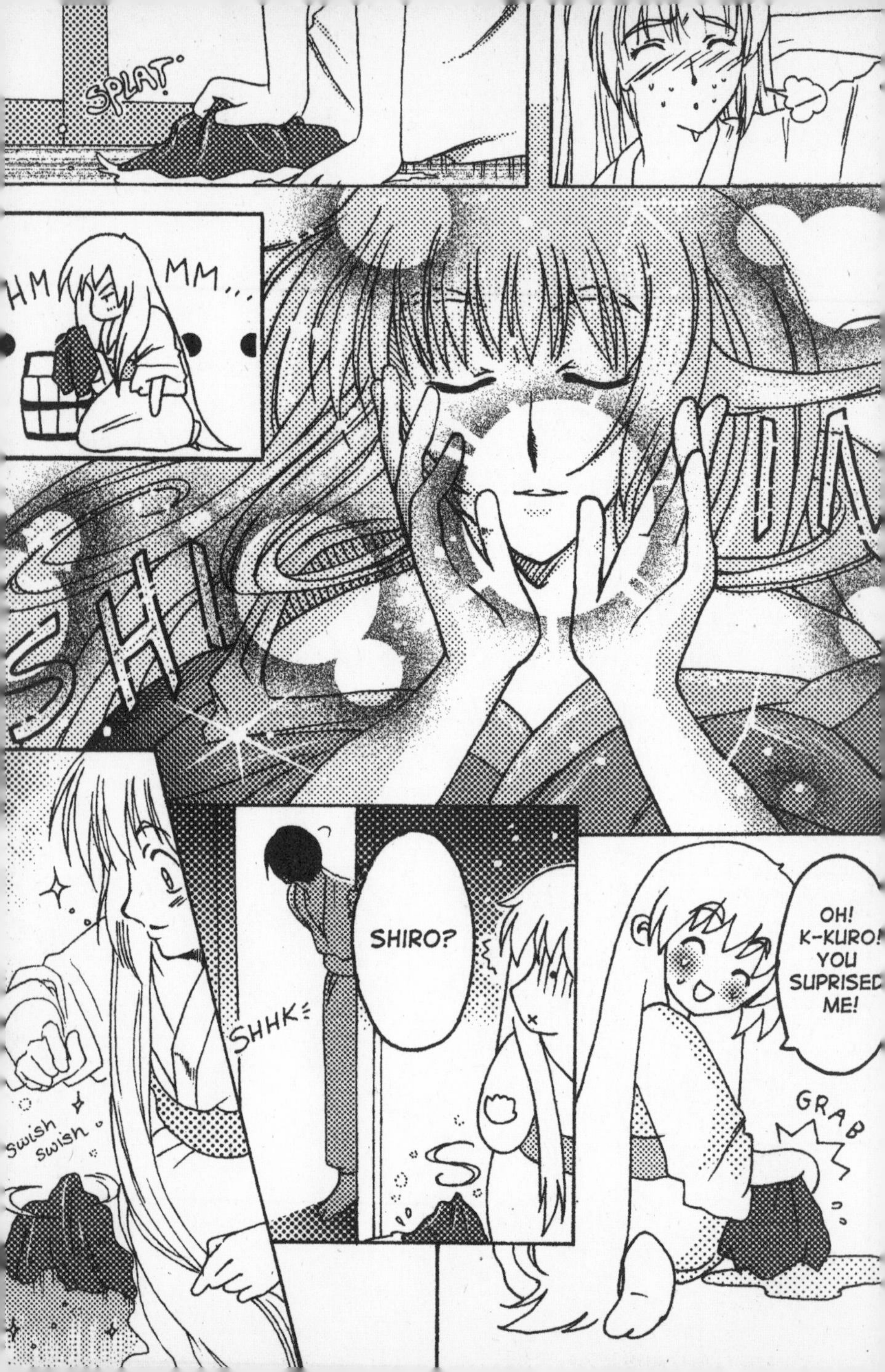
SPLAT!
HM MM...
SHI
swish swish
SHHK
SHIRO?
OH! K-KURO! YOU SUPRISED ME!
GRAB

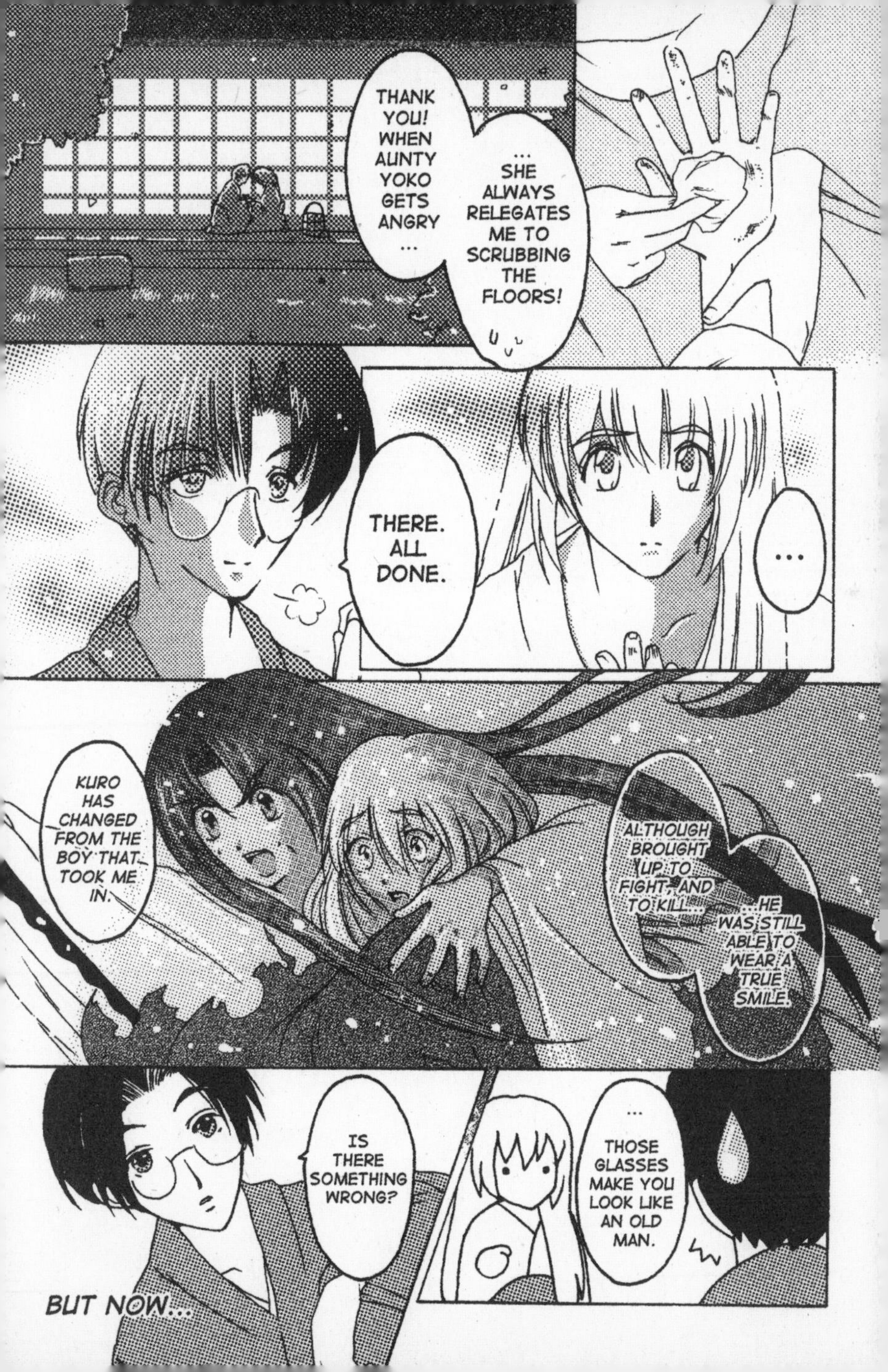
THANK YOU! WHEN AUNTY YOKO GETS ANGRY ...
... SHE ALWAYS RELEGATES ME TO SCRUBBING THE FLOORS!
THERE. ALL DONE.
...
KURO HAS CHANGED FROM THE BOY THAT TOOK ME IN.
ALTHOUGH BROUGHT UP TO FIGHT, AND TO KILL...
...HE WAS STILL ABLE TO WEAR A TRUE SMILE.
BUT NOW...
IS THERE SOMETHING WRONG?
... THOSE GLASSES MAKE YOU LOOK LIKE AN OLD MAN.

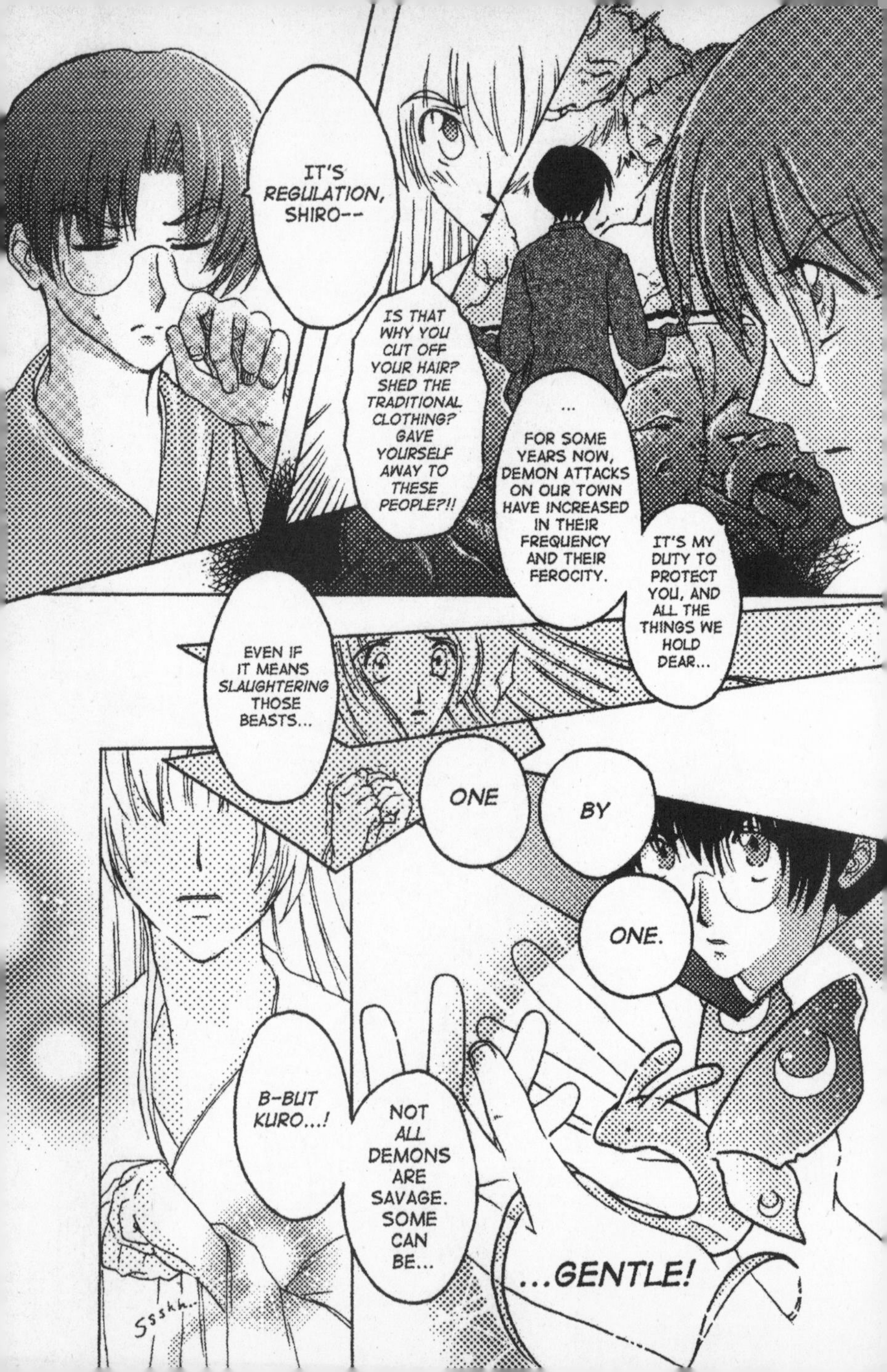
IT'S REGULATION, SHIRO--
IS THAT WHY YOU CUT OFF YOUR HAIR? SHED THE TRADITIONAL CLOTHING? GAVE YOURSELF AWAY TO THESE PEOPLE?!!
...
FOR SOME YEARS NOW, DEMON ATTACKS ON OUR TOWN HAVE INCREASED IN THEIR FREQUENCY AND THEIR FEROCITY.
IT'S MY DUTY TO PROTECT YOU, AND ALL THE THINGS WE HOLD DEAR...
EVEN IF IT MEANS SLAUGHTERING THOSE BEASTS...
ONE
BY
ONE.
B-BUT KURO...!
NOT ALL DEMONS ARE SAVAGE. SOME CAN BE...
...GENTLE!
Ssskh..

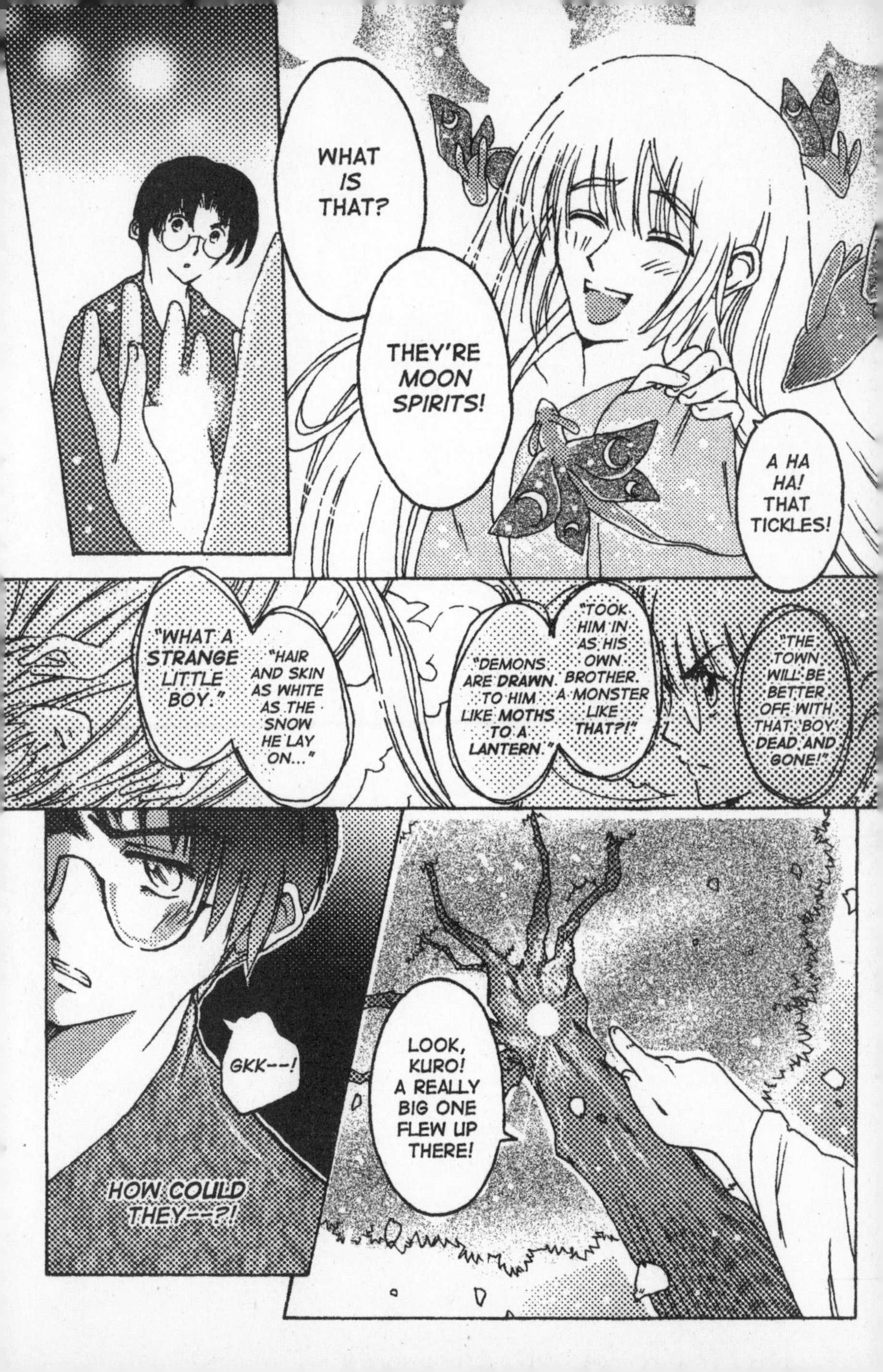
WHAT *IS* THAT?
THEY'RE *MOON SPIRITS!*
A HA HA! THAT TICKLES!
"WHAT A **STRANGE** LITTLE BOY."
"HAIR AND SKIN AS WHITE AS THE SNOW HE LAY ON..."
"DEMONS ARE **DRAWN** TO HIM LIKE **MOTHS** TO A **LANTERN.**"
"TOOK HIM IN AS HIS OWN BROTHER. A MONSTER LIKE THAT?!"
"THE TOWN WILL BE BETTER OFF WITH THAT BOY **DEAD AND GONE!**"
GKK--!
HOW COULD THEY--?!
LOOK, KURO! A REALLY BIG ONE FLEW UP THERE!

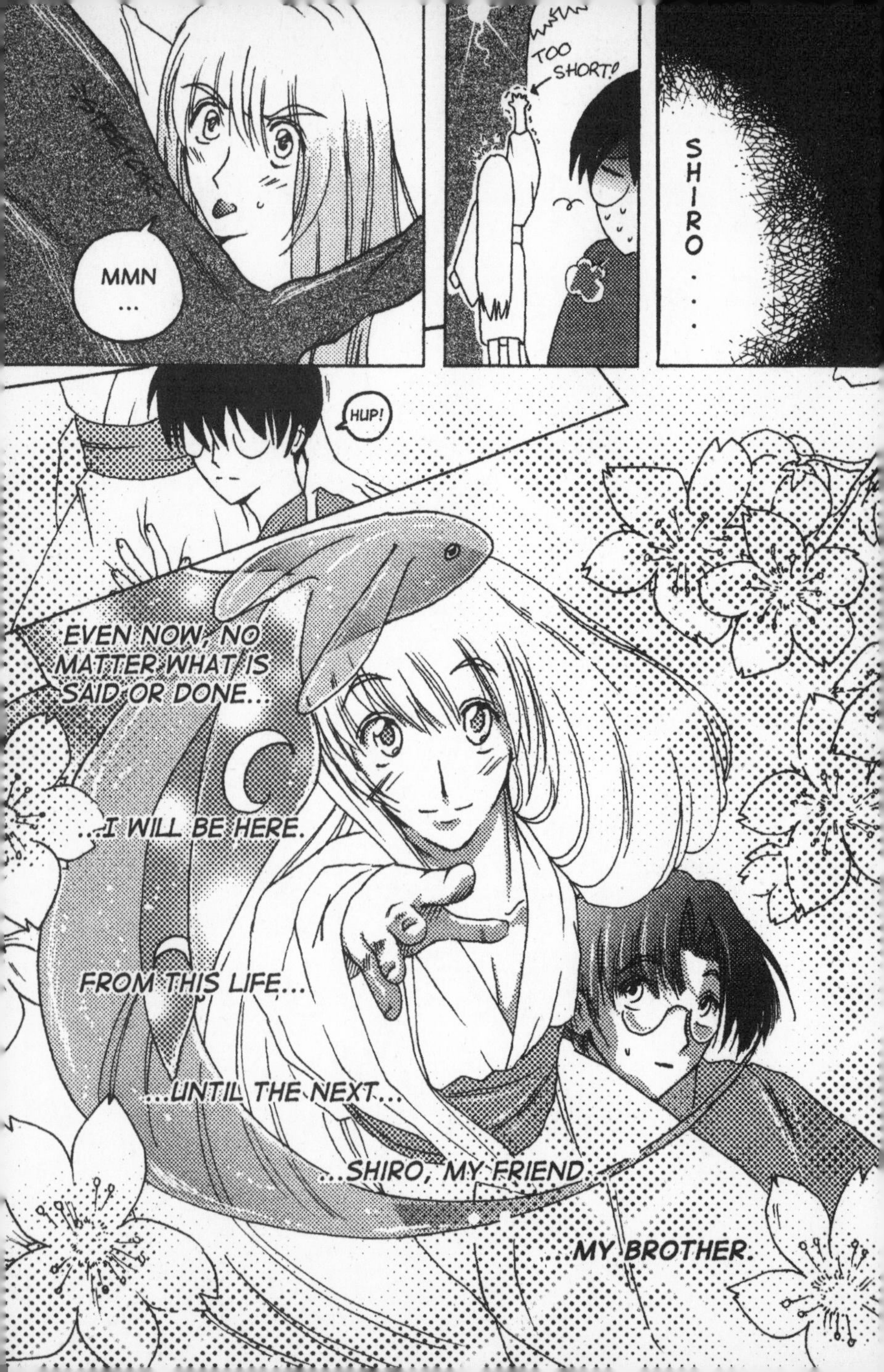
MMN
...
TOO SHORT!
SHIRO . . .
HUP!
EVEN NOW, NO MATTER WHAT IS SAID OR DONE...
...I WILL BE HERE.
FROM THIS LIFE...
...UNTIL THE NEXT...
...SHIRO, MY FRIEND...
...MY BROTHER.

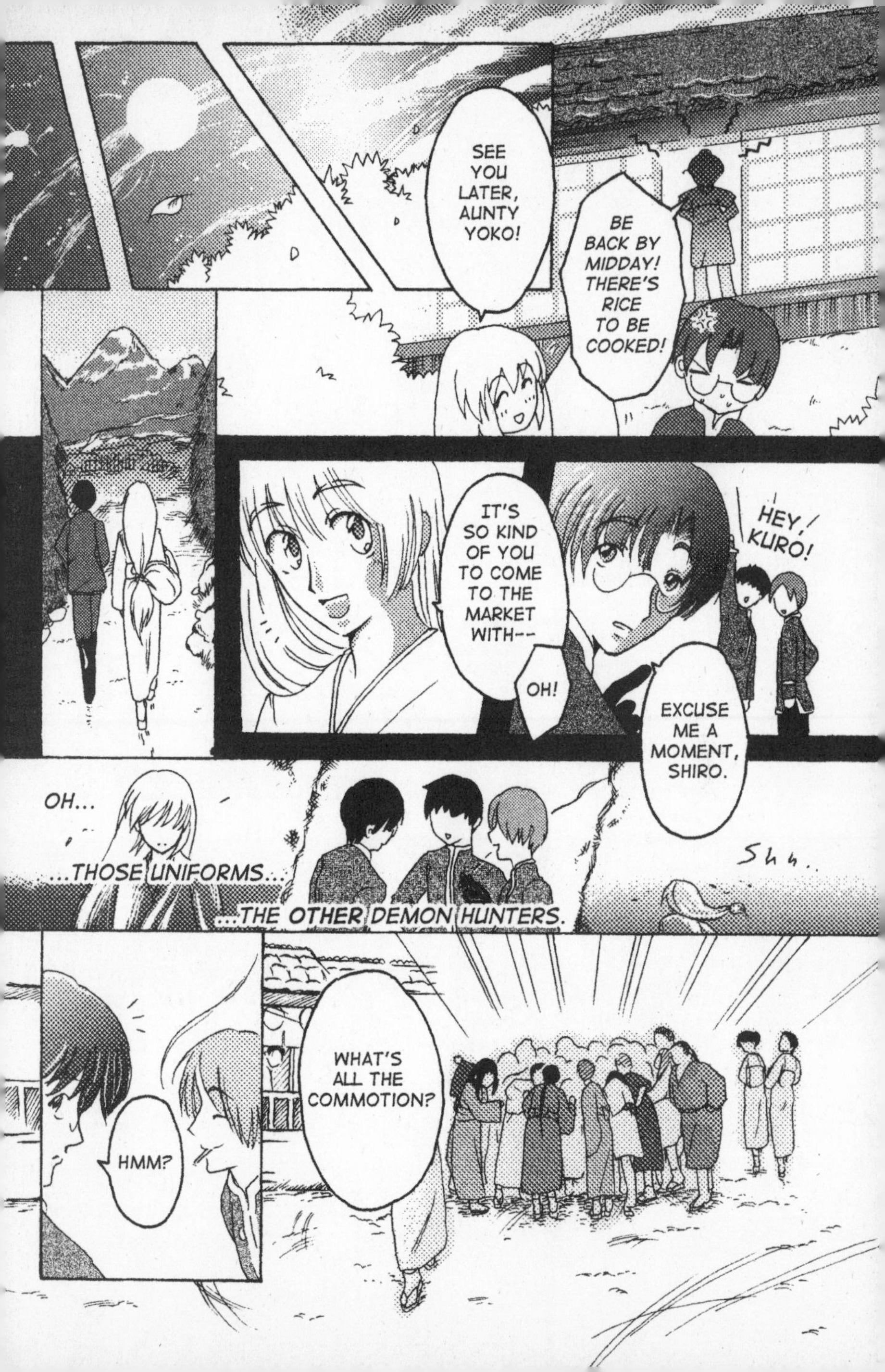
SEE YOU LATER, AUNTY YOKO!
BE BACK BY MIDDAY! THERE'S RICE TO BE COOKED!
IT'S SO KIND OF YOU TO COME TO THE MARKET WITH--
OH!
HEY, KURO!
EXCUSE ME A MOMENT, SHIRO.
OH...
...THOSE UNIFORMS...
...THE OTHER DEMON HUNTERS.
Shu..
HMM?
WHAT'S ALL THE COMMOTION?

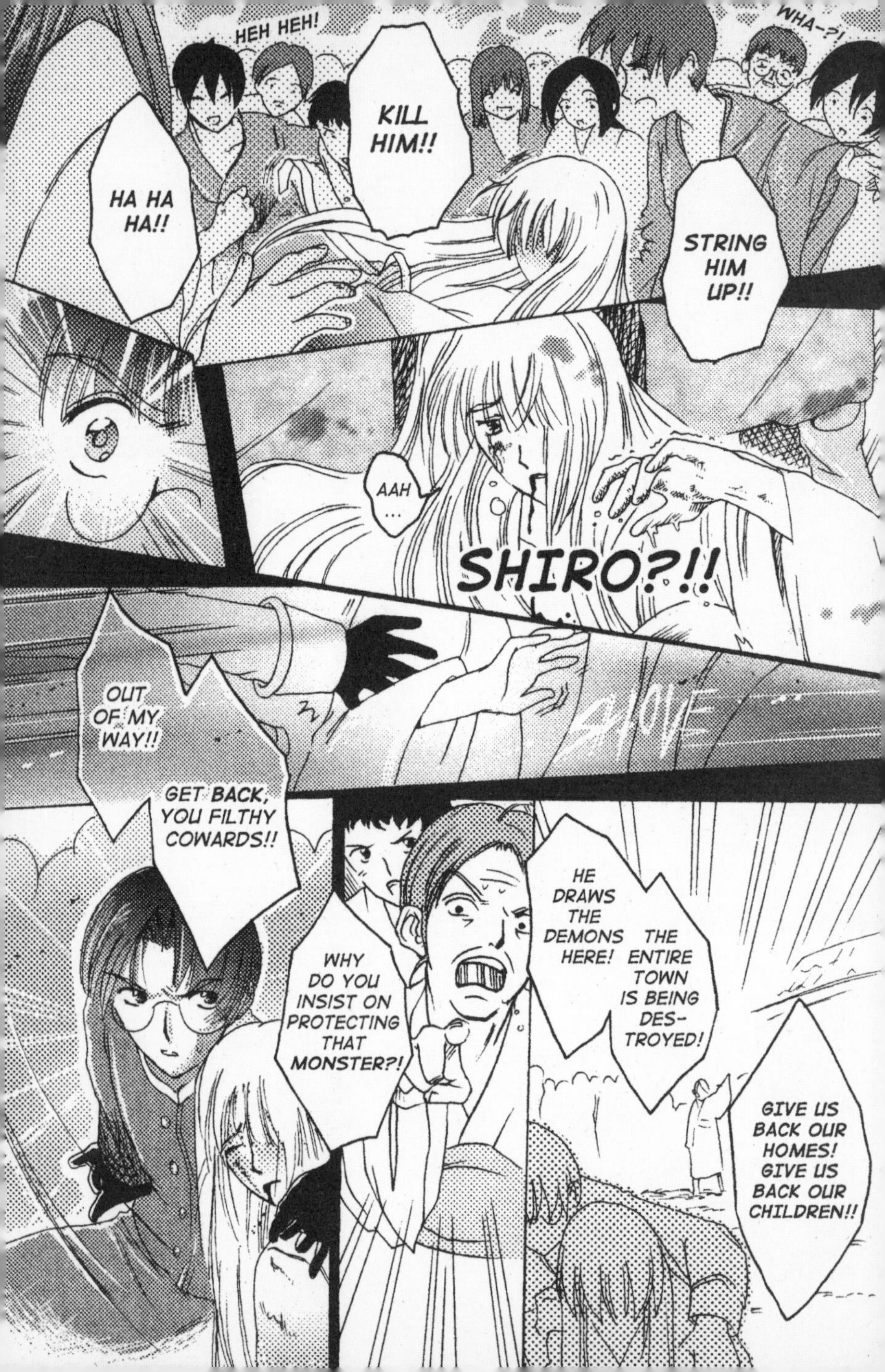
HEH HEH!
HA HA HA!!
KILL HIM!!
WHA-?!
STRING HIM UP!!
AAH ...
SHIRO?!!
OUT OF MY WAY!!
SHOVE
GET BACK, YOU FILTHY COWARDS!!
WHY DO YOU INSIST ON PROTECTING THAT MONSTER?!
HE DRAWS THE DEMONS HERE!
THE ENTIRE TOWN IS BEING DES-TROYED!
GIVE US BACK OUR HOMES! GIVE US BACK OUR CHILDREN!!

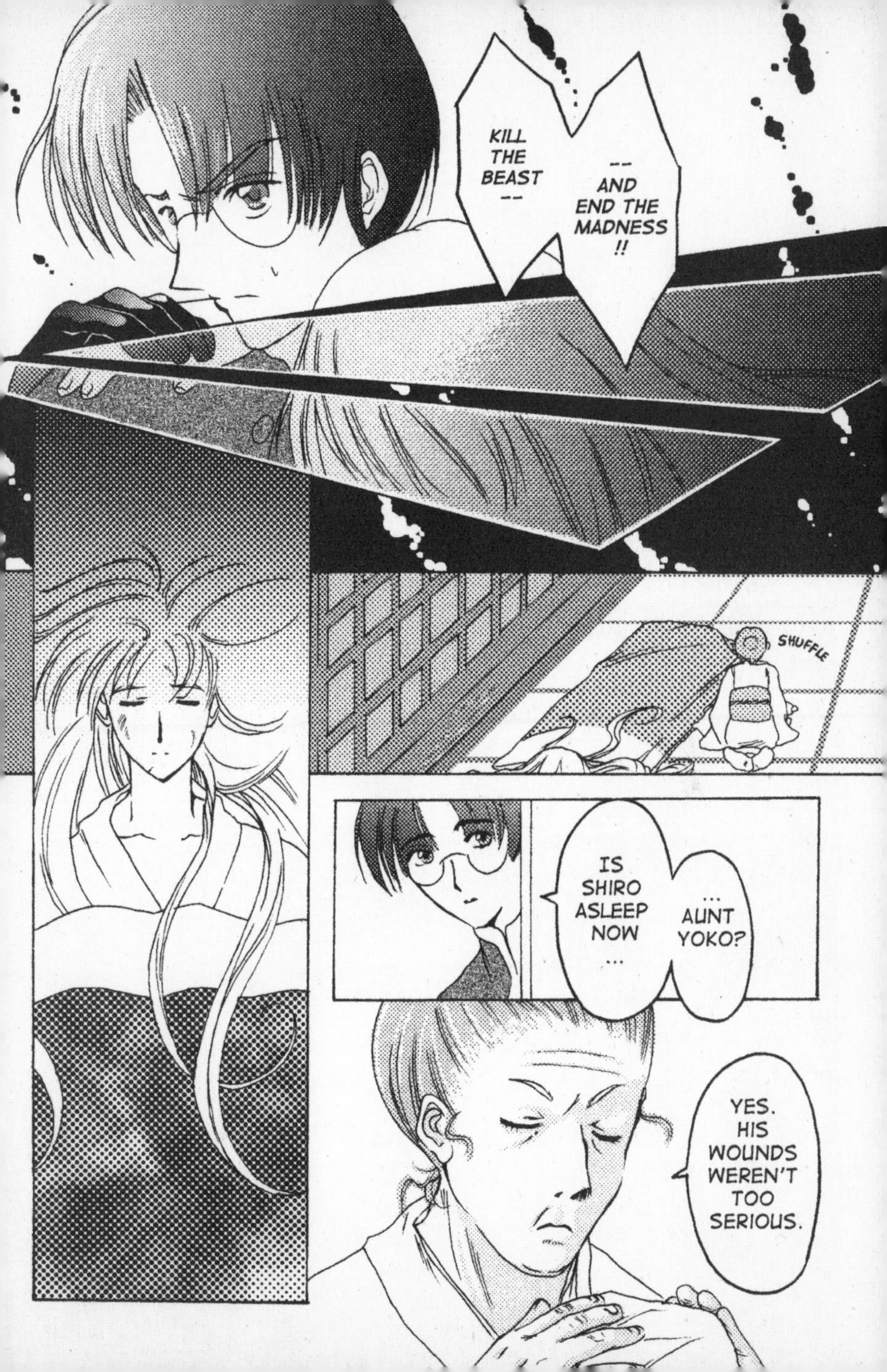
KILL THE BEAST --
-- AND END THE MADNESS !!
SHUFFLE
IS SHIRO ASLEEP NOW ...
... AUNT YOKO?
YES. HIS WOUNDS WEREN'T TOO SERIOUS.

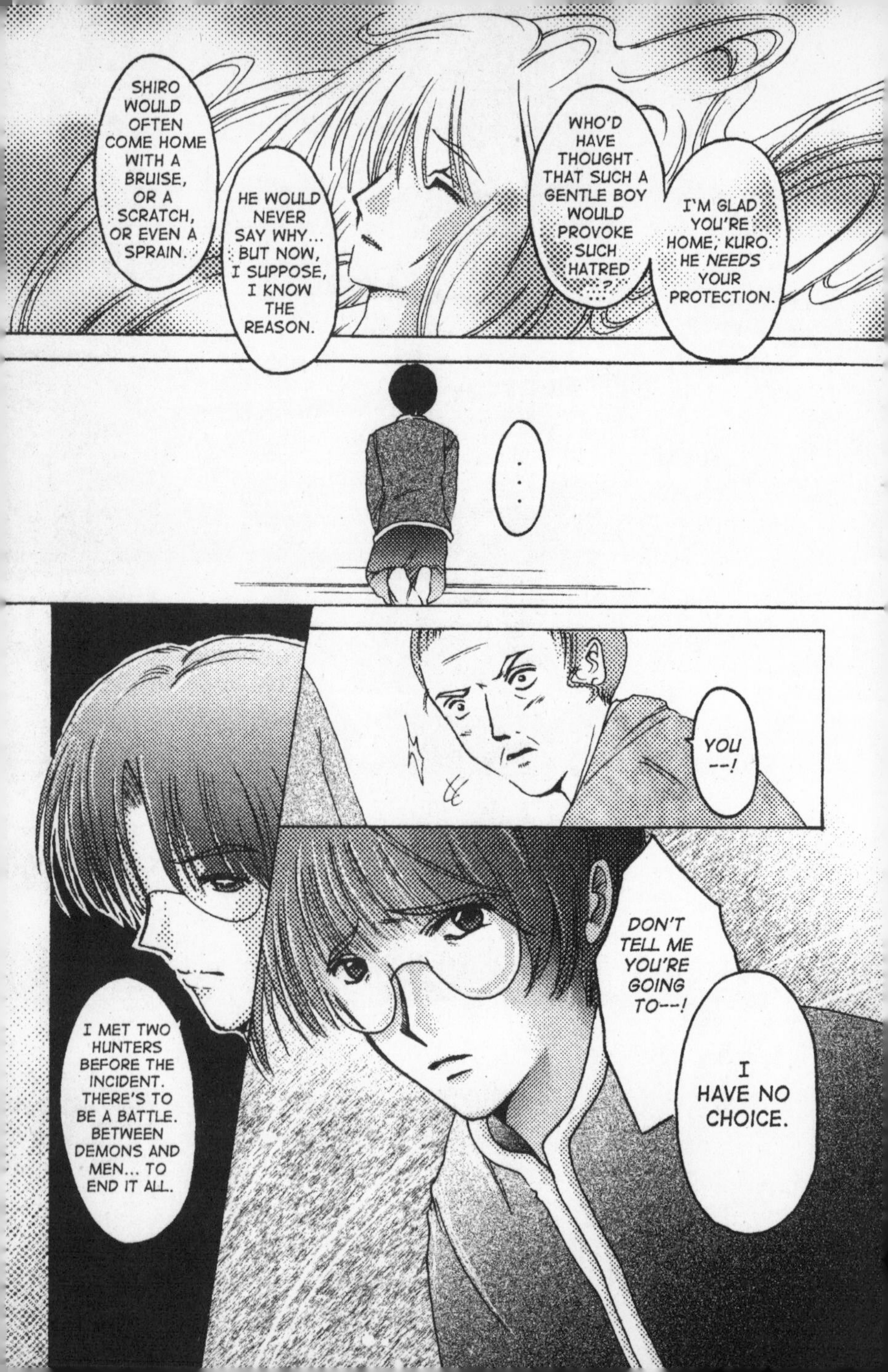
SHIRO WOULD OFTEN COME HOME WITH A BRUISE, OR A SCRATCH, OR EVEN A SPRAIN.
HE WOULD NEVER SAY WHY... BUT NOW, I SUPPOSE, I KNOW THE REASON.
WHO'D HAVE THOUGHT THAT SUCH A GENTLE BOY WOULD PROVOKE SUCH HATRED...?
I'M GLAD YOU'RE HOME, KURO. HE *NEEDS* YOUR PROTECTION.
...
YOU --!
DON'T TELL ME YOU'RE GOING TO--!
I MET TWO HUNTERS BEFORE THE INCIDENT. THERE'S TO BE A BATTLE. BETWEEN DEMONS AND MEN... TO END IT ALL.
I HAVE NO CHOICE.

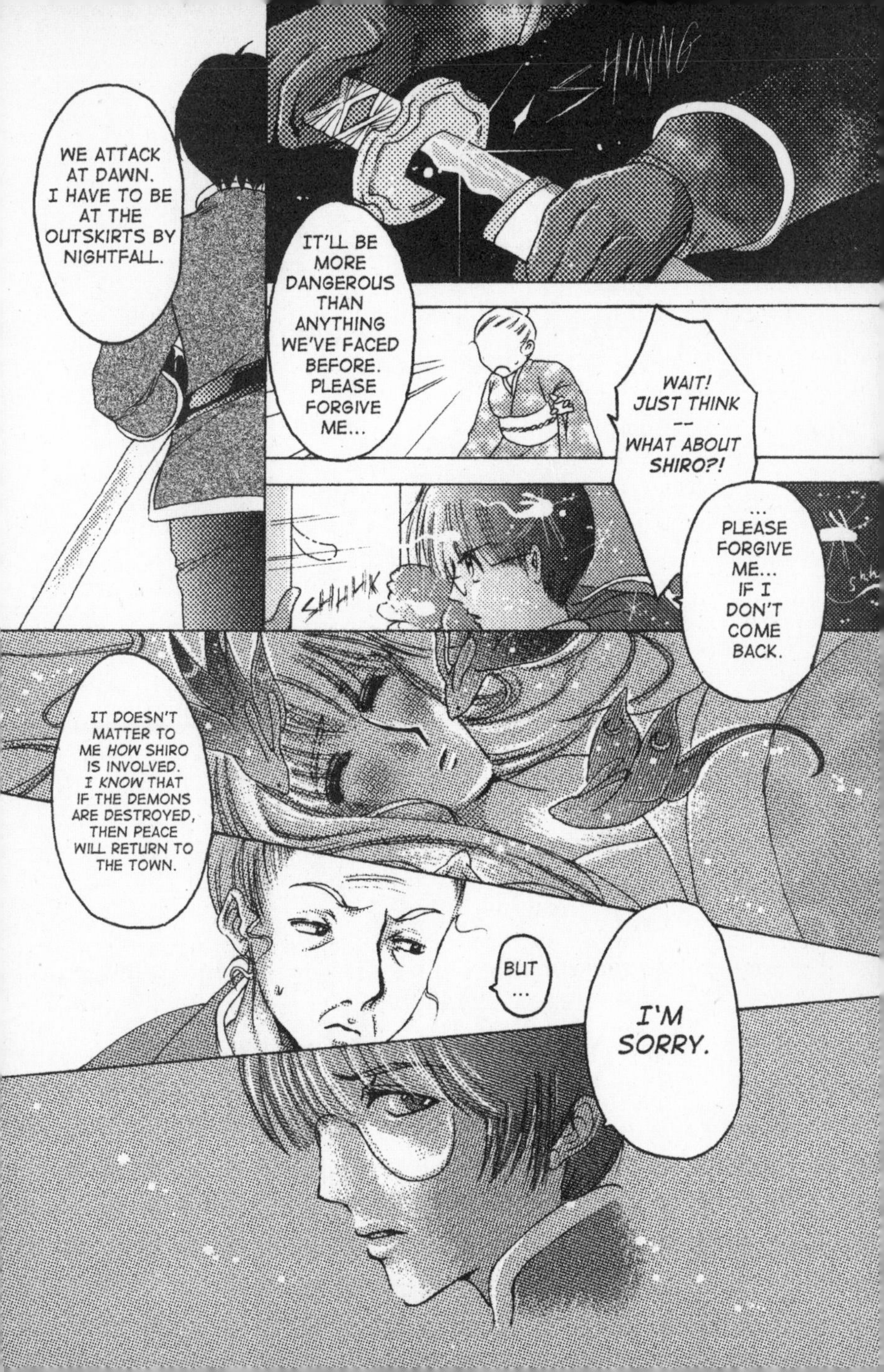
WE ATTACK AT DAWN. I HAVE TO BE AT THE OUTSKIRTS BY NIGHTFALL.
SHINNG
IT'LL BE MORE DANGEROUS THAN ANYTHING WE'VE FACED BEFORE. PLEASE FORGIVE ME...
WAIT! JUST THINK -- WHAT ABOUT SHIRO?!
SHHHK
... PLEASE FORGIVE ME... IF I DON'T COME BACK.
IT DOESN'T MATTER TO ME *HOW* SHIRO IS INVOLVED. I *KNOW* THAT IF THE DEMONS ARE DESTROYED, THEN PEACE WILL RETURN TO THE TOWN.
BUT ...
I'M SORRY.

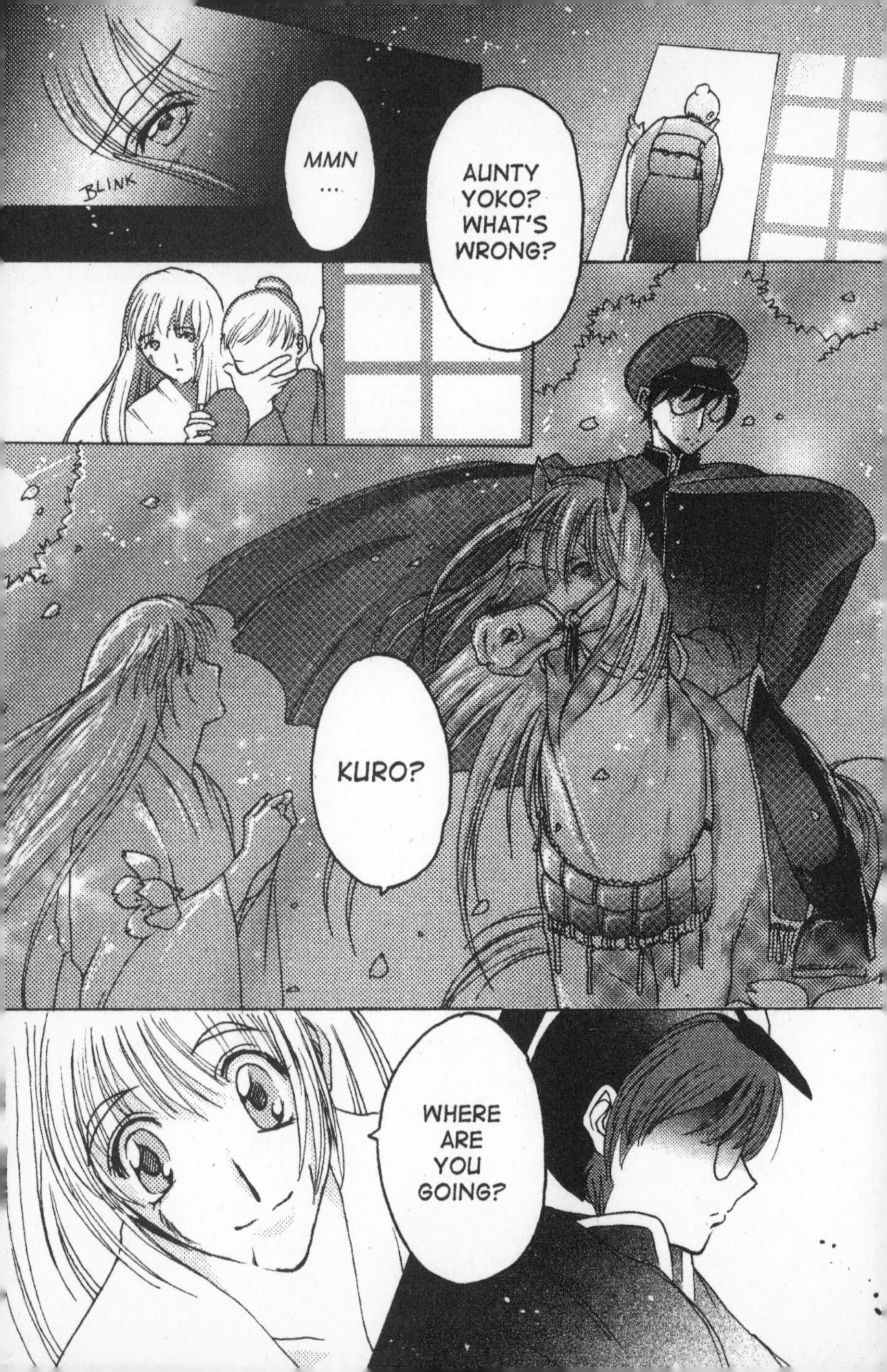
BLINK
MMN ...
AUNTY YOKO? WHAT'S WRONG?
KURO?
WHERE ARE YOU GOING?

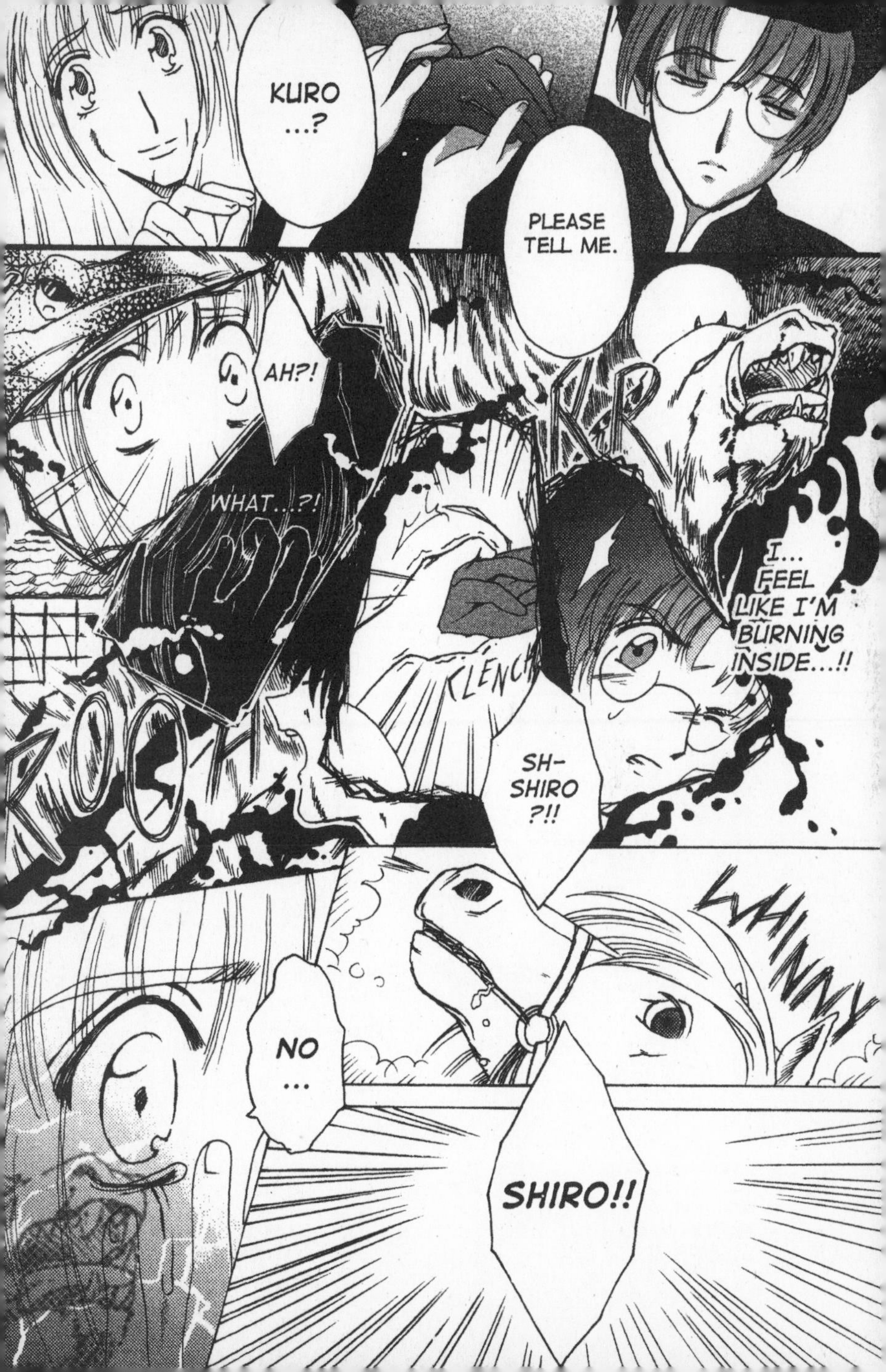
KURO ...?
PLEASE TELL ME.
AH?!
WHAT...?!
KLENCH
I... FEEL LIKE I'M BURNING INSIDE...!!
SH-SHIRO ?!!
NO ...
WHINNY
SHIRO!!

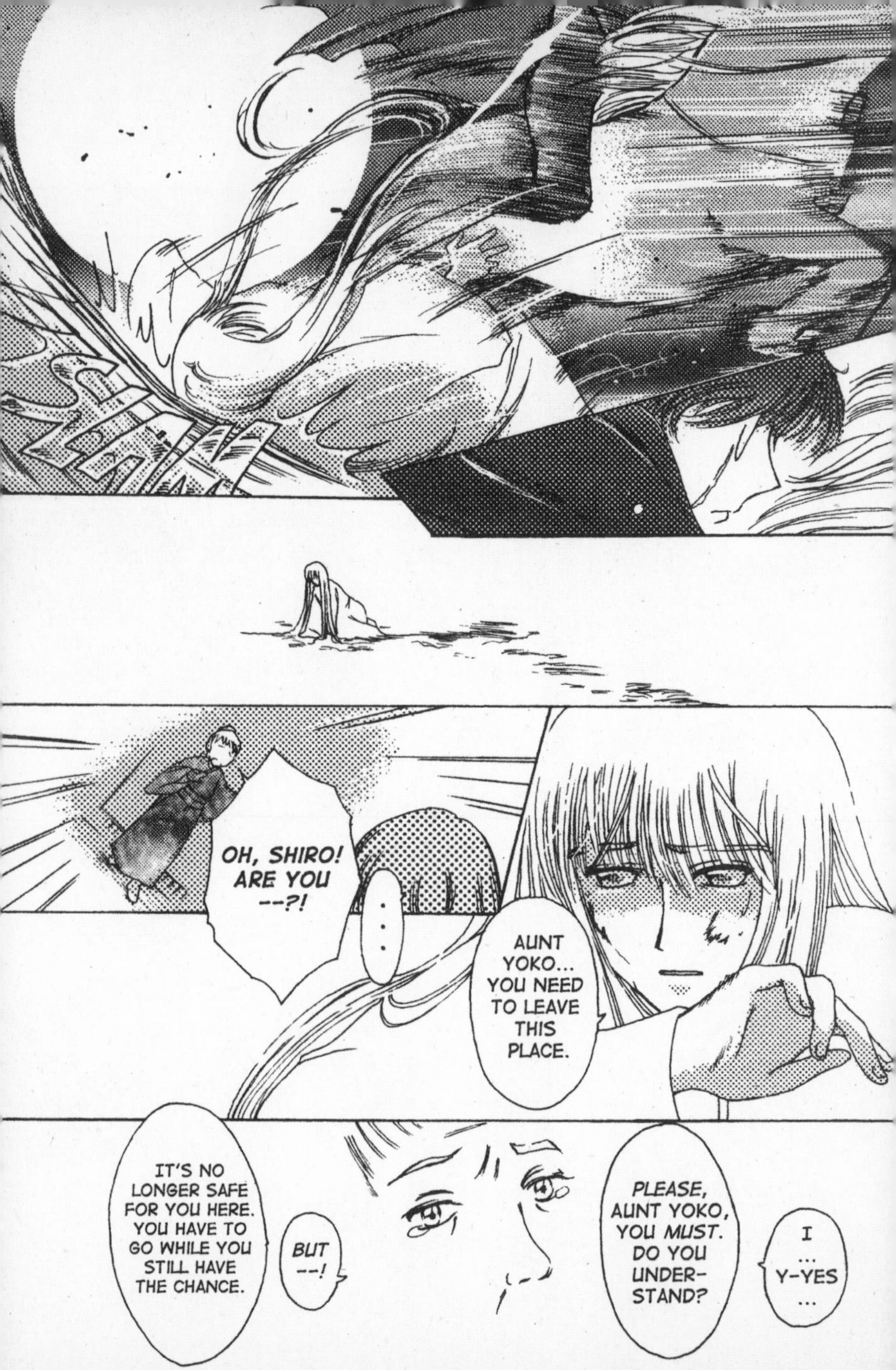
OH, SHIRO! ARE YOU --?!
...
AUNT YOKO... YOU NEED TO LEAVE THIS PLACE.
IT'S NO LONGER SAFE FOR YOU HERE. YOU HAVE TO GO WHILE YOU STILL HAVE THE CHANCE.
BUT --!
PLEASE, AUNT YOKO, YOU *MUST*. DO YOU UNDER-STAND?
I ... Y-YES ...

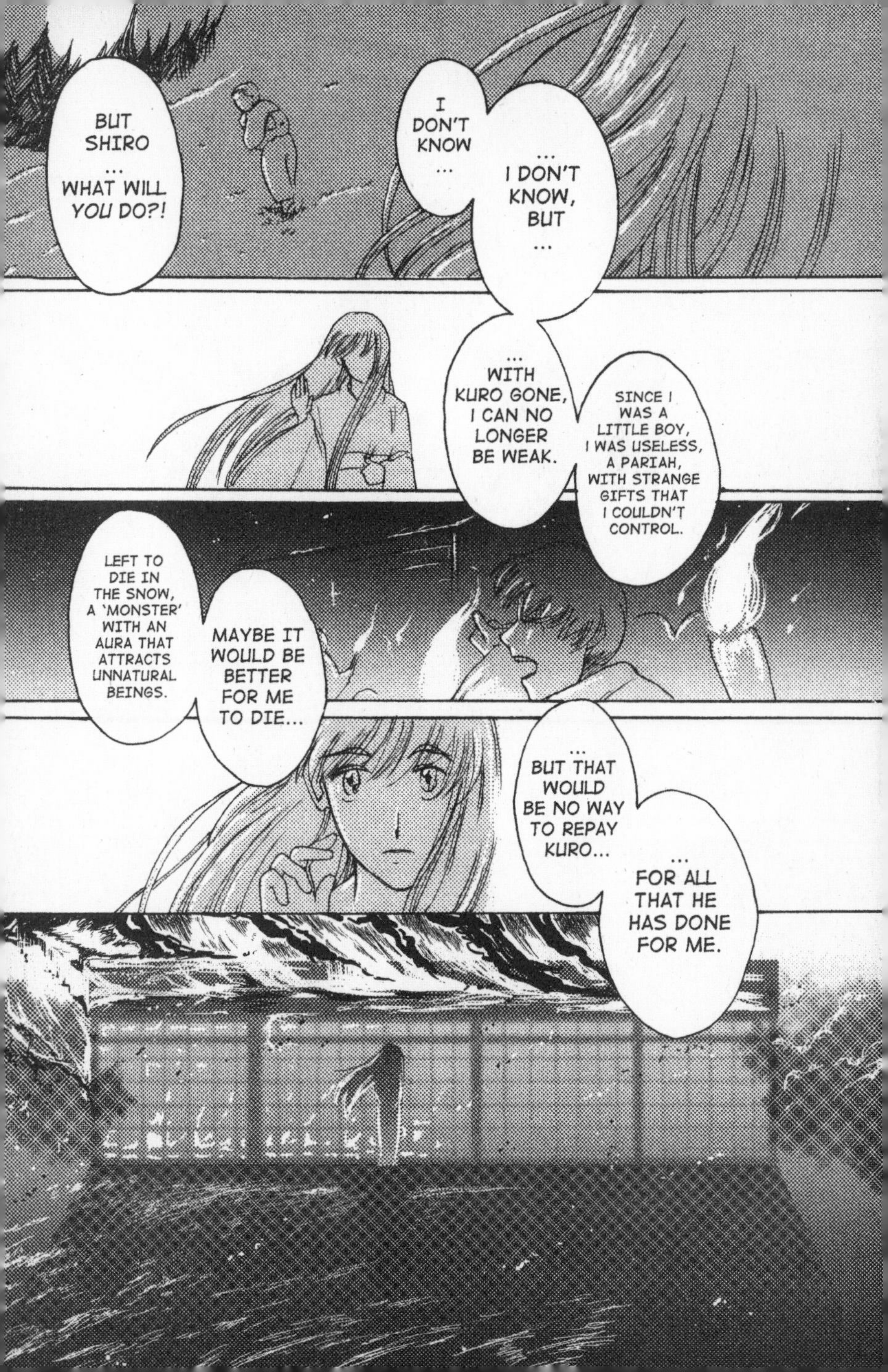
BUT SHIRO ... WHAT WILL *YOU* DO?!
I DON'T KNOW ...
... I DON'T KNOW, BUT ...
... WITH KURO GONE, I CAN NO LONGER BE WEAK.
SINCE I WAS A LITTLE BOY, I WAS USELESS, A PARIAH, WITH STRANGE GIFTS THAT I COULDN'T CONTROL.
LEFT TO DIE IN THE SNOW, A 'MONSTER' WITH AN AURA THAT ATTRACTS UNNATURAL BEINGS.
MAYBE IT WOULD BE BETTER FOR ME TO DIE...
... BUT THAT WOULD BE NO WAY TO REPAY KURO...
... FOR ALL THAT HE HAS DONE FOR ME.

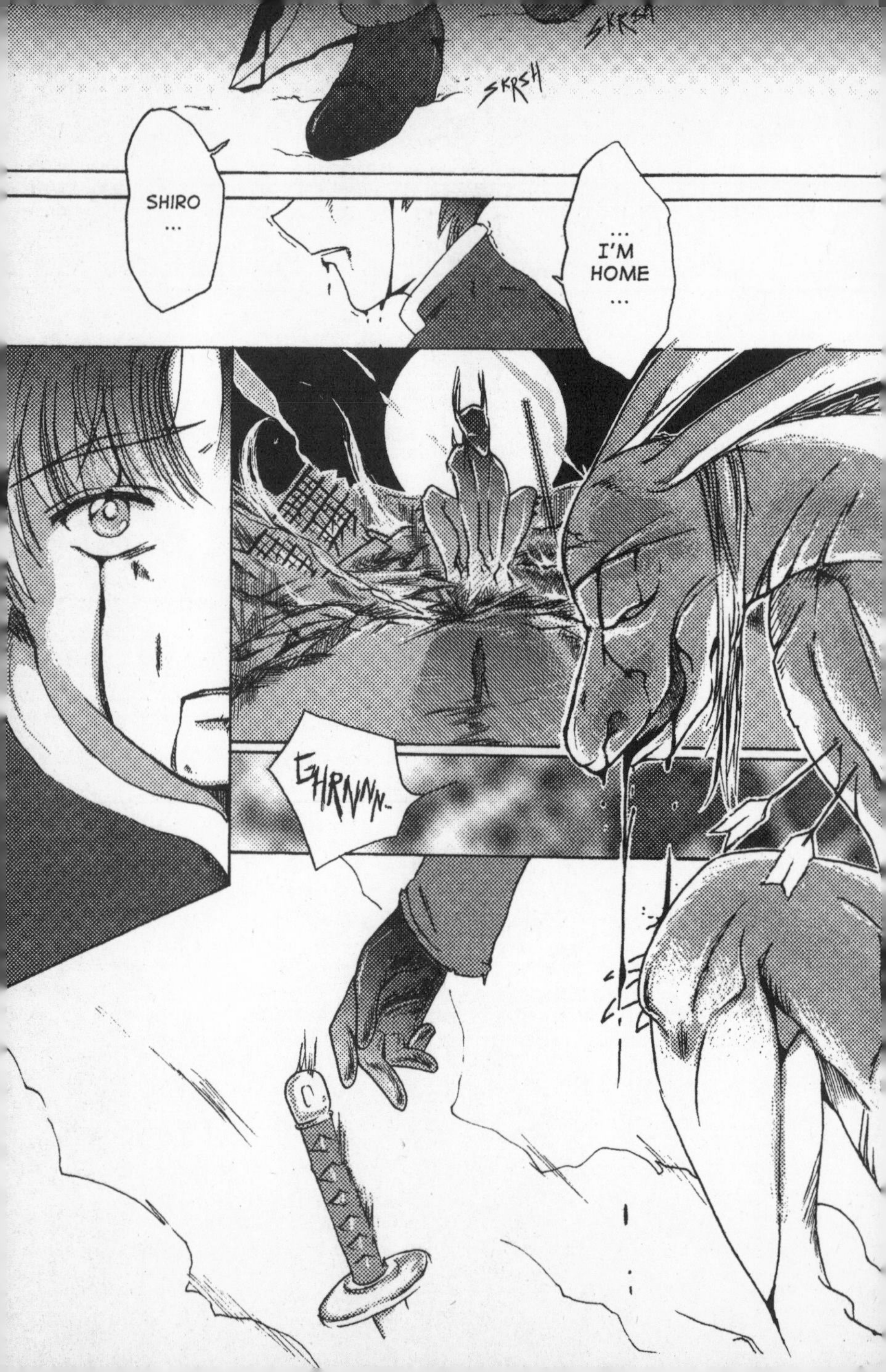
SKRSH
SKRSH
SHIRO ...
... I'M HOME ...
GHRNNN

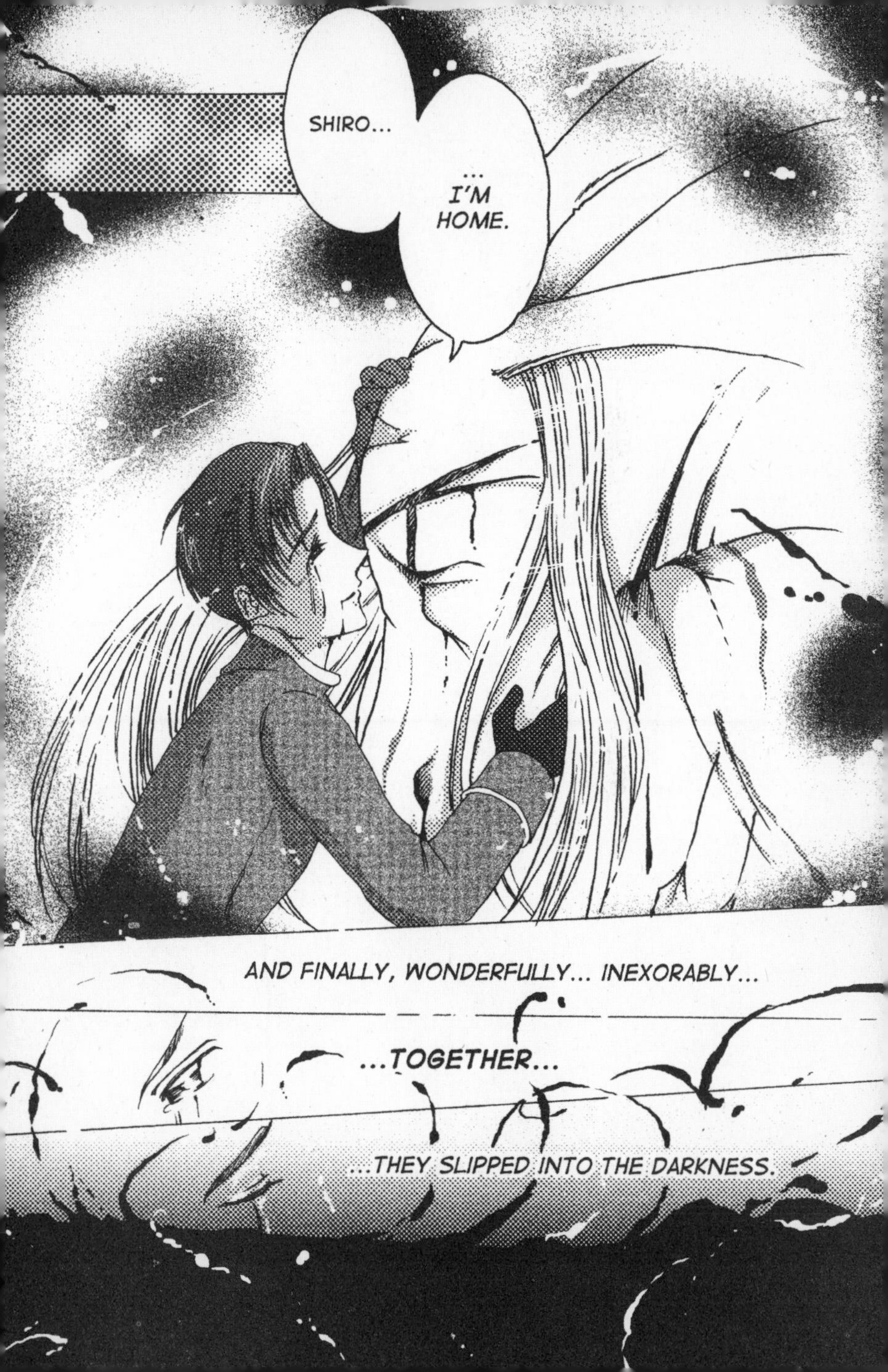
SHIRO...
... I'M HOME.
AND FINALLY, WONDERFULLY... INEXORABLY...
...TOGETHER...
...THEY SLIPPED INTO THE DARKNESS.

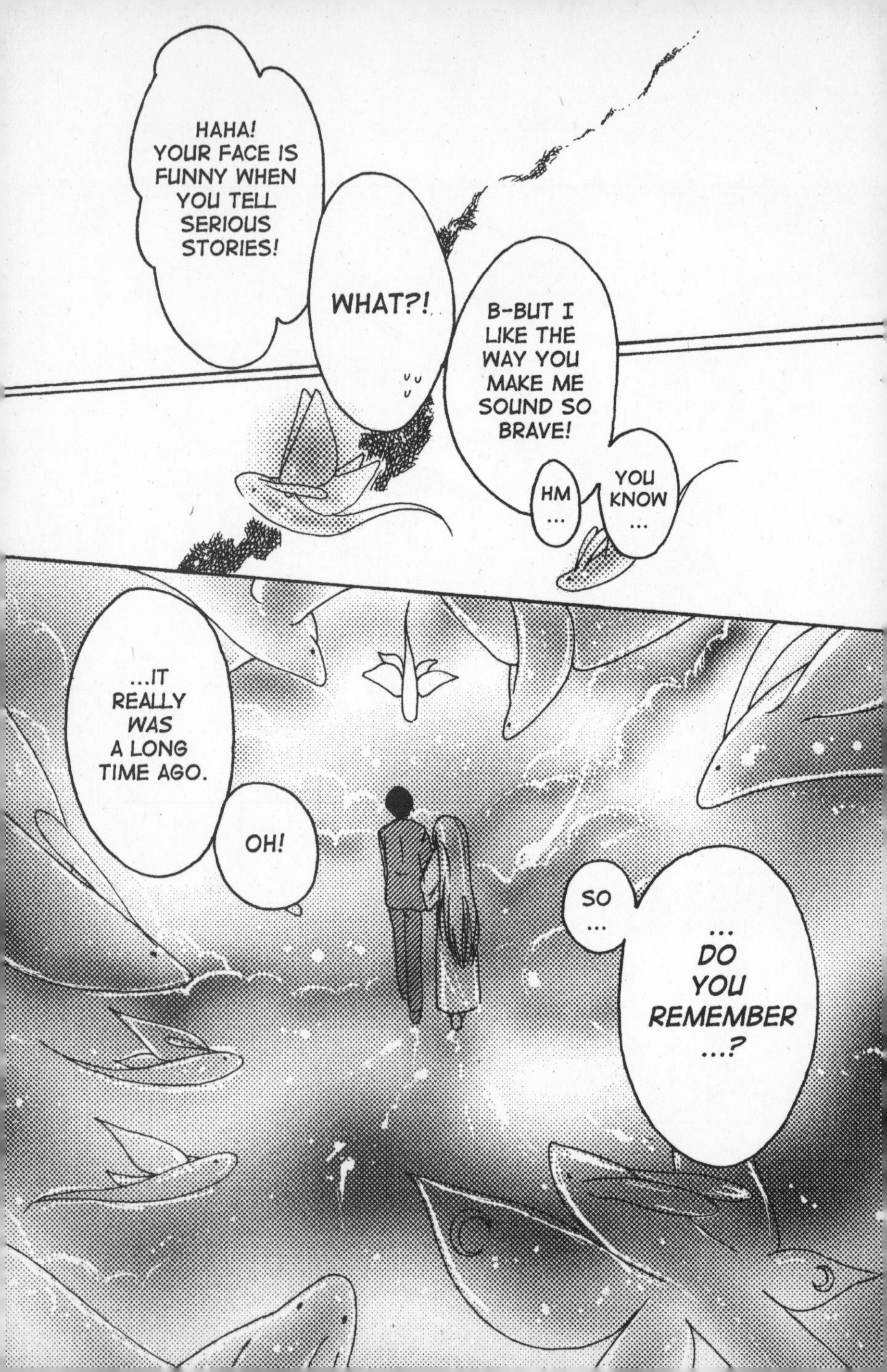
HAHA! YOUR FACE IS FUNNY WHEN YOU TELL SERIOUS STORIES!
WHAT?!
B-BUT I LIKE THE WAY YOU MAKE ME SOUND SO BRAVE!
HM...
YOU KNOW...
...IT REALLY WAS A LONG TIME AGO.
OH!
SO...
...DO YOU REMEMBER...?

REDEEMON :: Runner Up ::

....

Mai-yeng Tran was born in Swindon, England in 1982. She's now currently residing in London.
www.maiyeng.deviantart.com

Favorite manga:
Black Jack, Giant Robo: The Animation

Favorite manga artists:
Tezuka Osamu, Oda Eiichiro, Usuta Kyousuke

....

Author's Comments:
To be honest this story was originally intended for a fan comic, but after passing up on a couple of stories that I had in mind for *RSoM*, I settled for this one. The protagonist, Rogan, was a random character I made up years ago on an oekaki board, but I'm glad to finally put him to use. It may not be my best (I feel I could do better), but I hope it's enough to entertain!

Just a little fact about the title: Redeem + Demon = Redeemon
—*Mai-yeng Tran*

::

::

REDEEMON :: Runner Up ::

....

Judge's Comments:
Perhaps it was Mai-yeng Tran's character design that struck me, or maybe the Digimon-sounding title, but this work grabbed me at the first panel and had me until the end, and even after! Whether it's inking, toning, panel layout, composition, character design, dialogue, or what have you, Mai-yeng is clearly skilled in all of these elements. I actually gave her work a perfect score of 100 during judging, I was so pleased with it! And of the most striking features, the best had to be the camera demon that she was able to pull off flawlessly despite the drastic shift in styles. The warped and penciled crosshatching for the demon was an excellent visual technique, perfectly fitting the world within the camera Mai-yeng created. Choosing to include a fight scene in the story just goes to show how at home Mai-yeng feels with a variety of actions. And when a story can make you double over laughing, it's clearly done a brilliant job of moving you! Excellent job through and through!
—*Katherine Schilling*

Judge's Comments:
Don't try to overthink "Redeemon." If you question why you never see the main character's face or why a normal-looking couple would identify a stranger as a "cosplay bum," you've missed the point. "Redeemon" is just a fun, silly comedy—with some really cool stuff in terms of character design and concepts.

The biggest problem I have is with the rendering in the Flash Demon section. Tran would have done better to match the clean tone style of the rest of the entry rather than sketching out all the lines in the demon's body and backgrounds, and lettering the demon's balloons herself. This speaks to her difficulty with backgrounds in general, as they rarely appear and we end up with too many face-on-screentone panels. This is further aggravated by the fast pace of the story, as each panel is fairly dense. Perhaps my biggest complaint in this regard is the fight scene with the demon, in which all the action has been shrunk to fit on the page and no particular cool moves stand out. And then, unfortunately, the one time we are treated to a large image, it's a still.

However, Tran does a lot of things right, and in nineteen pages everything wraps up nicely, with a priceless shot of a boot-trodden face, too!
—*Hope Donovan*

::

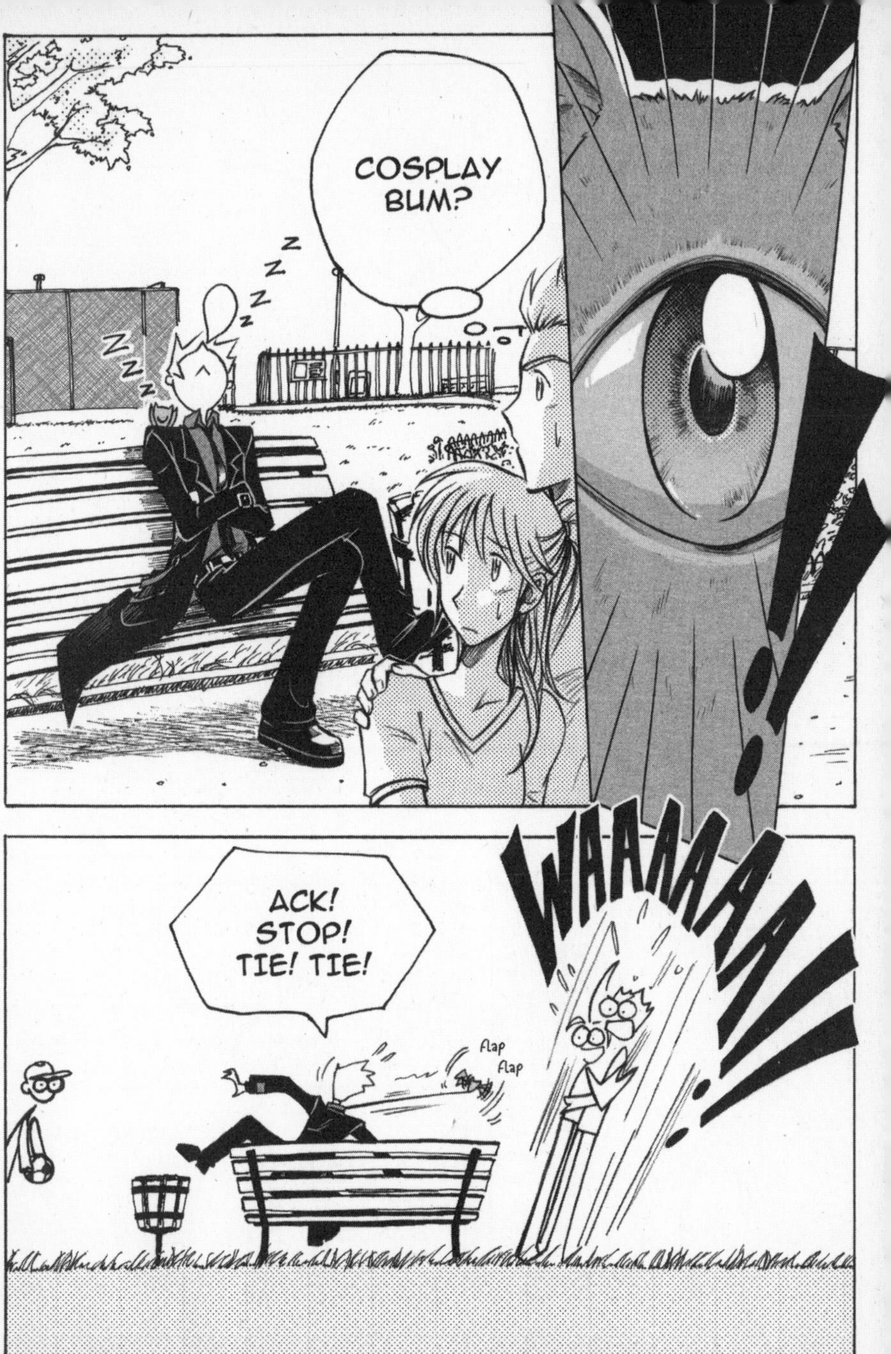
COSPLAY BUM?
ACK! STOP! TIE! TIE!
Flap Flap
WAAAAA!!

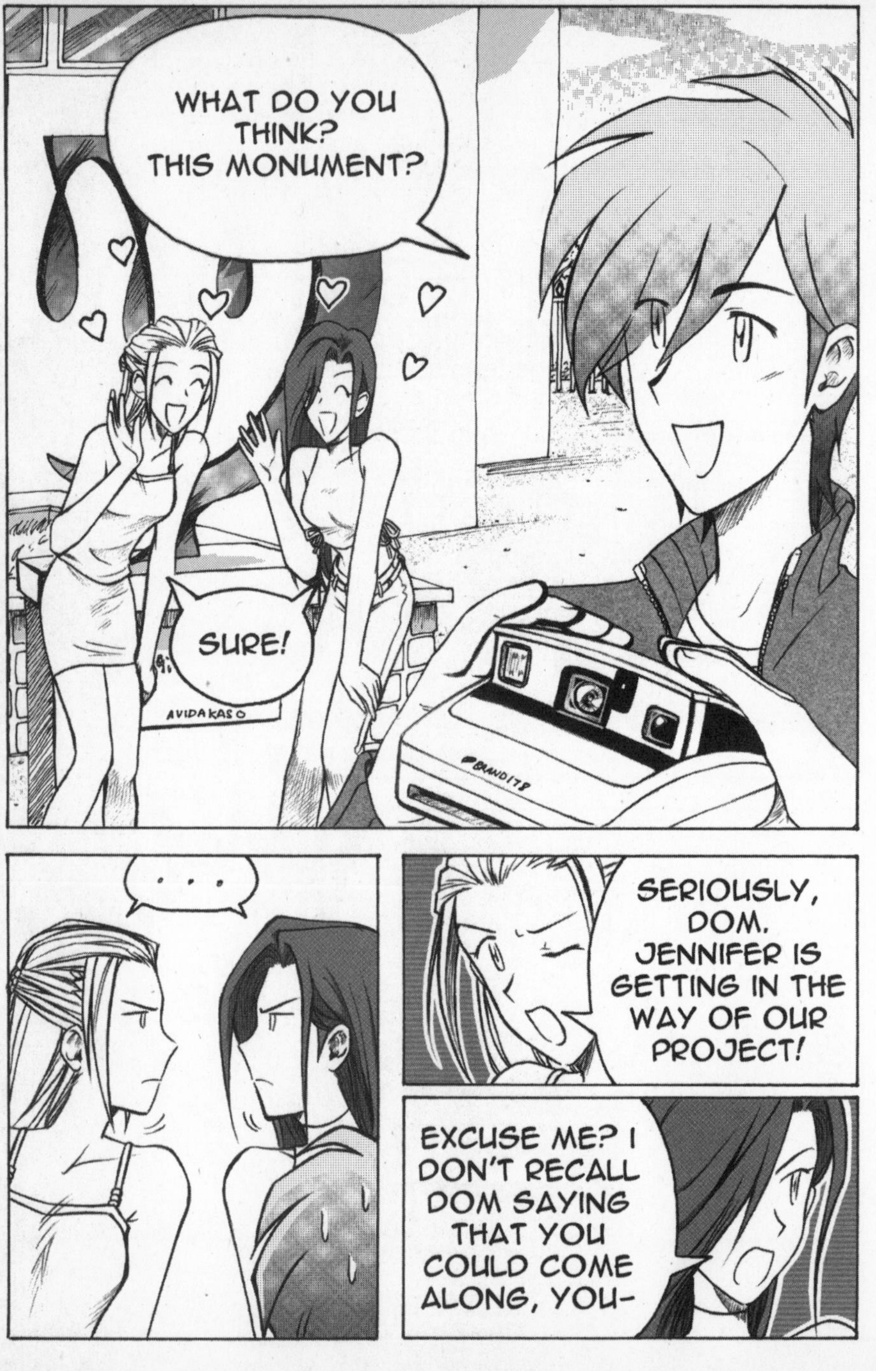
WHAT DO YOU THINK? THIS MONUMENT?
SURE!
. . .
SERIOUSLY, DOM. JENNIFER IS GETTING IN THE WAY OF OUR PROJECT!
EXCUSE ME? I DON'T RECALL DOM SAYING THAT YOU COULD COME ALONG, YOU-

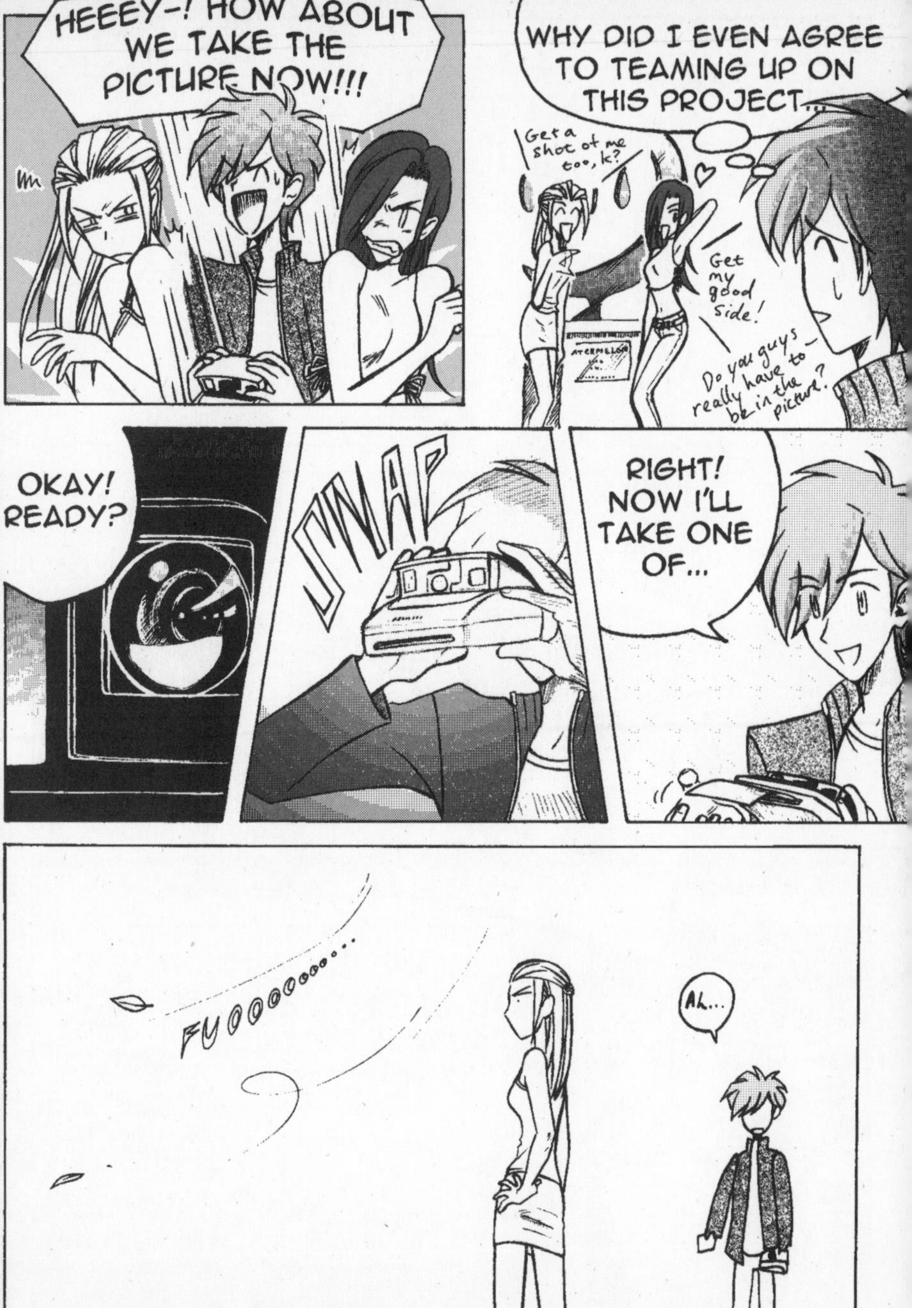
HEEEY-! HOW ABOUT WE TAKE THE PICTURE NOW!!!
WHY DID I EVEN AGREE TO TEAMING UP ON THIS PROJECT...
Get a shot of me too, k?
Get my good side!
Do you guys really have to be in the picture?
OKAY! READY?
SNAP
RIGHT! NOW I'LL TAKE ONE OF...
FUOOOOooo...
Ah...

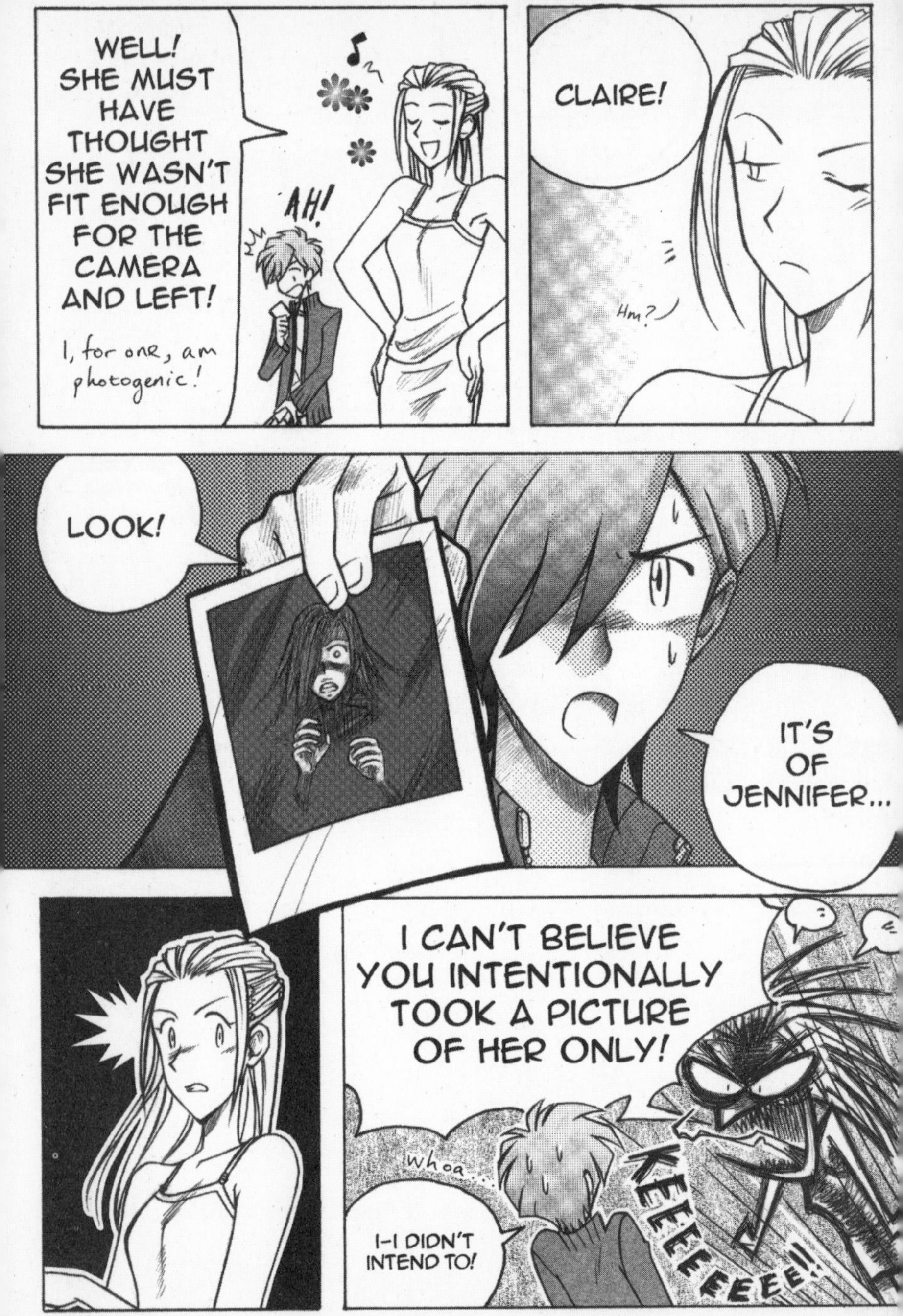
WELL! SHE MUST HAVE THOUGHT SHE WASN'T FIT ENOUGH FOR THE CAMERA AND LEFT!
I, for one, am photogenic!
AH!
CLAIRE!
Hm?
LOOK!
IT'S OF JENNIFER...
I CAN'T BELIEVE YOU INTENTIONALLY TOOK A PICTURE OF HER ONLY!
Whoa...
I-I DIDN'T INTEND TO!
KEEEEEEEEE!!

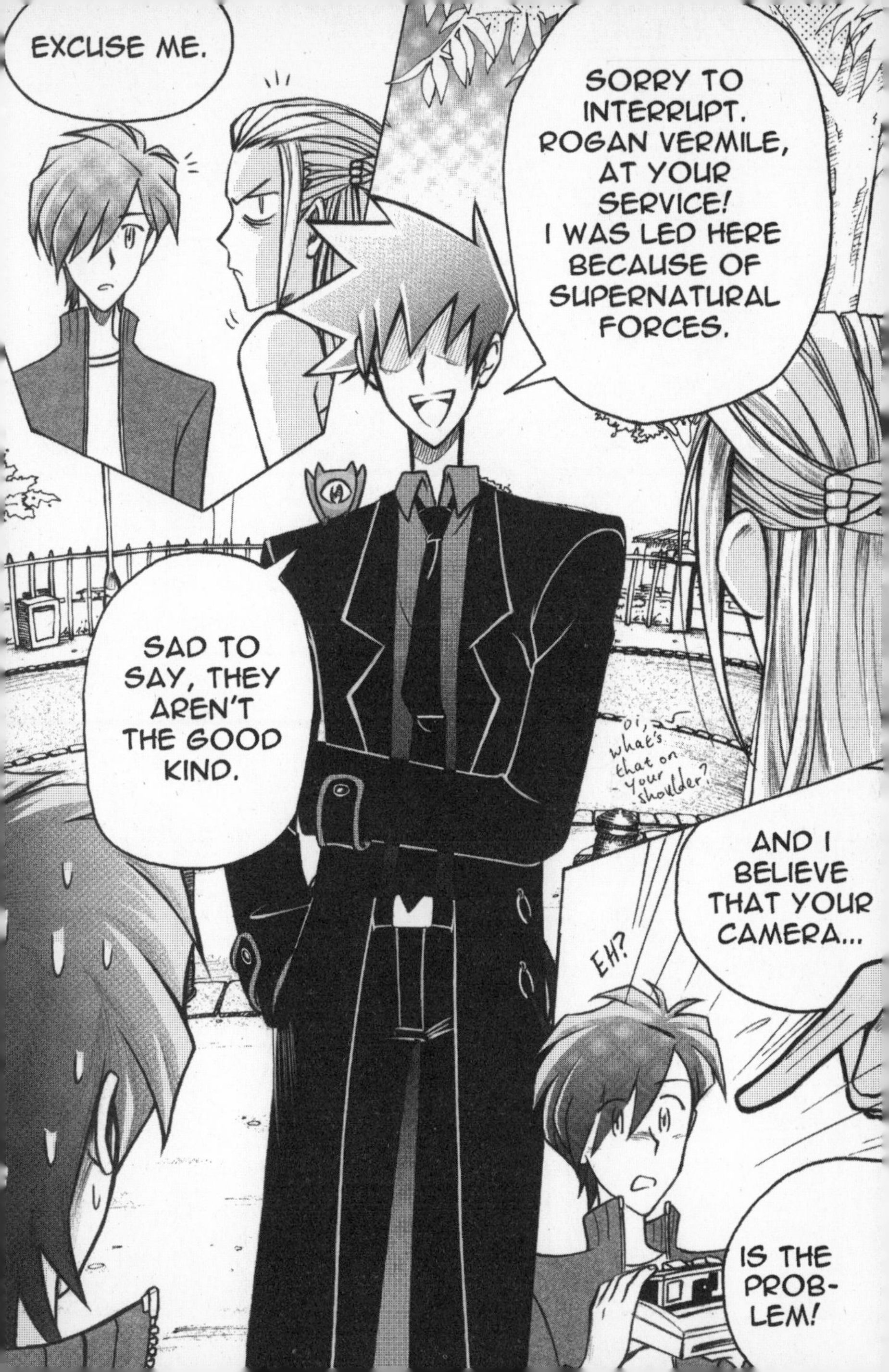
EXCUSE ME.
SORRY TO INTERRUPT. ROGAN VERMILE, AT YOUR SERVICE! I WAS LED HERE BECAUSE OF SUPERNATURAL FORCES.
SAD TO SAY, THEY AREN'T THE GOOD KIND.
oi, what's that on your shoulder?
EH?
AND I BELIEVE THAT YOUR CAMERA...
IS THE PROB-LEM!

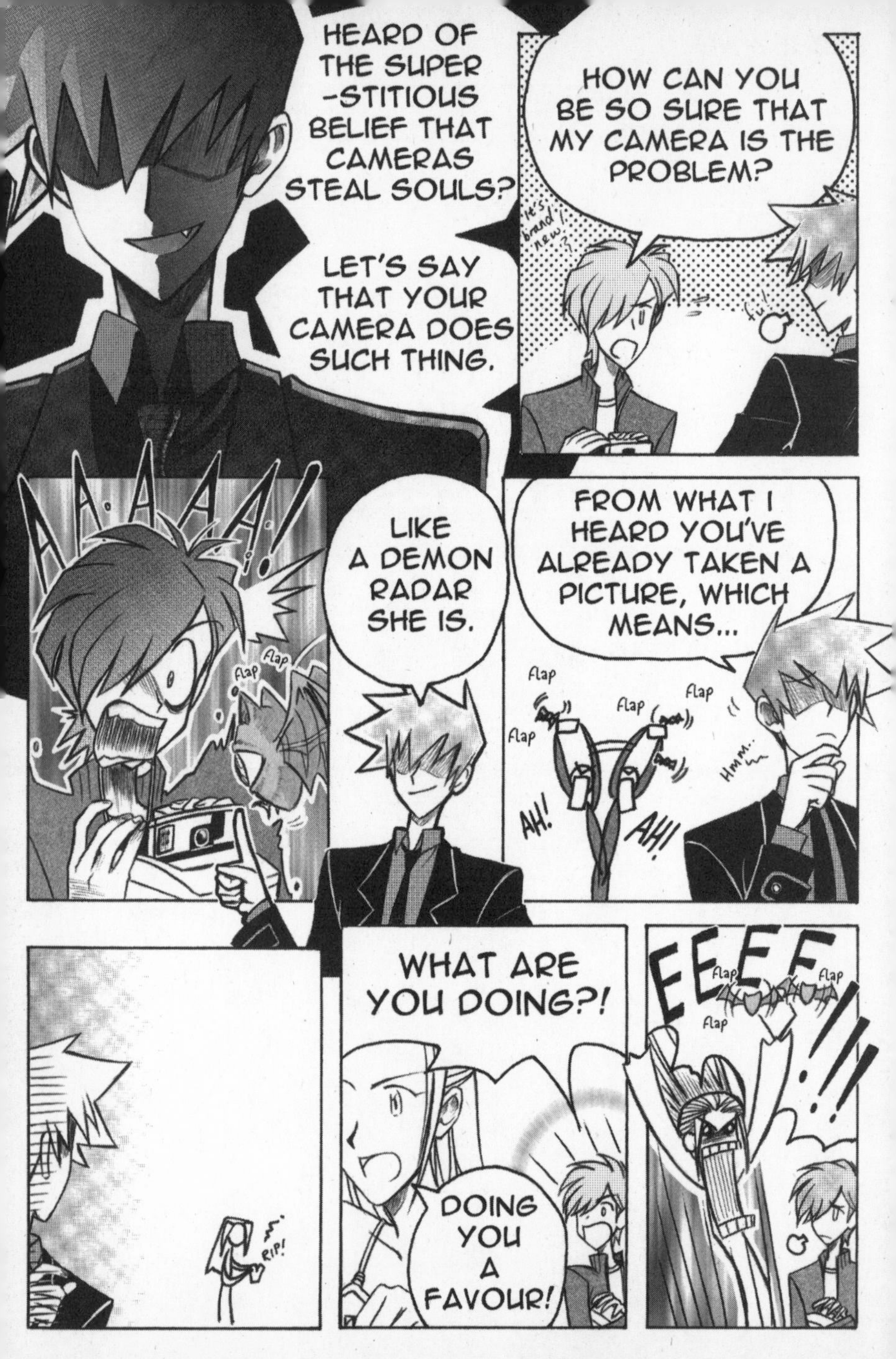
HEARD OF THE SUPER -STITIOUS BELIEF THAT CAMERAS STEAL SOULS?
LET'S SAY THAT YOUR CAMERA DOES SUCH THING.
HOW CAN YOU BE SO SURE THAT MY CAMERA IS THE PROBLEM?
It's brand new!
fu!
AAAAA!
Flap
Flap
LIKE A DEMON RADAR SHE IS.
FROM WHAT I HEARD YOU'VE ALREADY TAKEN A PICTURE, WHICH MEANS...
Flap
Flap
Flap
Flap
AH!
AH!
Hmm..
RIP!
WHAT ARE YOU DOING?!
DOING YOU A FAVOUR!
EEEE!!!
Flap
Flap
Flap

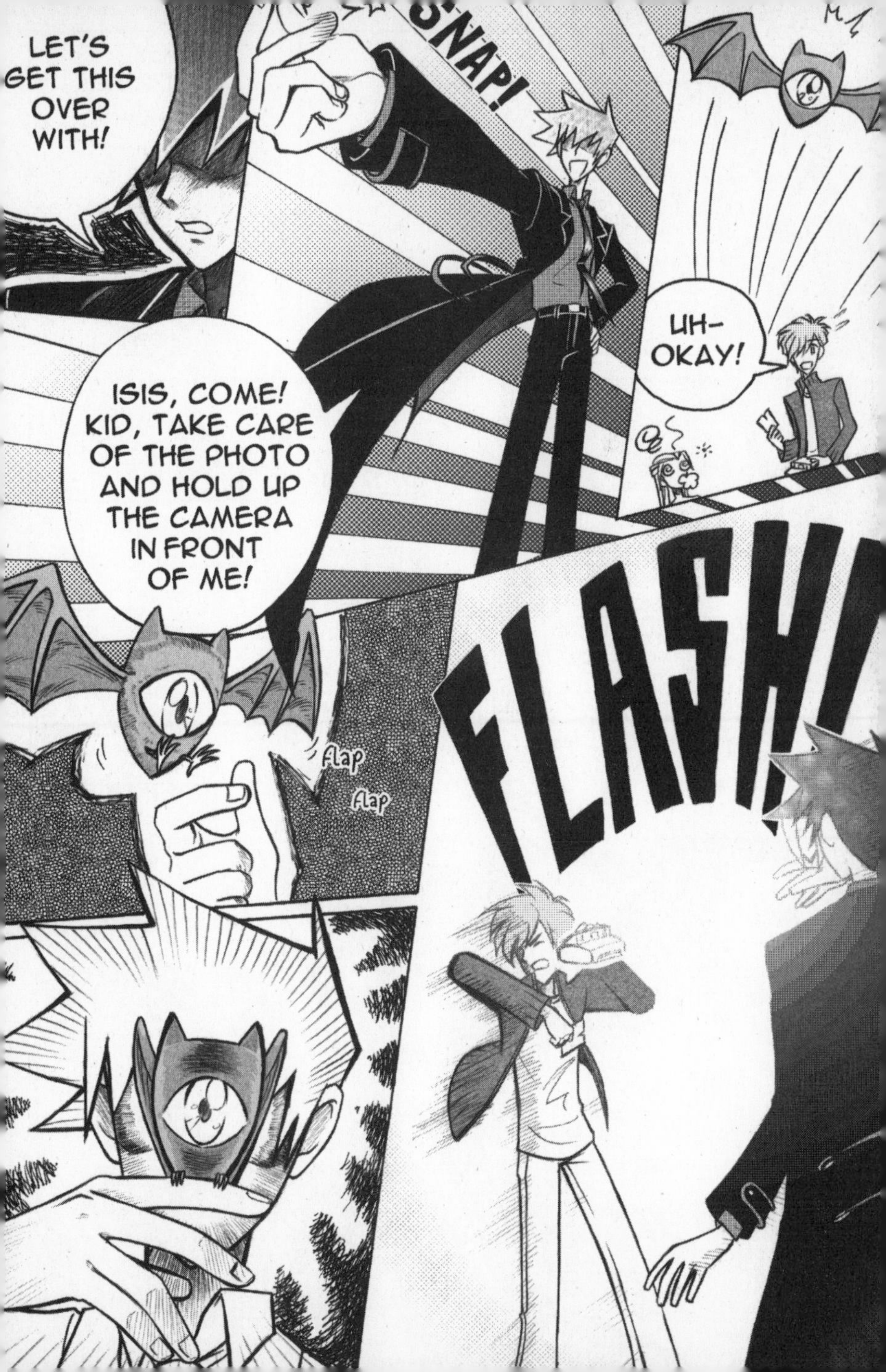
LET'S GET THIS OVER WITH!
SNAP!
ISIS, COME! KID, TAKE CARE OF THE PHOTO AND HOLD UP THE CAMERA IN FRONT OF ME!
UH-OKAY!
flap
flap
FLASH!

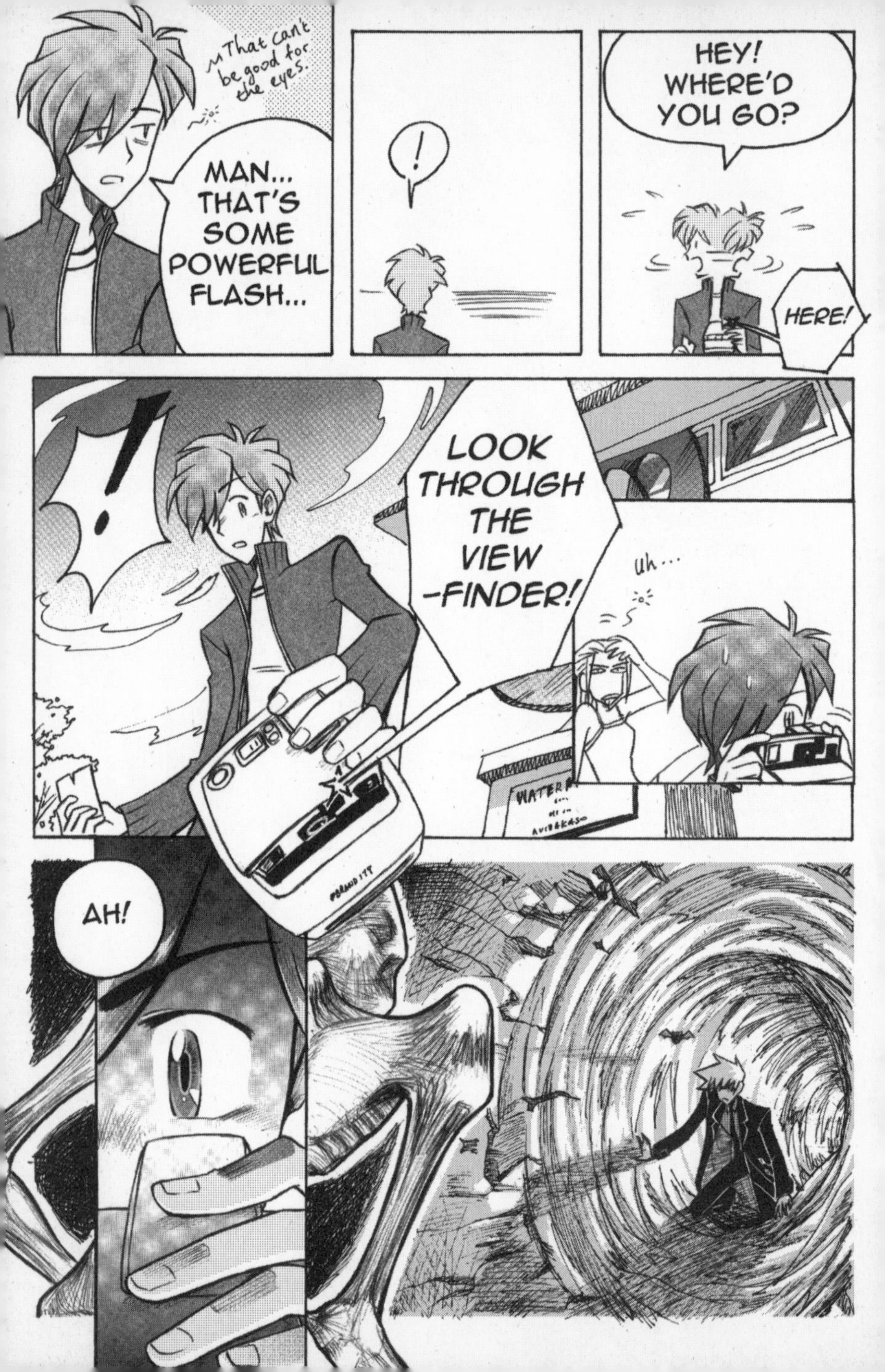
That can't be good for the eyes.
MAN... THAT'S SOME POWERFUL FLASH...
!
HEY! WHERE'D YOU GO?
HERE!
!
LOOK THROUGH THE VIEW -FINDER!
uh...
AH!

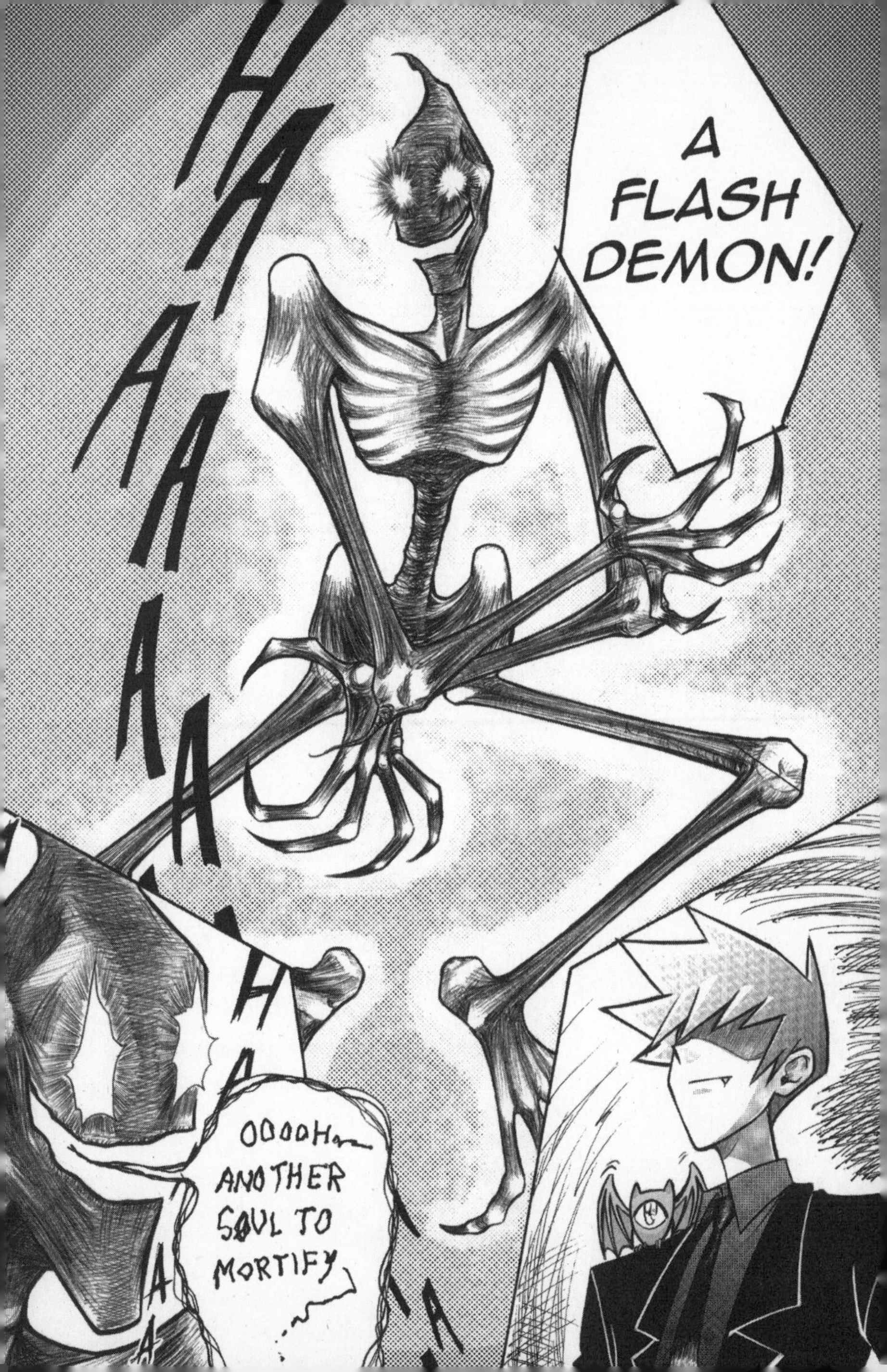
HAAAAAAA
A FLASH DEMON!
HAAAA
OOOOH~ ANOTHER SOUL TO MORTIFY

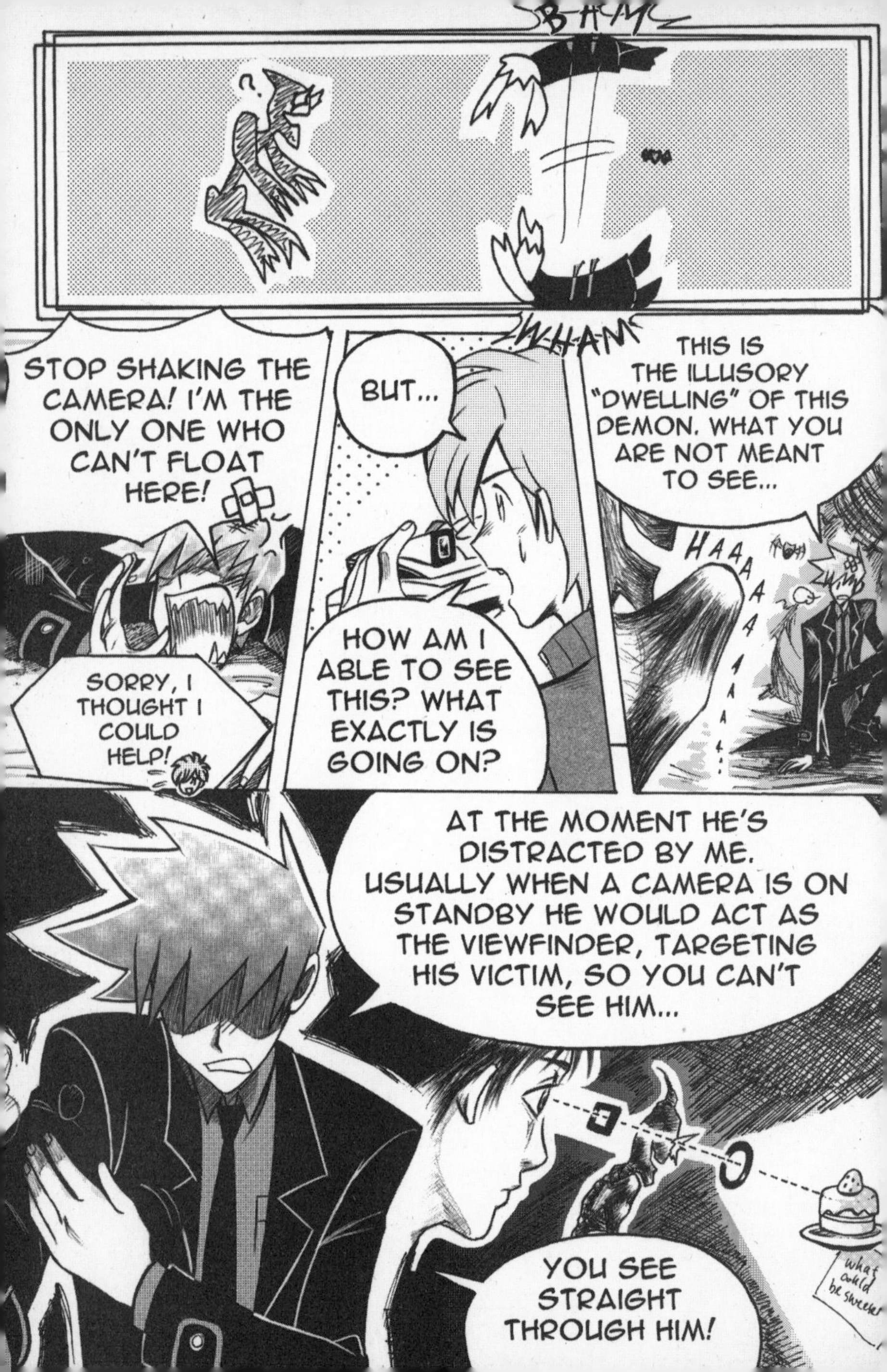
?
BAM
WHAM
STOP SHAKING THE CAMERA! I'M THE ONLY ONE WHO CAN'T FLOAT HERE!
SORRY, I THOUGHT I COULD HELP!
BUT...
HOW AM I ABLE TO SEE THIS? WHAT EXACTLY IS GOING ON?
THIS IS THE ILLUSORY "DWELLING" OF THIS DEMON. WHAT YOU ARE NOT MEANT TO SEE...
HAAAAAAAAAA
AT THE MOMENT HE'S DISTRACTED BY ME. USUALLY WHEN A CAMERA IS ON STANDBY HE WOULD ACT AS THE VIEWFINDER, TARGETING HIS VICTIM, SO YOU CAN'T SEE HIM...
YOU SEE STRAIGHT THROUGH HIM!
what could be sweeter

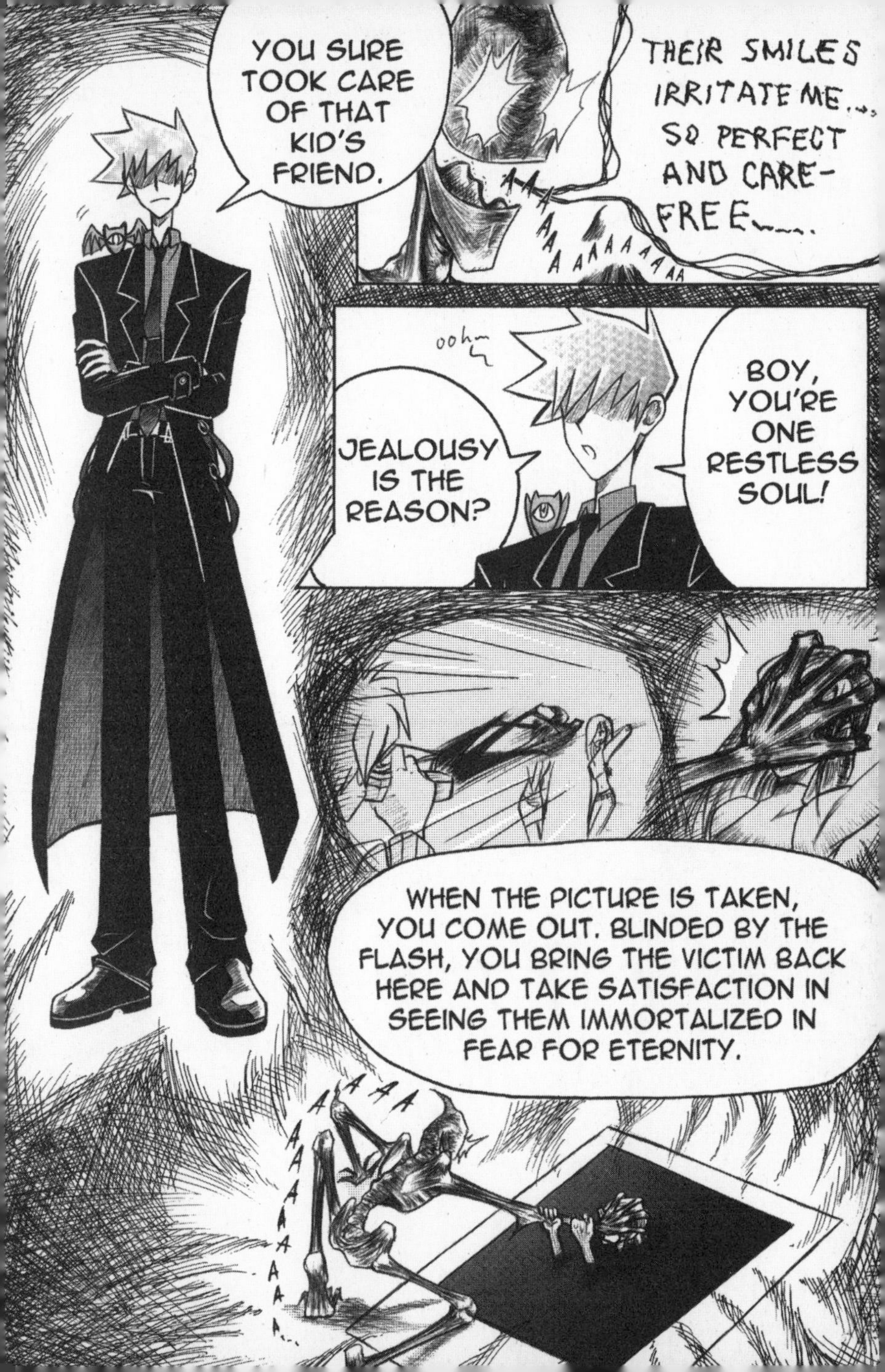
YOU SURE TOOK CARE OF THAT KID'S FRIEND.
THEIR SMILES IRRITATE ME... SO PERFECT AND CARE-FREE....
AAAAAAAAAAAAAA
JEALOUSY IS THE REASON?
BOY, YOU'RE ONE RESTLESS SOUL!
WHEN THE PICTURE IS TAKEN, YOU COME OUT. BLINDED BY THE FLASH, YOU BRING THE VICTIM BACK HERE AND TAKE SATISFACTION IN SEEING THEM IMMORTALIZED IN FEAR FOR ETERNITY.
AAAAAAAAAAAAA...

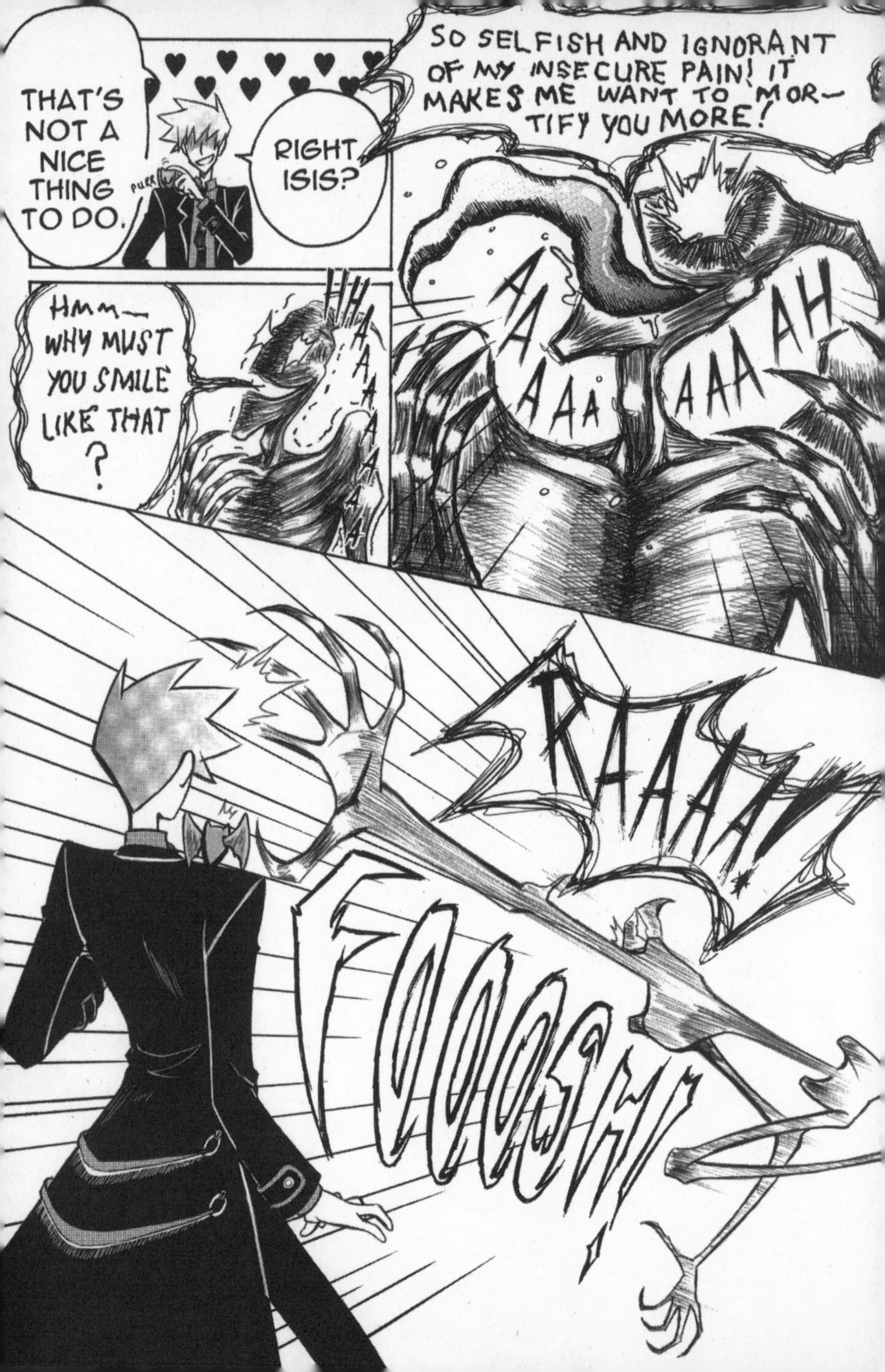
THAT'S NOT A NICE THING TO DO.
PURR
RIGHT ISIS?
Hmm— WHY MUST YOU SMILE LIKE THAT?
HHAAAAAAAAAA
SO SELFISH AND IGNORANT OF MY INSECURE PAIN! IT MAKES ME WANT TO MOR-TIFY YOU MORE!
AAAAAAAAAAAH
RAAAA!
FOOOOSH!

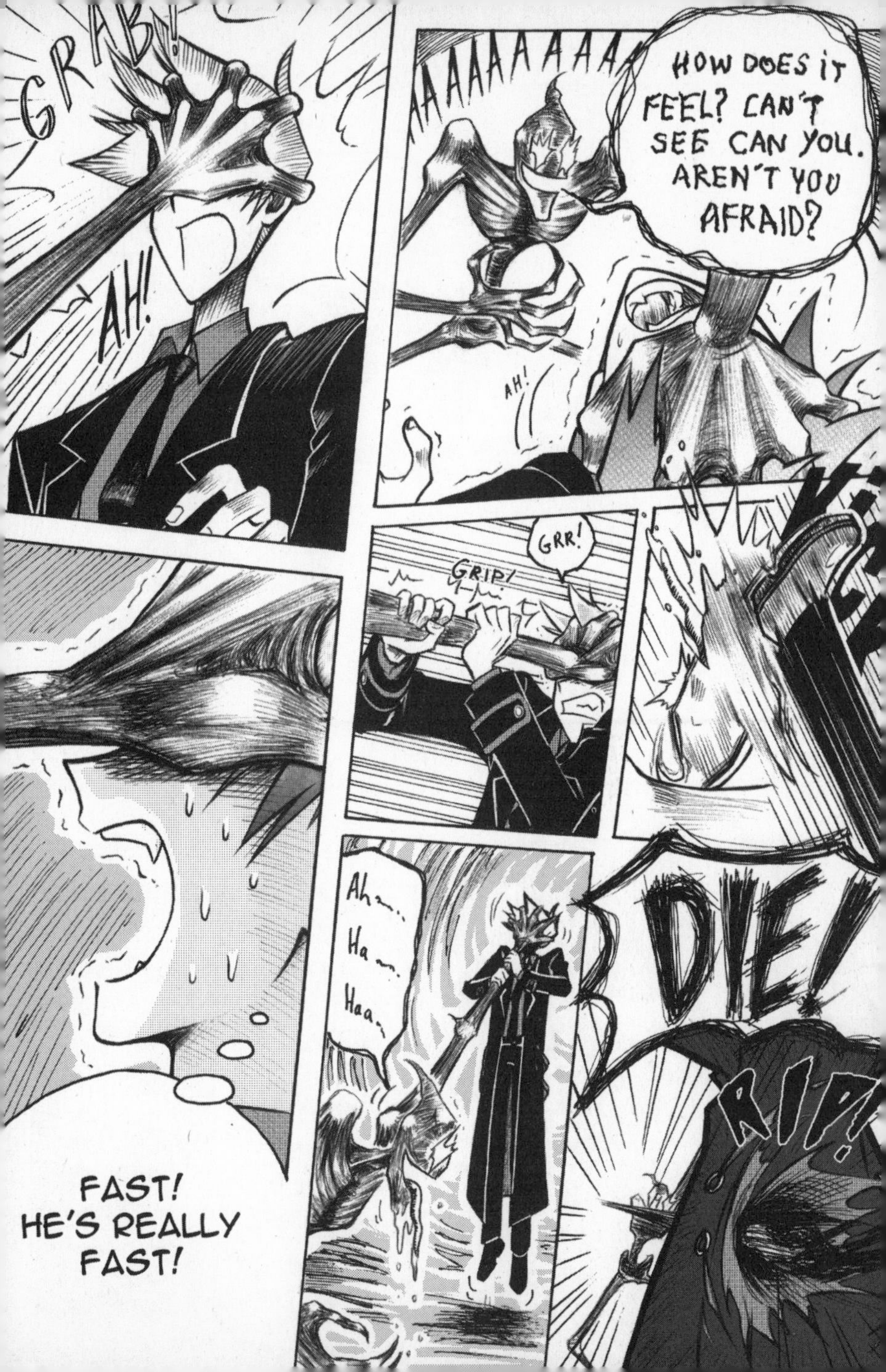
GRAB!
AH!
AAAAAAAAAA
HOW DOES IT FEEL? CAN'T SEE CAN YOU. AREN'T YOU AFRAID?
AH!
GRR!
GRIP!
FAST! HE'S REALLY FAST!
Ah... Ha... Haa...
DIE!
RIP!

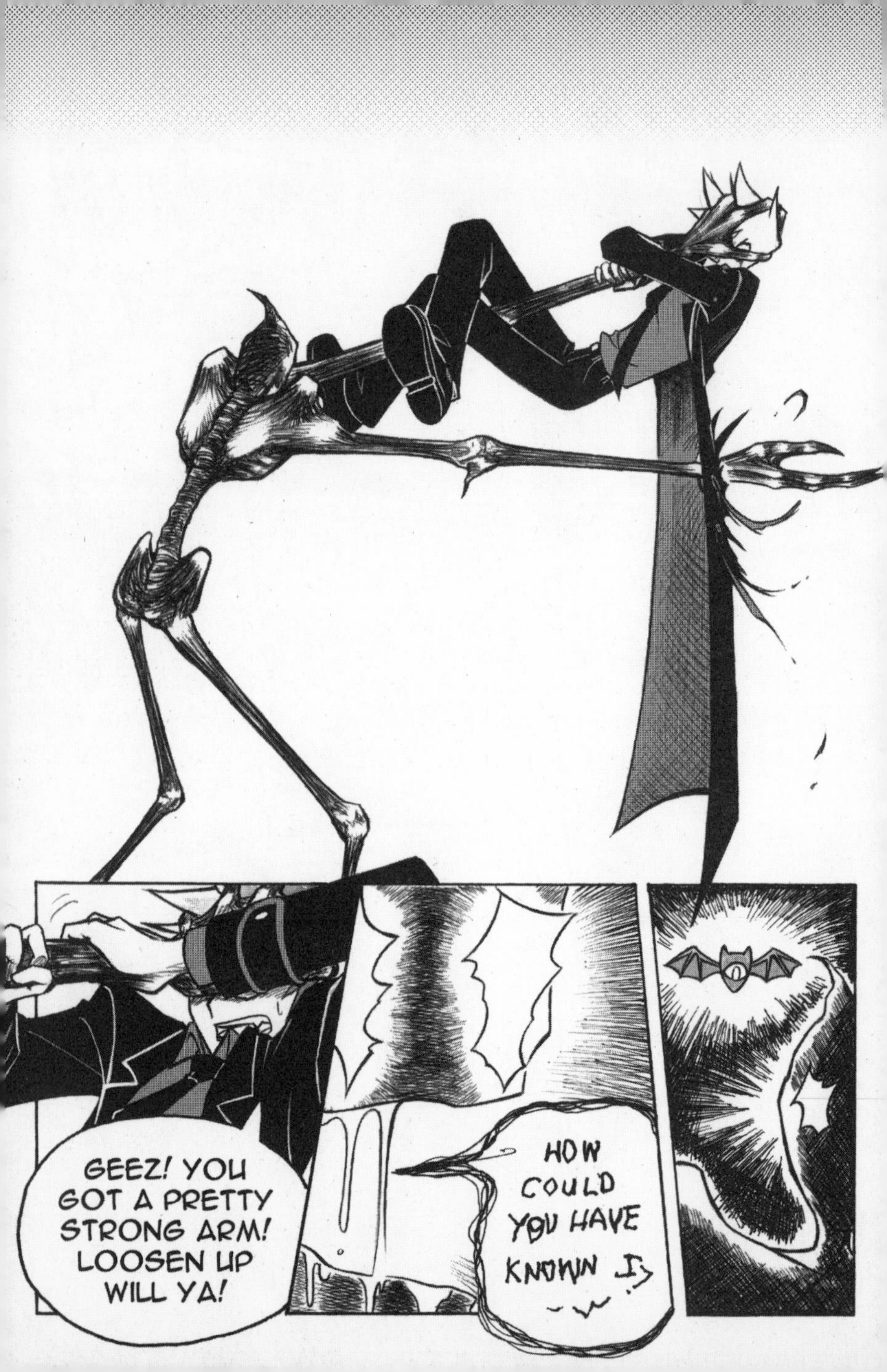
GEEZ! YOU GOT A PRETTY STRONG ARM! LOOSEN UP WILL YA!
HOW COULD YOU HAVE KNOWN

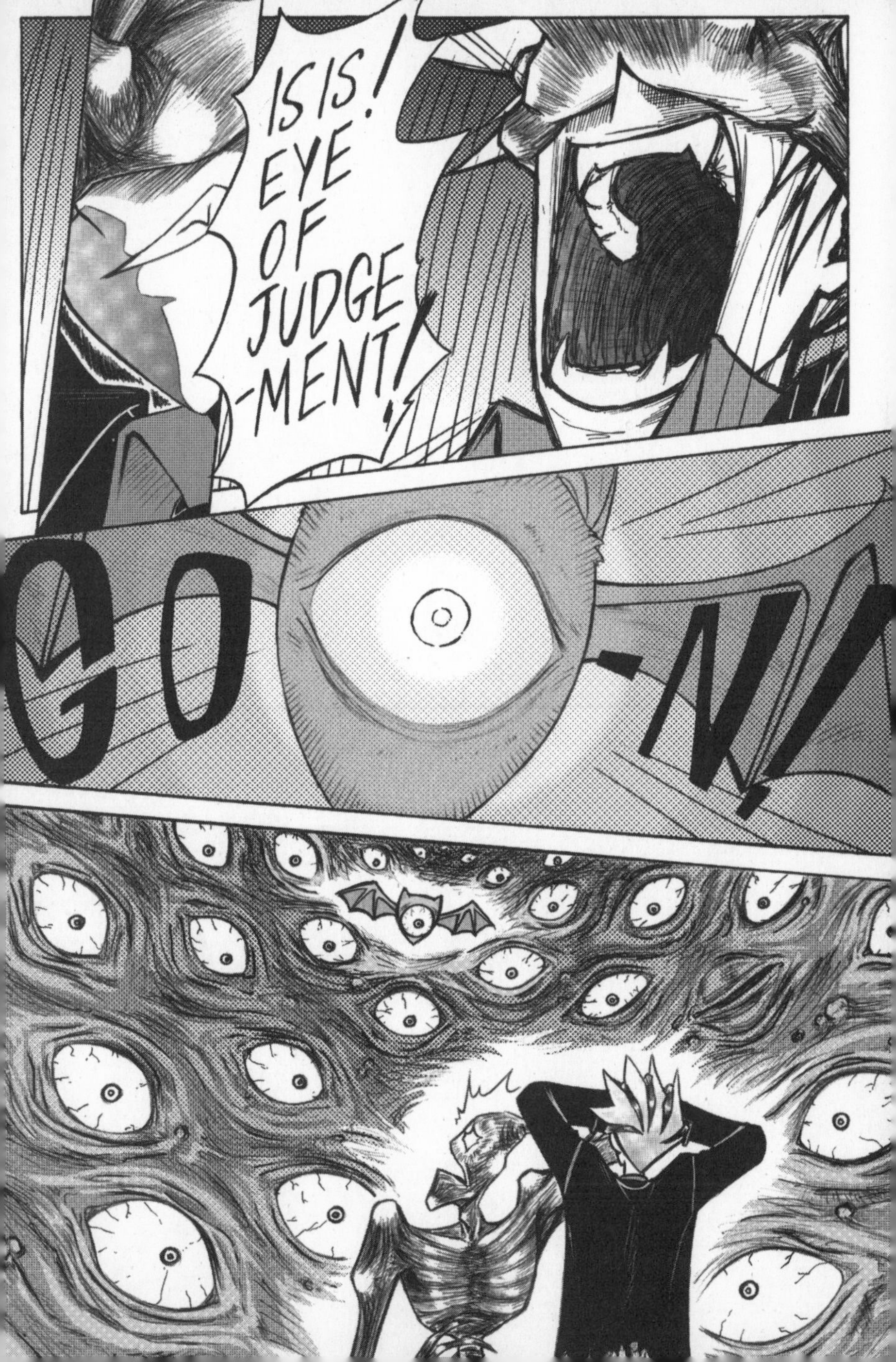
IS IS! EYE OF JUDGE-MENT!
GO-N!

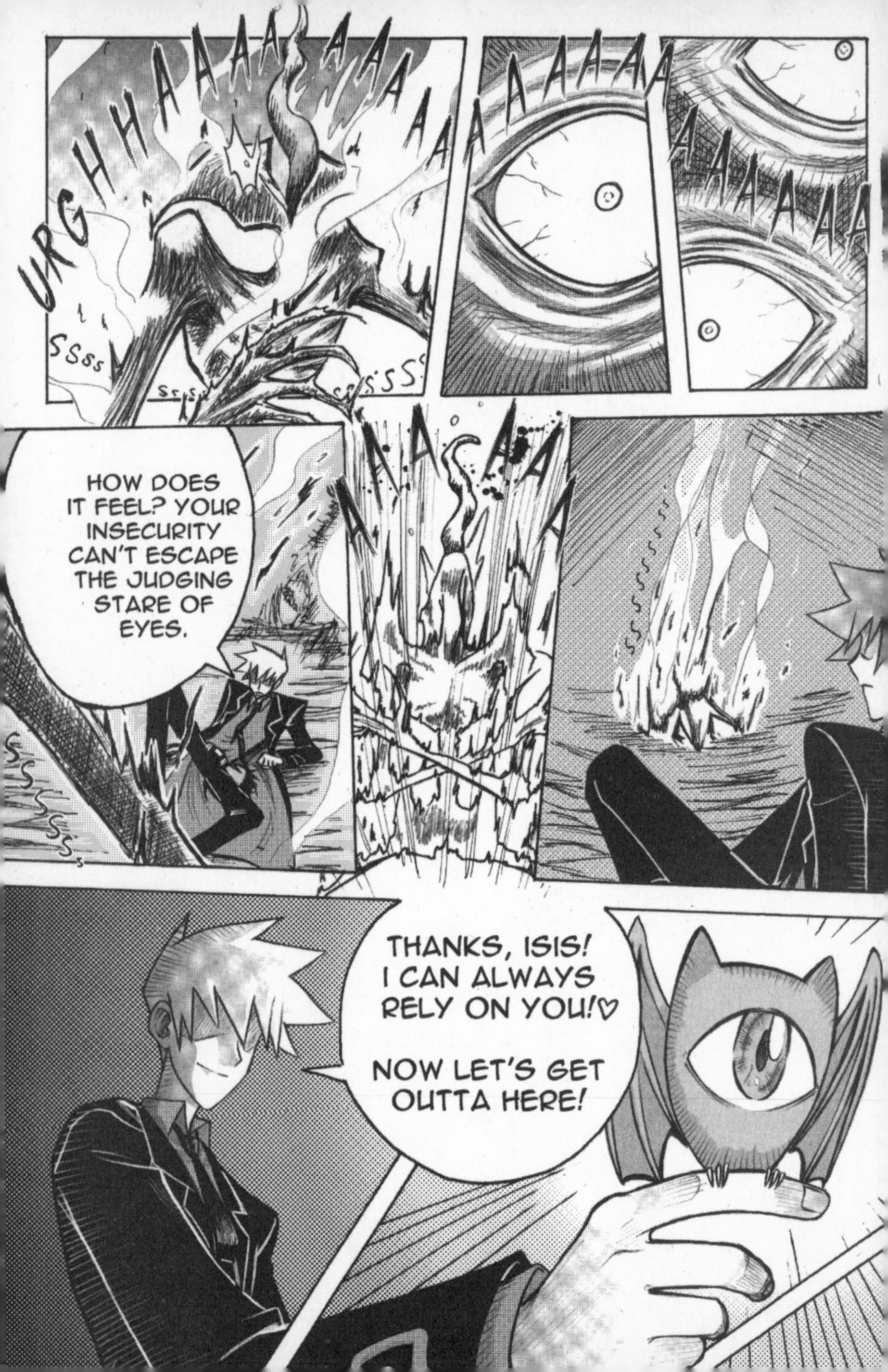
URGHHAAAAAAAAAAAAAAAAAAAAAAA
SSsss
SSSSS
HOW DOES IT FEEL? YOUR INSECURITY CAN'T ESCAPE THE JUDGING STARE OF EYES.
AAAAAAA
THANKS, ISIS! I CAN ALWAYS RELY ON YOU!♡
NOW LET'S GET OUTTA HERE!

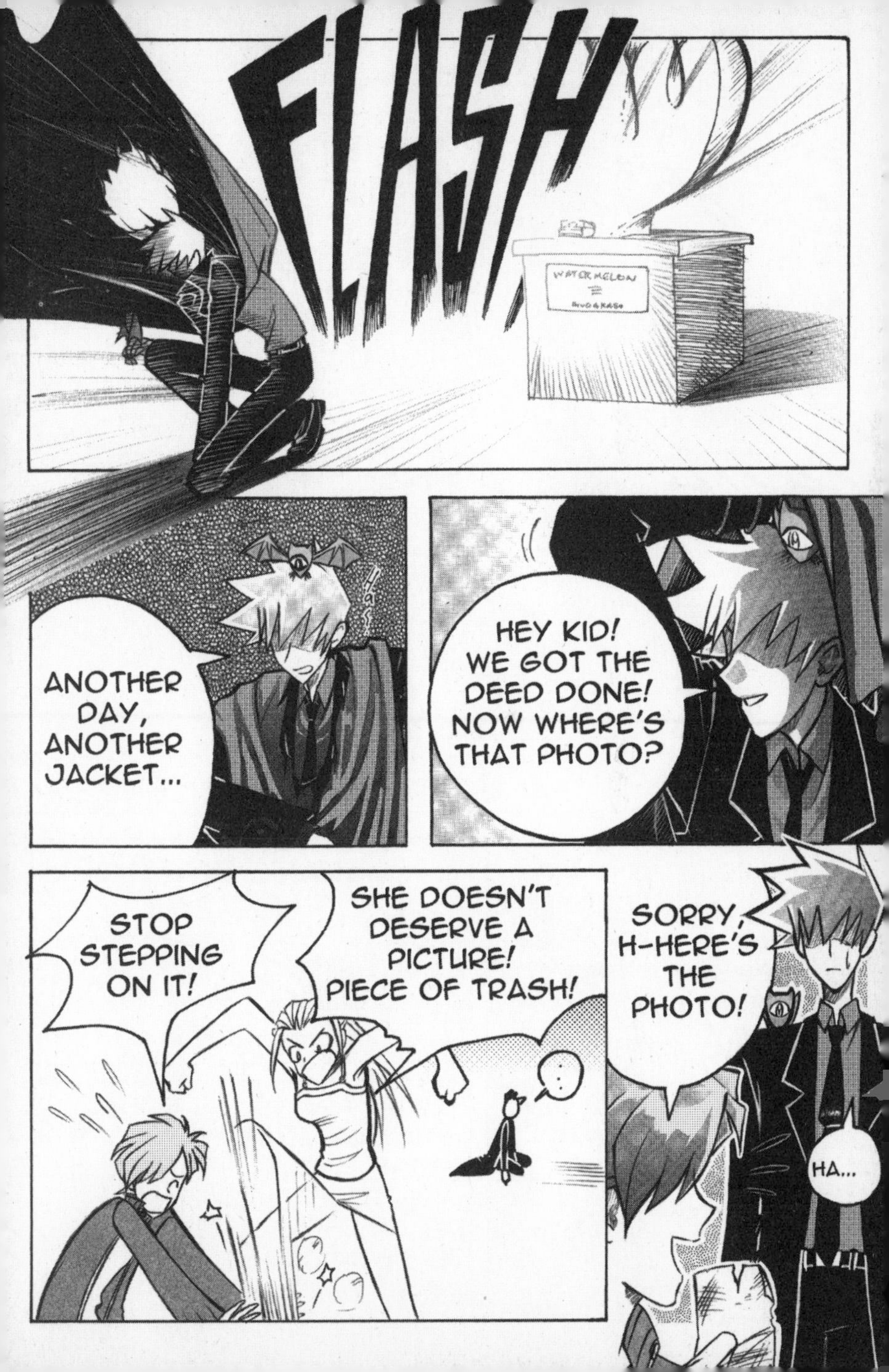
FLASH
ANOTHER DAY, ANOTHER JACKET...
HEY KID! WE GOT THE DEED DONE! NOW WHERE'S THAT PHOTO?
STOP STEPPING ON IT!
SHE DOESN'T DESERVE A PICTURE! PIECE OF TRASH!
...
SORRY, H-HERE'S THE PHOTO!
HA...

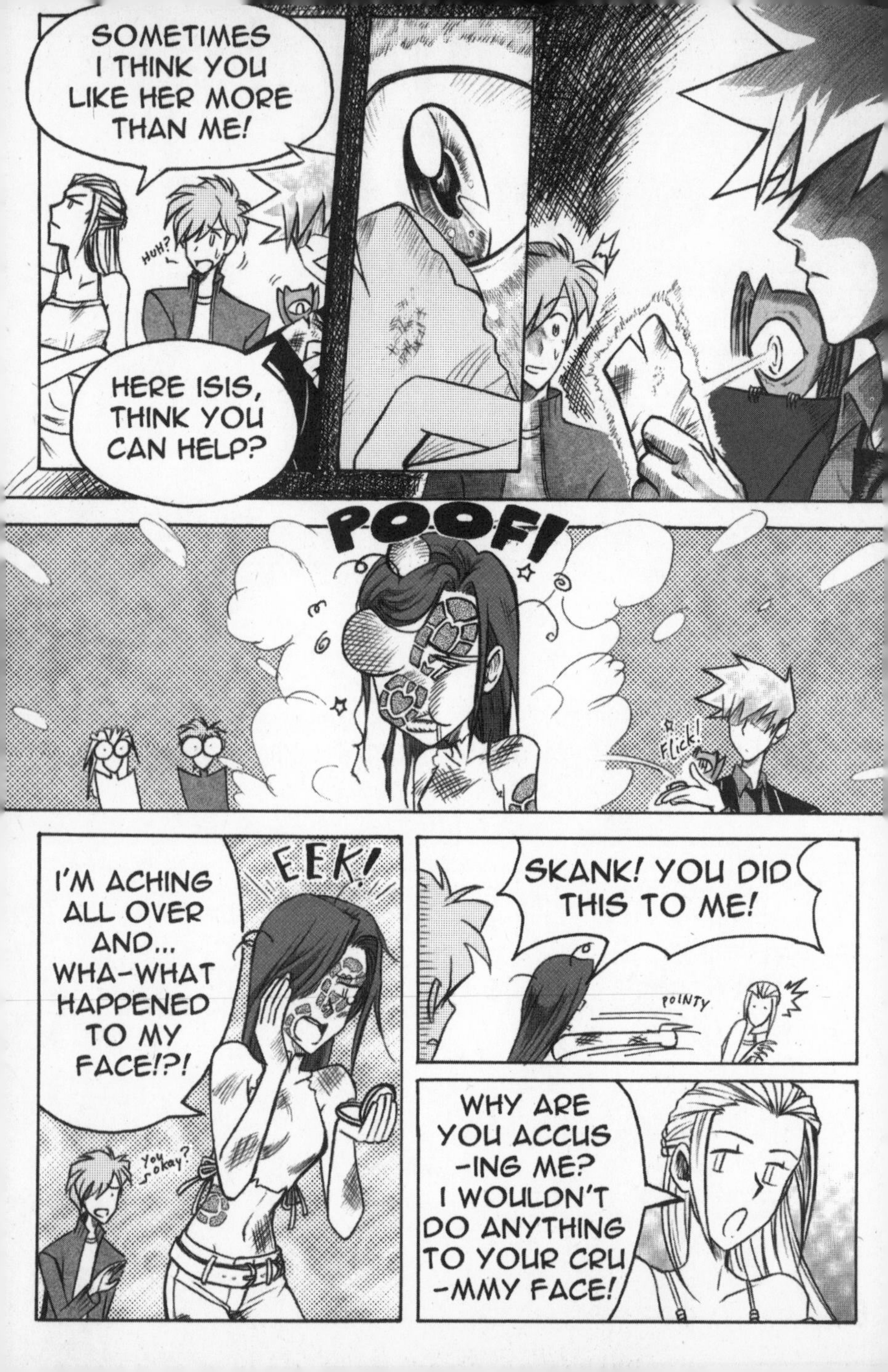
SOMETIMES I THINK YOU LIKE HER MORE THAN ME!
HUH?
HERE ISIS, THINK YOU CAN HELP?
POOF!
FLICK!
I'M ACHING ALL OVER AND... WHA-WHAT HAPPENED TO MY FACE!?!
EEK!
YOU OKAY?
SKANK! YOU DID THIS TO ME!
POINTY
WHY ARE YOU ACCUS -ING ME? I WOULDN'T DO ANYTHING TO YOUR CRU -MMY FACE!

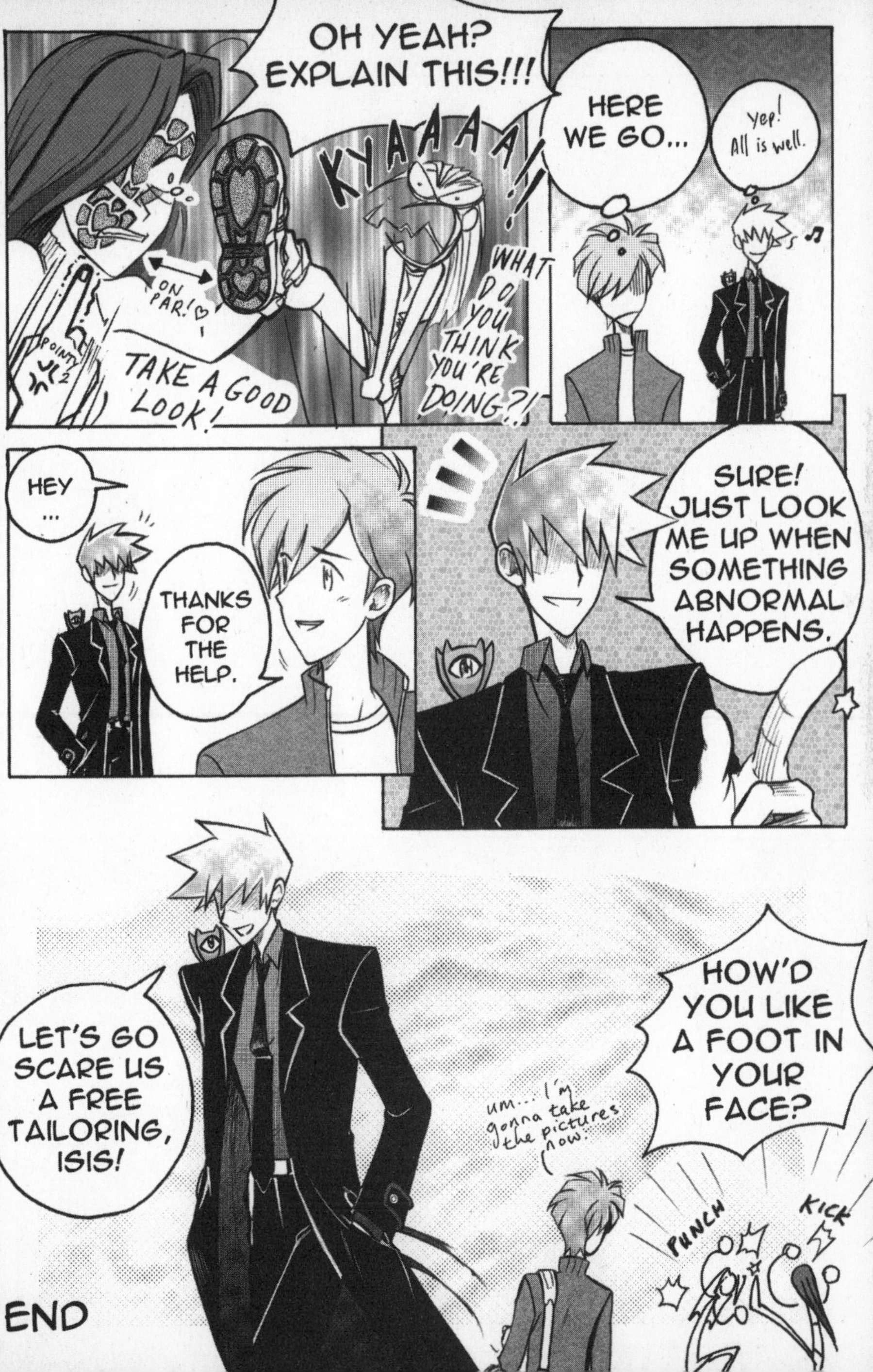
OH YEAH? EXPLAIN THIS!!!
ON PAR! ♡
POINT
TAKE A GOOD LOOK!
KYAAAAA!!!
WHAT DO YOU THINK YOU'RE DOING?!
HERE WE GO...
Yep! All is well.
HEY ...
THANKS FOR THE HELP.
SURE! JUST LOOK ME UP WHEN SOMETHING ABNORMAL HAPPENS.
LET'S GO SCARE US A FREE TAILORING, ISIS!
um... I'm gonna take the pictures now.
HOW'D YOU LIKE A FOOT IN YOUR FACE?
PUNCH
KICK
END

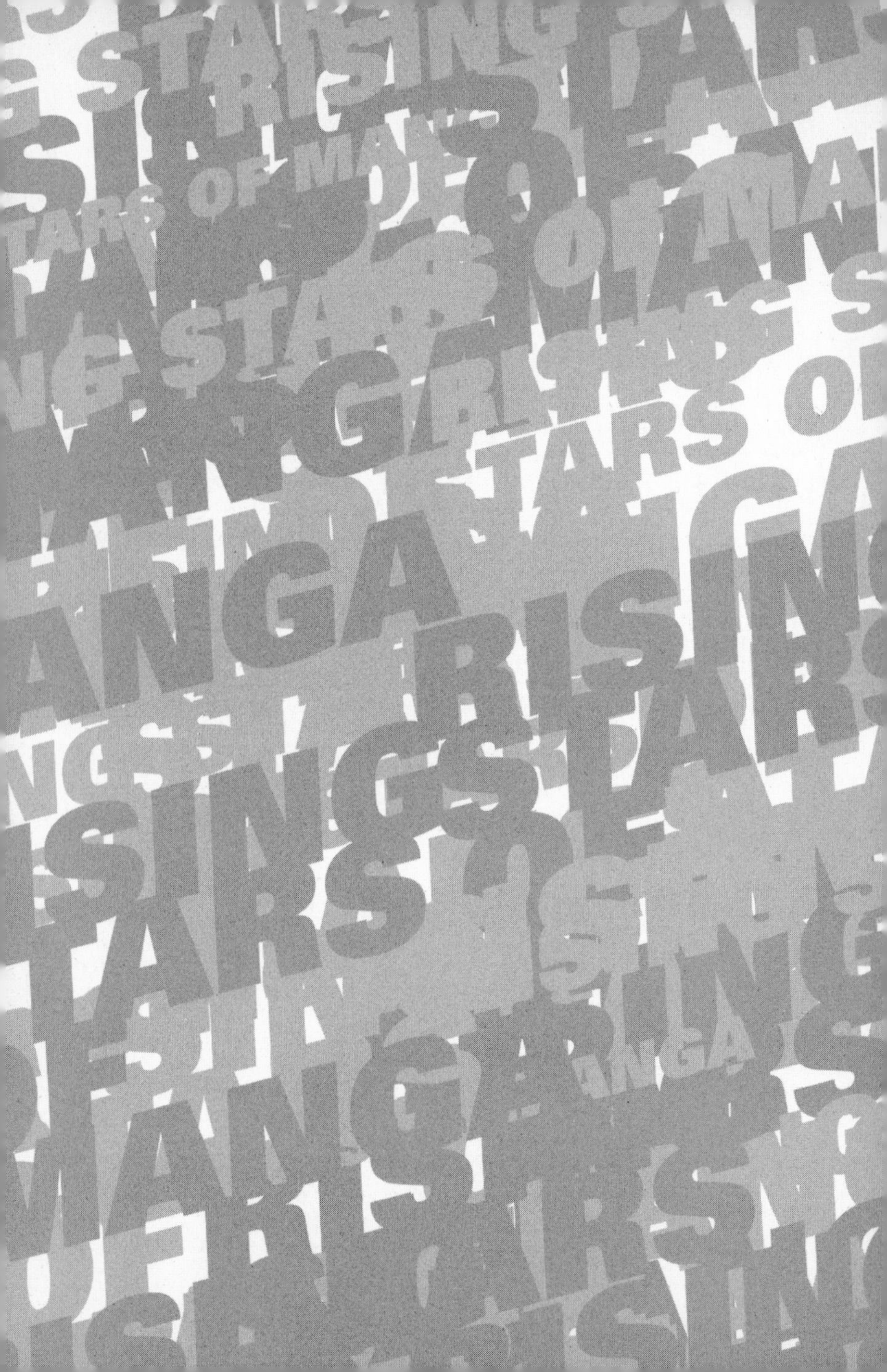
TARS O
ANGA
RIS

::

THE HOMECOMING :: Runner Up ::

....

Morag Lewis was born in Dundee, Scotland, in 1979. She is a
molecular biologist by trade, and is currently studying the genetics of
progressive deafness.
www.toothycat.net

Favorite manga:
Mars, Tokyo Babylon, Black Jack, Nausicaä of the Valley of Wind

Favorite manga artists:
Ashinano Hitoshi, Takeshi Obata

....

Author's Comments:
"The Homecoming" is a very old idea. I wrote it down some time ago,
and left it as a lonely little text file on my hard drive for several years.
I came back to it when trying to think of a good storyline—short stories are
not my strong point—and found I liked the idea of telling a science fiction
story. It was originally intended to be longer, but I think it works much better
as a short, standalone comic.
—*Morag Lewis*

::

::

THE HOMECOMING :: Runner Up ::

....

Judge's Comments:

Science fiction is a favorite genre of mine and something I really like to see done well. My very favorite science fiction stories are those that focus on the human side of the characters. "The Homecoming" presents a radically changed future world affected by some unspecified global cataclysm—a staple of science fiction—but looks at it from a lighthearted, human point of view. This is a big plus in my book. I liked the idea of an artifact-hunting game show, and the interaction of the main characters is very believable. The dialogue stays away from the "talking heads" trap too common in science fiction. I like the emotional impact of the grandfather's ashes, and I appreciate that our protagonists don't win the game—what they get out of their experience is more important than any prize, and that's a widely applicable theme.

Beyond the story, the art also has a lot of good points. The facial expressions and body language are good. There are some very nice backgrounds, and there's good use of solid black areas. The pacing is a bit rushed at the beginning, but the middle slows things down nicely, giving enough visual impact to important scenes. Unfortunately, however, the ending feels very rushed, with very little room to focus on important parts such as the final panel—this gives the impression that it's a 25-page story that has been compressed down to 20 pages. Anatomy is sometimes a bit off, like at the bottom of page 2. And has something happened to fashion sense in the future—should we believe that there will be no variation in space suit design? The lines throughout this entry are quite thin, which in manga is something that's very important—too many entries featured linework much too thick to fit with the manga style. Unfortunately, the lines here, while being thin, also come off as weak, tentative, and unconfident. There is also a near-entire lack of line weight variation, an important factor in professional inking.

The real dealbreaker for me, however, goes back to the story—I find it difficult to buy the details of the Earth's abandonment as presented. The costs involved in evacuating the entire planetary population are astronomical, yet this was accomplished in the grandfather's lifetime—either that or the planet was so contaminated that billions of people were killed off, and the extinction was so complete that mere game show participants can visit without fear of roving refugee bands; but if that were so, I wouldn't expect the ecosystem to have recovered nearly as quickly as it apparently has. Overall this entry had an interesting premise and good storytelling, but the artistic execution and world building show some gaps in the details.
—Peter Ahlstrom

Judge's Comments:

Science fiction isn't an easy genre to write, and it's not one in which we tend to get a lot of strong *RSOM* entries. It's difficult to build a coherent future world and establish clear characters in the space of 20 short pages, and, in general, many of the most successful entries stick to a simpler concept. "The Homecoming" impressed me right from the start by employing very clear, well-paced panel layouts, and presenting a well-rounded, engaging setting. The futuristic elements aren't the most spectacular I've ever seen, but they're handled in such a way that they accent the story without distracting the reader with too much detail. Returning to an Earth long dead is a fairly well-trod premise, but Morag Lewis presented us with a simple, coherent plot, and I enjoyed the resulting story.

However, in spite of solid layouts, the consistency of the art leaves quite a bit to be desired. Attractive character designs and a decent attempt at sci-fi technology are counterbalanced by panels where the characters are off-model and proportions are inconsistent. Further studies in life-drawing and anatomy would really give a boost to Morag's storytelling capabilities, enhancing a strong writing talent with added artistic flexibility and range. This entry shows the kind of promise that we look for in a Rising Star, so the next step for Morag would be to increase the all-around professional, polished aspects of her work.
—Lillian Diaz-Przybyl

::

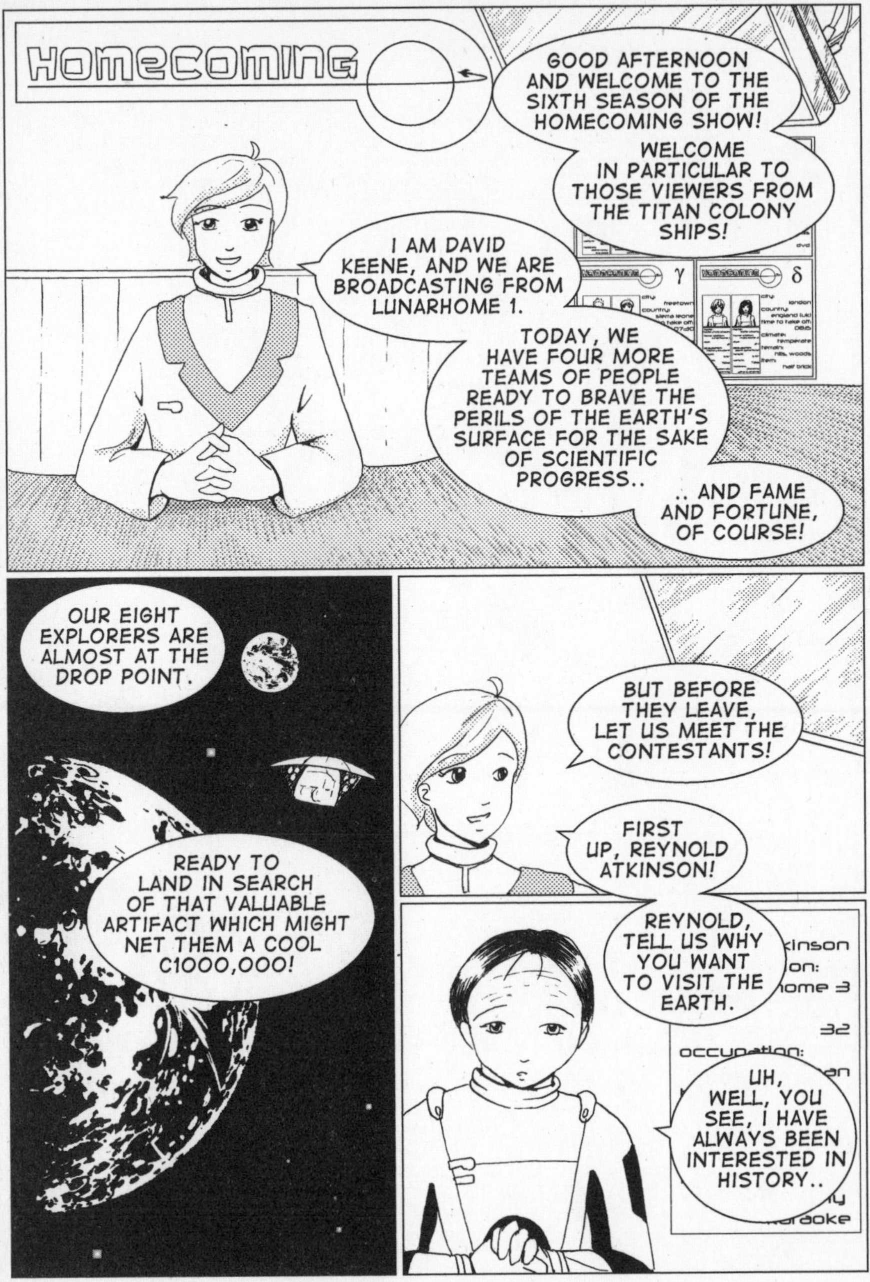
HOMECOMING
GOOD AFTERNOON AND WELCOME TO THE SIXTH SEASON OF THE HOMECOMING SHOW!
WELCOME IN PARTICULAR TO THOSE VIEWERS FROM THE TITAN COLONY SHIPS!
I AM DAVID KEENE, AND WE ARE BROADCASTING FROM LUNARHOME 1.
TODAY, WE HAVE FOUR MORE TEAMS OF PEOPLE READY TO BRAVE THE PERILS OF THE EARTH'S SURFACE FOR THE SAKE OF SCIENTIFIC PROGRESS..
.. AND FAME AND FORTUNE, OF COURSE!
OUR EIGHT EXPLORERS ARE ALMOST AT THE DROP POINT.
READY TO LAND IN SEARCH OF THAT VALUABLE ARTIFACT WHICH MIGHT NET THEM A COOL C1000,000!
BUT BEFORE THEY LEAVE, LET US MEET THE CONTESTANTS!
FIRST UP, REYNOLD ATKINSON!
REYNOLD, TELL US WHY YOU WANT TO VISIT THE EARTH.
UH, WELL, YOU SEE, I HAVE ALWAYS BEEN INTERESTED IN HISTORY..

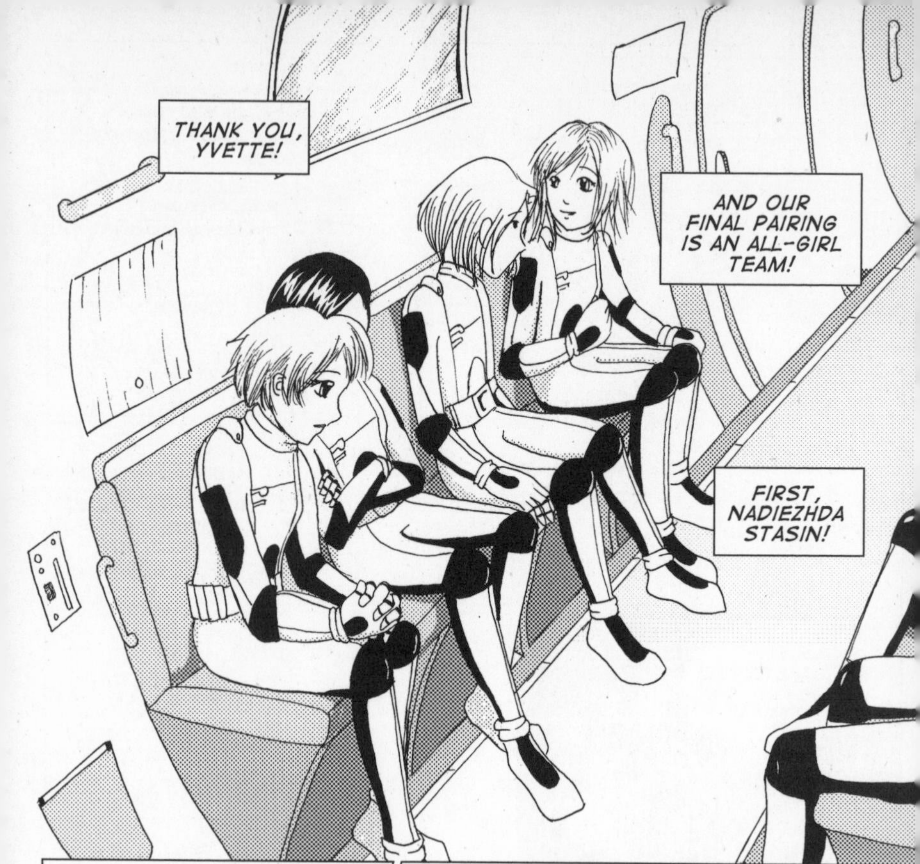
THANK YOU, YVETTE!
AND OUR FINAL PAIRING IS AN ALL-GIRL TEAM!
FIRST, NADIEZHDA STASIN!

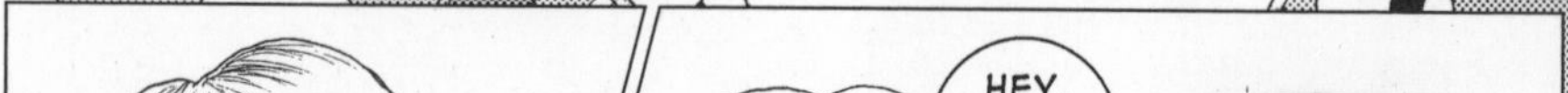
HEY, CALM DOWN.
THESE ARE PRE-RECORDED, REMEMBER?

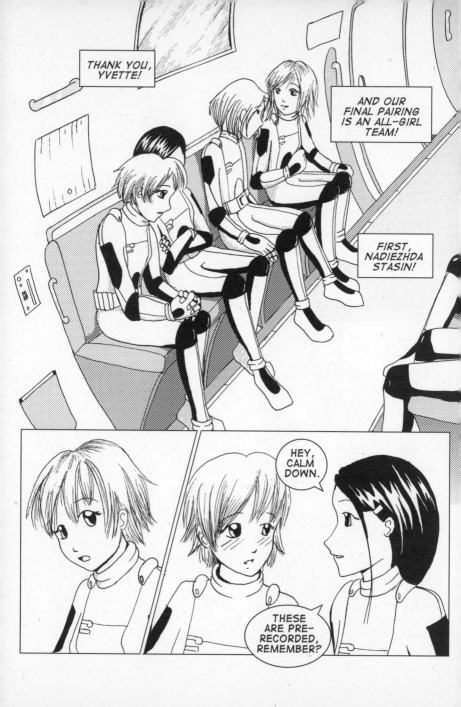

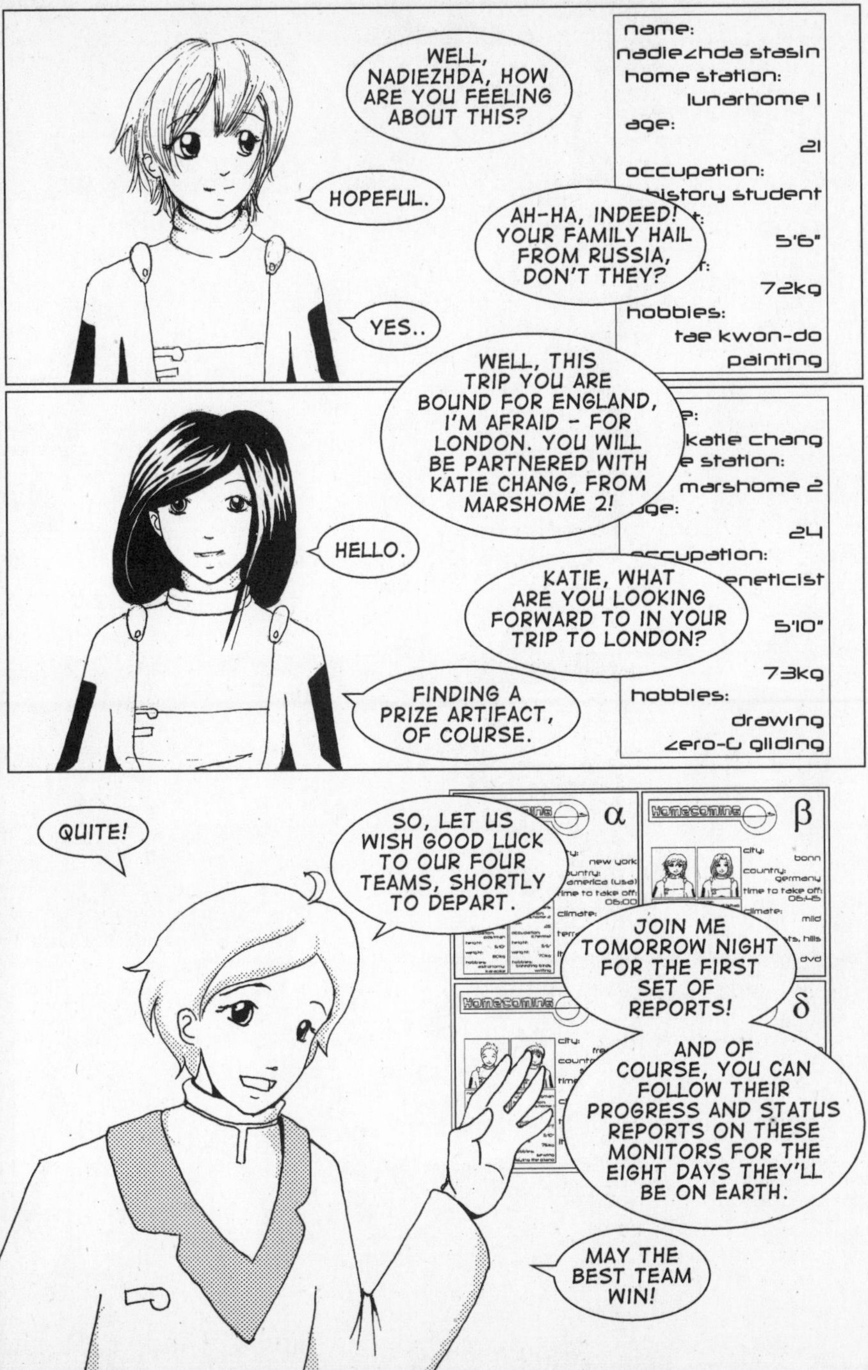
WELL, NADIEZHDA, HOW ARE YOU FEELING ABOUT THIS?
name:
nadiezhda stasin
home station:
lunarhome 1
age:
21
occupation:
history student
5'6"
72kg
hobbies:
tae kwon-do
painting
HOPEFUL.
AH-HA, INDEED! YOUR FAMILY HAIL FROM RUSSIA, DON'T THEY?
YES..
WELL, THIS TRIP YOU ARE BOUND FOR ENGLAND, I'M AFRAID - FOR LONDON. YOU WILL BE PARTNERED WITH KATIE CHANG, FROM MARSHOME 2!
katie chang
marshome 2
24
HELLO.
KATIE, WHAT ARE YOU LOOKING FORWARD TO IN YOUR TRIP TO LONDON?
5'10"
73kg
hobbies:
drawing
zero-G gliding
FINDING A PRIZE ARTIFACT, OF COURSE.
QUITE!
SO, LET US WISH GOOD LUCK TO OUR FOUR TEAMS, SHORTLY TO DEPART.
JOIN ME TOMORROW NIGHT FOR THE FIRST SET OF REPORTS!
AND OF COURSE, YOU CAN FOLLOW THEIR PROGRESS AND STATUS REPORTS ON THESE MONITORS FOR THE EIGHT DAYS THEY'LL BE ON EARTH.
MAY THE BEST TEAM WIN!

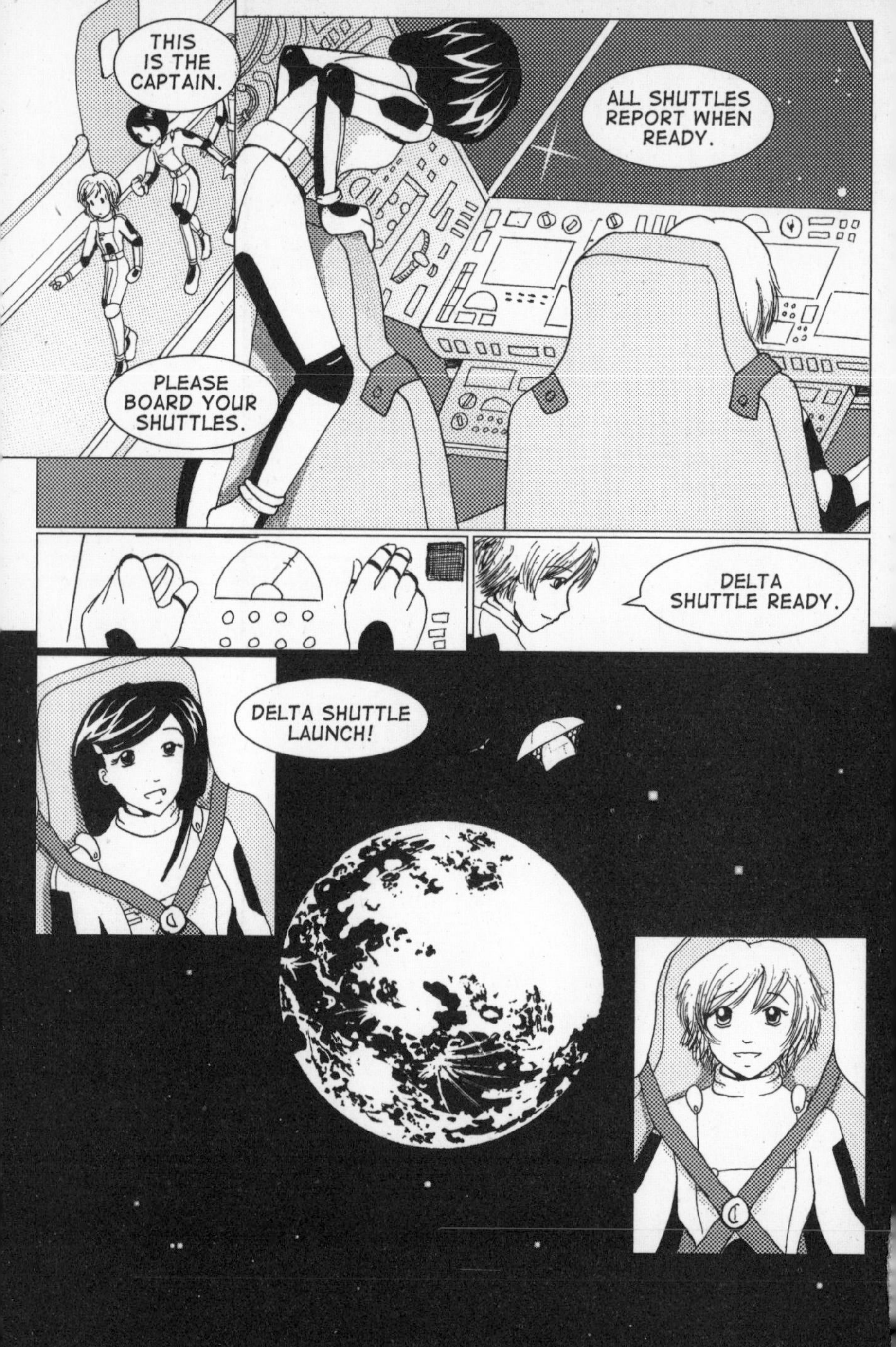
THIS IS THE CAPTAIN.
PLEASE BOARD YOUR SHUTTLES.
ALL SHUTTLES REPORT WHEN READY.
DELTA SHUTTLE READY.
DELTA SHUTTLE LAUNCH!

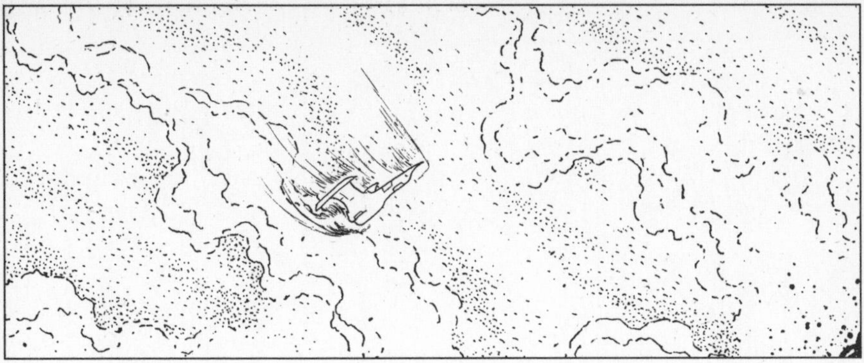

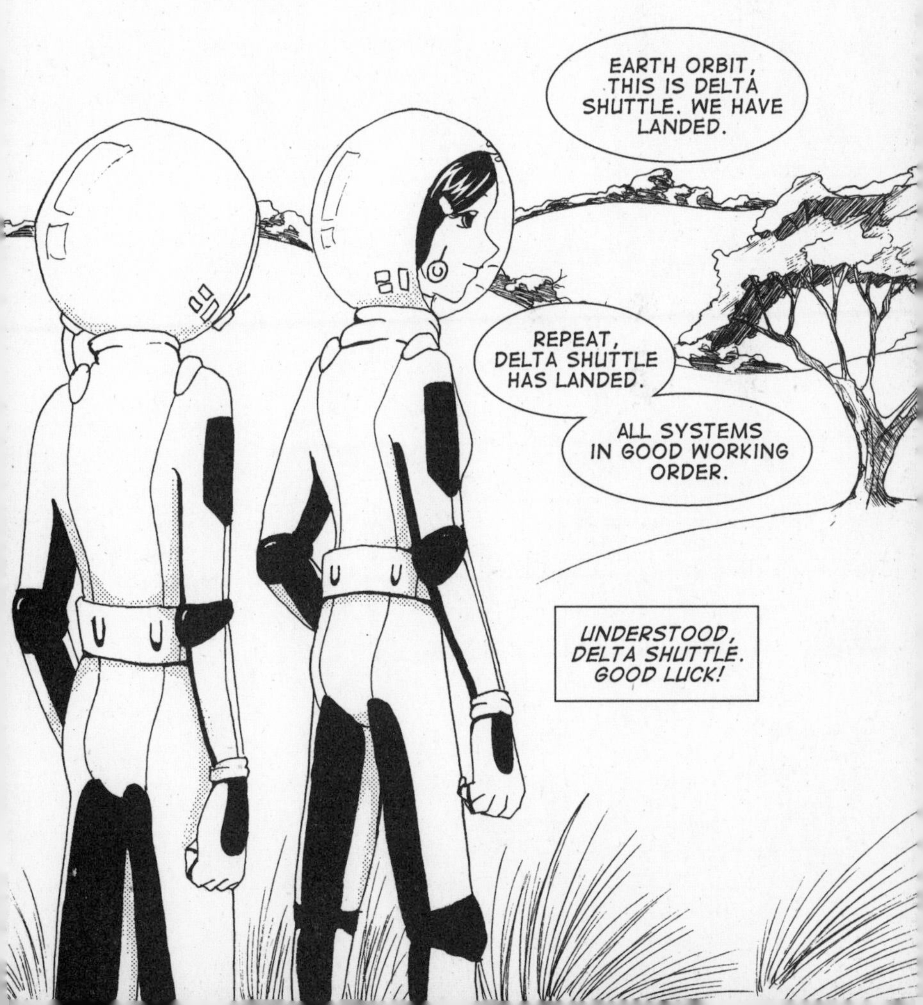
EARTH ORBIT, THIS IS DELTA SHUTTLE. WE HAVE LANDED.
REPEAT, DELTA SHUTTLE HAS LANDED.
ALL SYSTEMS IN GOOD WORKING ORDER.
UNDERSTOOD, DELTA SHUTTLE. GOOD LUCK!

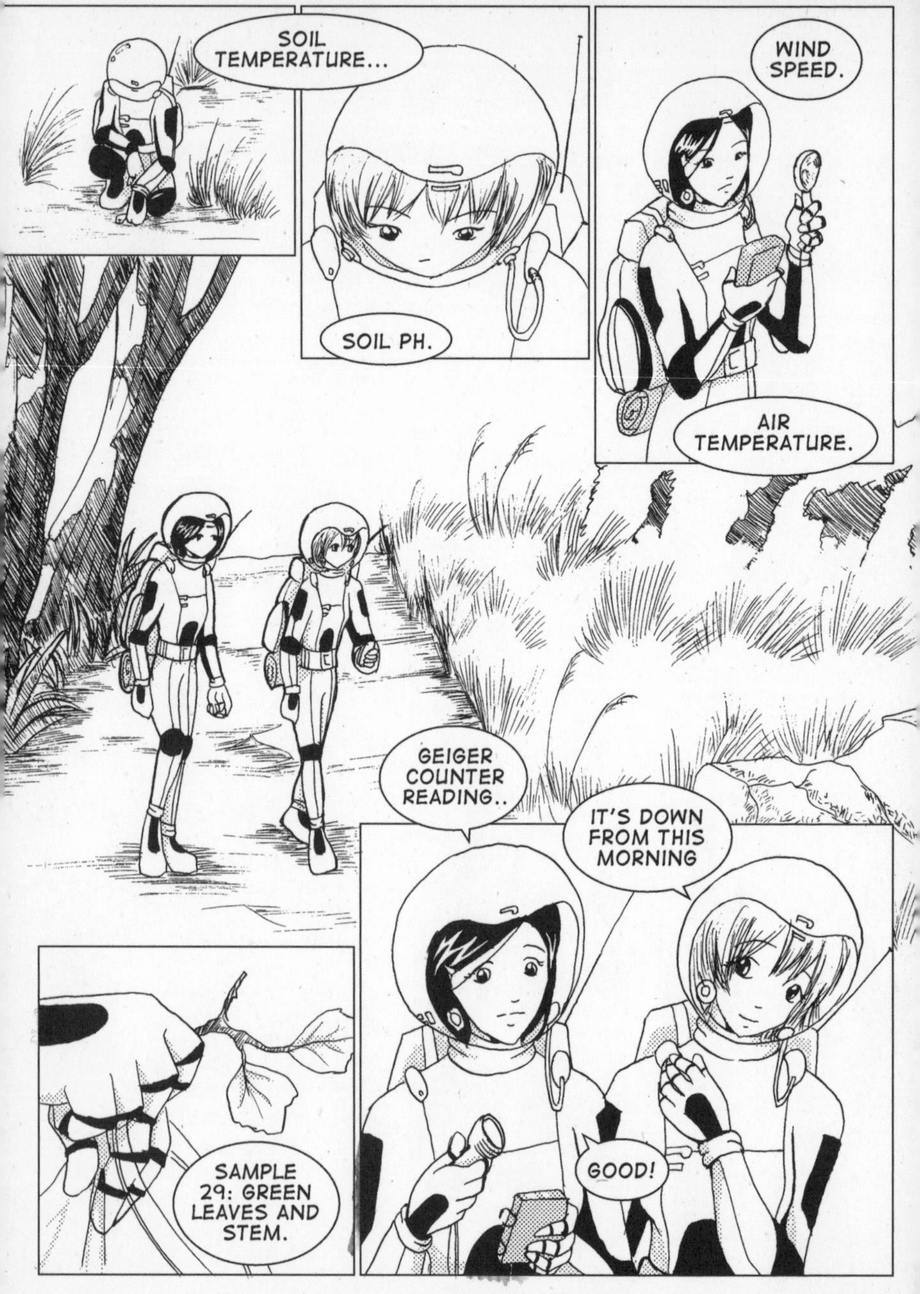
SOIL TEMPERATURE...
SOIL PH.
WIND SPEED.
AIR TEMPERATURE.
GEIGER COUNTER READING..
SAMPLE 29: GREEN LEAVES AND STEM.
IT'S DOWN FROM THIS MORNING
GOOD!

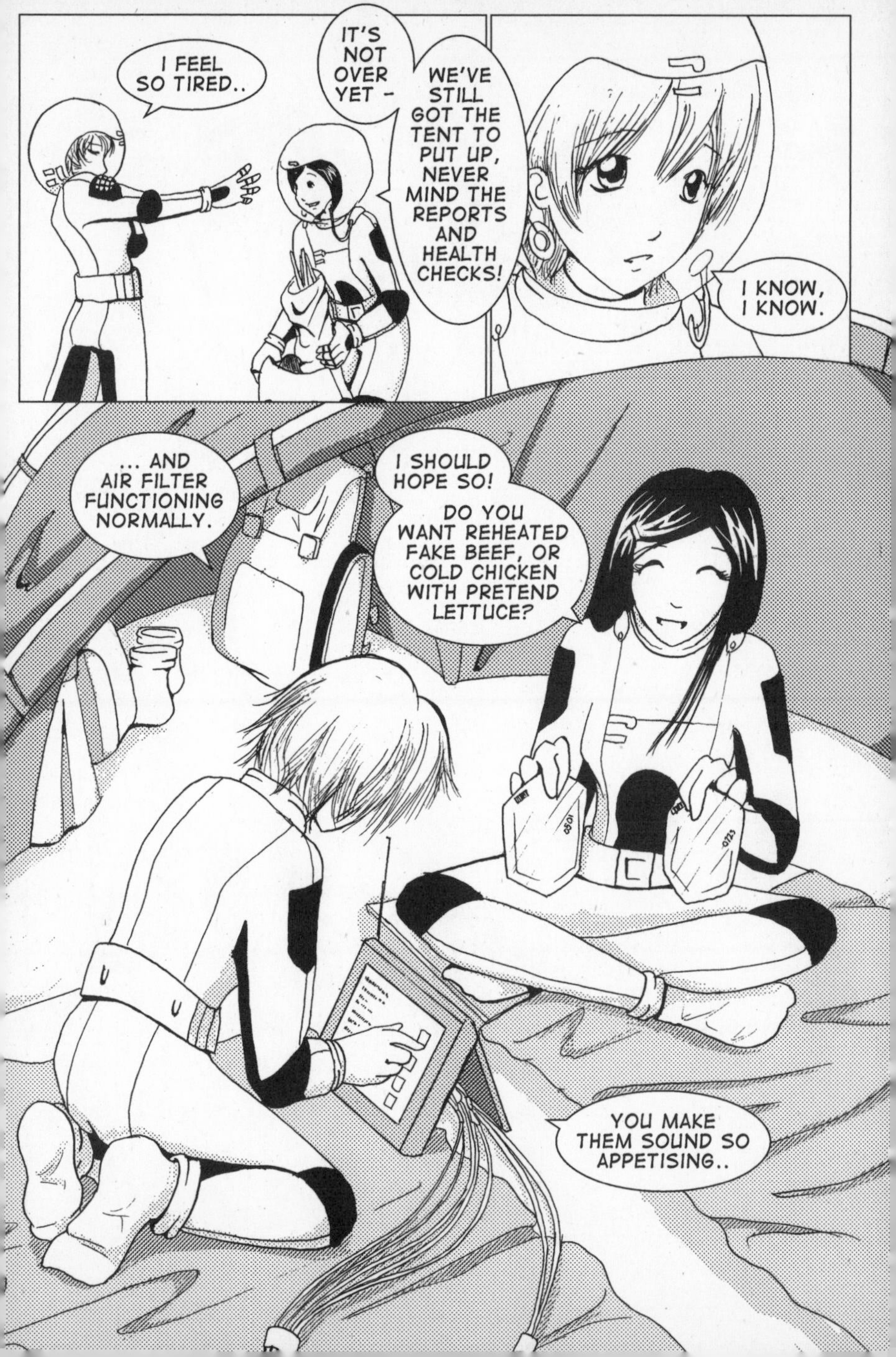
I FEEL SO TIRED..
IT'S NOT OVER YET -
WE'VE STILL GOT THE TENT TO PUT UP, NEVER MIND THE REPORTS AND HEALTH CHECKS!
I KNOW, I KNOW.
... AND AIR FILTER FUNCTIONING NORMALLY.
I SHOULD HOPE SO!
DO YOU WANT REHEATED FAKE BEEF, OR COLD CHICKEN WITH PRETEND LETTUCE?
YOU MAKE THEM SOUND SO APPETISING..

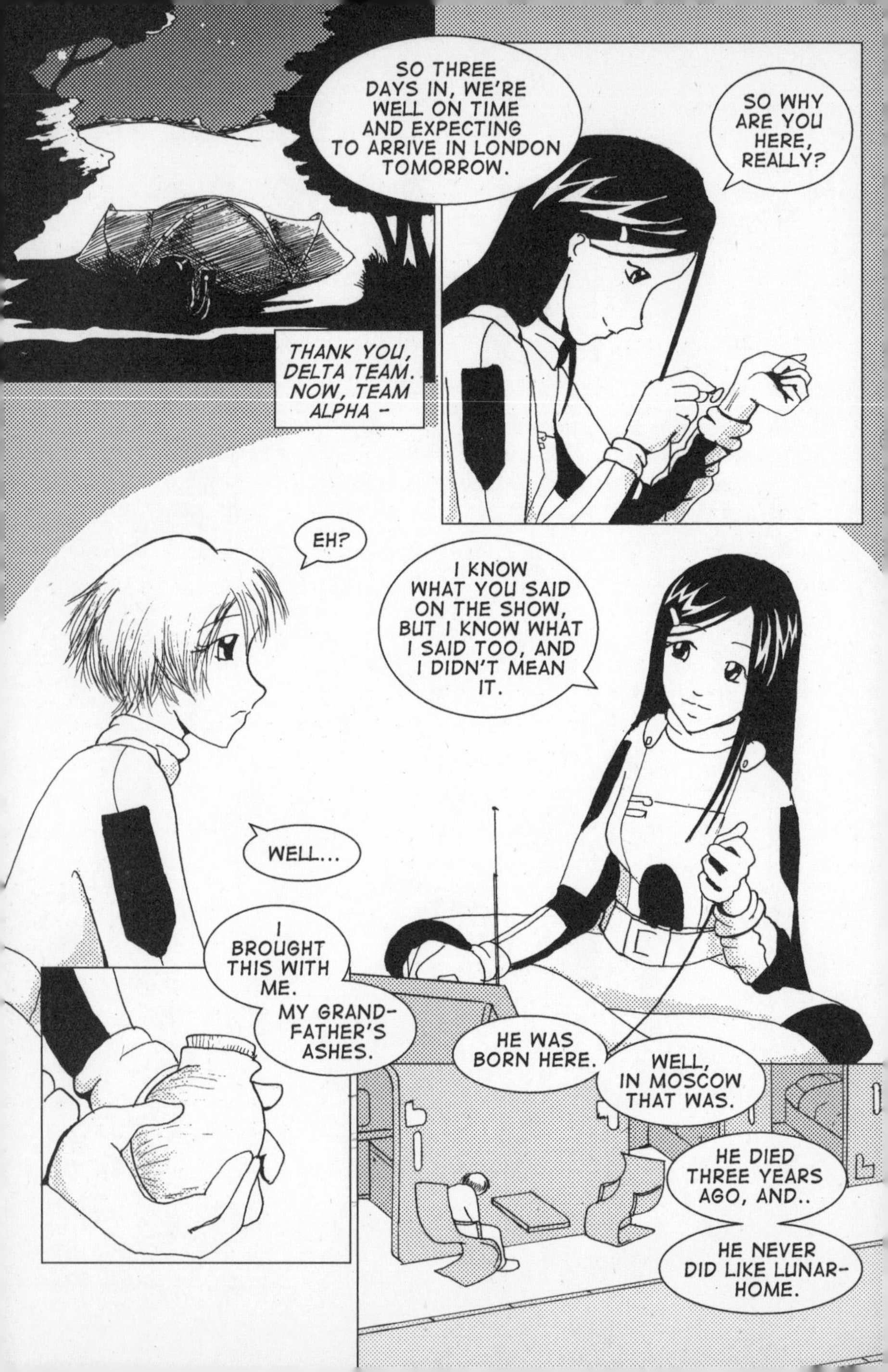
SO THREE DAYS IN, WE'RE WELL ON TIME AND EXPECTING TO ARRIVE IN LONDON TOMORROW.
THANK YOU, DELTA TEAM. NOW, TEAM ALPHA -
SO WHY ARE YOU HERE, REALLY?
EH?
I KNOW WHAT YOU SAID ON THE SHOW, BUT I KNOW WHAT I SAID TOO, AND I DIDN'T MEAN IT.
WELL...
I BROUGHT THIS WITH ME.
MY GRAND-FATHER'S ASHES.
HE WAS BORN HERE.
WELL, IN MOSCOW THAT WAS.
HE DIED THREE YEARS AGO, AND..
HE NEVER DID LIKE LUNAR-HOME.

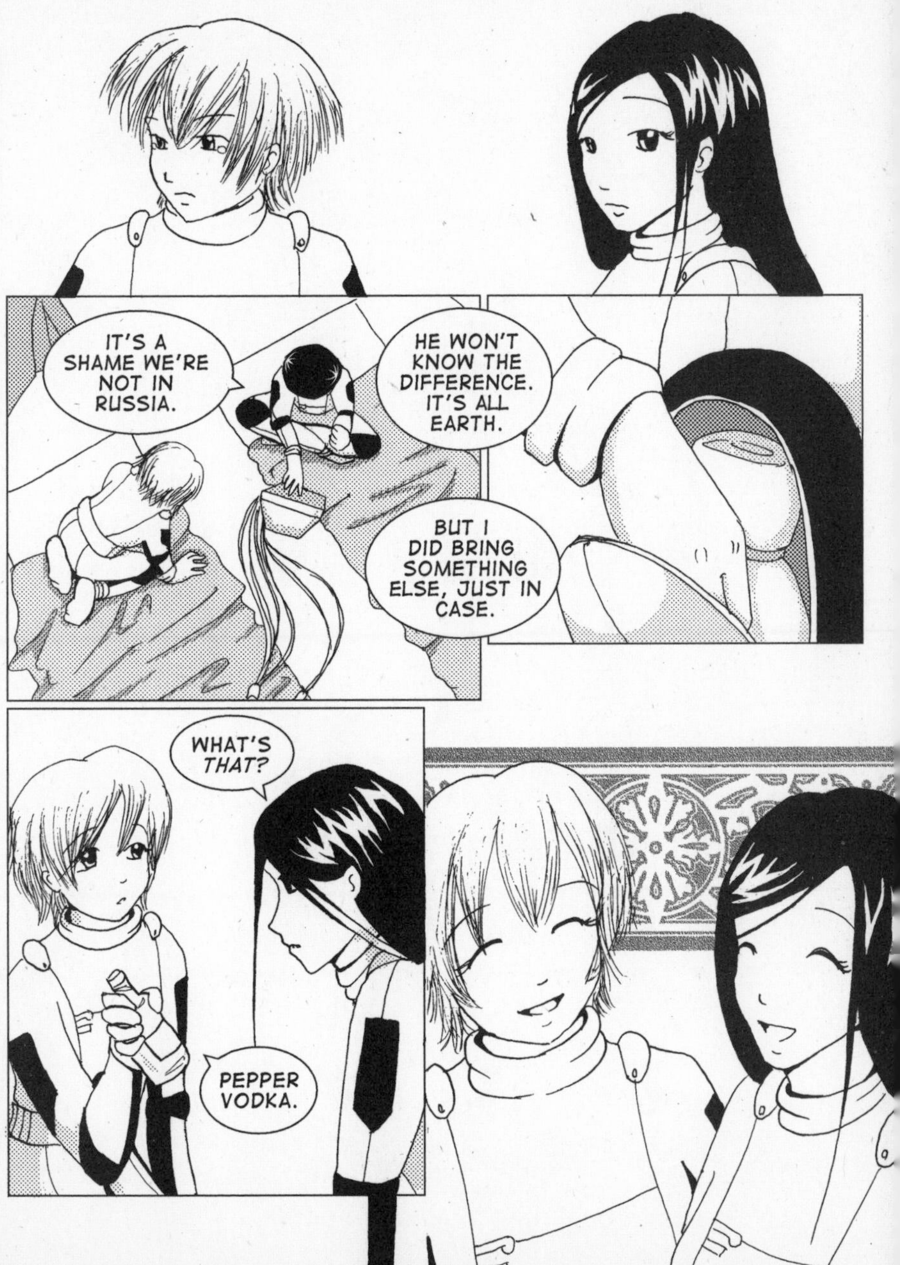
IT'S A SHAME WE'RE NOT IN RUSSIA.
HE WON'T KNOW THE DIFFERENCE. IT'S ALL EARTH.
BUT I DID BRING SOMETHING ELSE, JUST IN CASE.
WHAT'S *THAT*?
PEPPER VODKA.

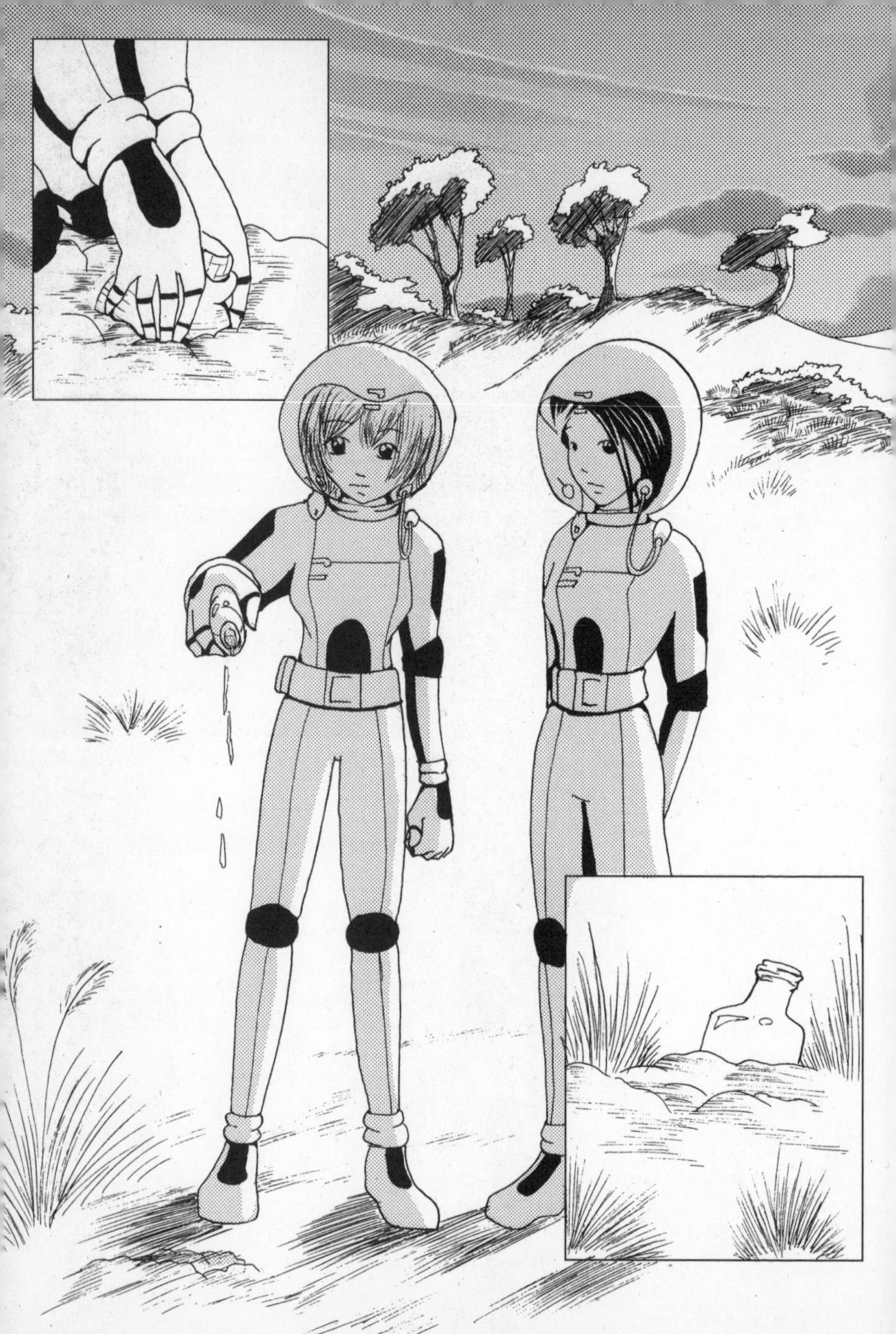

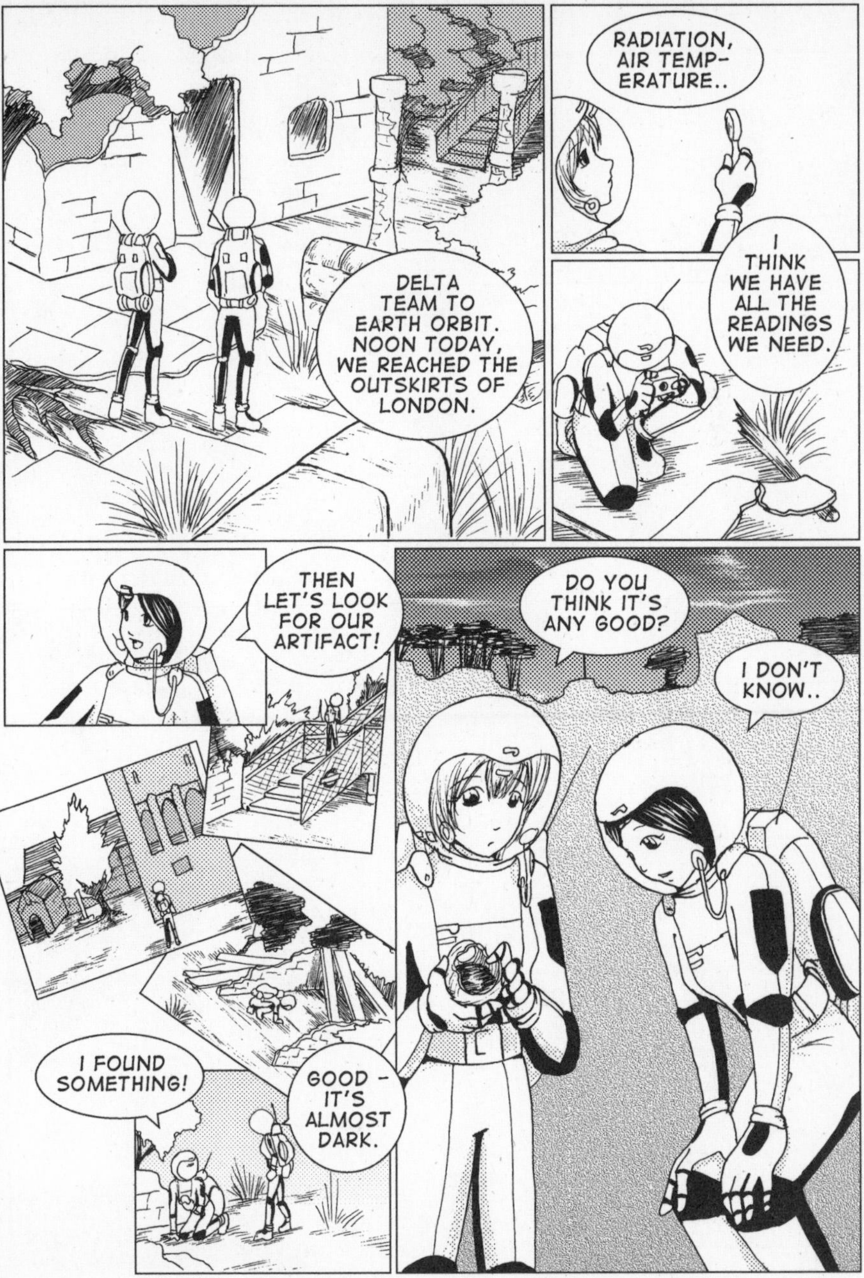
DELTA TEAM TO EARTH ORBIT. NOON TODAY, WE REACHED THE OUTSKIRTS OF LONDON.
RADIATION, AIR TEMP-ERATURE..
I THINK WE HAVE ALL THE READINGS WE NEED.
THEN LET'S LOOK FOR OUR ARTIFACT!
I FOUND SOMETHING!
GOOD - IT'S ALMOST DARK.
DO YOU THINK IT'S ANY GOOD?
I DON'T KNOW..

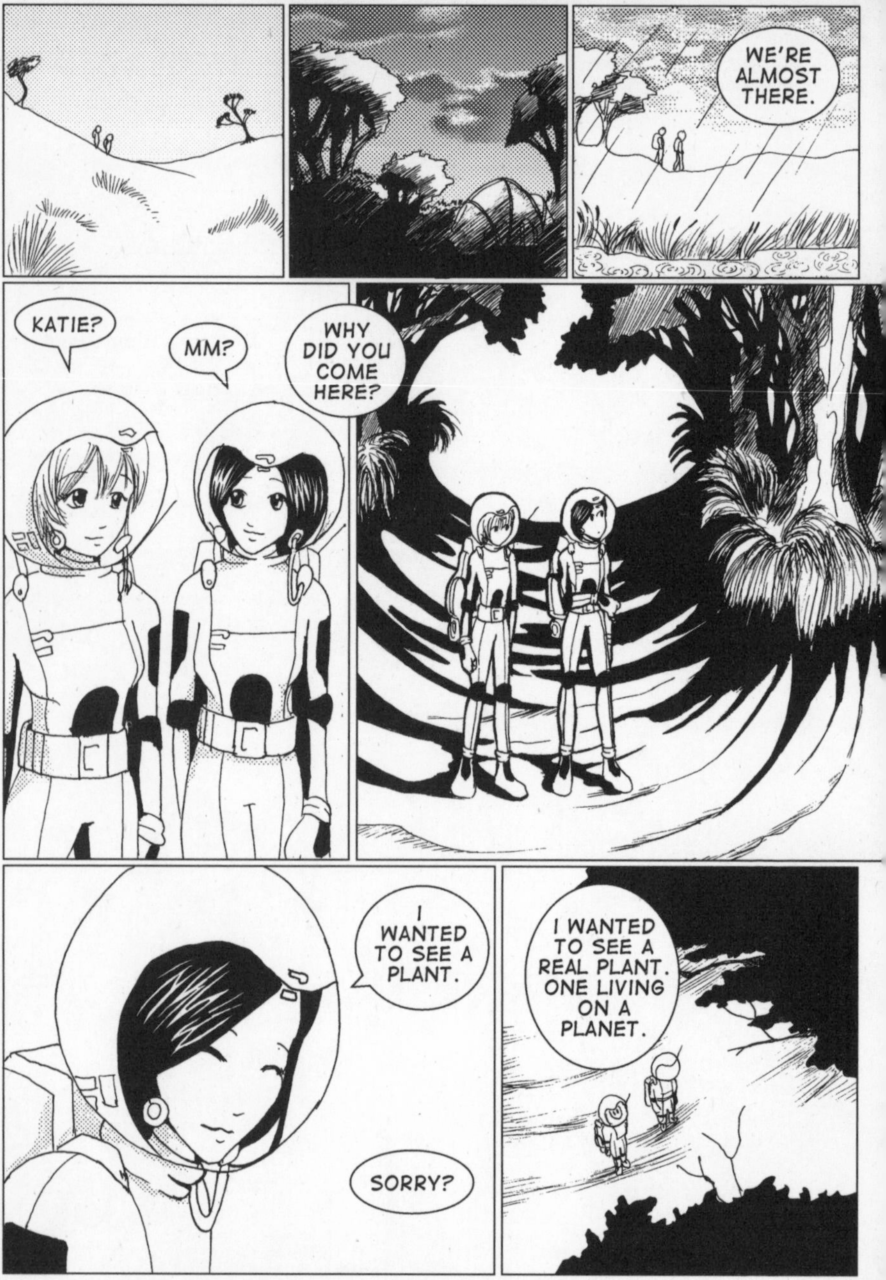
WE'RE ALMOST THERE.
KATIE?
MM?
WHY DID YOU COME HERE?
I WANTED TO SEE A PLANT.
SORRY?
I WANTED TO SEE A REAL PLANT. ONE LIVING ON A PLANET.

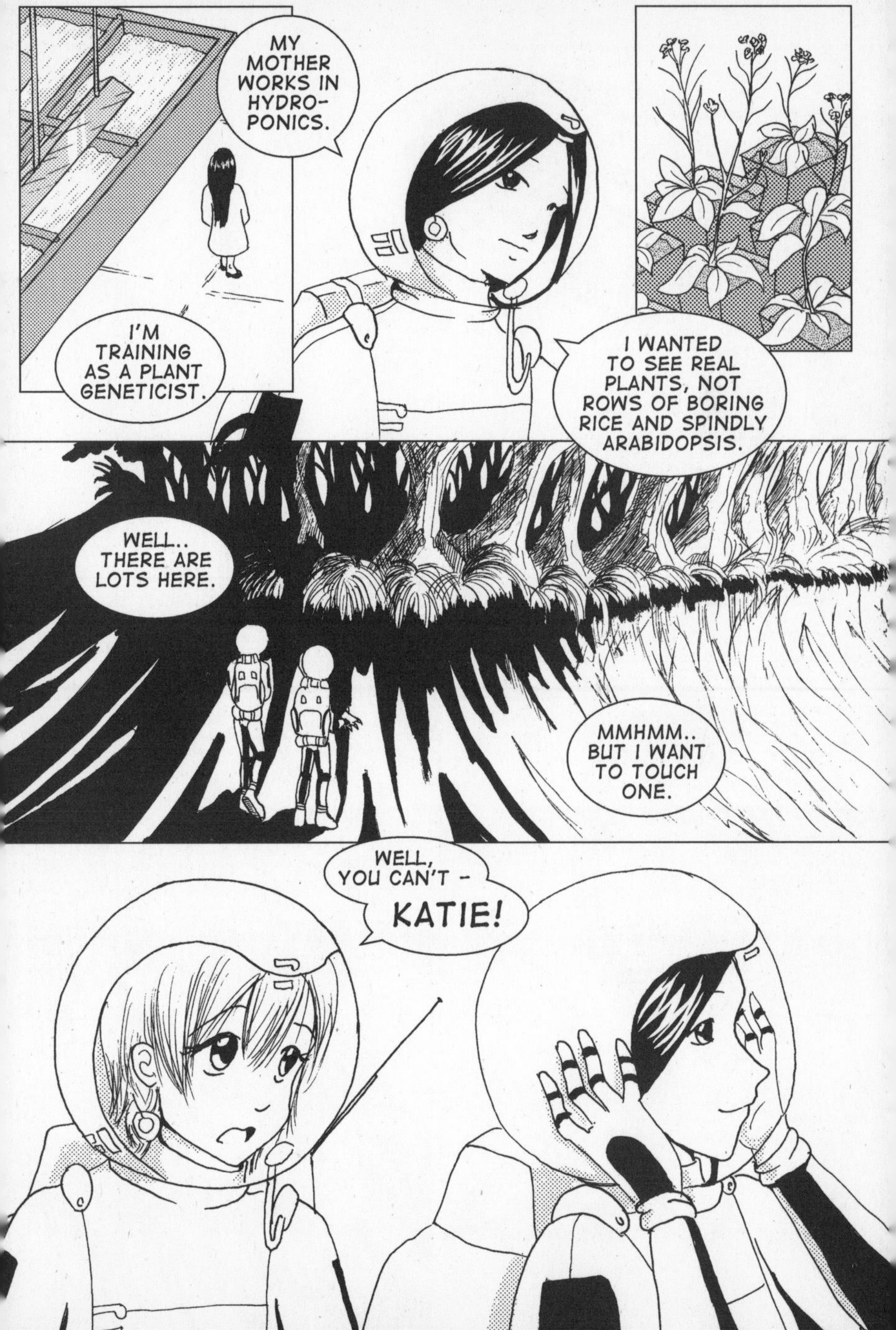
MY MOTHER WORKS IN HYDRO-PONICS.
I'M TRAINING AS A PLANT GENETICIST.
I WANTED TO SEE REAL PLANTS, NOT ROWS OF BORING RICE AND SPINDLY ARABIDOPSIS.
WELL.. THERE ARE LOTS HERE.
MMHMM.. BUT I WANT TO TOUCH ONE.
WELL, YOU CAN'T -
KATIE!

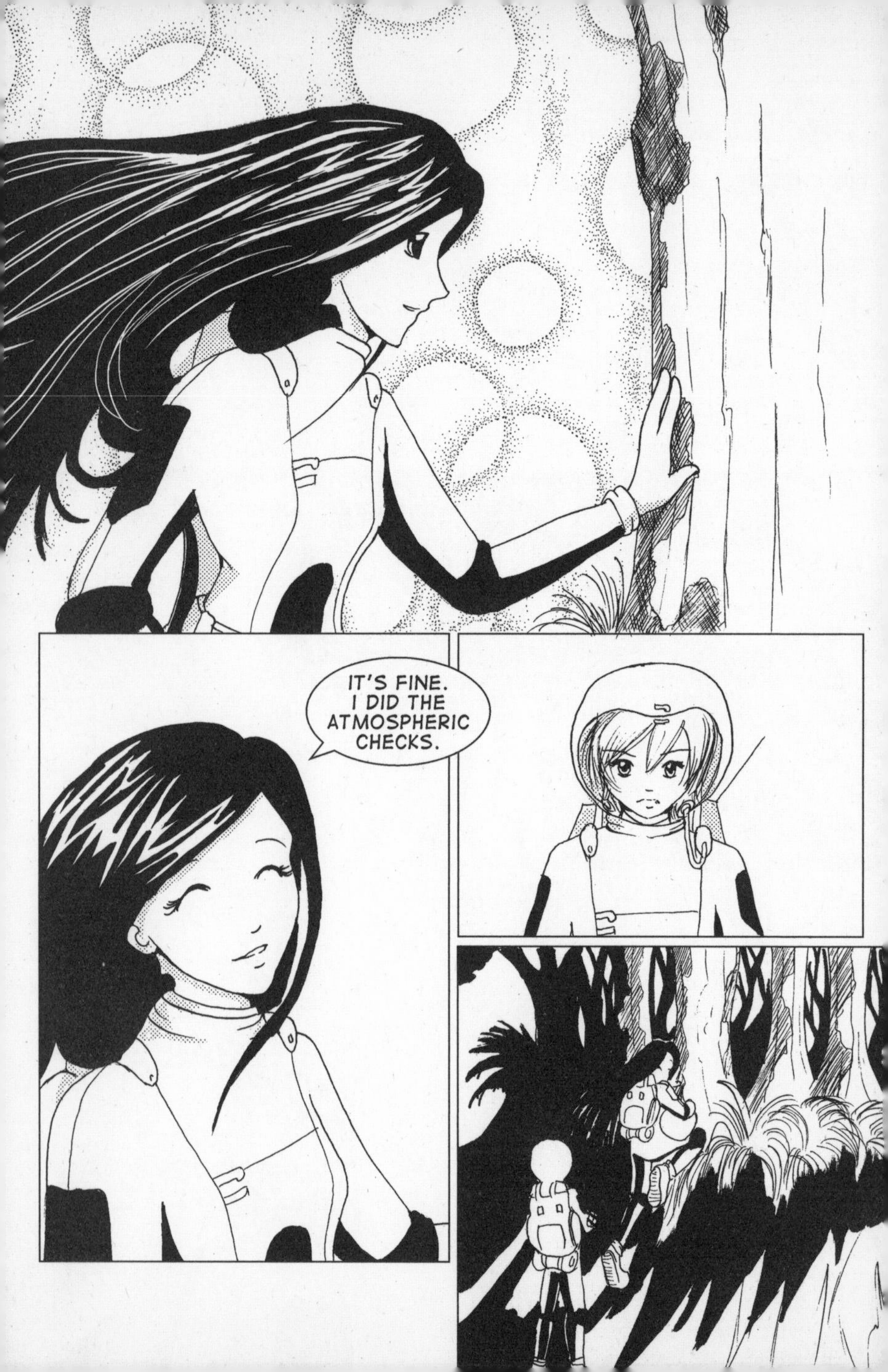
IT'S FINE. I DID THE ATMOSPHERIC CHECKS.

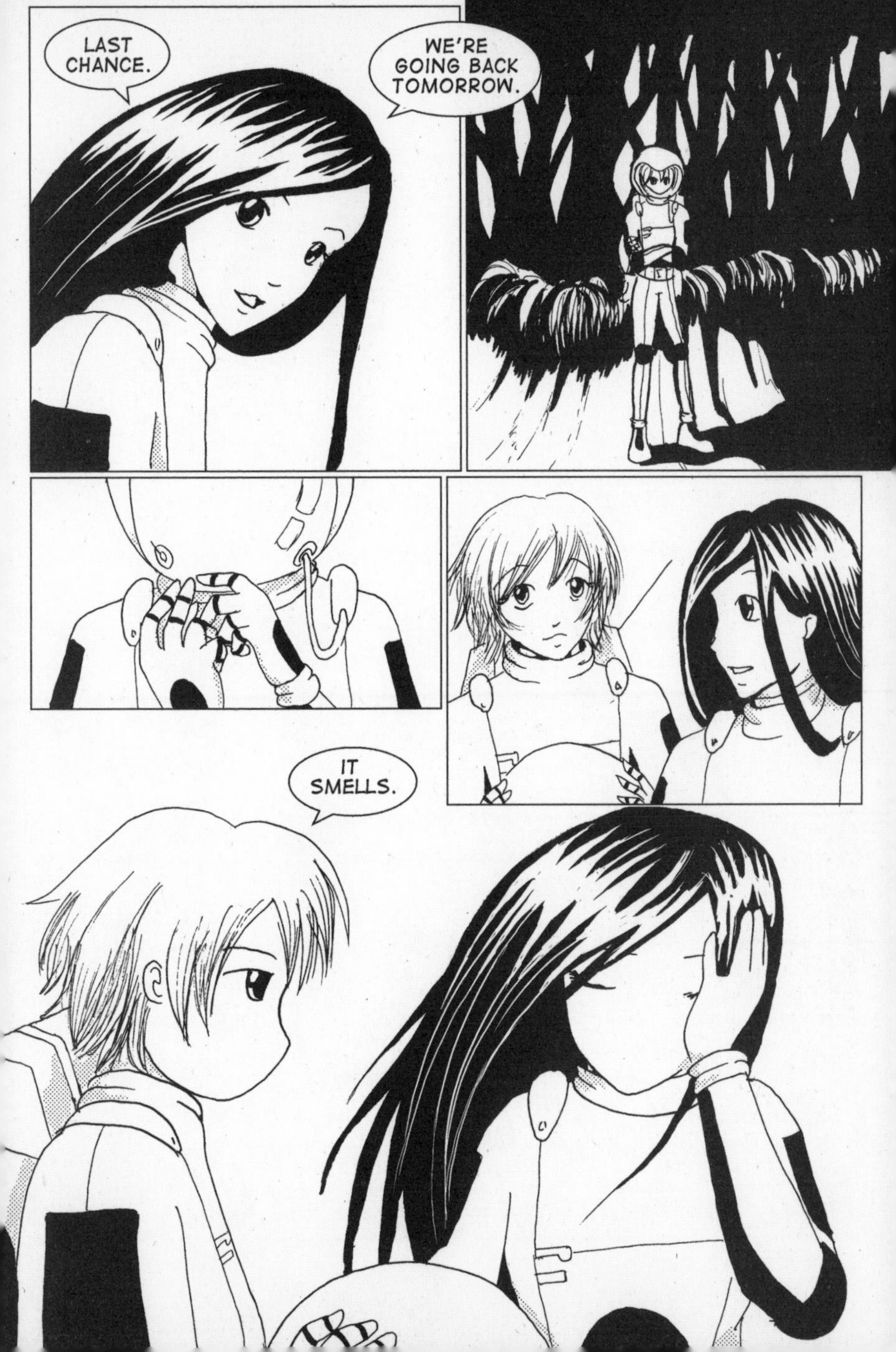
LAST CHANCE.
WE'RE GOING BACK TOMORROW.
IT SMELLS.

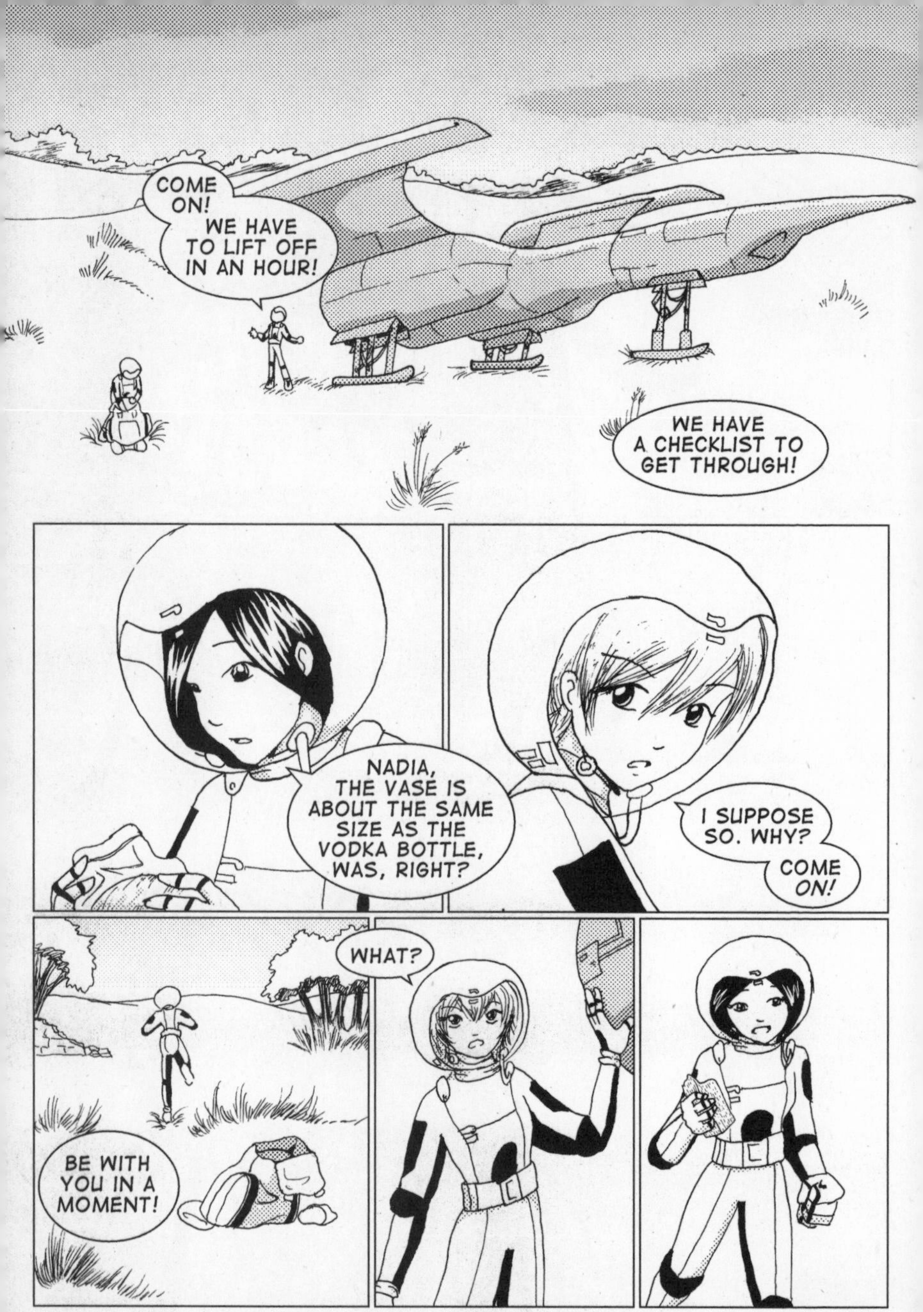
COME ON! WE HAVE TO LIFT OFF IN AN HOUR!
WE HAVE A CHECKLIST TO GET THROUGH!
NADIA, THE VASE IS ABOUT THE SAME SIZE AS THE VODKA BOTTLE, WAS, RIGHT?
I SUPPOSE SO. WHY?
COME ON!
BE WITH YOU IN A MOMENT!
WHAT?

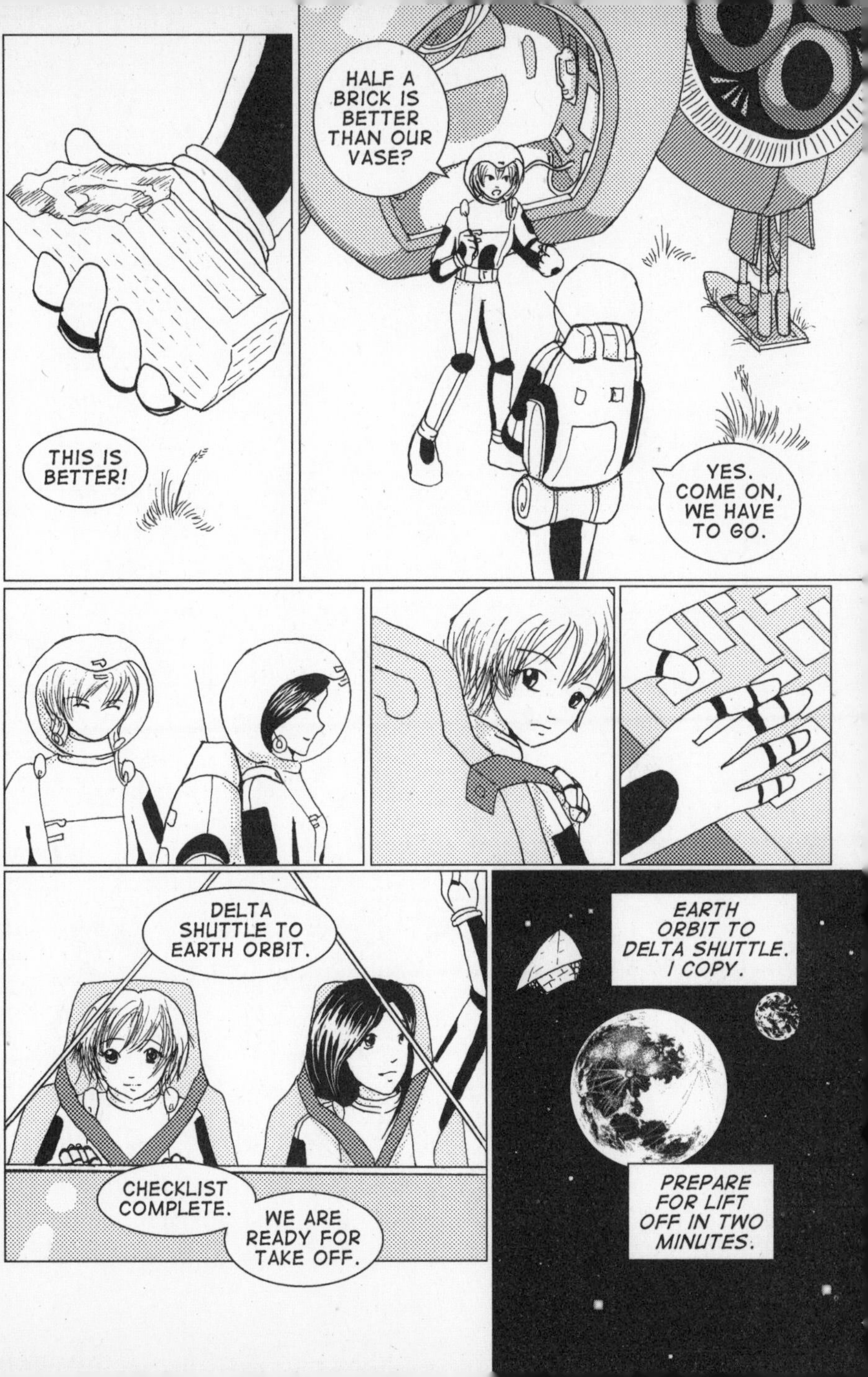
THIS IS BETTER!
HALF A BRICK IS BETTER THAN OUR VASE?
YES. COME ON, WE HAVE TO GO.
DELTA SHUTTLE TO EARTH ORBIT.
CHECKLIST COMPLETE.
WE ARE READY FOR TAKE OFF.
EARTH ORBIT TO DELTA SHUTTLE. I COPY.
PREPARE FOR LIFT OFF IN TWO MINUTES.

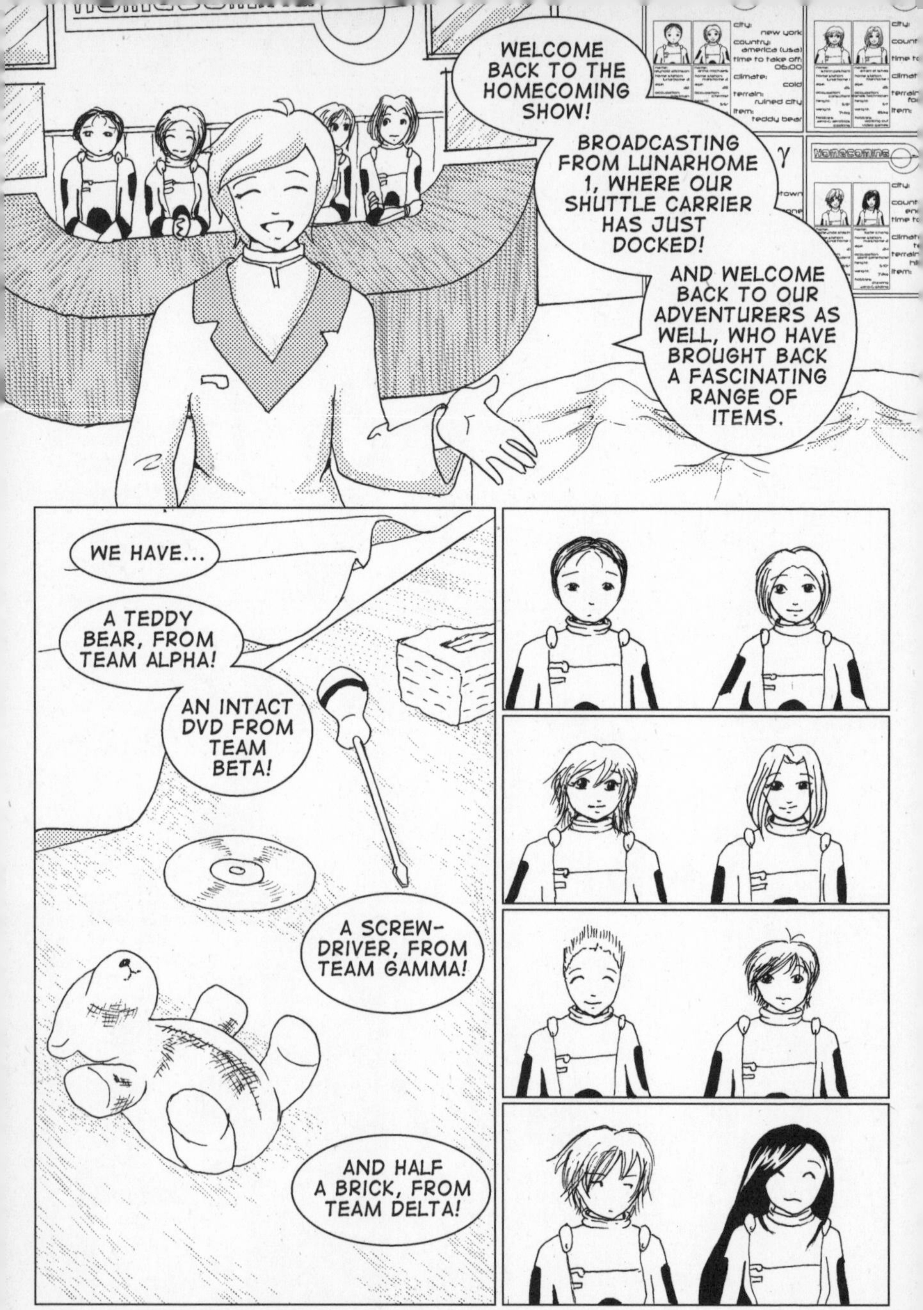
WELCOME BACK TO THE HOMECOMING SHOW!
BROADCASTING FROM LUNARHOME 1, WHERE OUR SHUTTLE CARRIER HAS JUST DOCKED!
AND WELCOME BACK TO OUR ADVENTURERS AS WELL, WHO HAVE BROUGHT BACK A FASCINATING RANGE OF ITEMS.
WE HAVE...
A TEDDY BEAR, FROM TEAM ALPHA!
AN INTACT DVD FROM TEAM BETA!
A SCREW-DRIVER, FROM TEAM GAMMA!
AND HALF A BRICK, FROM TEAM DELTA!

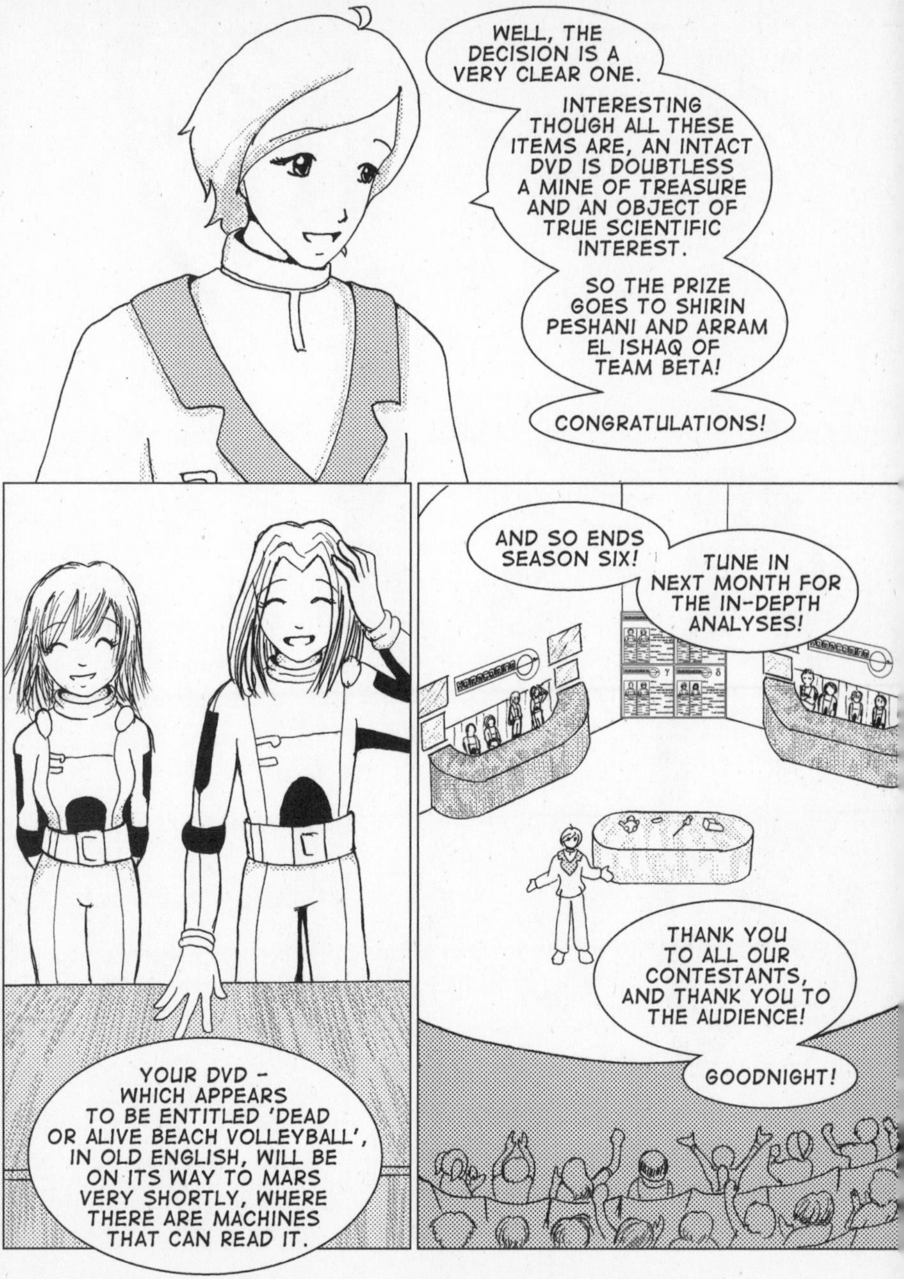
WELL, THE DECISION IS A VERY CLEAR ONE.
INTERESTING THOUGH ALL THESE ITEMS ARE, AN INTACT DVD IS DOUBTLESS A MINE OF TREASURE AND AN OBJECT OF TRUE SCIENTIFIC INTEREST.
SO THE PRIZE GOES TO SHIRIN PESHANI AND ARRAM EL ISHAQ OF TEAM BETA!
CONGRATULATIONS!
YOUR DVD - WHICH APPEARS TO BE ENTITLED 'DEAD OR ALIVE BEACH VOLLEYBALL', IN OLD ENGLISH, WILL BE ON ITS WAY TO MARS VERY SHORTLY, WHERE THERE ARE MACHINES THAT CAN READ IT.
AND SO ENDS SEASON SIX!
TUNE IN NEXT MONTH FOR THE IN-DEPTH ANALYSES!
THANK YOU TO ALL OUR CONTESTANTS, AND THANK YOU TO THE AUDIENCE!
GOODNIGHT!

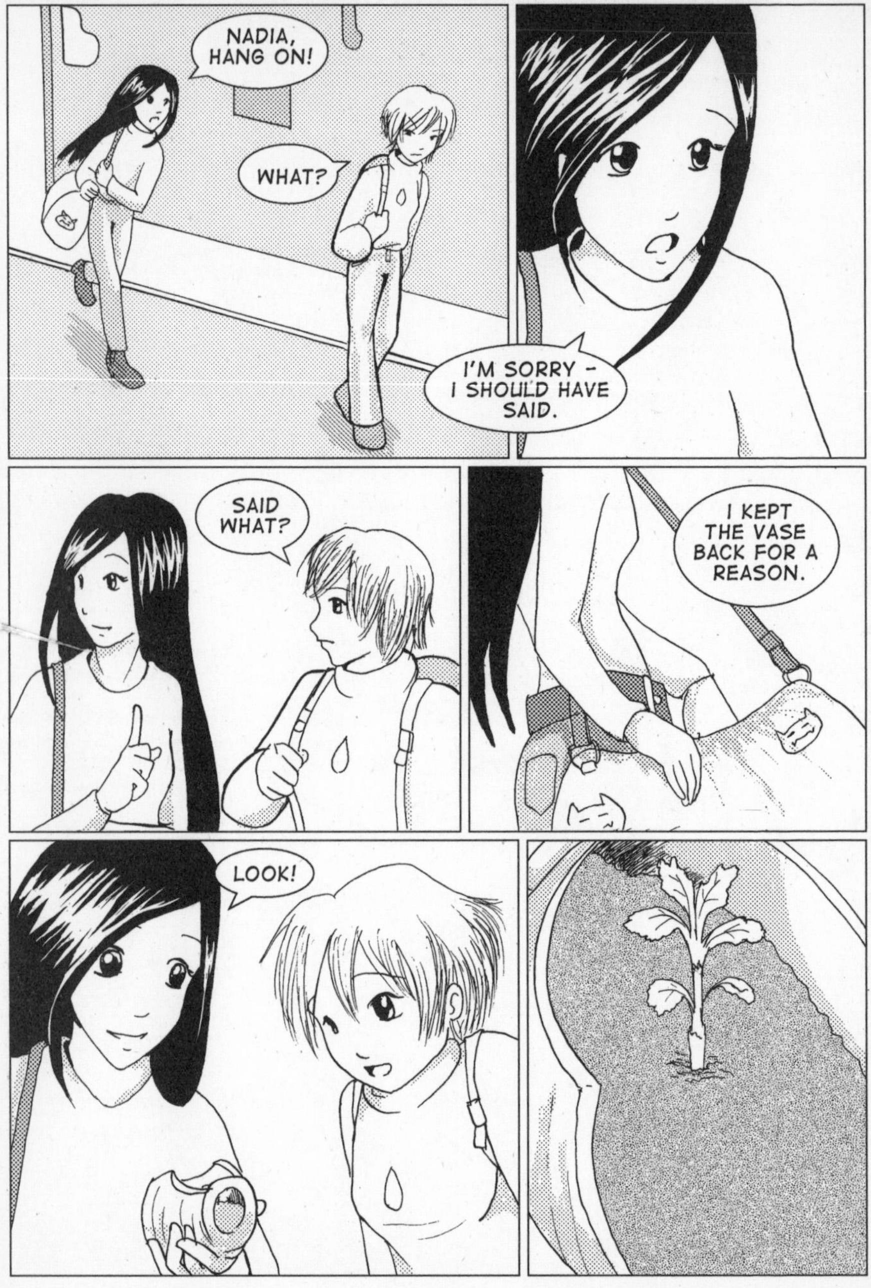
NADIA, HANG ON!
WHAT?
I'M SORRY - I SHOULD HAVE SAID.
SAID WHAT?
I KEPT THE VASE BACK FOR A REASON.
LOOK!

PROMISE ME :: Runner Up ::

....

Khalid Kassim was born in Rome, Italy in 1988. He is currently still in education (college). He studies digital media and art & design.

Favorite manga:
Death Note

Favorite manga artist:
Takeshi Obata

....

Author's Comments:
"Promise Me" was born while I was working on a pitch for a completely different story, the main characters in my pitch gave me the idea for the short story. I thought *RSoM* would be a great challenge to create a short story, which I rarely do.
—*Khalid Kassim*

::

PROMISE ME :: Runner Up ::

....

Judge's Comments:
"Promise Me" is an ambitious character study. It tackles serious, non black-and-white issues while not attempting to explain or solve them. Instead, it takes you deep into the heart of its characters' world—and at times, that world becomes as real and sympathetic as anything in life.

Of course, to augment that sense of reality, Kassim pulls off some striking art decisions. The flashback on page three is powerful not only for its content, but also its black frames, gray panels, accelerated pace and absence of dialogue. Kassim also made excellent use of facial expressions and body language, particularly with Rayn, his tough-as-nails yet soft-hearted hero. From the first page, you can tell that Rayn is a man of strong passion and few words, and his interactions on the pages that follow only bolster that impression—from his rueful smile at ex-wife Amelia to his tender expression at seeing his brother Zayan for the last time.

There are some spelling and punctuation errors, and at one point the scar on the left side of Rayn's head disappears completely. But those are just nitpicks—more than anything, I would have liked to see more focus in the story's structure. In particular, the narrator's identity is unclear. Is it Eddy, the former inmate that Rayn saved at the expense of his own life? Were there multiple speakers? It could be Eddy in the beginning, then Amelia, and then Zayan. It's even possible that the entire narration takes place in Rayn's mind—after all, he is the one we follow most consistently, and sometimes he is alone. Regardless, this ambiguity in perspective serves to dilute, rather than reinforce, the story's key moment—the promise between the two brothers.

I also am unclear on the identity of the little boy at the end. Is it supposed to be Rayn, or Zayan? It looks more like Zayan...but the story follows Rayn, so...hmm. Finally, I admit to being completely stumped as to why the story ends with the mother disappearing. I wish I did understand, because I'm sure the intended conclusion would have been truly satisfying. Unfortunately, to me it served as the anticlimax to an otherwise touching and powerful tale.
—*Carol Fox*

Judge's Comments:
This was one of my early favorites in the judging process. The subject matter is not something I've seen in manga before, and the realism reflected here—no daring escape attempt, no last-second reprieve—is refreshing. The characters hint at great depth, and the courage with which Rayn is facing his death is admirable. The art is also quite serviceable, with a manga flair that I like, but showing that the author has come up with his own personal style. The facial expressions are outstanding, and there's good use of the "show-don't-tell" sawhorse of writing advice. The solid blacks and line weight variation are skillfully employed. The anatomy is often quite good, but it sometimes comes off as a little odd, like on the top of page 15. Panels show good depth, but sometimes background images get a bit flat, like in the story's first panel. The balloons have adequate breathing room within them, which is good, but some pages come off as rather crowded. There is some decent panel size variation, but the panel shapes are plain and there's the occasional read order problem, such as on page eight. The "grab the panel edge" effect on page two doesn't work for me here, and while I appreciate the way the story does not rely on "talking heads" to present information, the point of view is often unclear—it's hard to tell which characters the various bits of narration belong to. The sound effects are visually rather plain, though page 18's are excellent. The grammar and punctuation also need some work. Finally, the last two pages are very confusing, hinting at some kind of unresolved family issue—at this point the author is perhaps trying to do too much with the story; the end of a work is not the best place to try to bring up backstory details. But notwithstanding its shortcomings, this entry evoked a powerful emotional response in its readers, and the ability to do that is a skill every creator should pursue.
—*Peter Ahlstrom*

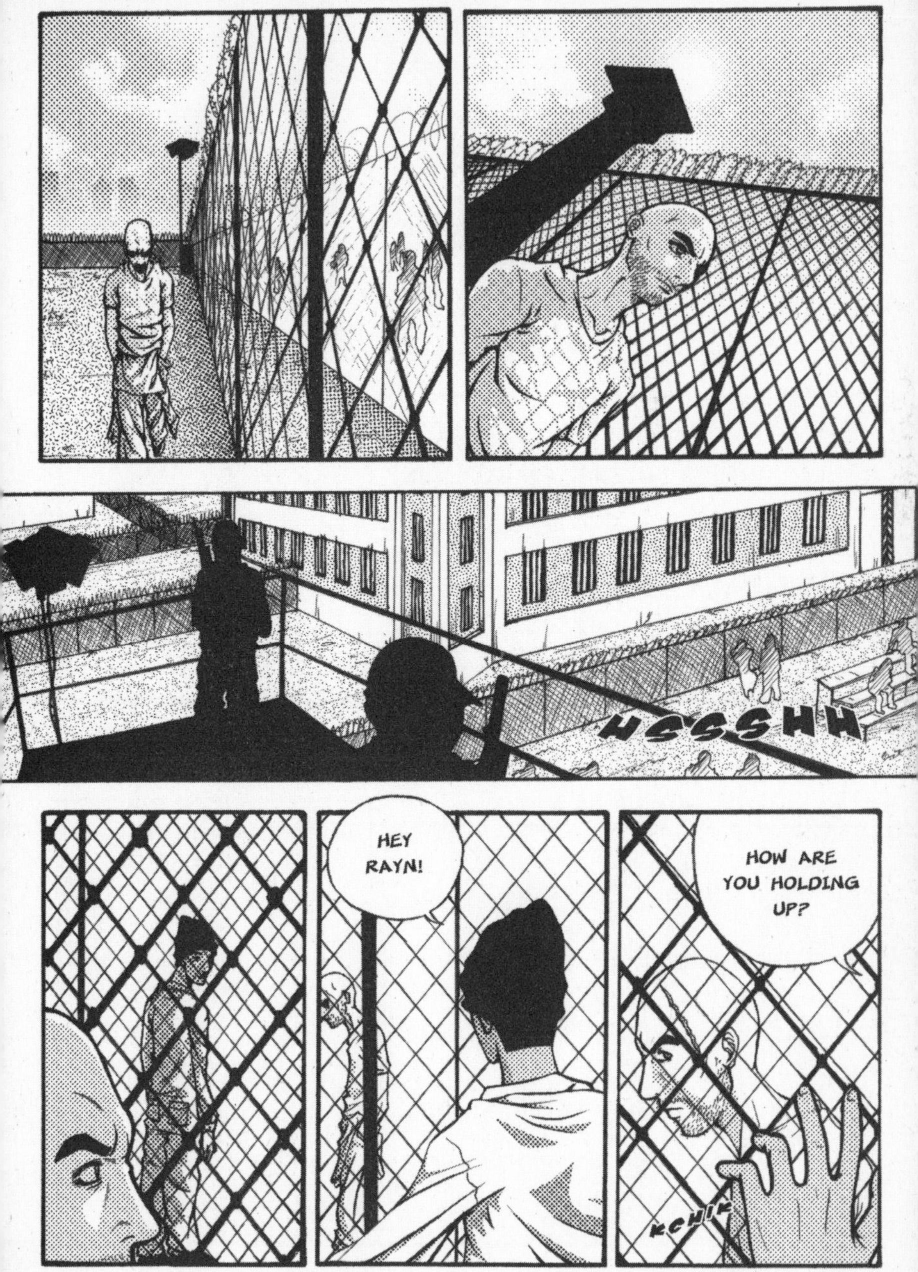
HSSSHH
HEY RAYN!
HOW ARE YOU HOLDING UP?
KCHIK

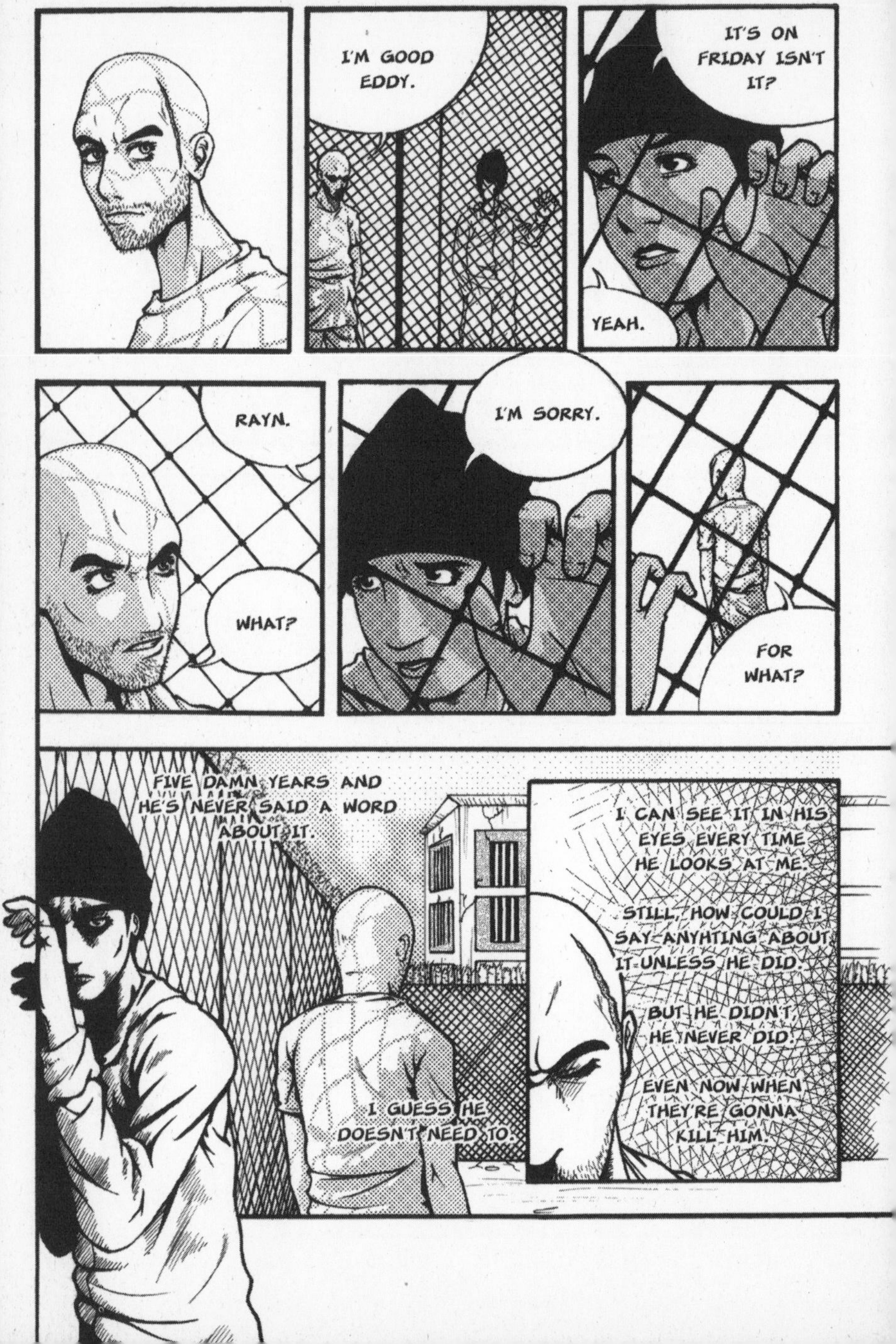
I'M GOOD EDDY.
IT'S ON FRIDAY ISN'T IT?
YEAH.
RAYN.
WHAT?
I'M SORRY.
FOR WHAT?
FIVE DAMN YEARS AND HE'S NEVER SAID A WORD ABOUT IT.
I GUESS HE DOESN'T NEED TO.
I CAN SEE IT IN HIS EYES EVERY TIME HE LOOKS AT ME.
STILL, HOW COULD I SAY ANYHTING ABOUT IT UNLESS HE DID.
BUT HE DIDN'T, HE NEVER DID.
EVEN NOW WHEN THEY'RE GONNA KILL HIM.

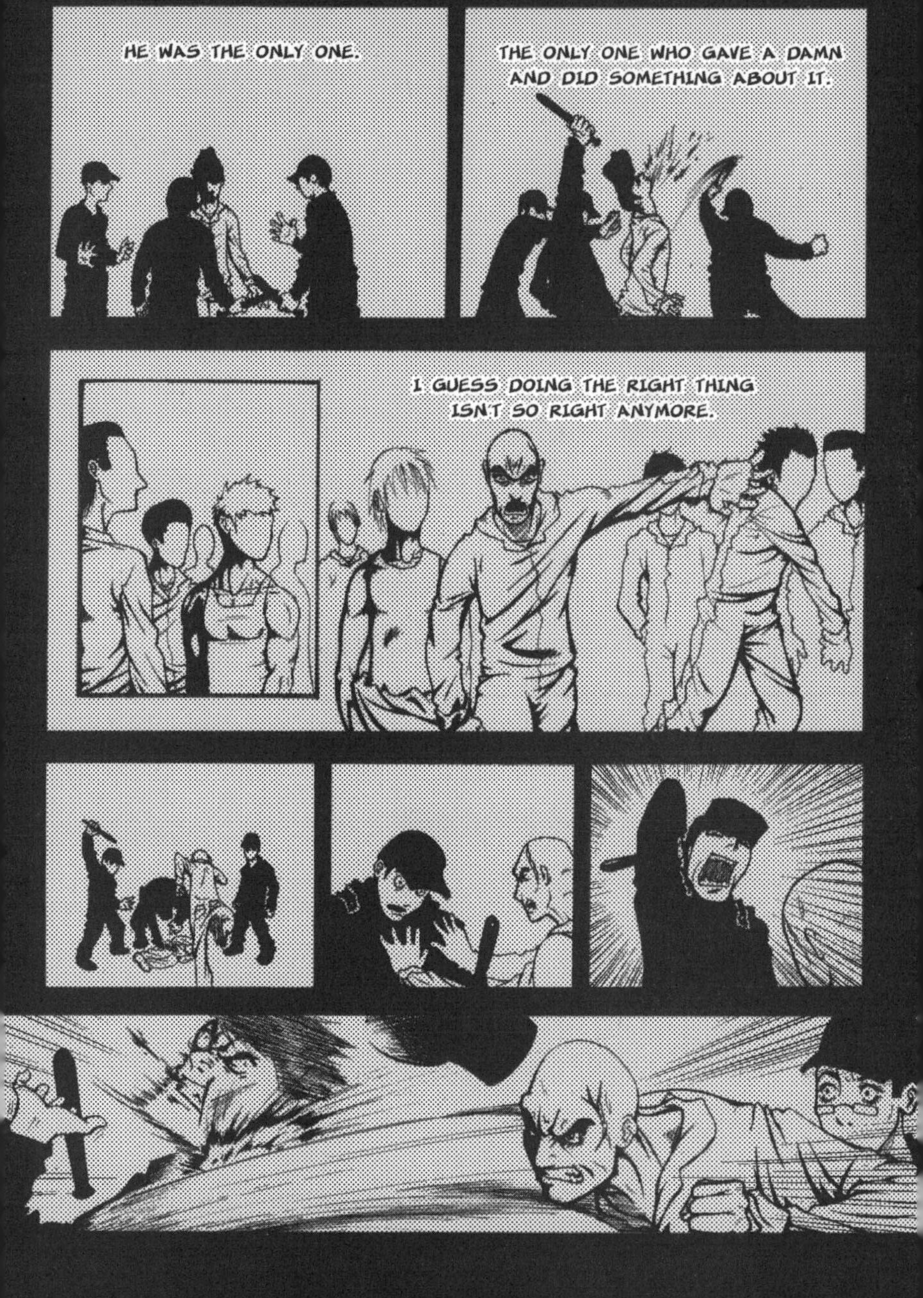
HE WAS THE ONLY ONE.
THE ONLY ONE WHO GAVE A DAMN AND DID SOMETHING ABOUT IT.
I GUESS DOING THE RIGHT THING ISN'T SO RIGHT ANYMORE.

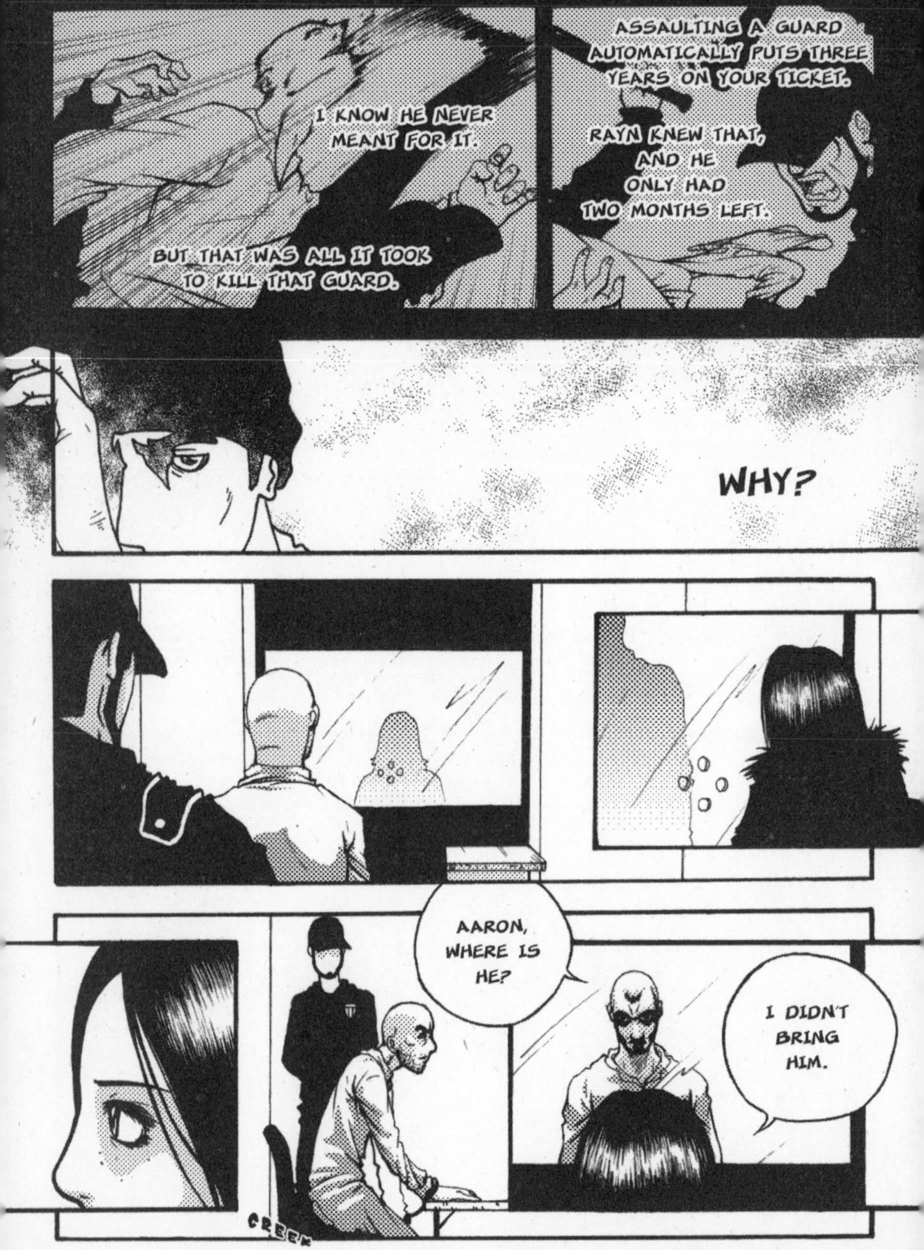
I KNOW HE NEVER MEANT FOR IT.
BUT THAT WAS ALL IT TOOK TO KILL THAT GUARD.
ASSAULTING A GUARD AUTOMATICALLY PUTS THREE YEARS ON YOUR TICKET.
RAYN KNEW THAT, AND HE ONLY HAD TWO MONTHS LEFT.
WHY?
CREEK
AARON, WHERE IS HE?
I DIDN'T BRING HIM.

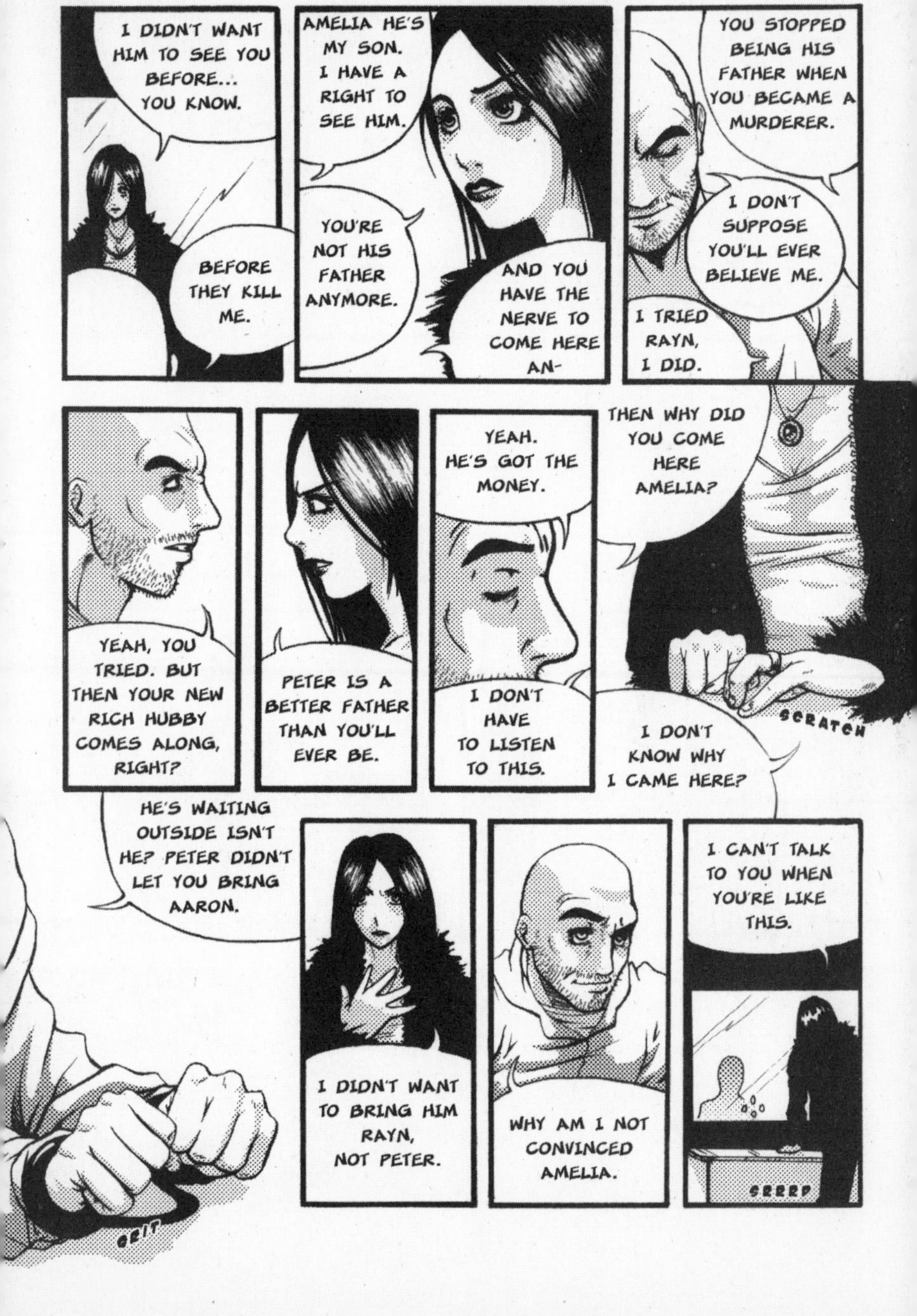
I DIDN'T WANT HIM TO SEE YOU BEFORE... YOU KNOW.
BEFORE THEY KILL ME.
AMELIA HE'S MY SON. I HAVE A RIGHT TO SEE HIM.
YOU'RE NOT HIS FATHER ANYMORE.
AND YOU HAVE THE NERVE TO COME HERE AN-
YOU STOPPED BEING HIS FATHER WHEN YOU BECAME A MURDERER.
I DON'T SUPPOSE YOU'LL EVER BELIEVE ME.
I TRIED RAYN, I DID.
YEAH, YOU TRIED. BUT THEN YOUR NEW RICH HUBBY COMES ALONG, RIGHT?
PETER IS A BETTER FATHER THAN YOU'LL EVER BE.
YEAH. HE'S GOT THE MONEY.
I DON'T HAVE TO LISTEN TO THIS.
THEN WHY DID YOU COME HERE AMELIA?
SCRATCH
I DON'T KNOW WHY I CAME HERE?
HE'S WAITING OUTSIDE ISN'T HE? PETER DIDN'T LET YOU BRING AARON.
GRIT
I DIDN'T WANT TO BRING HIM RAYN, NOT PETER.
WHY AM I NOT CONVINCED AMELIA.
I CAN'T TALK TO YOU WHEN YOU'RE LIKE THIS.
SRRRP

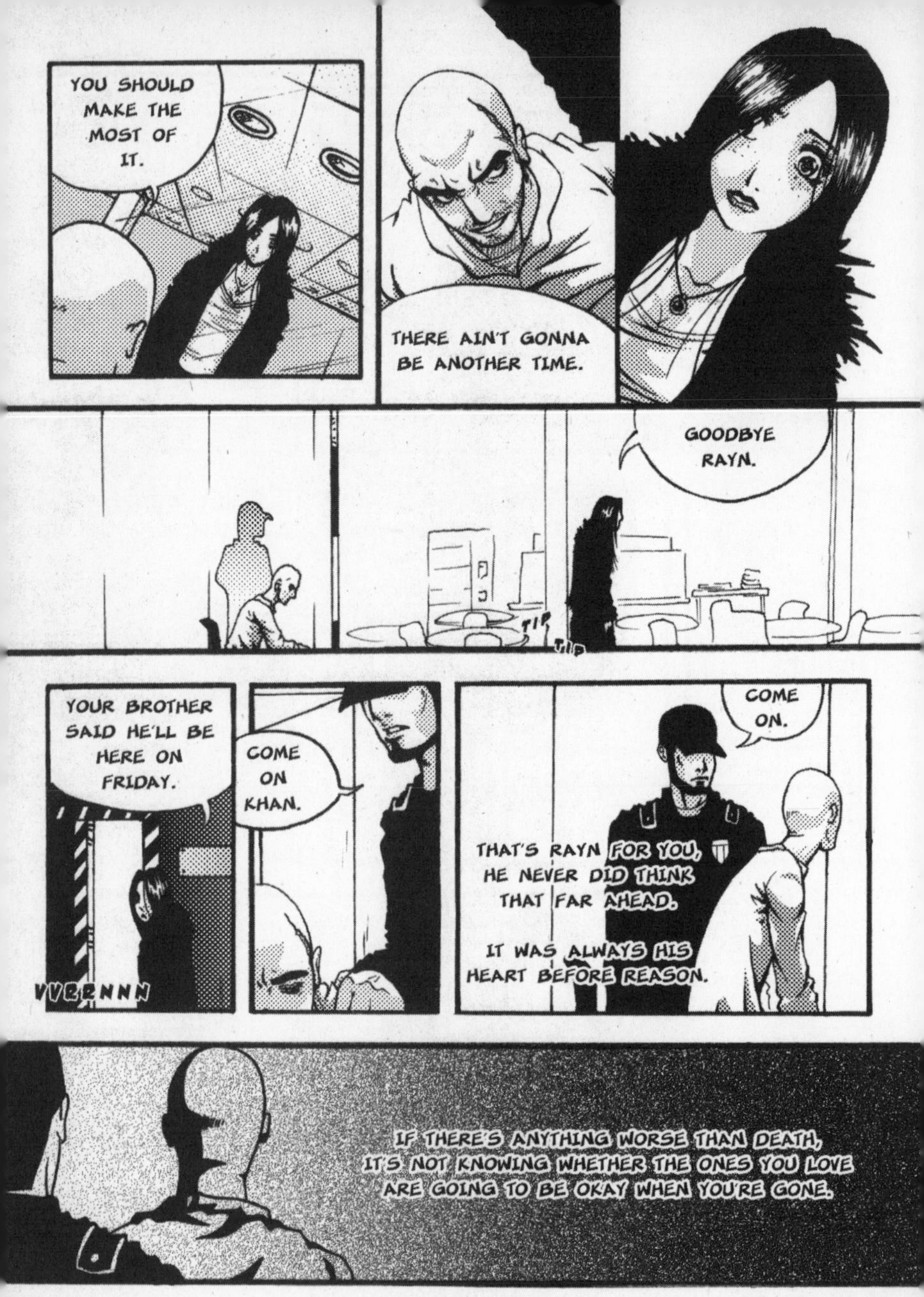
YOU SHOULD MAKE THE MOST OF IT.
THERE AIN'T GONNA BE ANOTHER TIME.
GOODBYE RAYN.
TIP
TIP
YOUR BROTHER SAID HE'LL BE HERE ON FRIDAY.
VVRRNNN
COME ON KHAN.
COME ON.
THAT'S RAYN FOR YOU, HE NEVER DID THINK THAT FAR AHEAD.
IT WAS ALWAYS HIS HEART BEFORE REASON.
IF THERE'S ANYTHING WORSE THAN DEATH, IT'S NOT KNOWING WHETHER THE ONES YOU LOVE ARE GOING TO BE OKAY WHEN YOU'RE GONE.

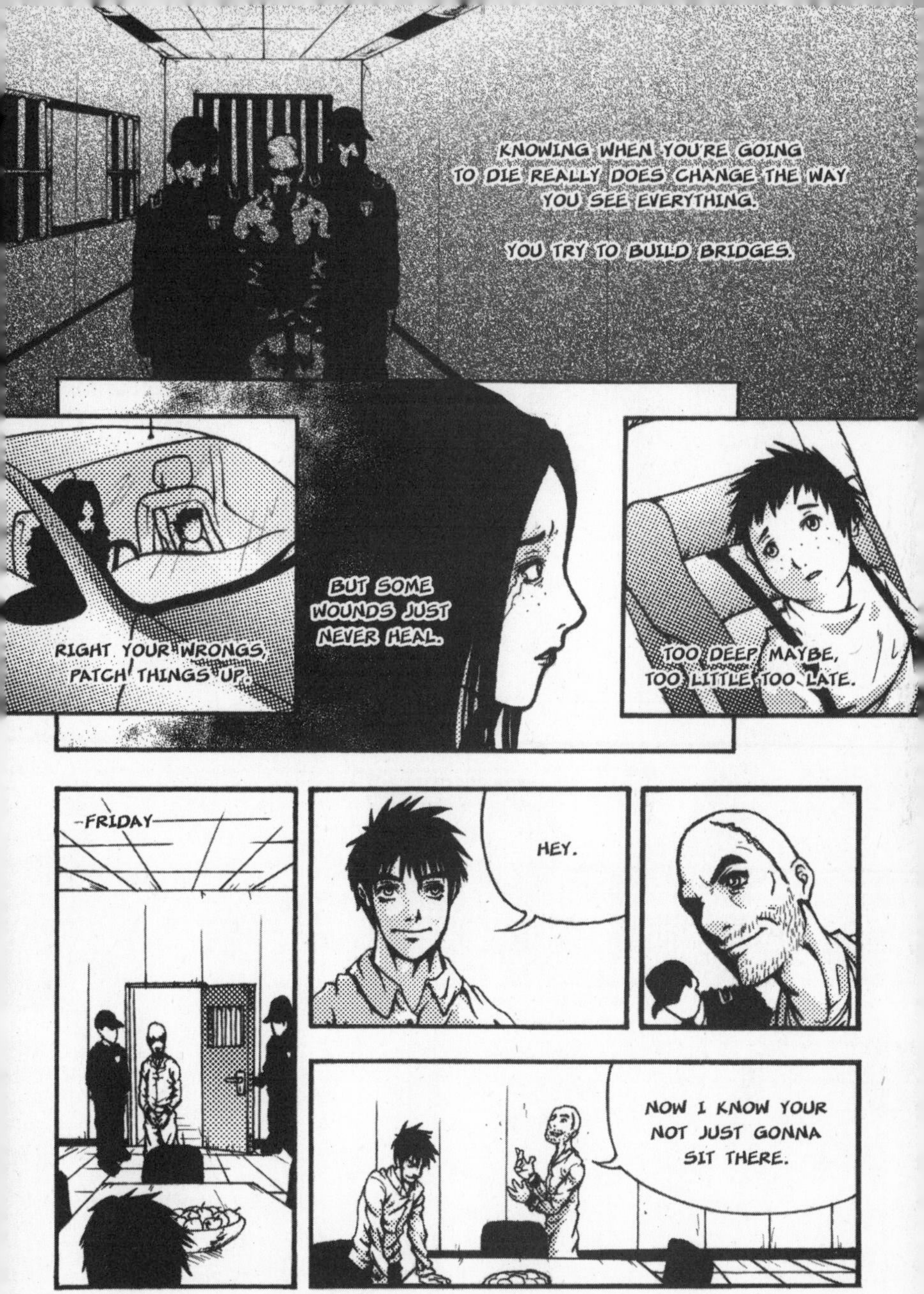
KNOWING WHEN YOU'RE GOING TO DIE REALLY DOES CHANGE THE WAY YOU SEE EVERYTHING.
YOU TRY TO BUILD BRIDGES.
RIGHT YOUR WRONGS, PATCH THINGS UP.
BUT SOME WOUNDS JUST NEVER HEAL.
TOO DEEP MAYBE, TOO LITTLE TOO LATE.
-FRIDAY-
HEY.
NOW I KNOW YOUR NOT JUST GONNA SIT THERE.

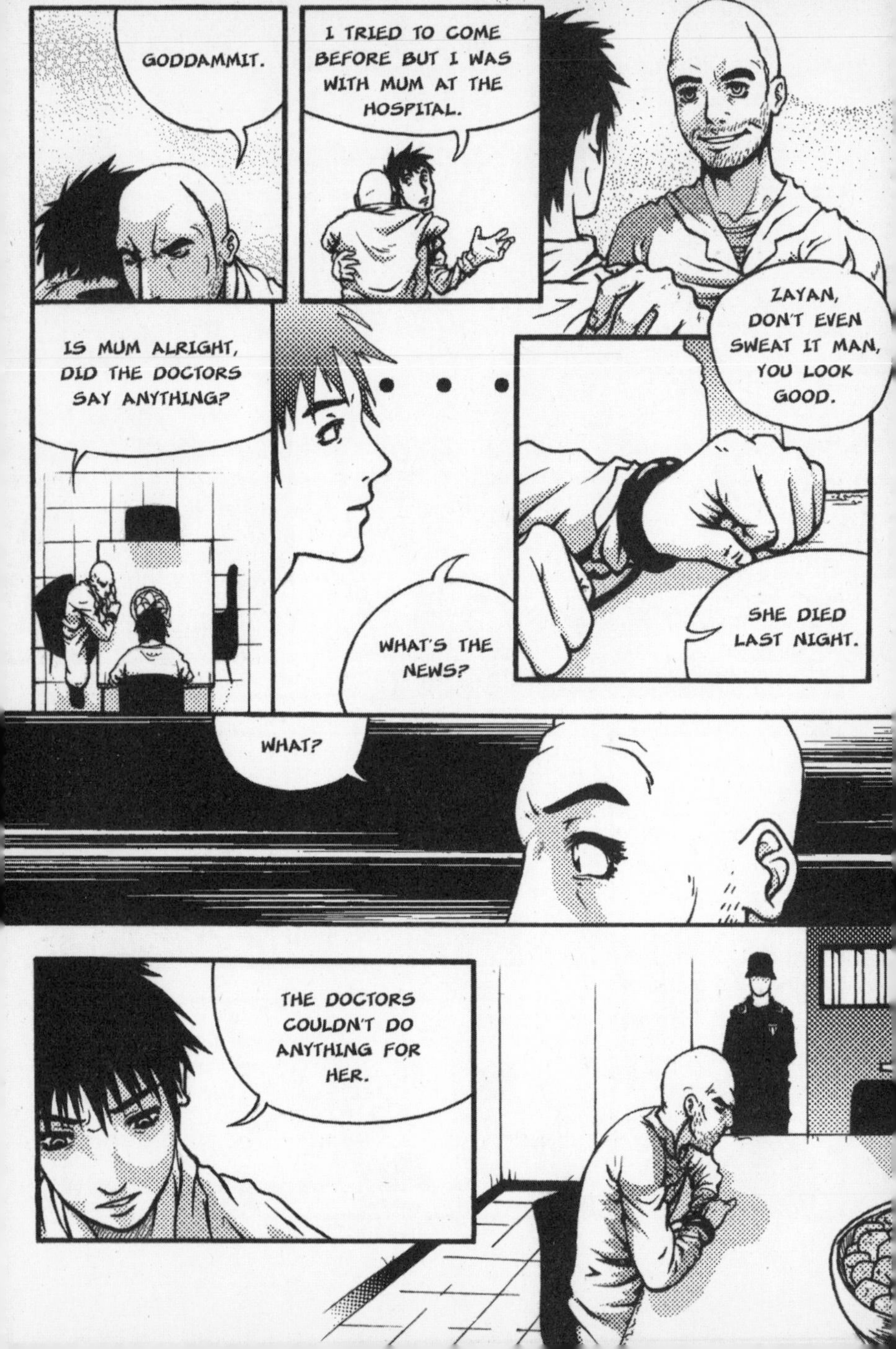
GODDAMMIT.
I TRIED TO COME BEFORE BUT I WAS WITH MUM AT THE HOSPITAL.
ZAYAN, DON'T EVEN SWEAT IT MAN, YOU LOOK GOOD.
IS MUM ALRIGHT, DID THE DOCTORS SAY ANYTHING?
...
WHAT'S THE NEWS?
SHE DIED LAST NIGHT.
WHAT?
THE DOCTORS COULDN'T DO ANYTHING FOR HER.

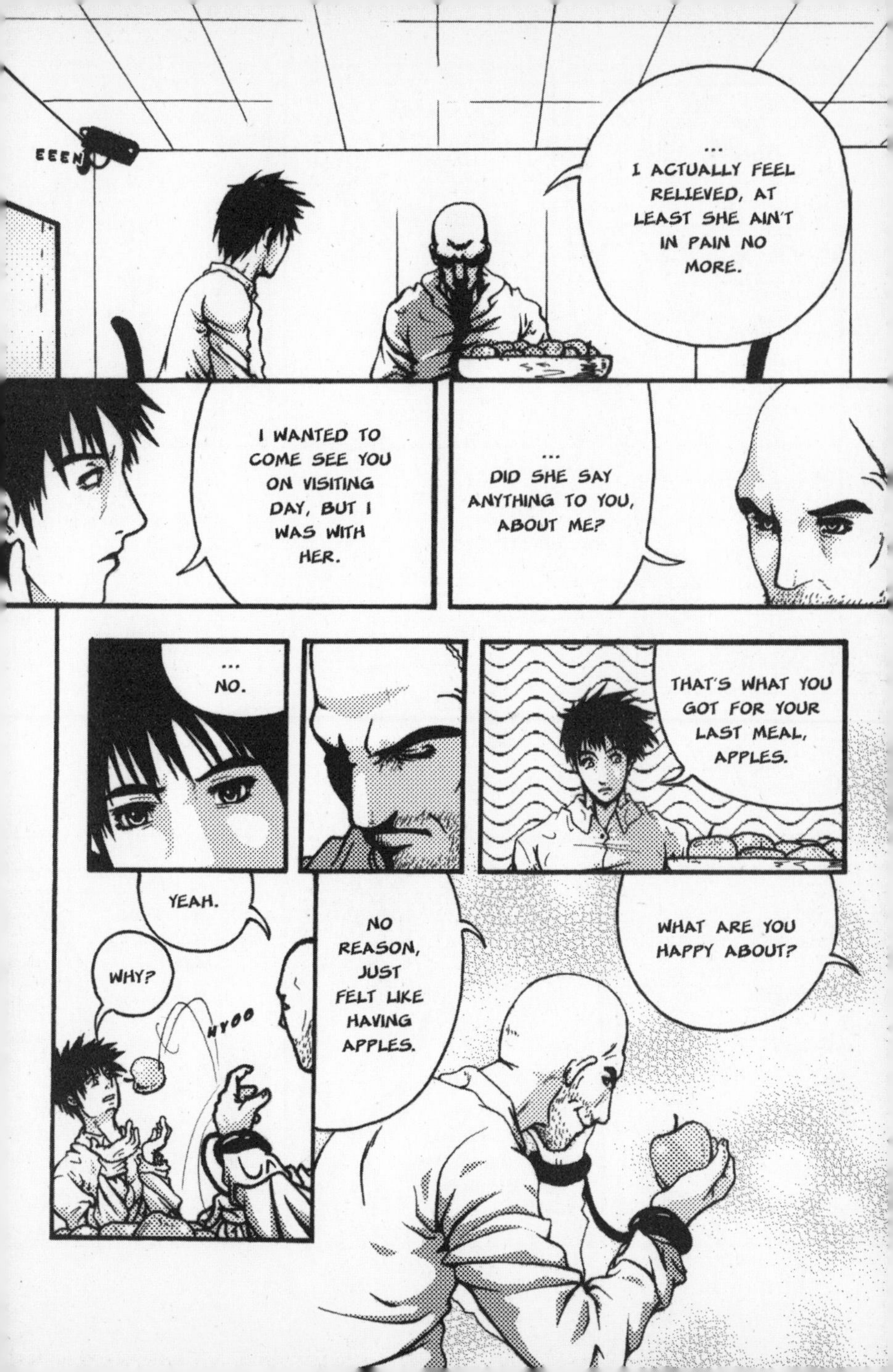
EEEN
...
I ACTUALLY FEEL RELIEVED, AT LEAST SHE AIN'T IN PAIN NO MORE.
I WANTED TO COME SEE YOU ON VISITING DAY, BUT I WAS WITH HER.
...
DID SHE SAY ANYTHING TO YOU, ABOUT ME?
...
NO.
THAT'S WHAT YOU GOT FOR YOUR LAST MEAL, APPLES.
YEAH.
WHY?
HYOO
NO REASON, JUST FELT LIKE HAVING APPLES.
WHAT ARE YOU HAPPY ABOUT?

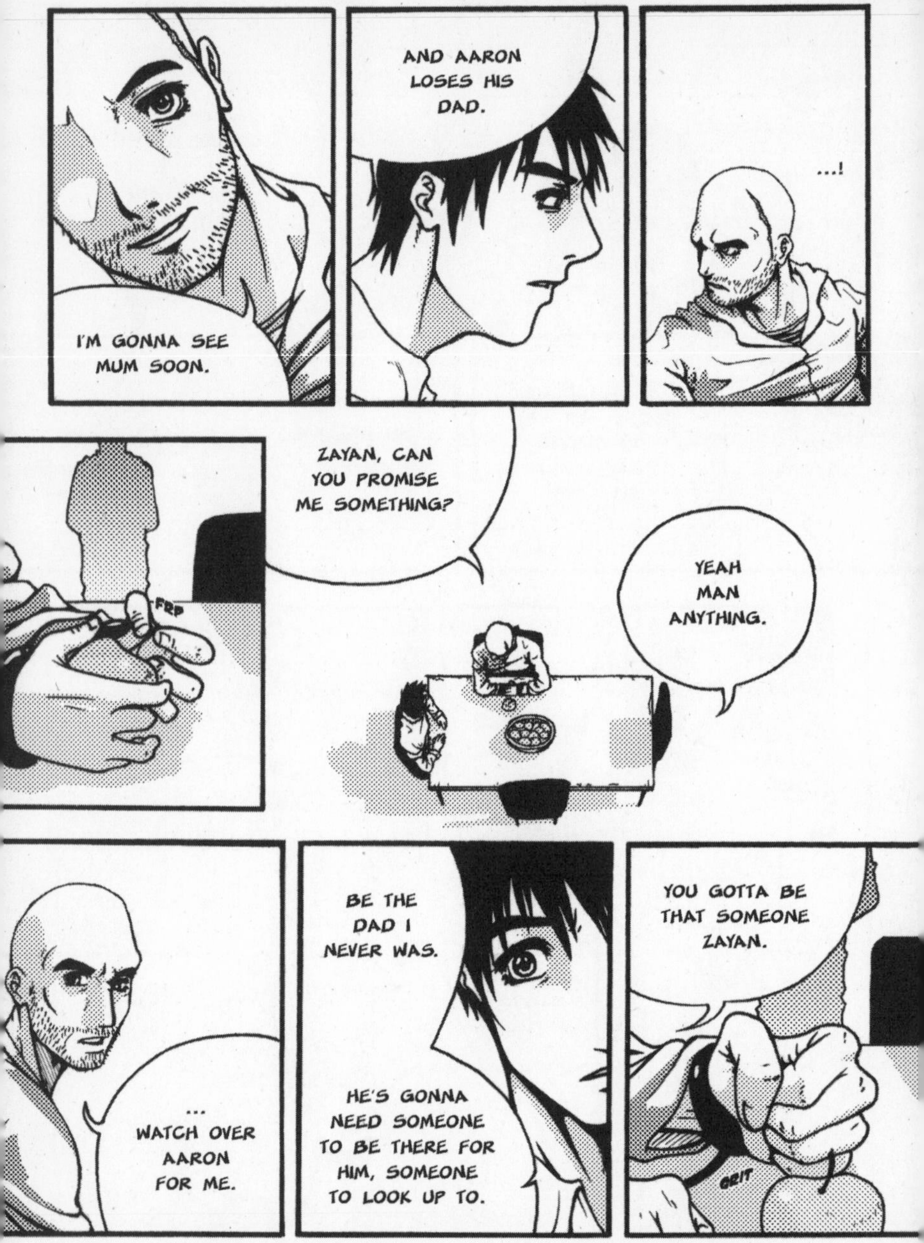
I'M GONNA SEE MUM SOON.
AND AARON LOSES HIS DAD.
...!
FRP
ZAYAN, CAN YOU PROMISE ME SOMETHING?
YEAH MAN ANYTHING.
... WATCH OVER AARON FOR ME.
BE THE DAD I NEVER WAS.
HE'S GONNA NEED SOMEONE TO BE THERE FOR HIM, SOMEONE TO LOOK UP TO.
YOU GOTTA BE THAT SOMEONE ZAYAN.
GRIT

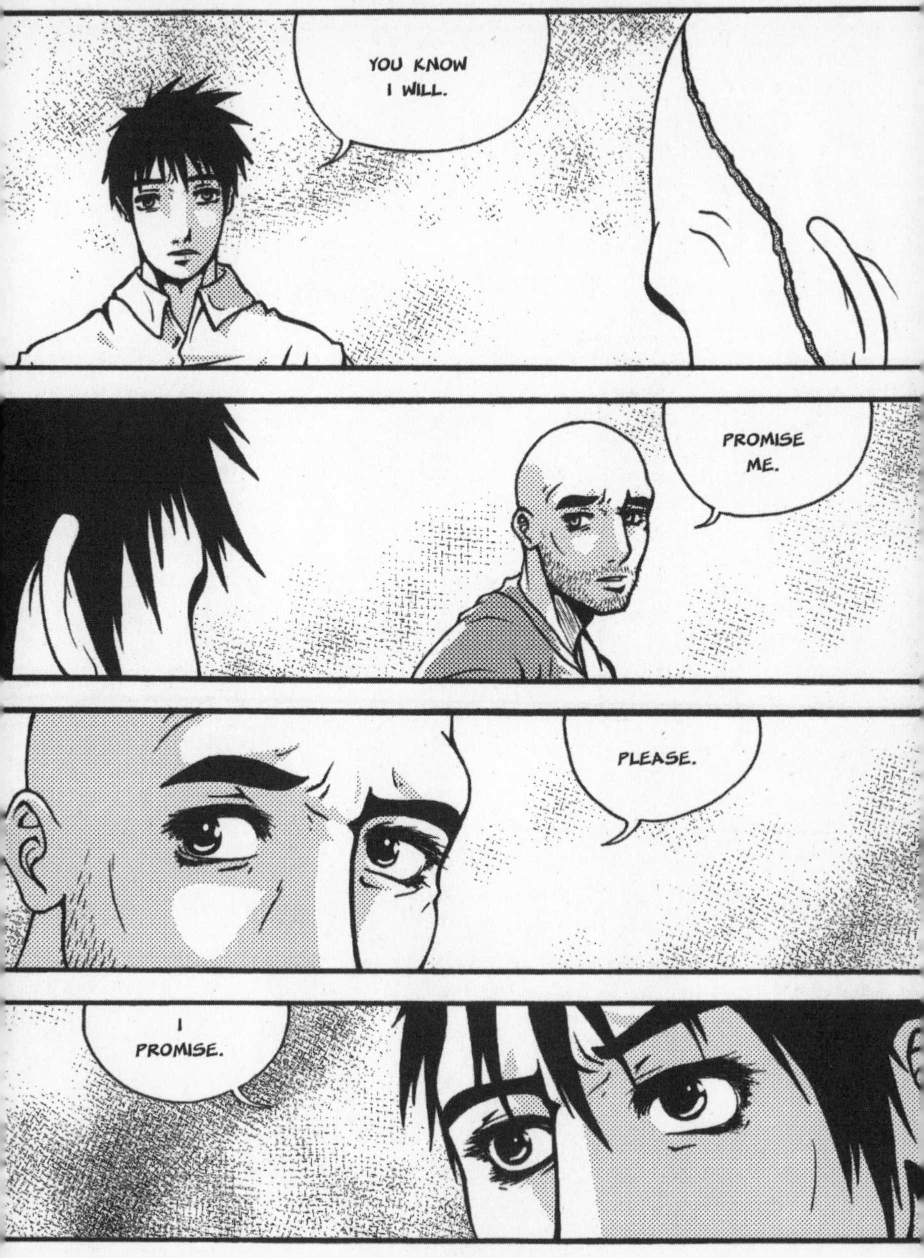
YOU KNOW I WILL.
PROMISE ME.
PLEASE.
I PROMISE.

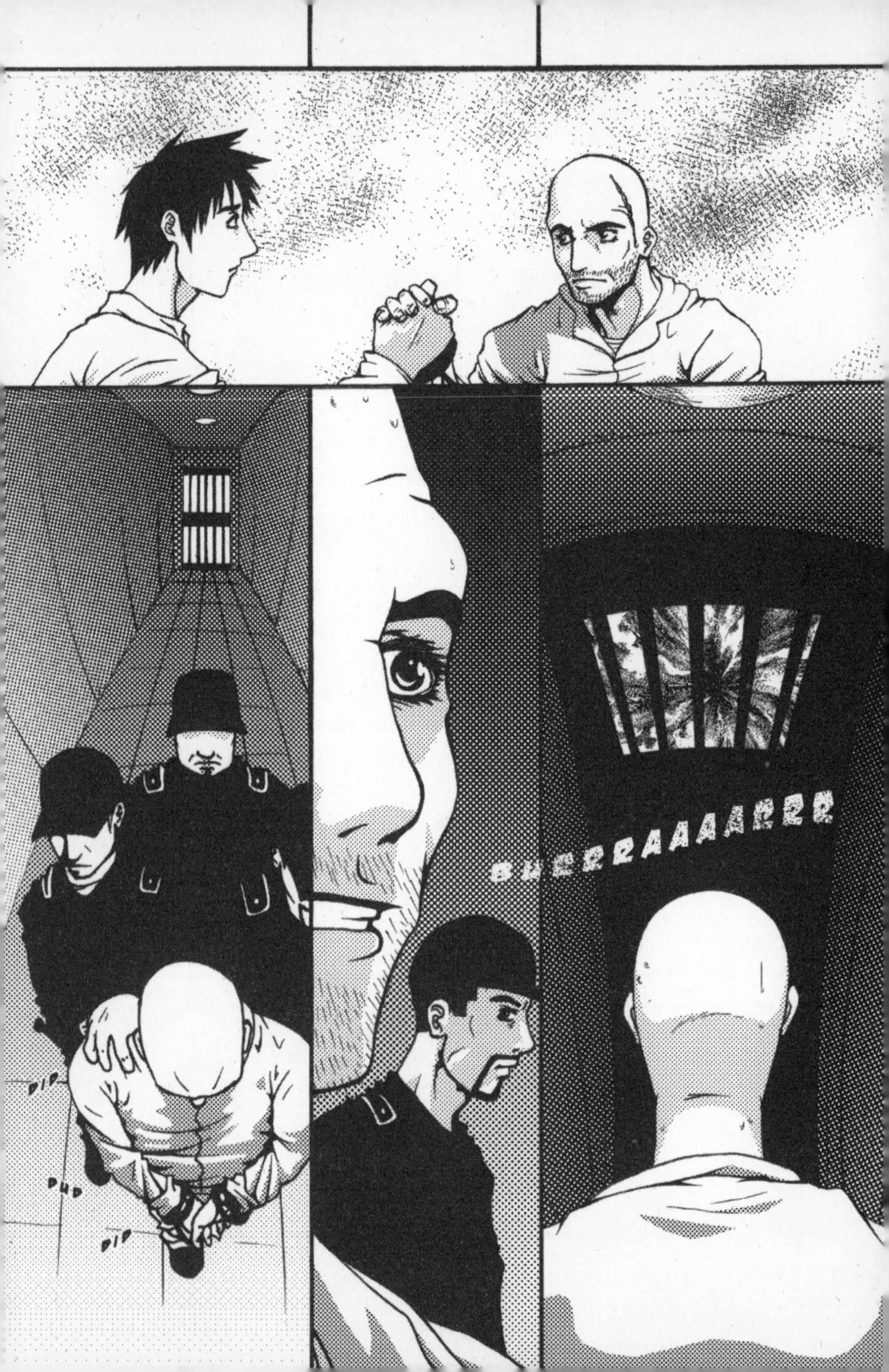
DID
DUD
DID
GWERRAAAARRR

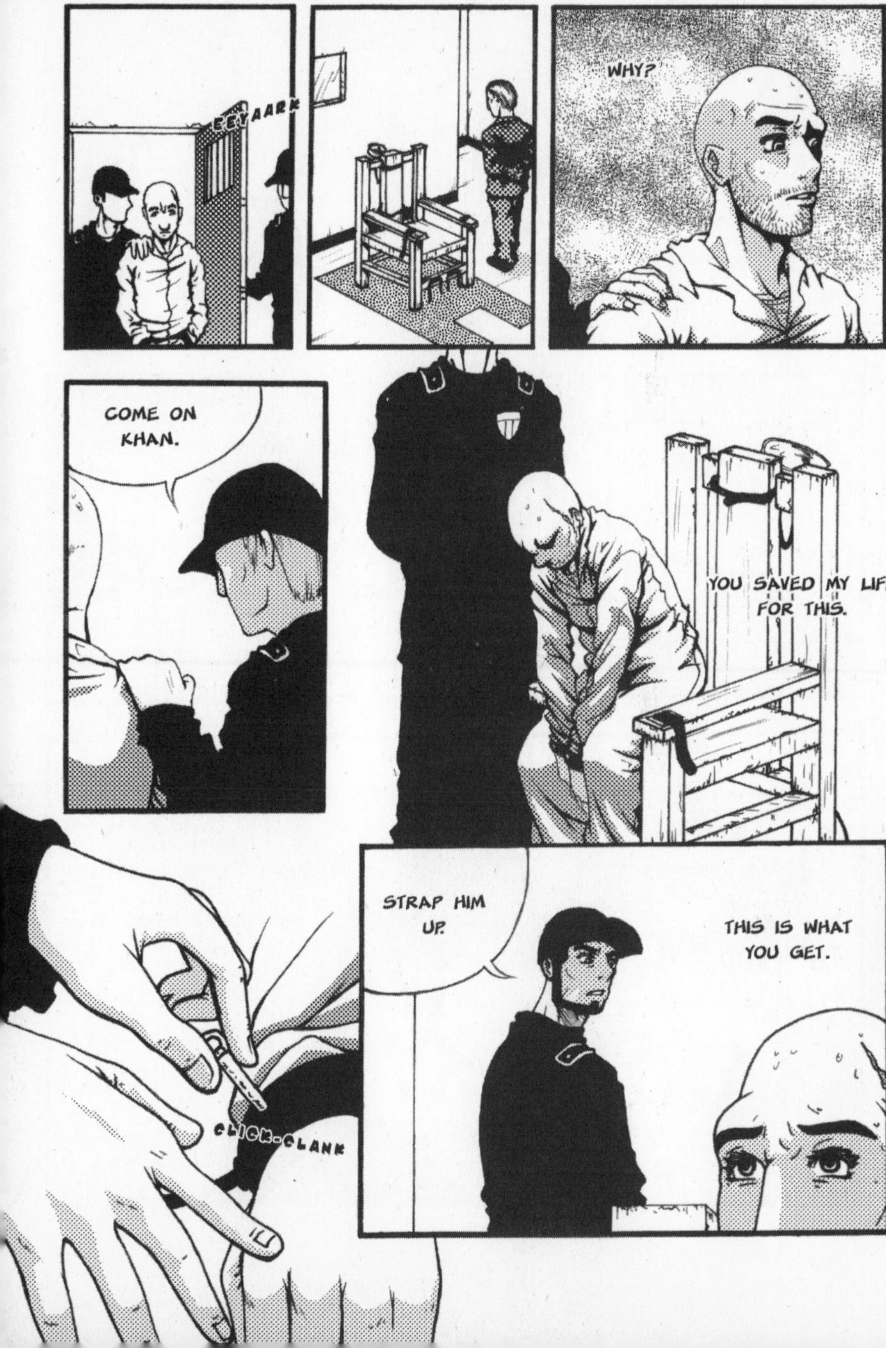
EEYAARK
WHY?
COME ON KHAN.
YOU SAVED MY LIFE FOR THIS.
STRAP HIM UP.
THIS IS WHAT YOU GET.
CLICK-CLANK

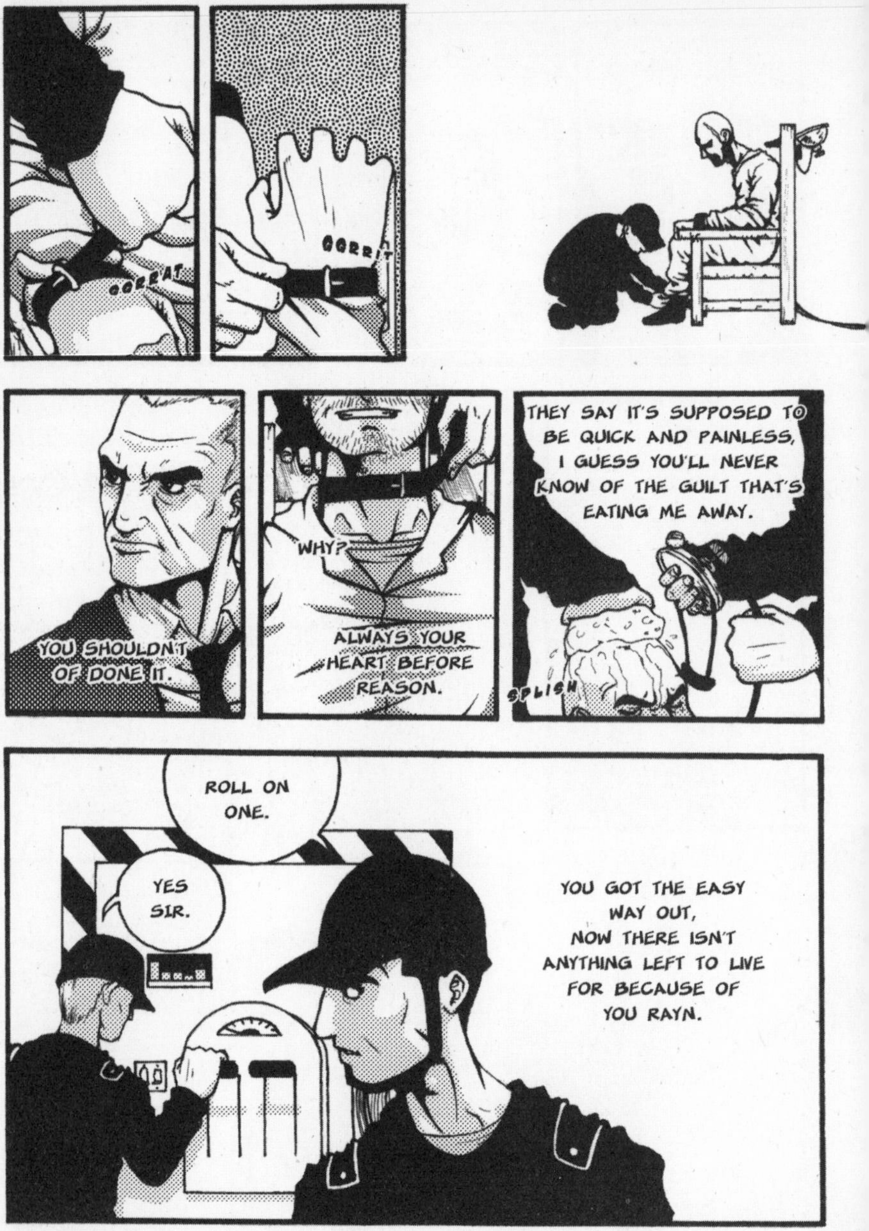
GGRRAT
GGRRIT
YOU SHOULDN'T OF DONE IT.
WHY?
ALWAYS YOUR HEART BEFORE REASON.
THEY SAY IT'S SUPPOSED TO BE QUICK AND PAINLESS, I GUESS YOU'LL NEVER KNOW OF THE GUILT THAT'S EATING ME AWAY.
SPLISH
ROLL ON ONE.
YES SIR.
YOU GOT THE EASY WAY OUT, NOW THERE ISN'T ANYTHING LEFT TO LIVE FOR BECAUSE OF YOU RAYN.

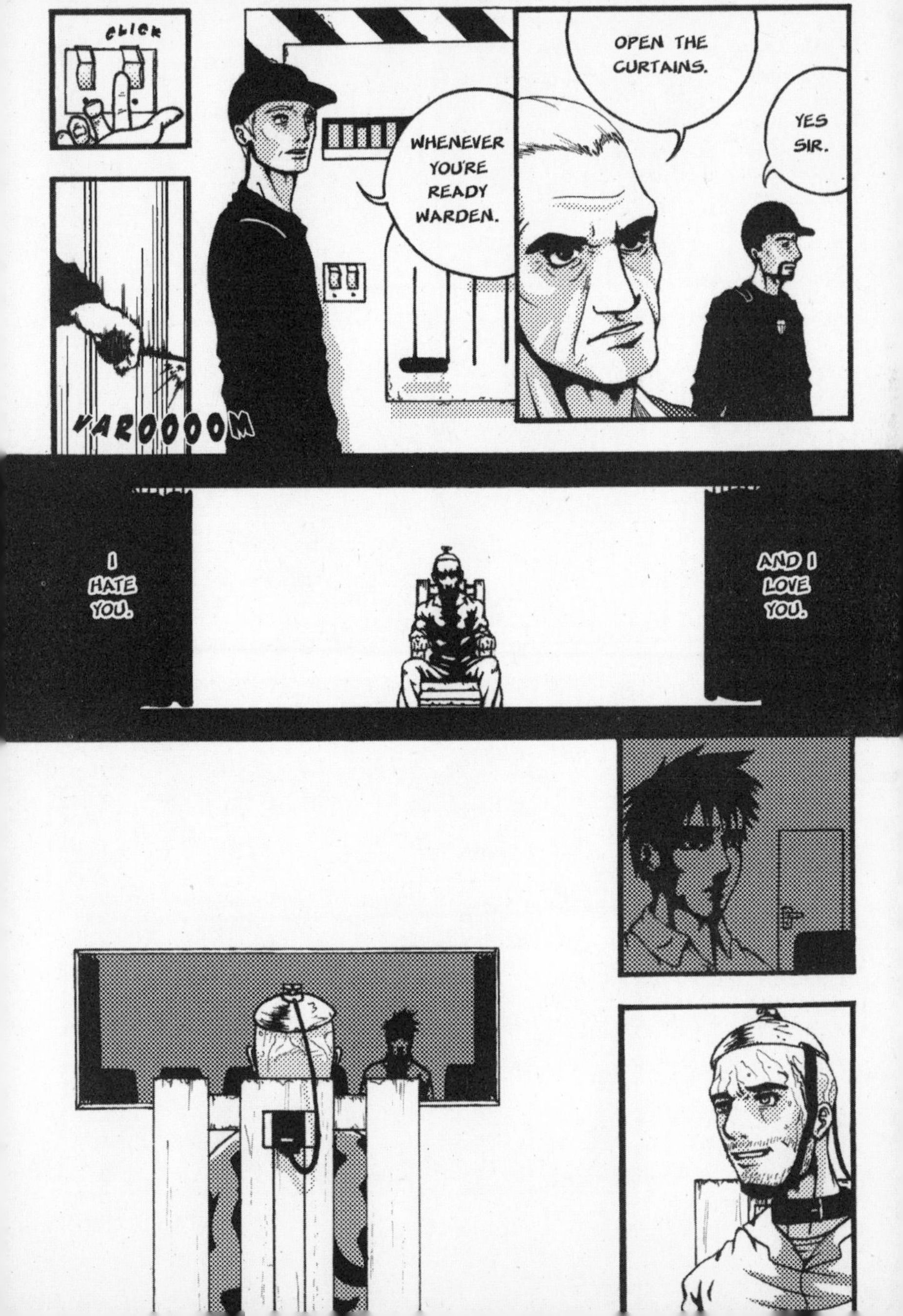
CLICK
VAROOOOM
WHENEVER YOU'RE READY WARDEN.
OPEN THE CURTAINS.
YES SIR.
I HATE YOU.
AND I LOVE YOU.

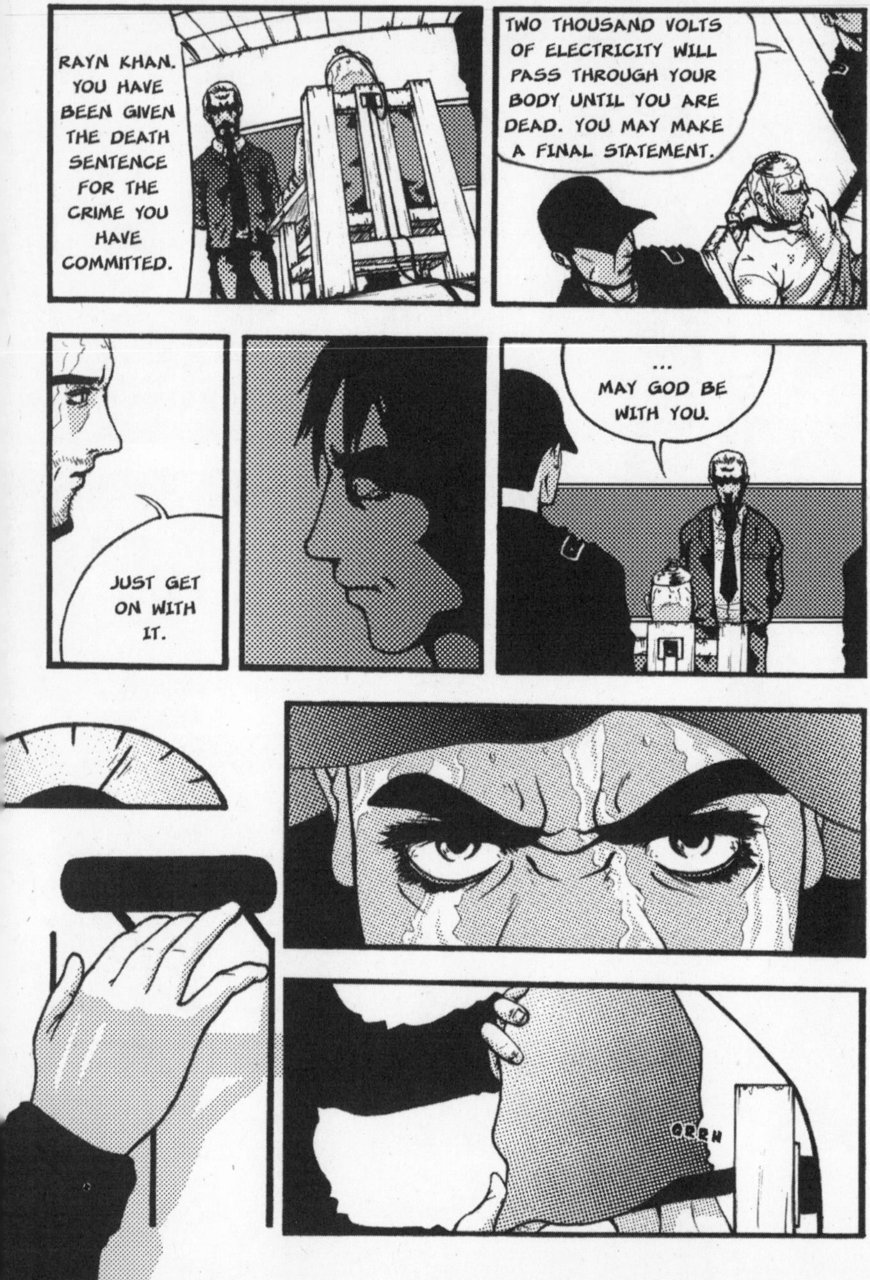
RAYN KHAN. YOU HAVE BEEN GIVEN THE DEATH SENTENCE FOR THE CRIME YOU HAVE COMMITTED.
TWO THOUSAND VOLTS OF ELECTRICITY WILL PASS THROUGH YOUR BODY UNTIL YOU ARE DEAD. YOU MAY MAKE A FINAL STATEMENT.
JUST GET ON WITH IT.
... MAY GOD BE WITH YOU.
GRRH

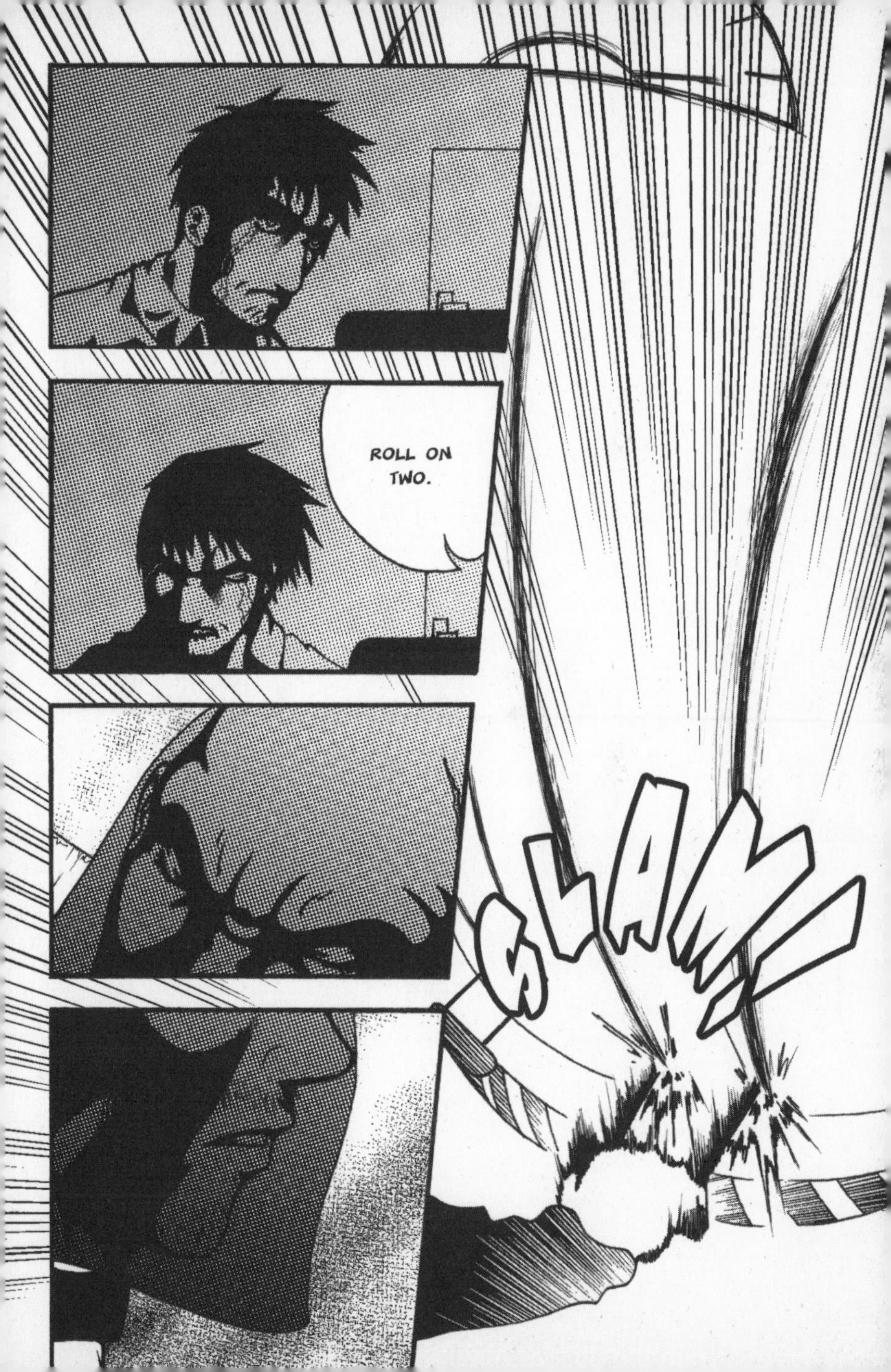
ROLL ON TWO.
SLAM!!

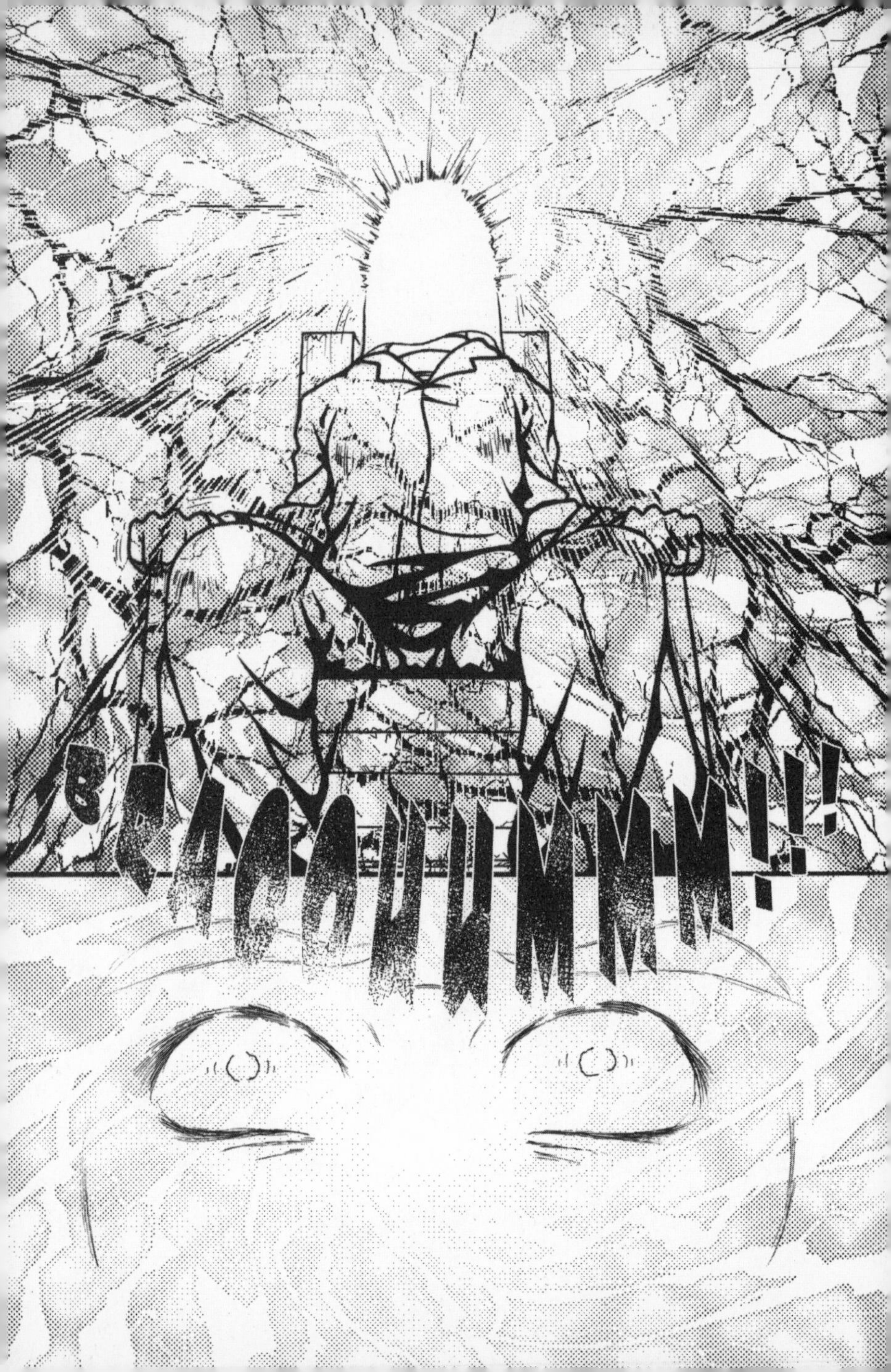
BRAOOUWMMM!!!

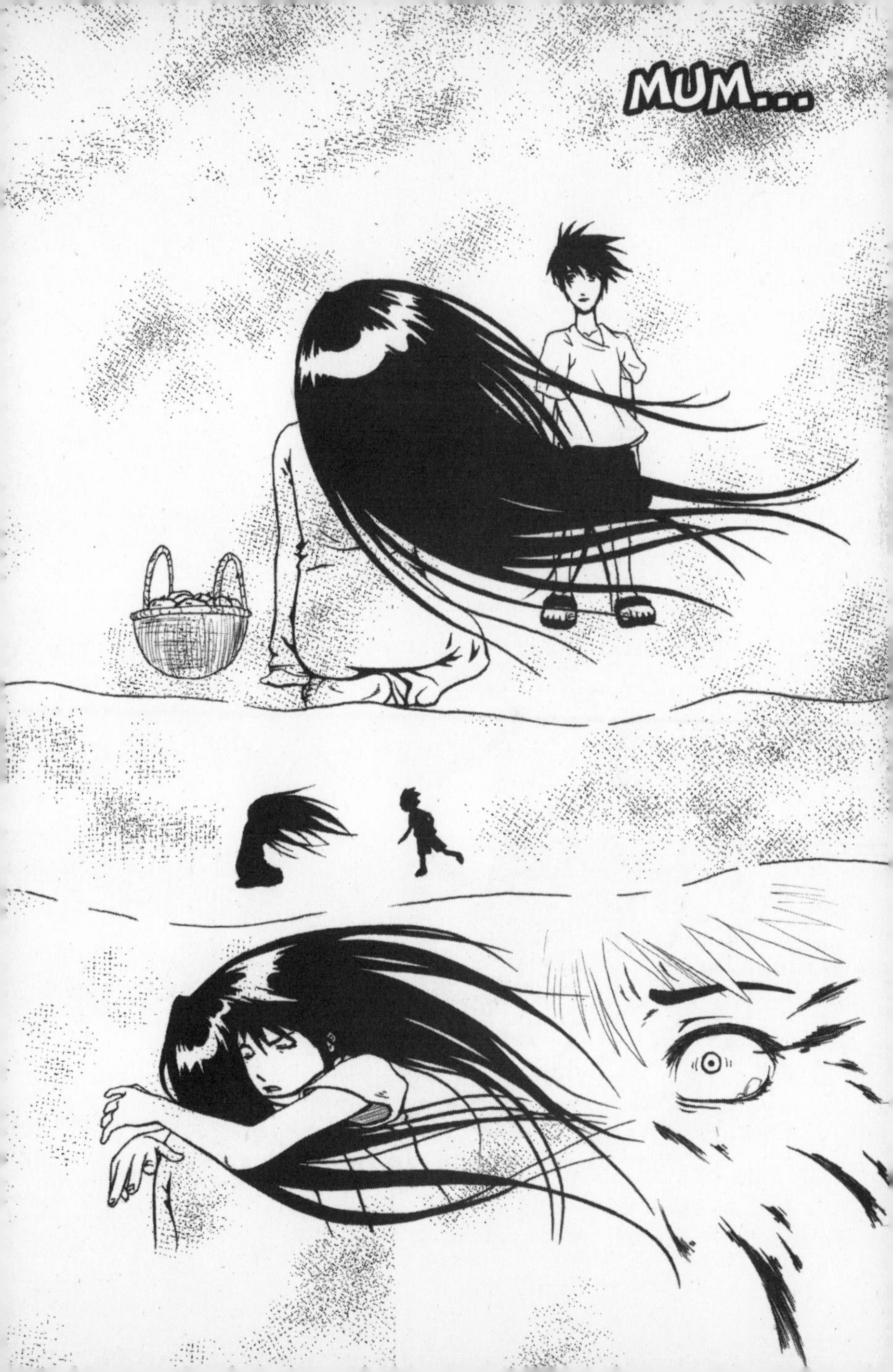
MUM...

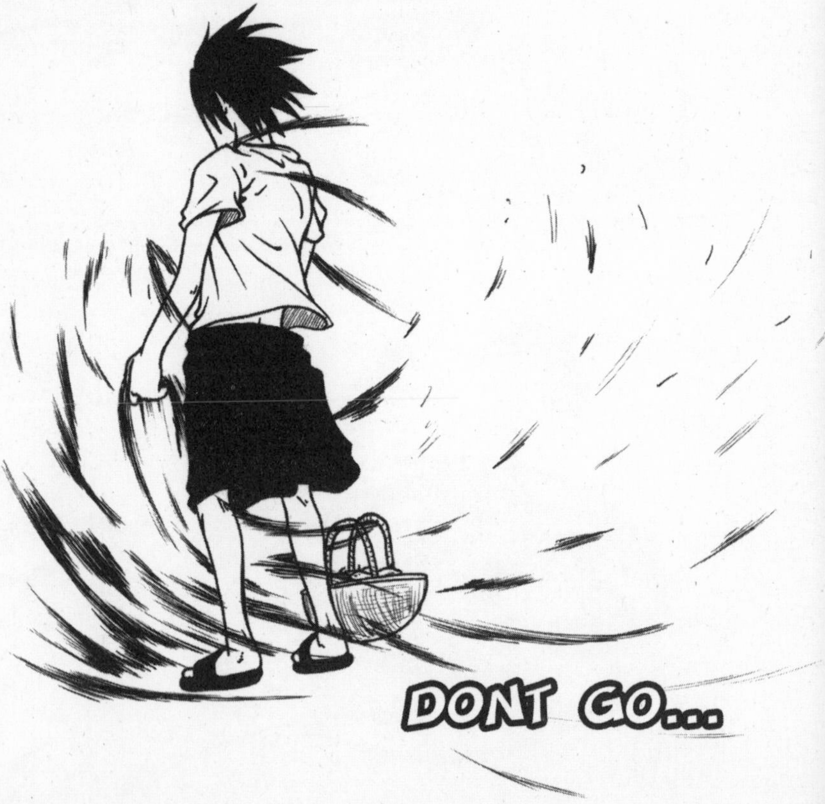
DONT GO...

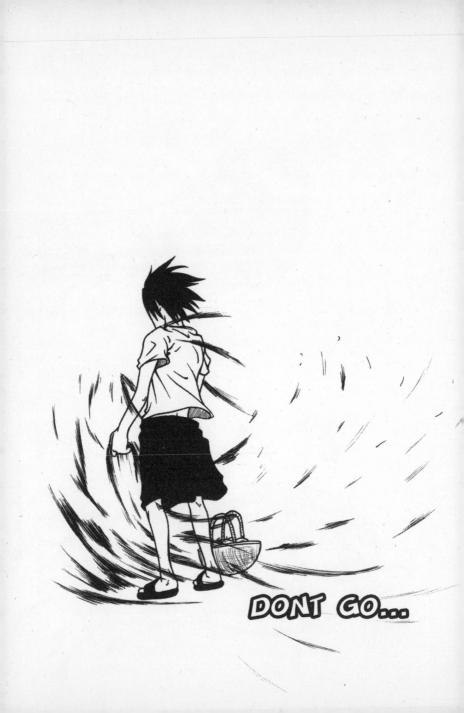

HAPPILY EVER AFTER :: Runner Up ::

....

Joanna Zhou was born in Jinan, China in 1984 and currently lives in London, England. She is a final year student at Chelsea College of Art & Design.
www.chocolatepixels.com

Favorite manga:
Wish, Weiss Kreuz, Angel Nest, Gothic Sports

Favorite manga artists:
Erica Sakurazawa, Hayao Miyazaki, Takashi Murakami (not a manga-ka, but equally inspirational!)

....

Author's Comments:
"Happily Ever After" was inspired by my childhood growing up in Vienna, Austria, which has a strong traditional culture in ballroom dancing. I wanted to create a manga that was both happy and sad, set against a glamorous backdrop. Graduation or prom is a common experience so I hope that some readers will be able to relate to the magic of that night!
—*Joanna Zhou*

::

135

::

HAPPILY EVER AFTER :: Runner Up ::

....

Judge's Comments:
"Happily Ever After" reads to me like a contemporary fairytale infused with a strong dose of harsh reality. All the staples of a good European fable are there: a princess, her prince, a ball. The title suggests that this is all very intentional, while at the same time, proves to be one of the most misleadingly sarcastic titles in the history of *Rising Stars*. This story of young lovers does not have a happy ending—it has a real one, and the tale is all the richer for it.

Who hasn't had a good relationship end simply because it developed at an inconvenient time? It's this relatability, along with "Happily Ever After"'s excellent visual storytelling, that earned it a spot in this book. However, it's a flawed entry. While Joanna Zhou's manga layouts are second-to-none, her actual rendering could use some polish. It's inconsistent, and I can't help feeling that it could be improved if just a little more time was spent on each page. Let's see some actual backgrounds instead of manga tones. Let's see some line weight variety in the inks. There's a large amount of talent at work here that's evident in the stronger pages (page 2, 10, 13 and 15 are standouts). It should be brought to every page. That goes for the writing as well. This is a great subject for a short manga, and Joanna certainly makes us care for her protagonist, but this entry is overwritten. Nowhere is the "picture worth a thousand words" adage more crucial than in manga, and I wish Joanna had stuck to it when scripting "Happily Ever After."

That said, I have to admit that "Happily Ever After"'s flaws kind of make it more endearing to me. Life isn't fairytale perfect, and while I doubt it was intentional, the rough spots in Joanna's entry actually help her in making that point to us. Is "Happily Ever After" perfect? No. Is it a great success? Absolutely.
—Tim Beedle

Judge's Comments:
This was Joanna Zhou's second entry into *Rising Stars*. Last year, she submitted a cute sort of "City Mouse, Country Mouse" tale. Much to our delight, this year's entry capitalized on her strong points while showing decidedly improved art.

Zhou's linework is clean and flowing, her page layouts balanced and her use of tones and lettering professional. What she knows are her strenghts, she does very well and accomplishes with style. But areas that she knows she's weaker in—like backgrounds—she shies away from. It's good to see a manga-ka who knows her strengths, but we also felt she owed it to herself to be a bit more adventurous and not, for instance, chibify the majority of her supporting characters.

The real triumph, of course, is how easy "Happily Ever After" is to sympathize with. Her characters feel real, and the situation is light-hearted and humorous while still being pretty serious. The greatest reservation most of the judges had was how wordy her entry was, but we felt her clean, slick art was something that should be recognized. Zhou's work is a joy to read, and we're proud she decided to share it with us.
—Hope Donovan

136

::

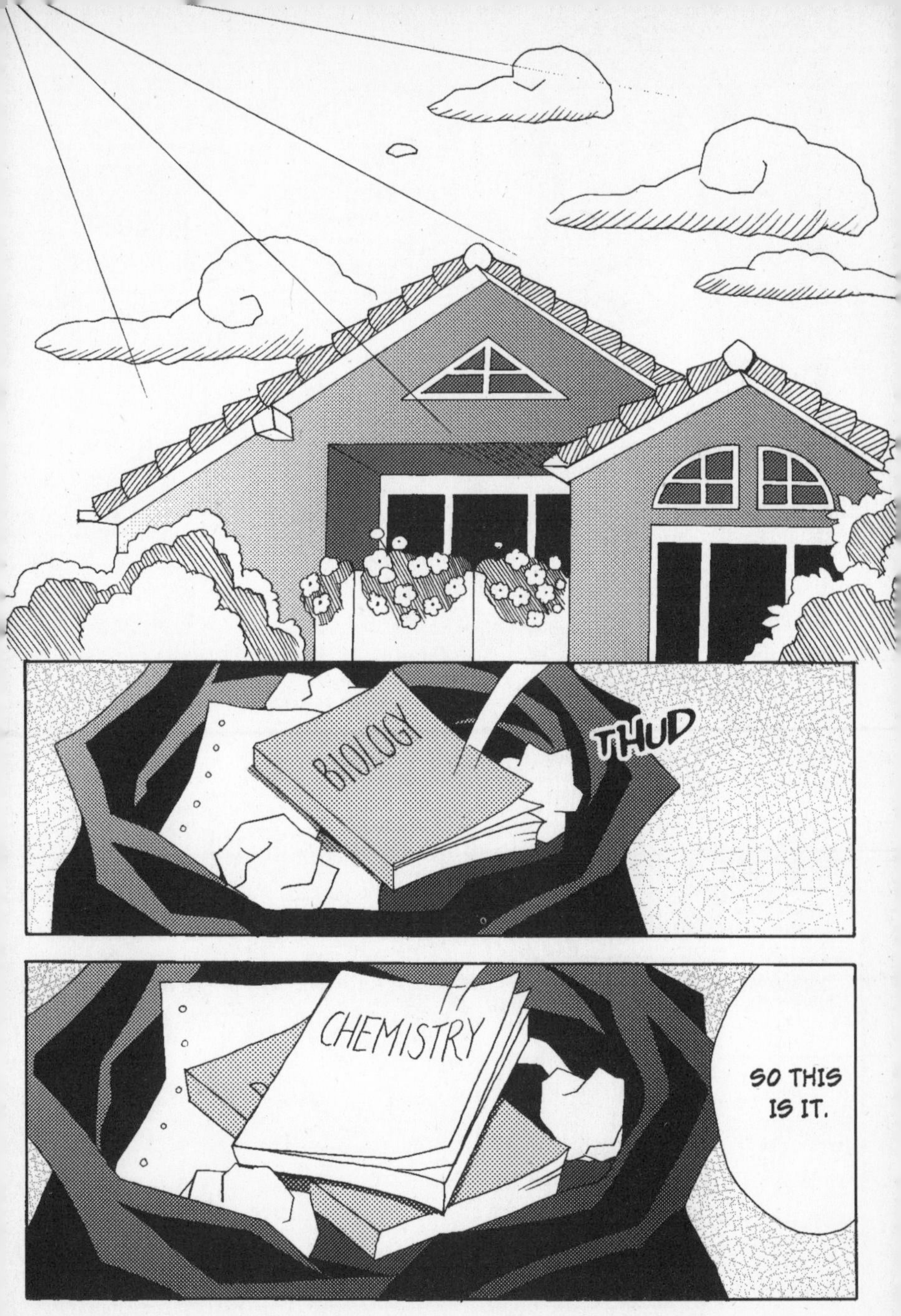
BIOLOGY
THUD
CHEMISTRY
SO THIS IS IT.

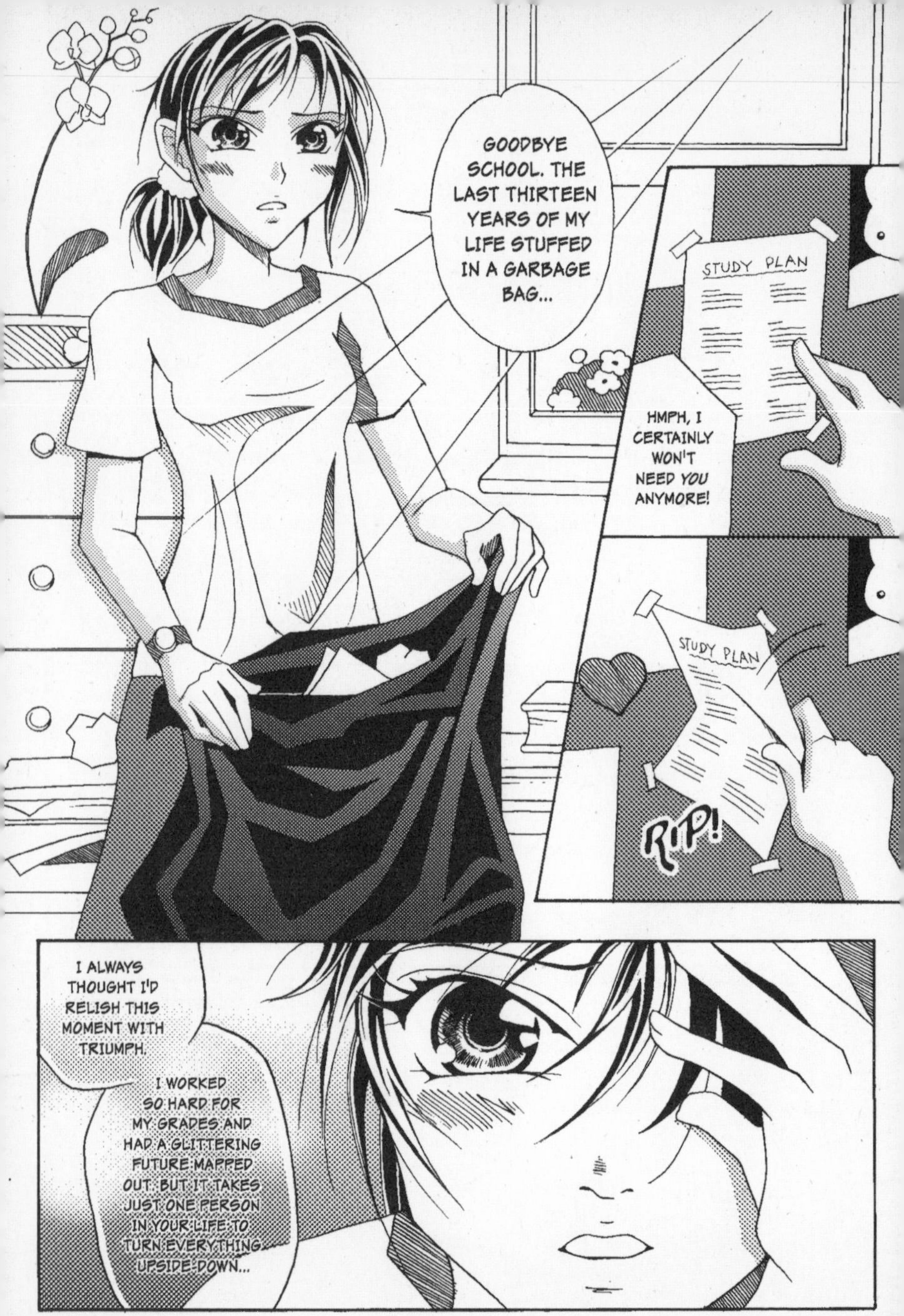
GOODBYE SCHOOL. THE LAST THIRTEEN YEARS OF MY LIFE STUFFED IN A GARBAGE BAG...
STUDY PLAN
HMPH, I CERTAINLY WON'T NEED *YOU* ANYMORE!
STUDY PLAN
RIP!
I ALWAYS THOUGHT I'D RELISH THIS MOMENT WITH TRIUMPH.
I WORKED SO HARD FOR MY GRADES AND HAD A GLITTERING FUTURE MAPPED OUT. BUT IT TAKES JUST ONE PERSON IN YOUR LIFE TO TURN EVERYTHING UPSIDE-DOWN...

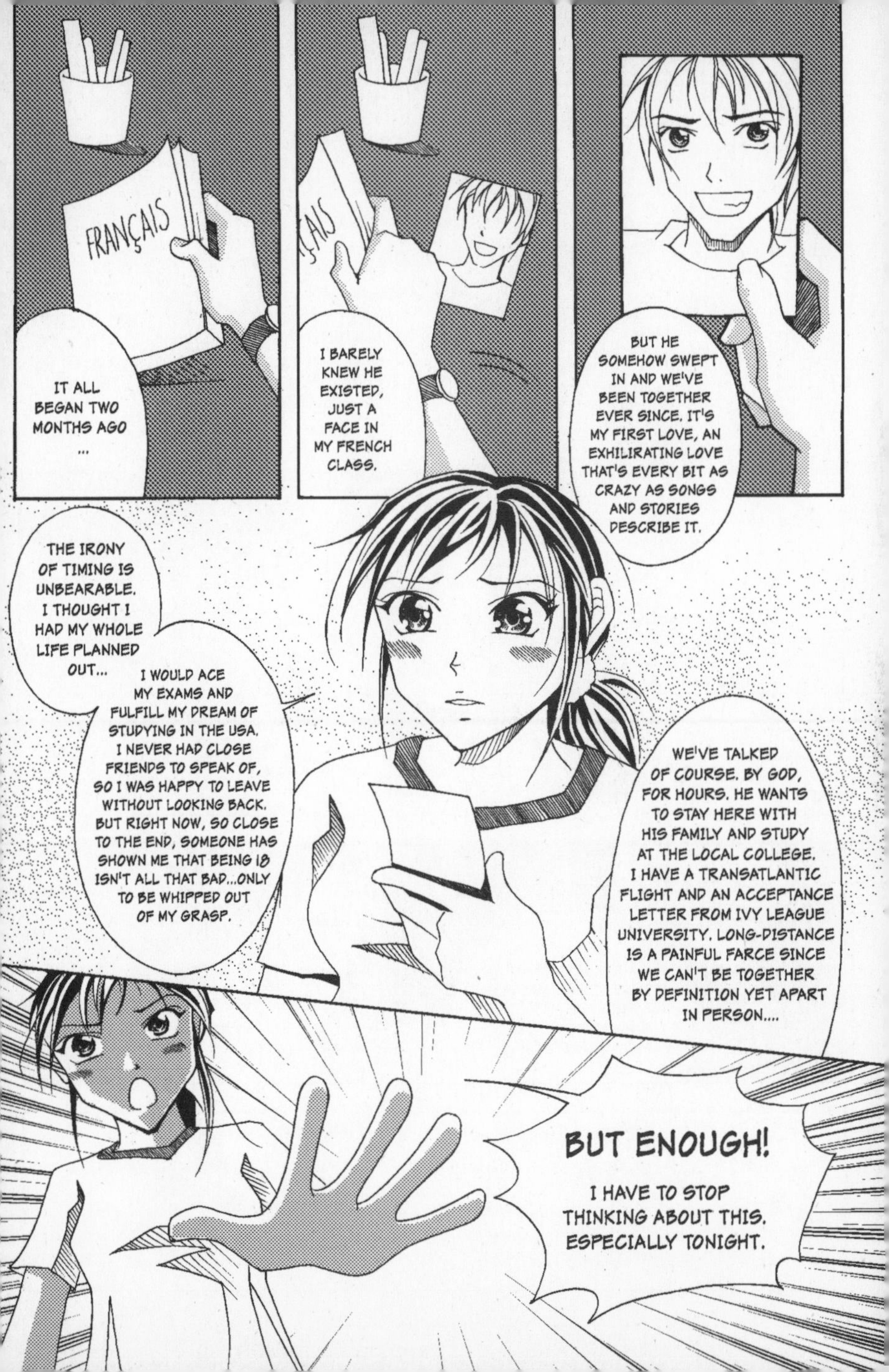
FRANÇAIS
IT ALL BEGAN TWO MONTHS AGO ...
ÇAIS
I BARELY KNEW HE EXISTED, JUST A FACE IN MY FRENCH CLASS.
BUT HE SOMEHOW SWEPT IN AND WE'VE BEEN TOGETHER EVER SINCE. IT'S MY FIRST LOVE, AN EXHILIRATING LOVE THAT'S EVERY BIT AS CRAZY AS SONGS AND STORIES DESCRIBE IT.
THE IRONY OF TIMING IS UNBEARABLE. I THOUGHT I HAD MY WHOLE LIFE PLANNED OUT...
I WOULD ACE MY EXAMS AND FULFILL MY DREAM OF STUDYING IN THE USA. I NEVER HAD CLOSE FRIENDS TO SPEAK OF, SO I WAS HAPPY TO LEAVE WITHOUT LOOKING BACK. BUT RIGHT NOW, SO CLOSE TO THE END, SOMEONE HAS SHOWN ME THAT BEING 18 ISN'T ALL THAT BAD...ONLY TO BE WHIPPED OUT OF MY GRASP.
WE'VE TALKED OF COURSE. BY GOD, FOR HOURS. HE WANTS TO STAY HERE WITH HIS FAMILY AND STUDY AT THE LOCAL COLLEGE. I HAVE A TRANSATLANTIC FLIGHT AND AN ACCEPTANCE LETTER FROM IVY LEAGUE UNIVERSITY. LONG-DISTANCE IS A PAINFUL FARCE SINCE WE CAN'T BE TOGETHER BY DEFINITION YET APART IN PERSON....
BUT ENOUGH!
I HAVE TO STOP THINKING ABOUT THIS. ESPECIALLY TONIGHT.

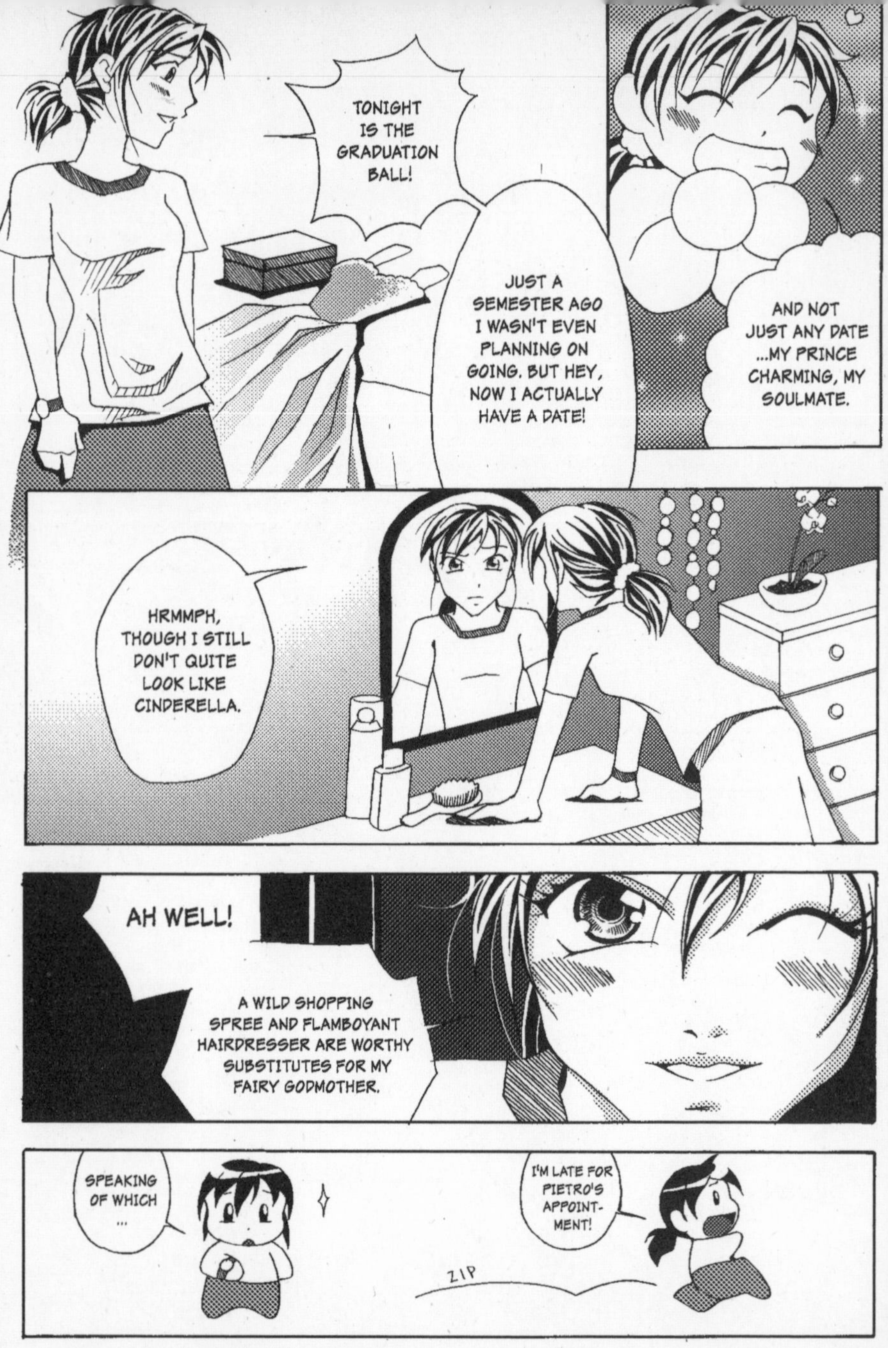
TONIGHT IS THE GRADUATION BALL!
JUST A SEMESTER AGO I WASN'T EVEN PLANNING ON GOING. BUT HEY, NOW I ACTUALLY HAVE A DATE!
AND NOT JUST ANY DATE ...MY PRINCE CHARMING, MY SOULMATE.
HRMMPH, THOUGH I STILL DON'T QUITE LOOK LIKE CINDERELLA.
AH WELL!
A WILD SHOPPING SPREE AND FLAMBOYANT HAIRDRESSER ARE WORTHY SUBSTITUTES FOR MY FAIRY GODMOTHER.
SPEAKING OF WHICH ...
I'M LATE FOR PIETRO'S APPOINT-MENT!
ZIP

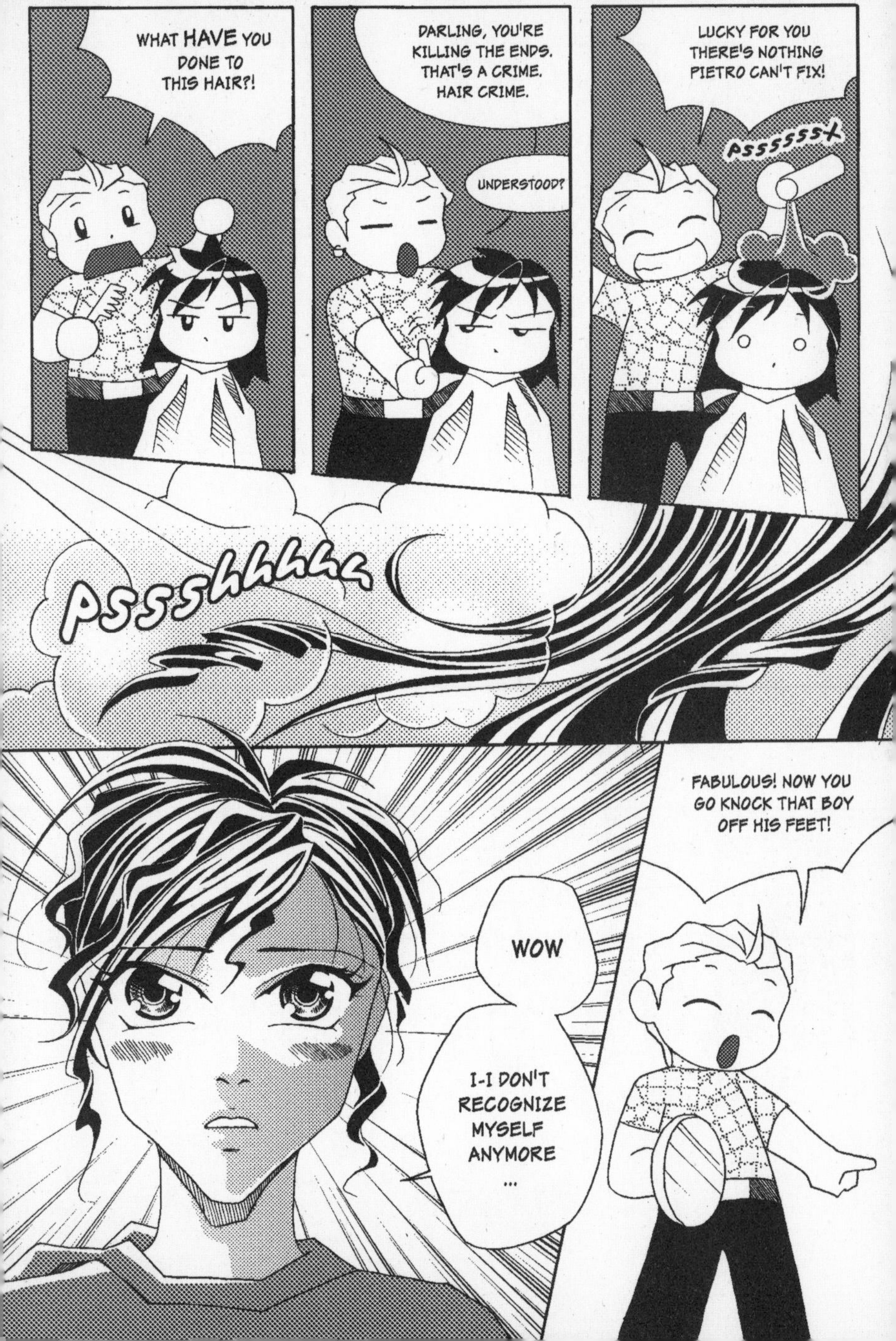

WHAT HAVE YOU DONE TO THIS HAIR?!
DARLING, YOU'RE KILLING THE ENDS. THAT'S A CRIME. HAIR CRIME.
UNDERSTOOD?
LUCKY FOR YOU THERE'S NOTHING PIETRO CAN'T FIX!
PSSSSSST
PSSSHHHHH
WOW
I-I DON'T RECOGNIZE MYSELF ANYMORE ...
FABULOUS! NOW YOU GO KNOCK THAT BOY OFF HIS FEET!

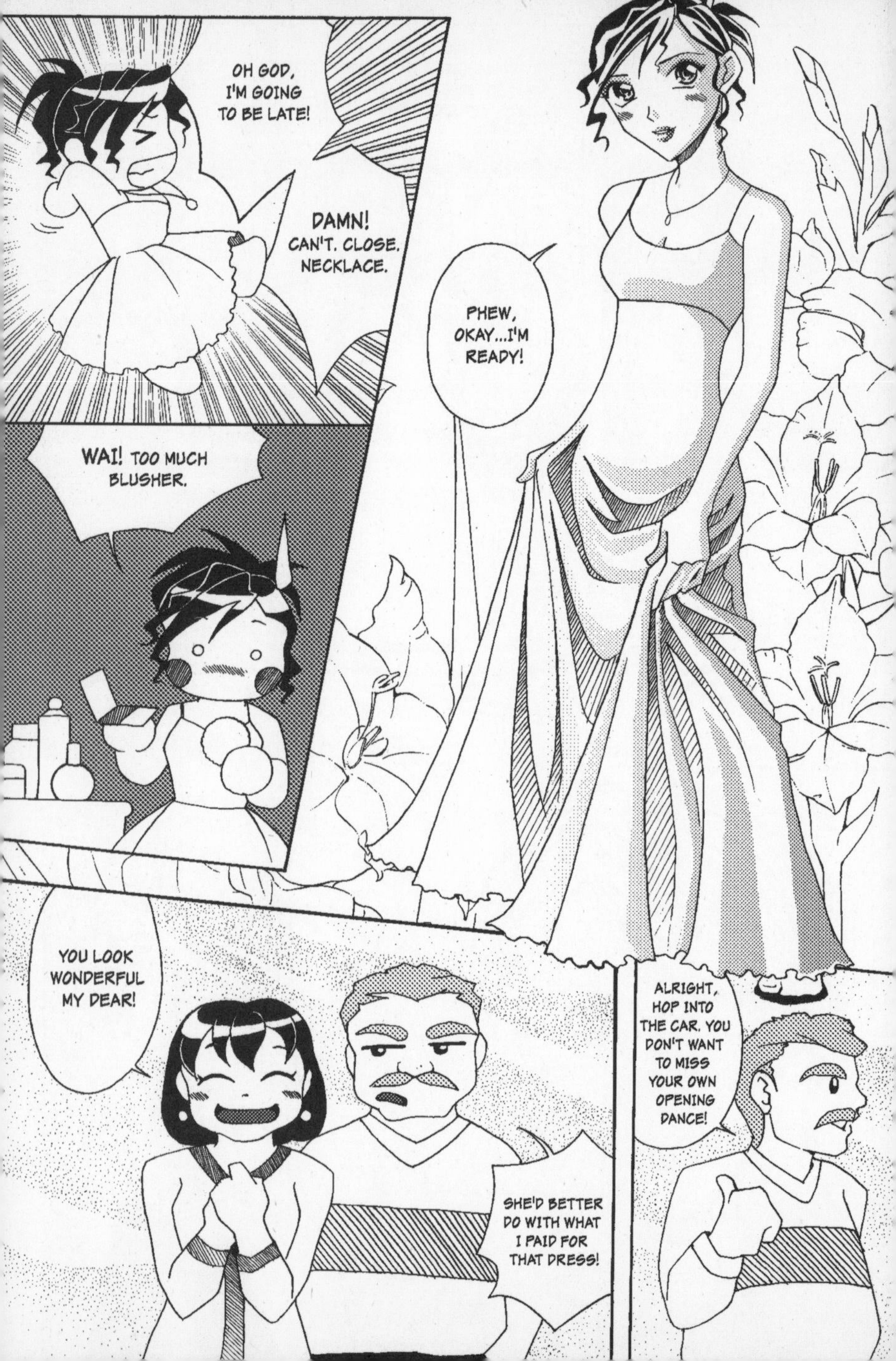
OH GOD, I'M GOING TO BE LATE!
DAMN! CAN'T. CLOSE. NECKLACE.
WAI! TOO MUCH BLUSHER.
PHEW, OKAY...I'M READY!
YOU LOOK WONDERFUL MY DEAR!
SHE'D BETTER DO WITH WHAT I PAID FOR THAT DRESS!
ALRIGHT, HOP INTO THE CAR. YOU DON'T WANT TO MISS YOUR OWN OPENING DANCE!

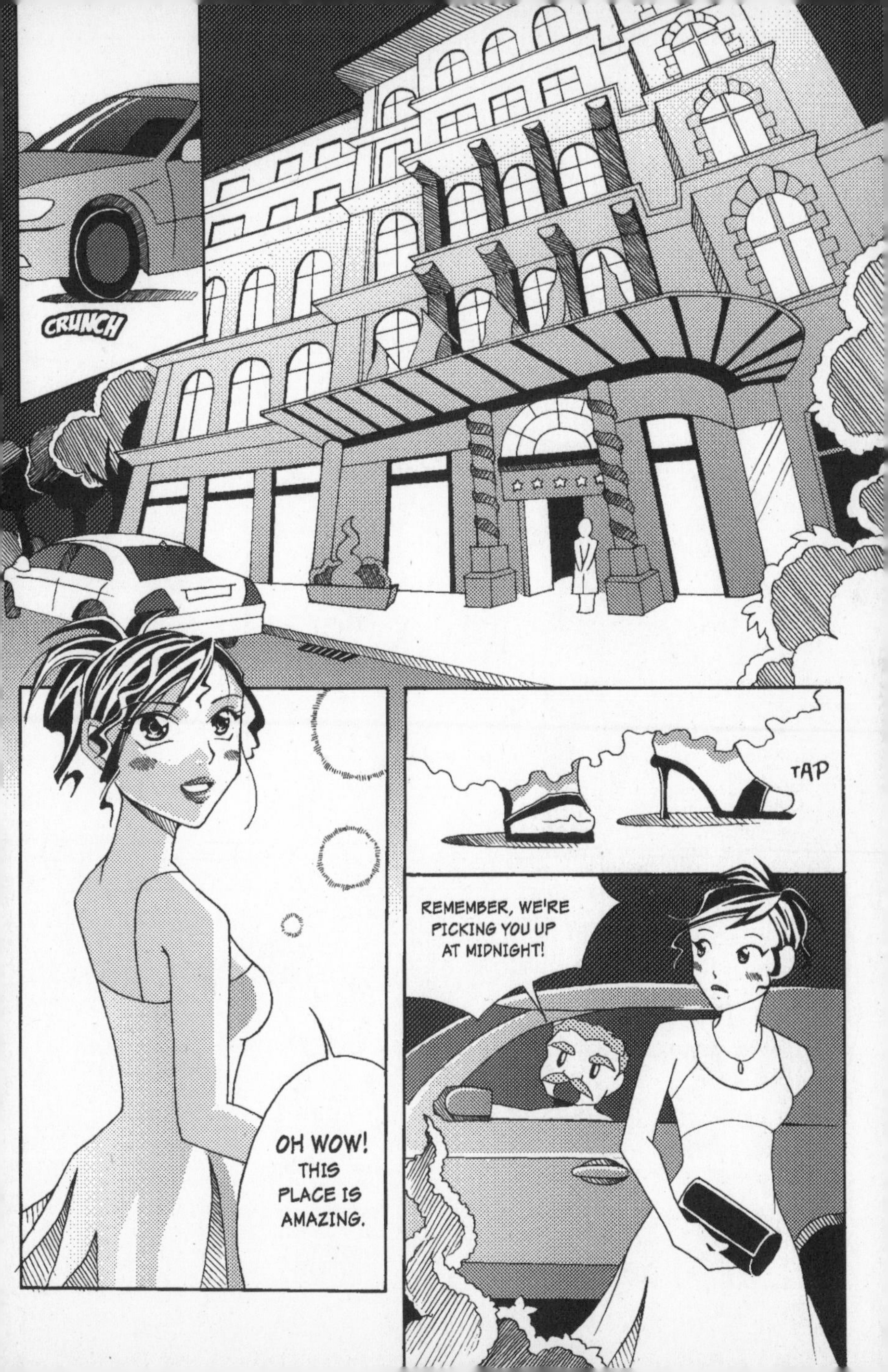
CRUNCH
OH WOW! THIS PLACE IS AMAZING.
TAP
REMEMBER, WE'RE PICKING YOU UP AT MIDNIGHT!

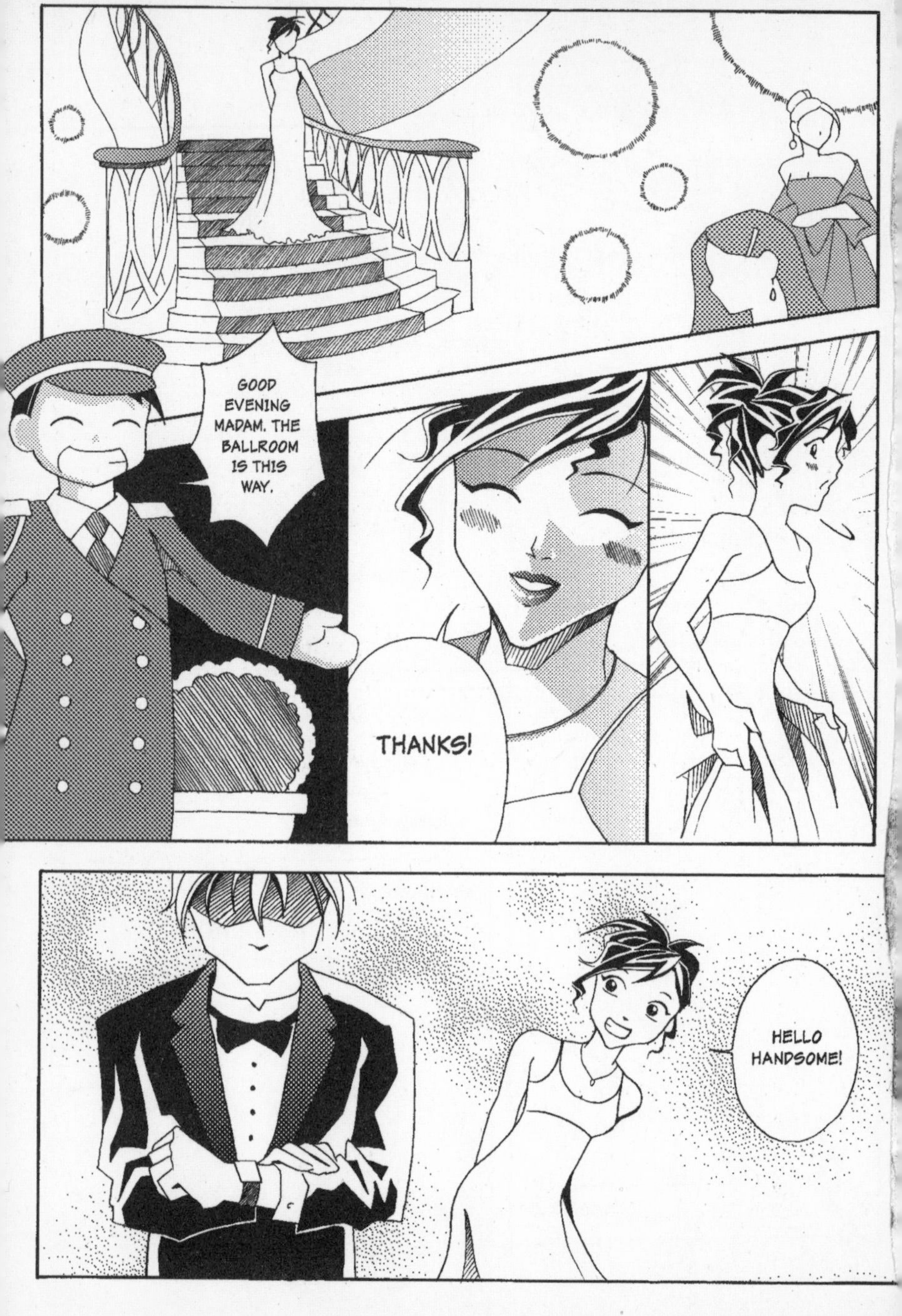
GOOD EVENING MADAM. THE BALLROOM IS THIS WAY.
THANKS!
HELLO HANDSOME!

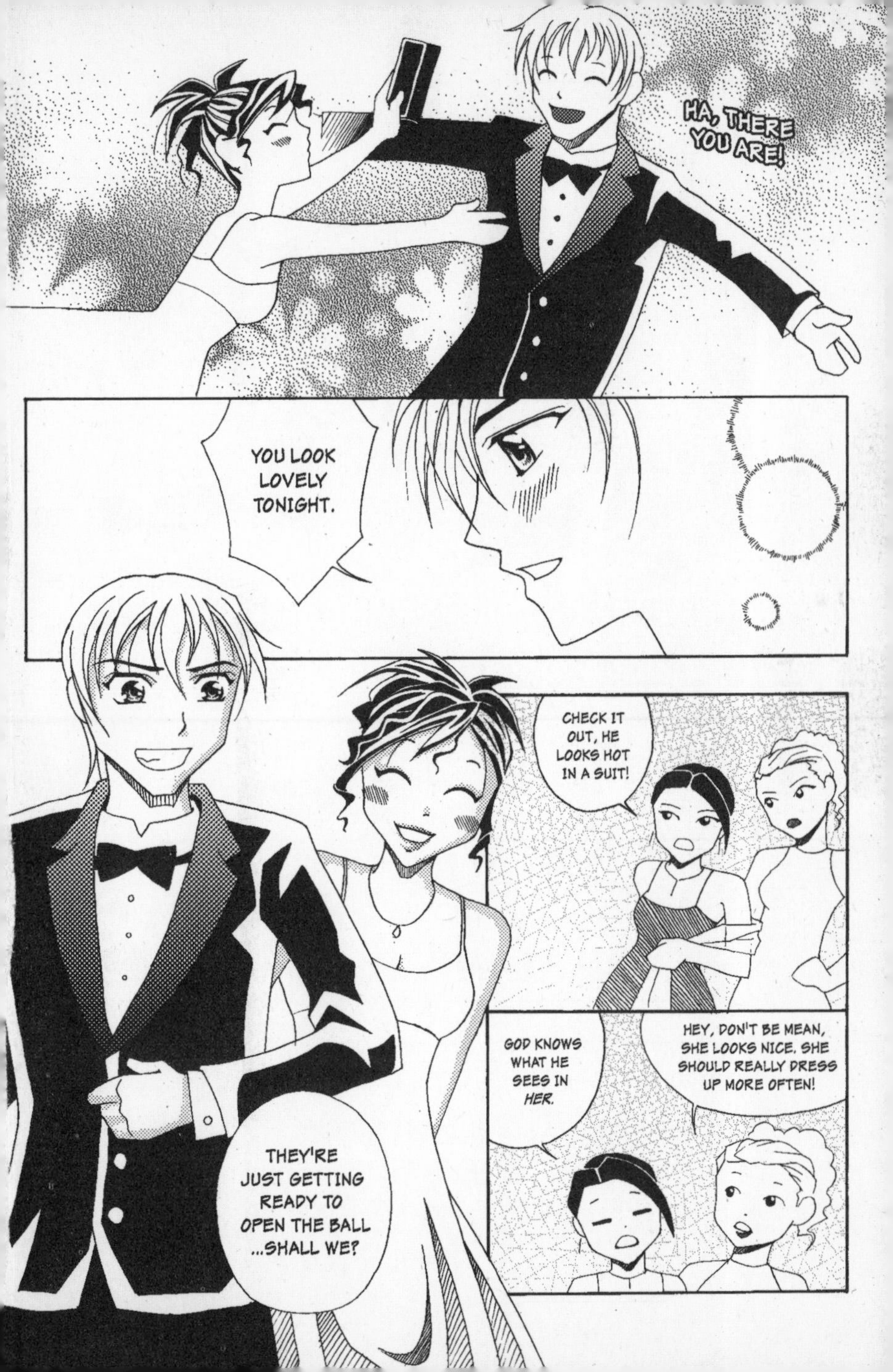
HA, THERE YOU ARE!
YOU LOOK LOVELY TONIGHT.
THEY'RE JUST GETTING READY TO OPEN THE BALL ...SHALL WE?
CHECK IT OUT, HE LOOKS HOT IN A SUIT!
GOD KNOWS WHAT HE SEES IN *HER*.
HEY, DON'T BE MEAN, SHE LOOKS NICE. SHE SHOULD REALLY DRESS UP MORE OFTEN!

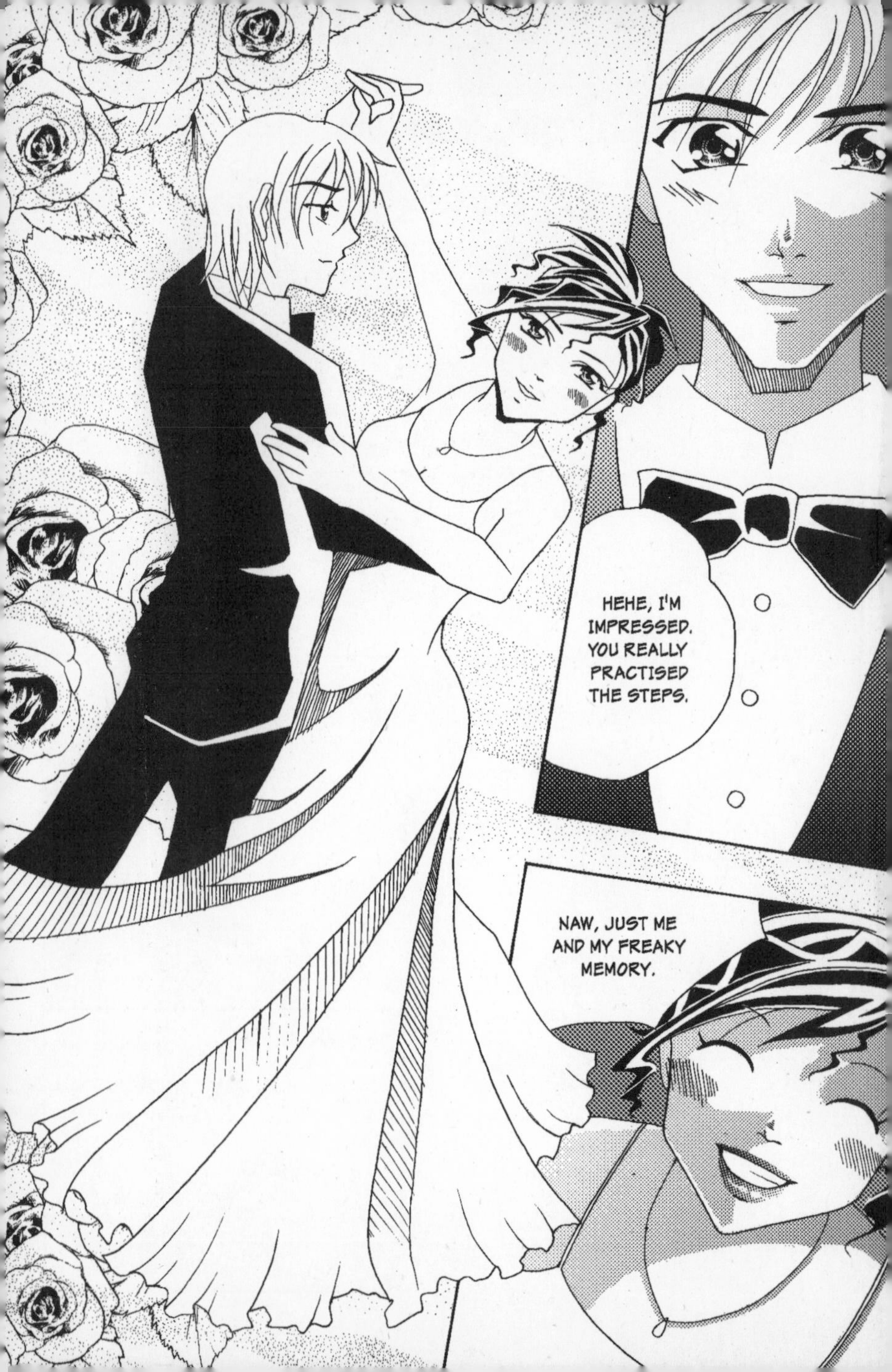
HEHE, I'M IMPRESSED. YOU REALLY PRACTISED THE STEPS.
NAW, JUST ME AND MY FREAKY MEMORY.

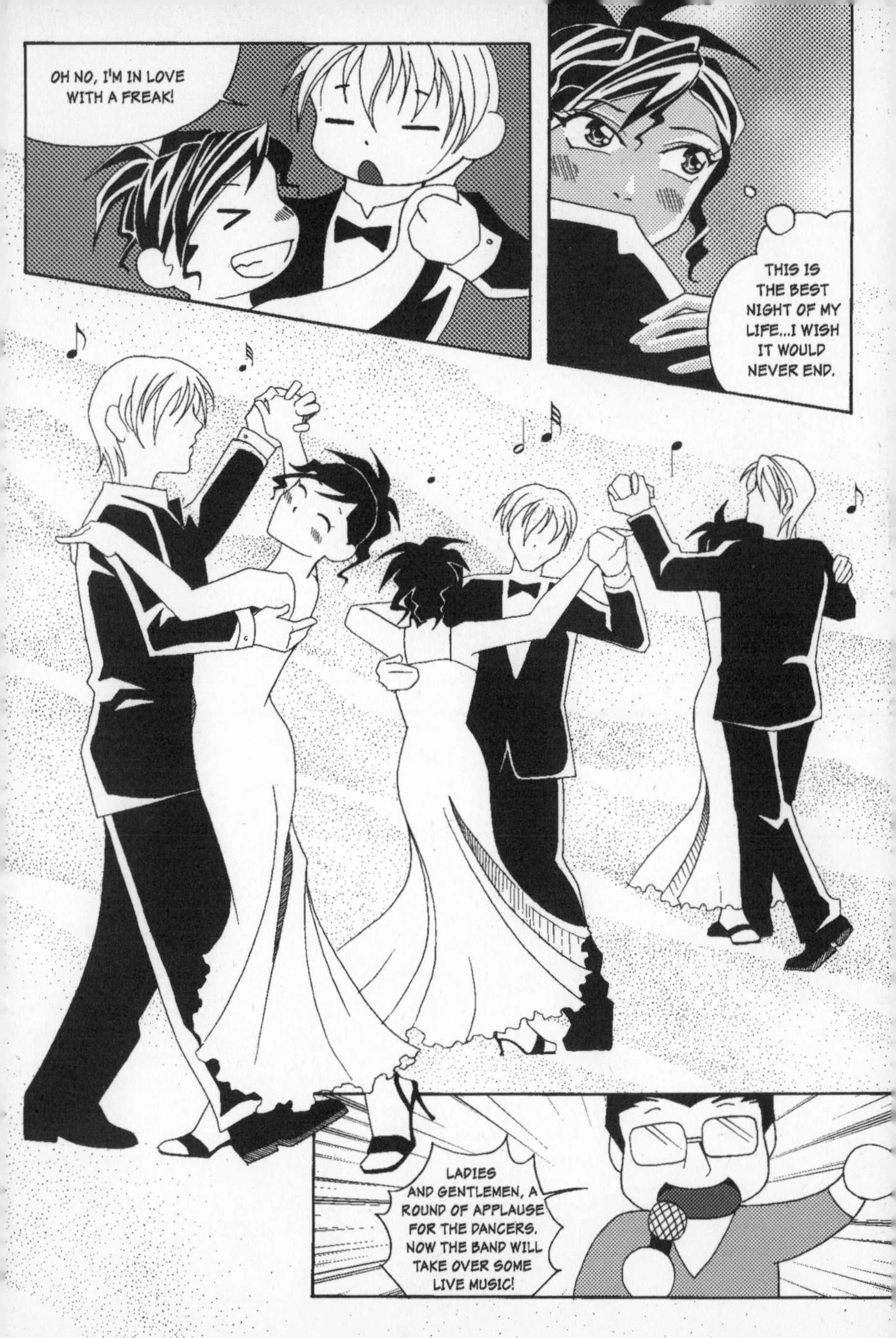
OH NO, I'M IN LOVE WITH A FREAK!
THIS IS THE BEST NIGHT OF MY LIFE...I WISH IT WOULD NEVER END.
LADIES AND GENTLEMEN, A ROUND OF APPLAUSE FOR THE DANCERS. NOW THE BAND WILL TAKE OVER SOME LIVE MUSIC!

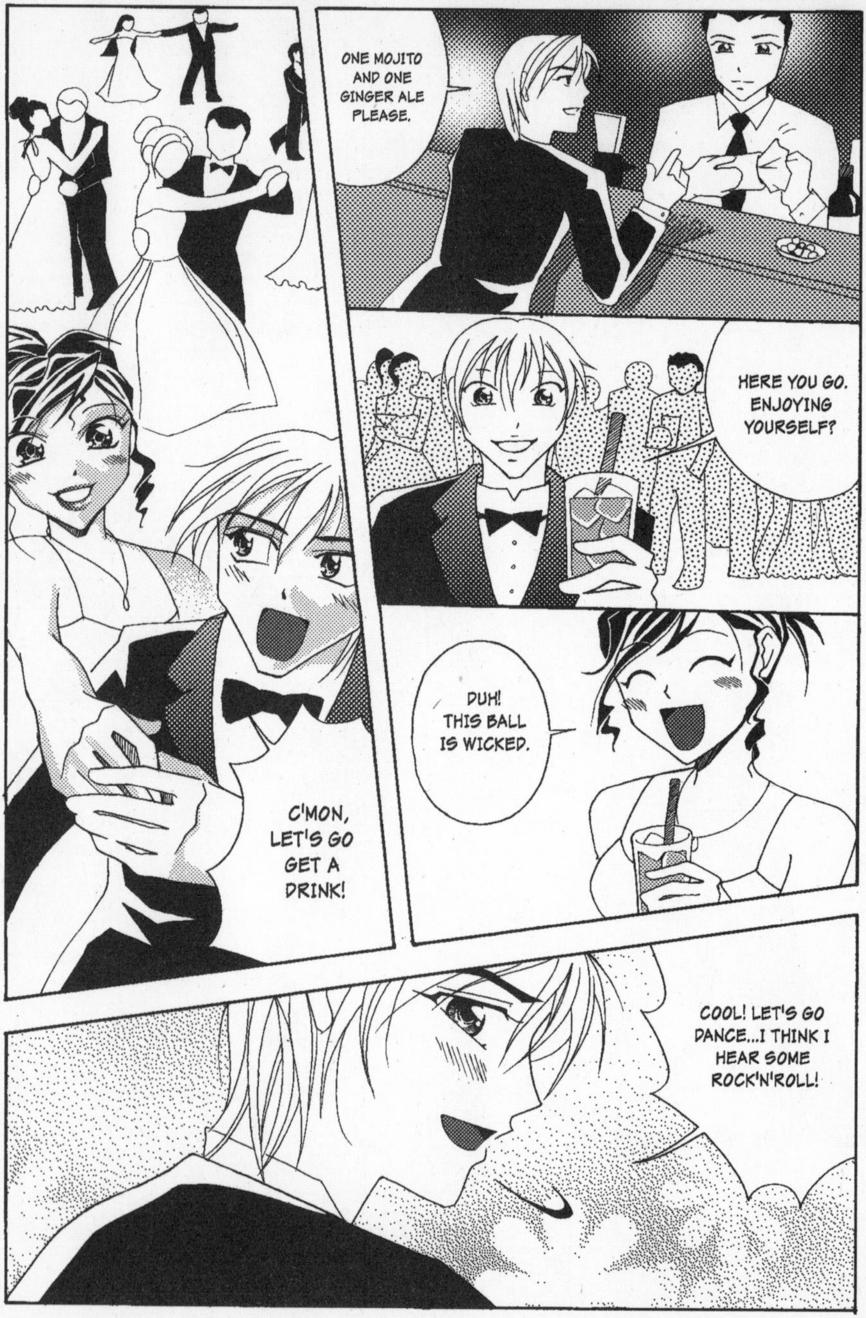

C'MON, LET'S GO GET A DRINK!
ONE MOJITO AND ONE GINGER ALE PLEASE.
HERE YOU GO. ENJOYING YOURSELF?
DUH! THIS BALL IS WICKED.
COOL! LET'S GO DANCE...I THINK I HEAR SOME ROCK'N'ROLL!

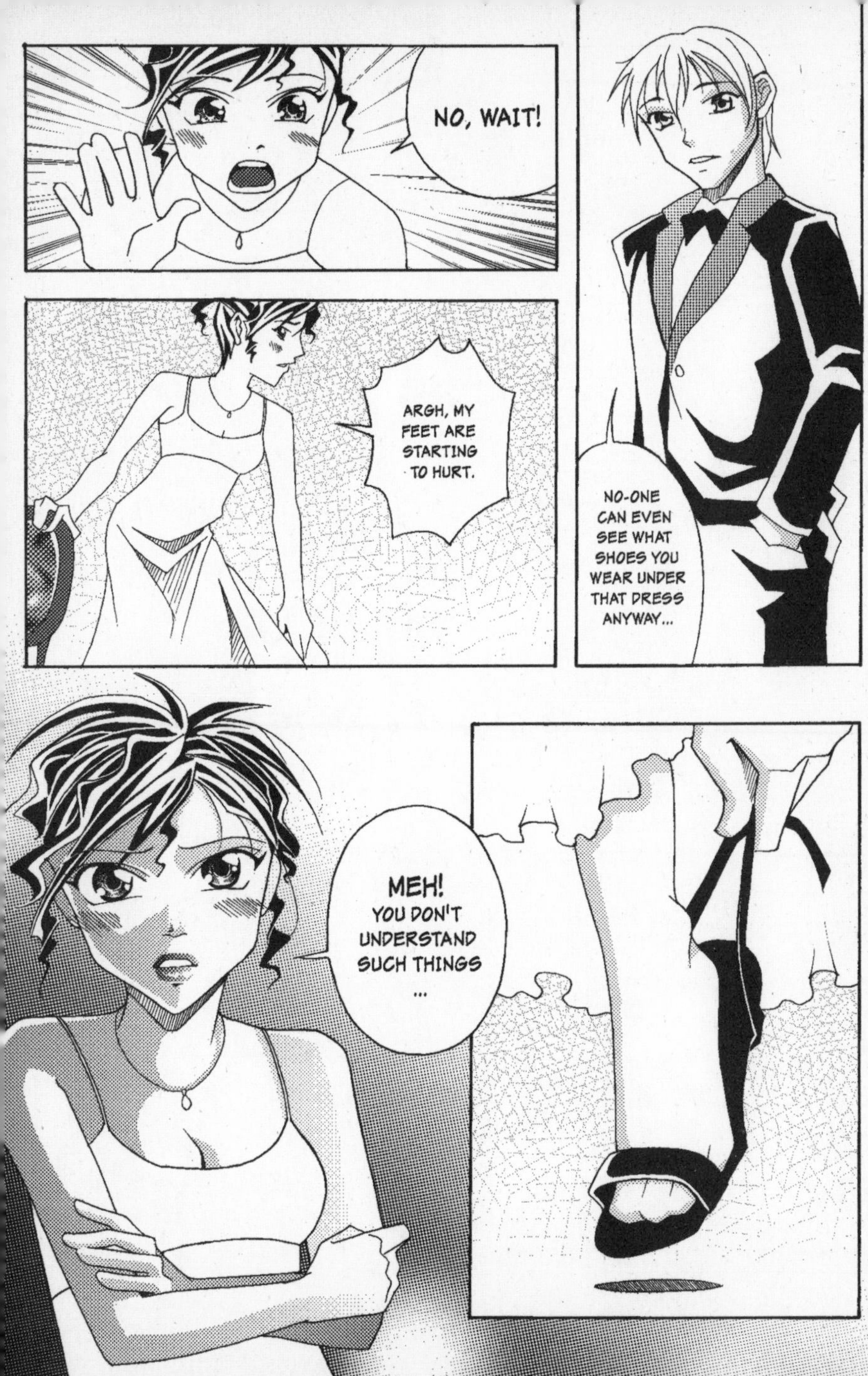
NO, WAIT!
ARGH, MY FEET ARE STARTING TO HURT.
NO-ONE CAN EVEN SEE WHAT SHOES YOU WEAR UNDER THAT DRESS ANYWAY...
MEH! YOU DON'T UNDERSTAND SUCH THINGS ...

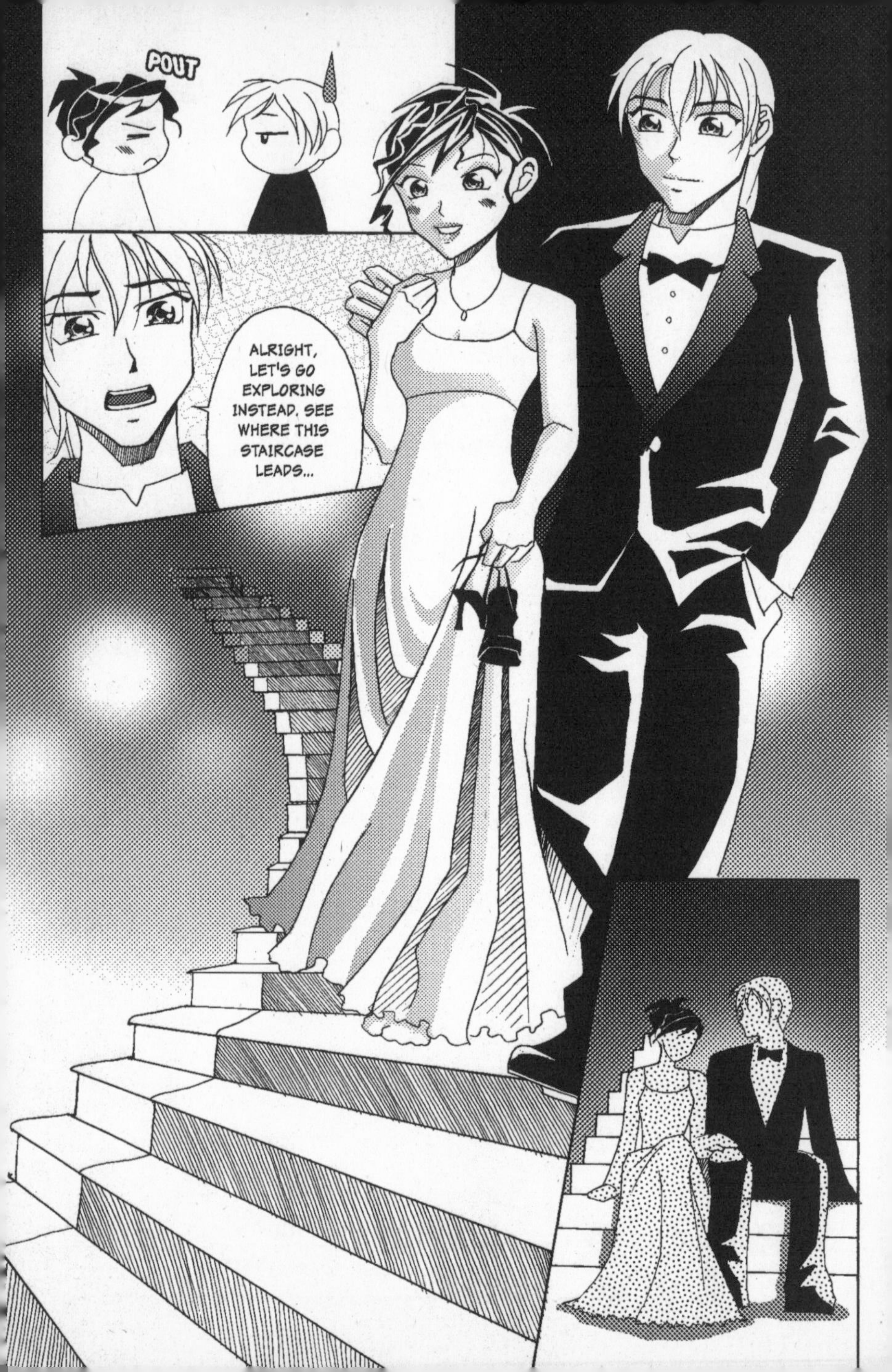
POUT
ALRIGHT, LET'S GO EXPLORING INSTEAD. SEE WHERE THIS STAIRCASE LEADS...

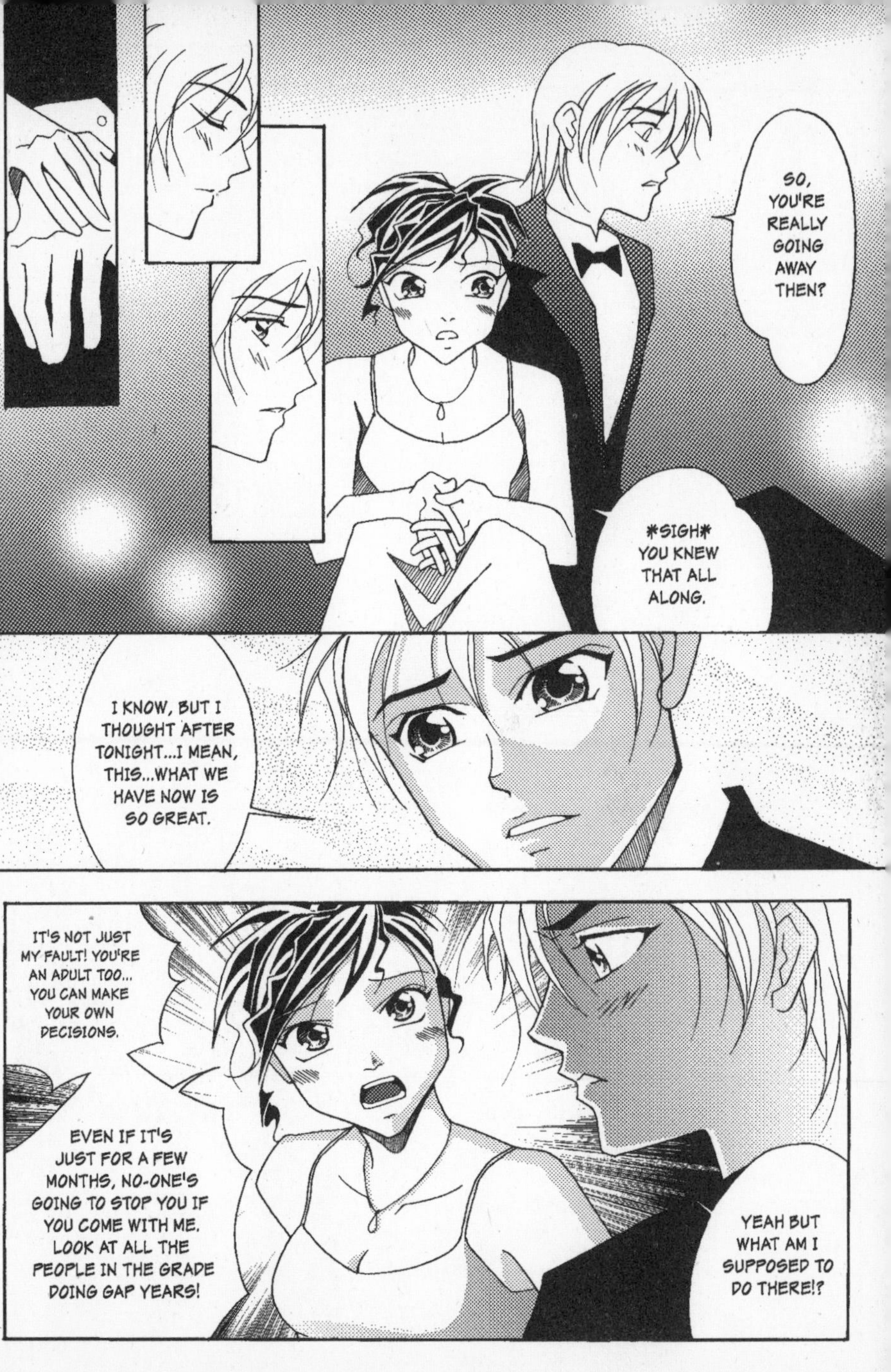
SO, YOU'RE REALLY GOING AWAY THEN?
SIGH YOU KNEW THAT ALL ALONG.
I KNOW, BUT I THOUGHT AFTER TONIGHT...I MEAN, THIS...WHAT WE HAVE NOW IS SO GREAT.
IT'S NOT JUST MY FAULT! YOU'RE AN ADULT TOO... YOU CAN MAKE YOUR OWN DECISIONS.
EVEN IF IT'S JUST FOR A FEW MONTHS, NO-ONE'S GOING TO STOP YOU IF YOU COME WITH ME. LOOK AT ALL THE PEOPLE IN THE GRADE DOING GAP YEARS!
YEAH BUT WHAT AM I SUPPOSED TO DO THERE!?

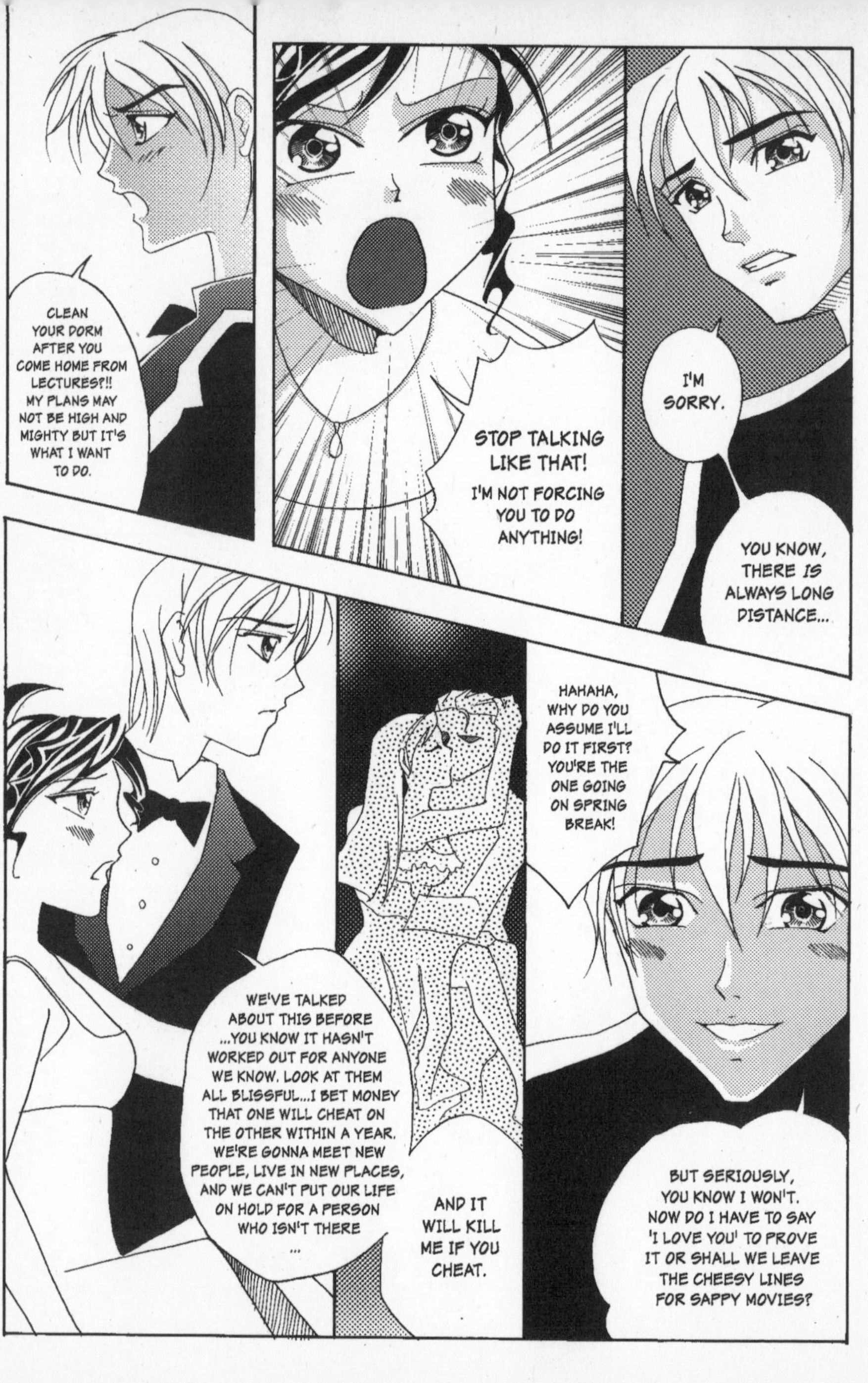
CLEAN YOUR DORM AFTER YOU COME HOME FROM LECTURES?!! MY PLANS MAY NOT BE HIGH AND MIGHTY BUT IT'S WHAT I WANT TO DO.
STOP TALKING LIKE THAT!
I'M NOT FORCING YOU TO DO ANYTHING!
I'M SORRY.
YOU KNOW, THERE *IS* ALWAYS LONG DISTANCE...
WE'VE TALKED ABOUT THIS BEFORE ...YOU KNOW IT HASN'T WORKED OUT FOR ANYONE WE KNOW. LOOK AT THEM ALL BLISSFUL...I BET MONEY THAT ONE WILL CHEAT ON THE OTHER WITHIN A YEAR. WE'RE GONNA MEET NEW PEOPLE, LIVE IN NEW PLACES, AND WE CAN'T PUT OUR LIFE ON HOLD FOR A PERSON WHO ISN'T THERE ...
AND IT WILL KILL ME IF YOU CHEAT.
HAHAHA, WHY DO YOU ASSUME I'LL DO IT FIRST? YOU'RE THE ONE GOING ON SPRING BREAK!
BUT SERIOUSLY, YOU KNOW I WON'T. NOW DO I HAVE TO SAY 'I LOVE YOU' TO PROVE IT OR SHALL WE LEAVE THE CHEESY LINES FOR SAPPY MOVIES?

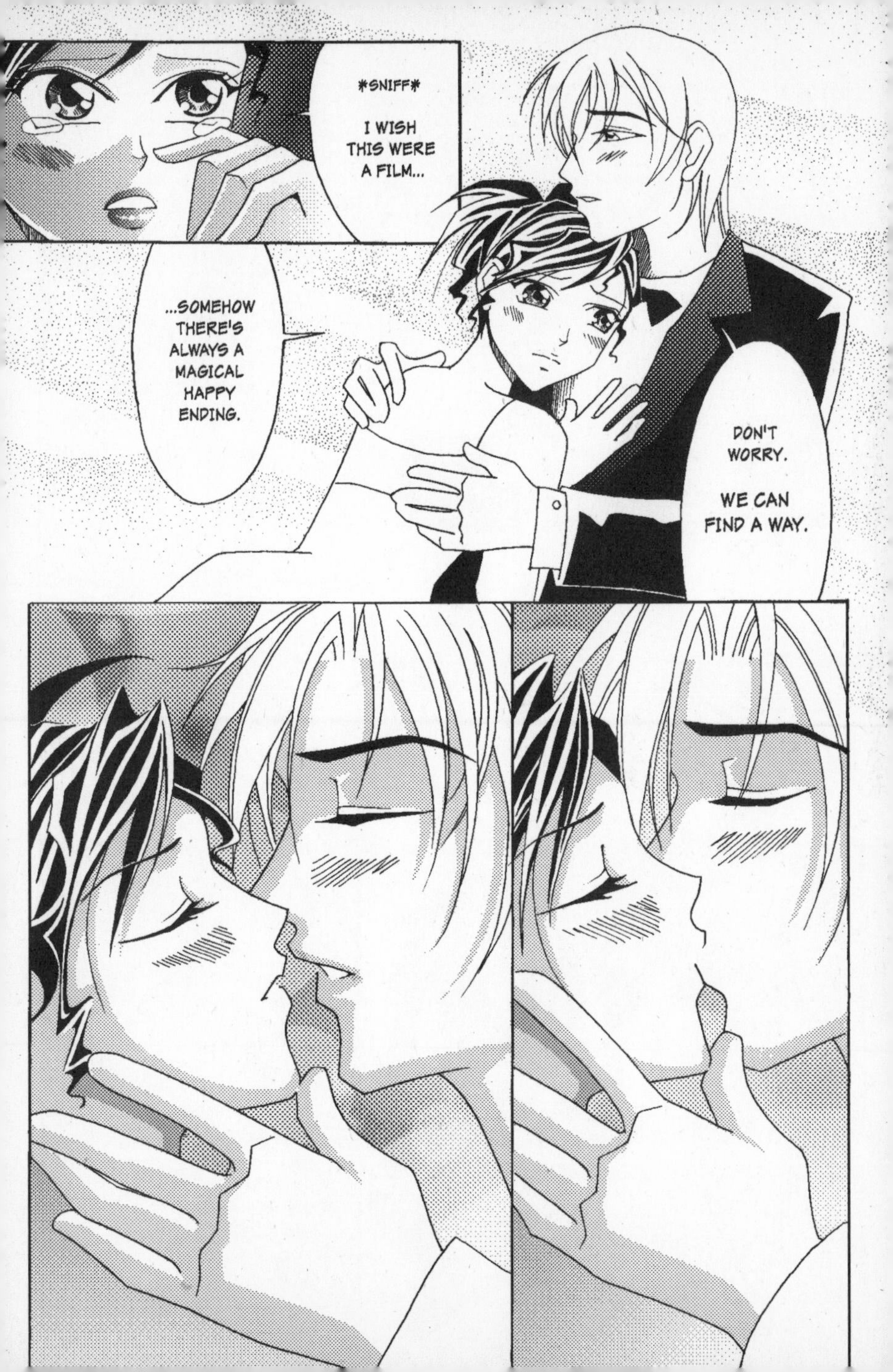
SNIFF
I WISH THIS WERE A FILM...
...SOMEHOW THERE'S ALWAYS A MAGICAL HAPPY ENDING.
DON'T WORRY.
WE CAN FIND A WAY.

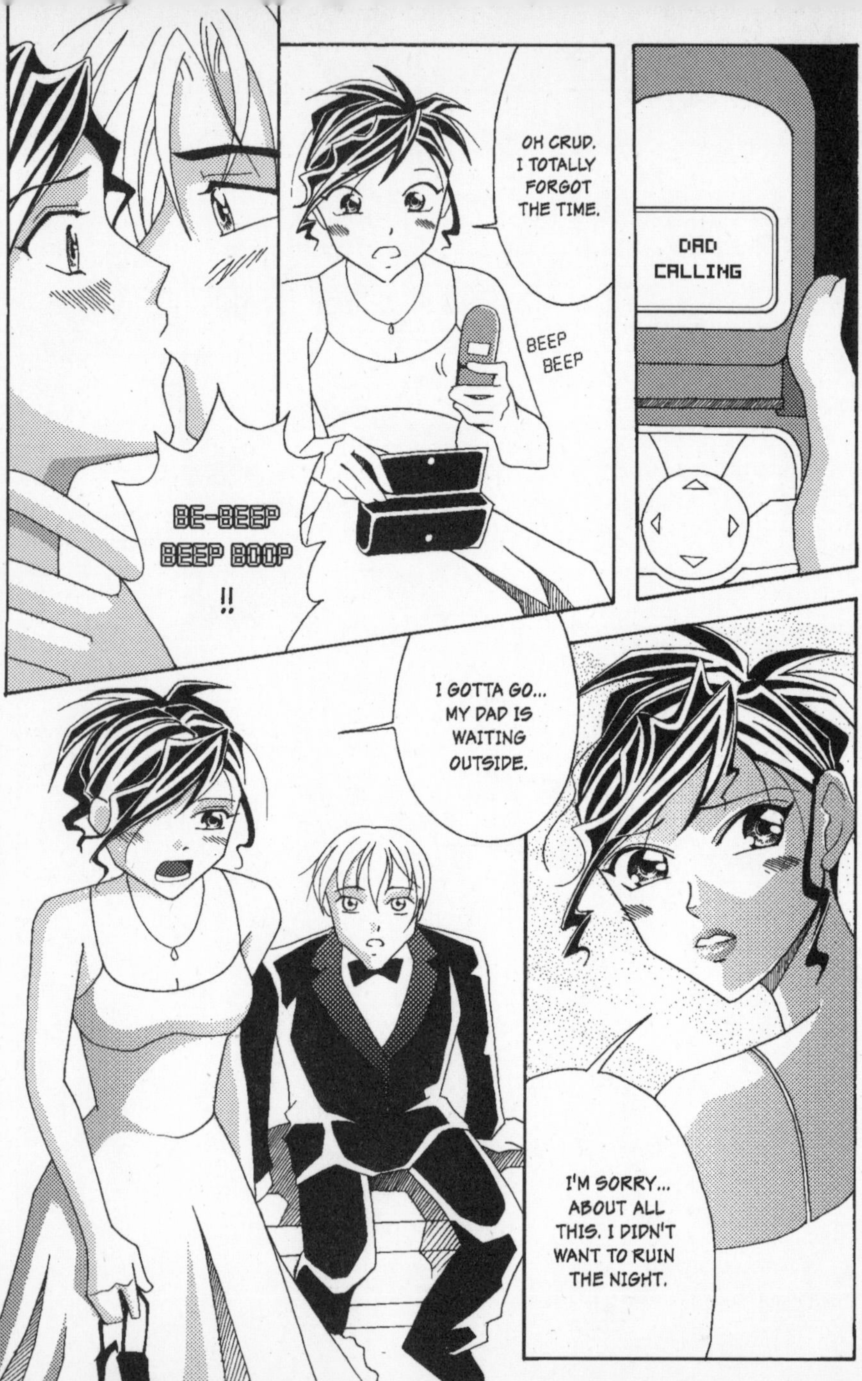
BE-BEEP
BEEP BOOP
!!
OH CRUD. I TOTALLY FORGOT THE TIME.
BEEP BEEP
DAD CALLING
I GOTTA GO... MY DAD IS WAITING OUTSIDE.
I'M SORRY... ABOUT ALL THIS. I DIDN'T WANT TO RUIN THE NIGHT.

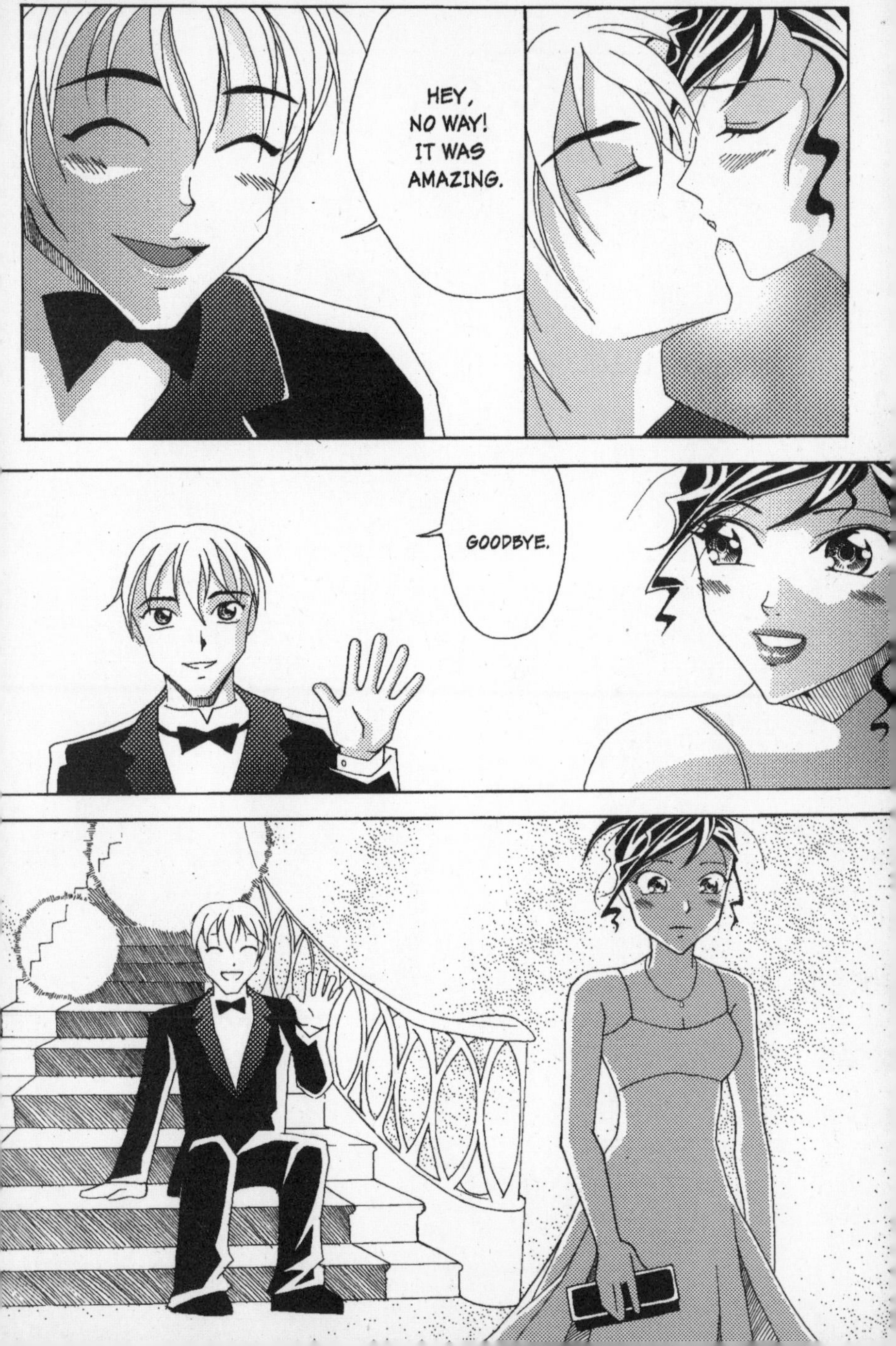
HEY, NO WAY! IT WAS AMAZING.
GOODBYE.

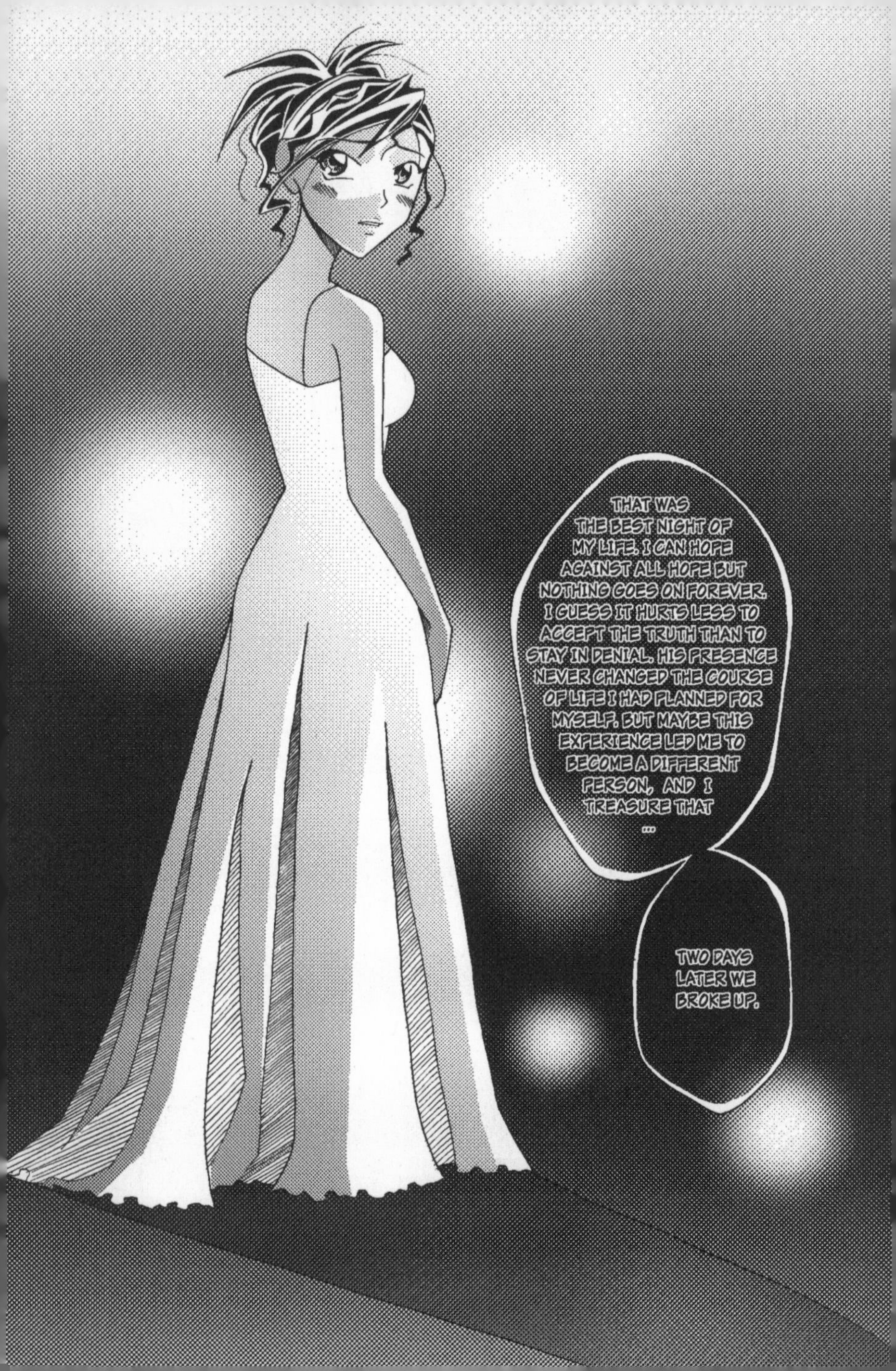
THAT WAS THE BEST NIGHT OF MY LIFE. I CAN HOPE AGAINST ALL HOPE BUT NOTHING GOES ON FOREVER. I GUESS IT HURTS LESS TO ACCEPT THE TRUTH THAN TO STAY IN DENIAL. HIS PRESENCE NEVER CHANGED THE COURSE OF LIFE I HAD PLANNED FOR MYSELF. BUT MAYBE THIS EXPERIENCE LED ME TO BECOME A DIFFERENT PERSON, AND I TREASURE THAT ...
TWO DAYS LATER WE BROKE UP.

::

EXPERIMENT 1817295#7205 :: People's Choice Winner ::

....

Suzanne Lam was born in Manchester, England in 1987. She currently
lives in West Yorkshire and has been drawing manga-styled comics
seriously for 3 years.
www.dblstudio.com

Favorite manga:
Houshin Engi

Favorite manga artist:
Ryu Fujisaki, Masashi Kishimoto, Takeshi Obata and more...

....

Author's Comments:
Writing has never been a strong point of mine, so writing a short story that
had to be no longer than 20 pages was a real challenge for me. I wanted to
change it completely when I was halfway through the story, but I didn't have
much time to. The characters have been taken from another story of mine.
—*Suzanne Lam*

::

::

EXPERIMENT 1817295#7205 :: People's Choice Award ::

....

Judge's Comments:
We judges make our call on what should be in the book before the online readers pick the People's Choice entry, but I have to admit, I was pretty sure that "Experiment" was going to get the People's Choice award long before the final votes were cast. With solid, appealing character designs, good use of slapstick humor, and the RPG parody jokes, I enjoyed this entry a lot overall, and I was impressed by how thoroughly Suzanne hit all of the "manga" buttons. So why did we judges not put it in the book ourselves? Well, honestly, it was a close thing, and we always go back and forth a lot on our picks for the top seven, but while Suzanne's panel layouts were cool, it wasn't always easy to follow what was going on, and there are some anatomy issues with the figures in places. While the designs were appealing, it felt like a cop-out to intentionally make the RPG look "generic," even though that was part of the joke. And the drawback to frenetic comic pacing is that the reader never gets a chance to really identify with any of the characters. Parody is the low-hanging fruit of *RSOM*—it's easy to do something fun and clever in the limited space available. Unfortunately, that doesn't always show off real storytelling skills to their best advantage, and for all of its style, "Experiment" was hurt as an entry because of that. However, I was really pleased to see an overall very strong entry get a little bit of extra recognition. Suzanne definitely deserves her place as a Rising Star!
—*Lillian Diaz-Przybyl*

Judge's Comments:
Sure the exuberantly long title made me roll my eyes, but I knew this story had to be in the book the moment I saw the first page! From the character design to composition to lettering this entry screamed, "This person knows what she's doing!" Perhaps some found the inking to be a little too thick at times, but I found it appropriate to the situation (mostly for the comedic air). And when the time arose for precise details, I found Suzanne pulled it off flawlessly—just look at those ice trees on the two-page spread! Plus, who could resist the flexible character expressions with designs reminiscent of Naruto? Every great artist has a great source of inspiration behind her!

Art aside, I found the topic was a refreshing take on the RPG-parody genre. Mind you, past entries I'd seen never went beyond flashy character design, but Suzanne's hilarious insight into the world of RPGs was refreshing and exciting! And I must commend her for tackling an action scene (the bane of many aspiring manga-ka) with familiar but tactful execution. Kudos to Suzanne, I know we'll be seeing more of her work in the future!
—*Katherine Schilling*

::

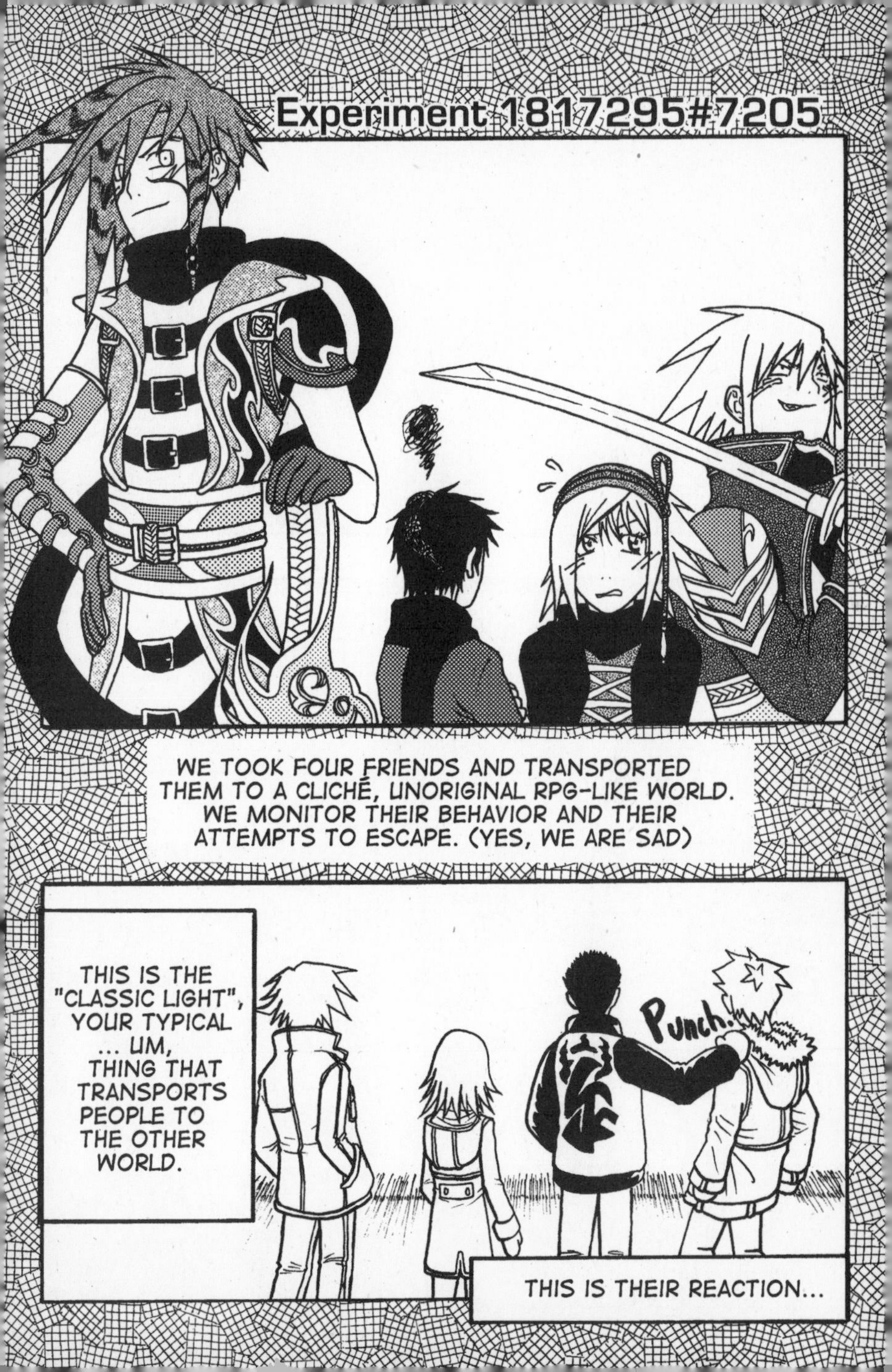
Experiment 1817295#7205
WE TOOK FOUR FRIENDS AND TRANSPORTED THEM TO A CLICHÉ, UNORIGINAL RPG-LIKE WORLD. WE MONITOR THEIR BEHAVIOR AND THEIR ATTEMPTS TO ESCAPE. (YES, WE ARE SAD)
THIS IS THE "CLASSIC LIGHT", YOUR TYPICAL ... UM, THING THAT TRANSPORTS PEOPLE TO THE OTHER WORLD.
Punch.
THIS IS THEIR REACTION...

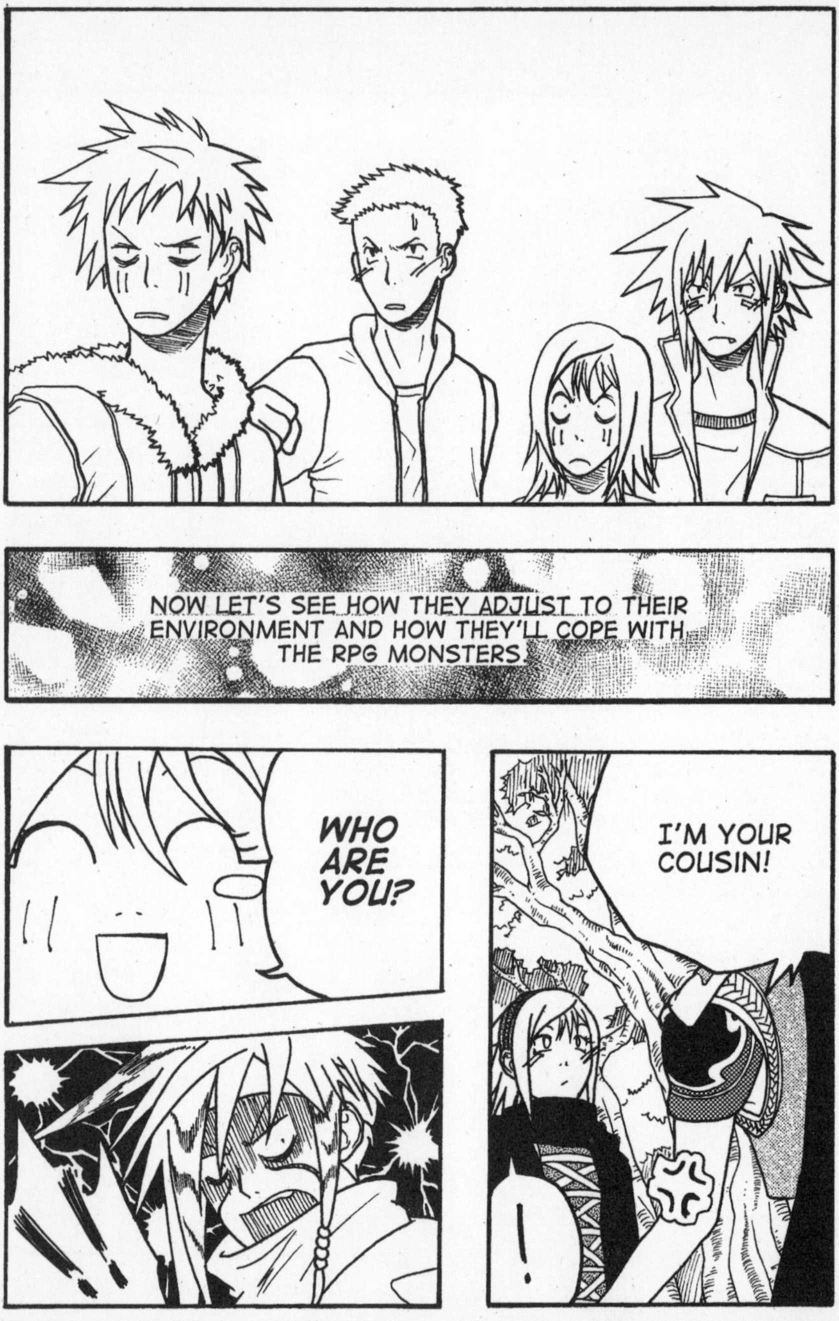
NOW LET'S SEE HOW THEY ADJUST TO THEIR ENVIRONMENT AND HOW THEY'LL COPE WITH THE RPG MONSTERS.
WHO ARE YOU?
I'M YOUR COUSIN!
!

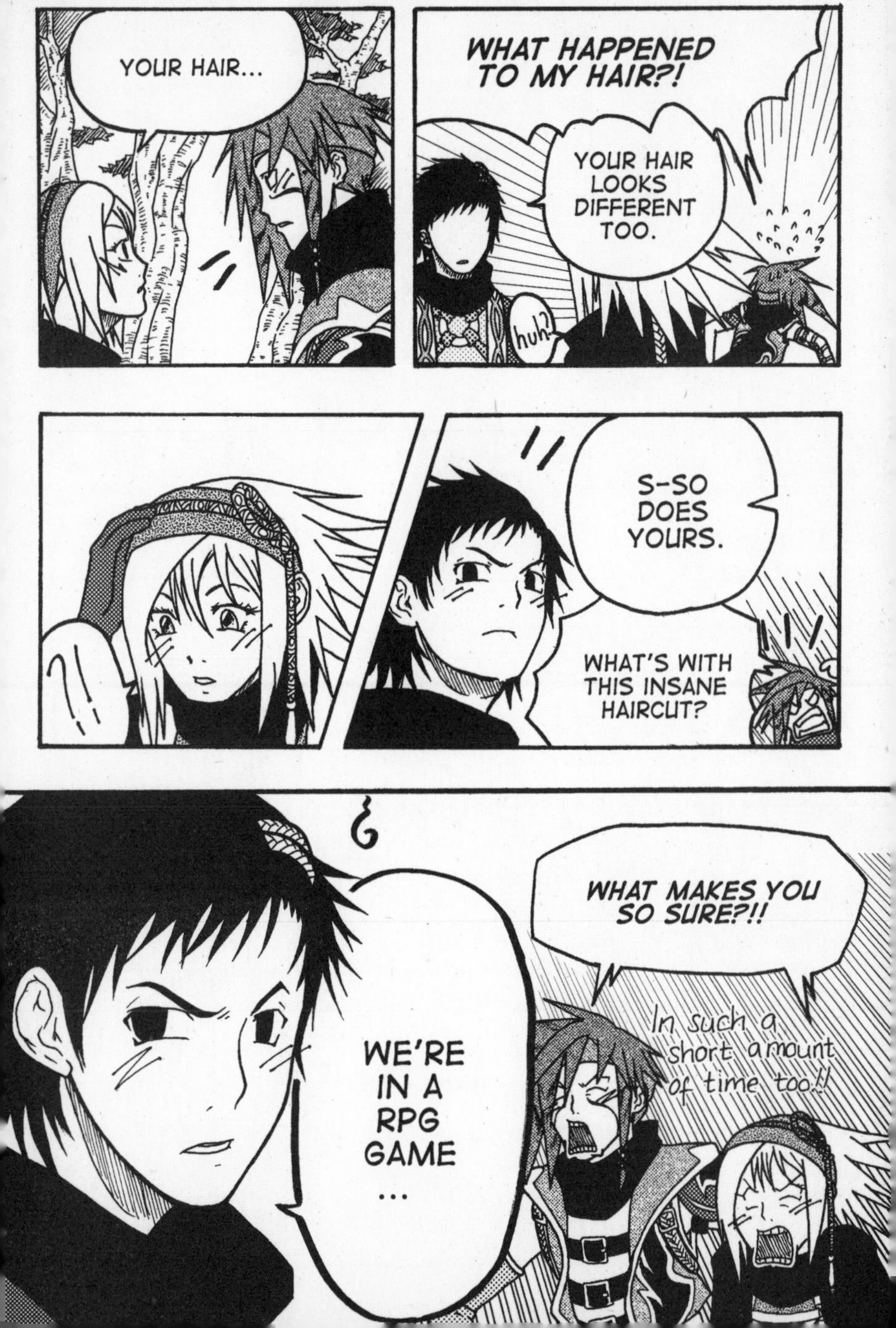
YOUR HAIR...
WHAT HAPPENED TO MY HAIR?!
YOUR HAIR LOOKS DIFFERENT TOO.
huh?
S-SO DOES YOURS.
WHAT'S WITH THIS INSANE HAIRCUT?
WE'RE IN A RPG GAME ...
WHAT MAKES YOU SO SURE?!!
In such a short amount of time too!!

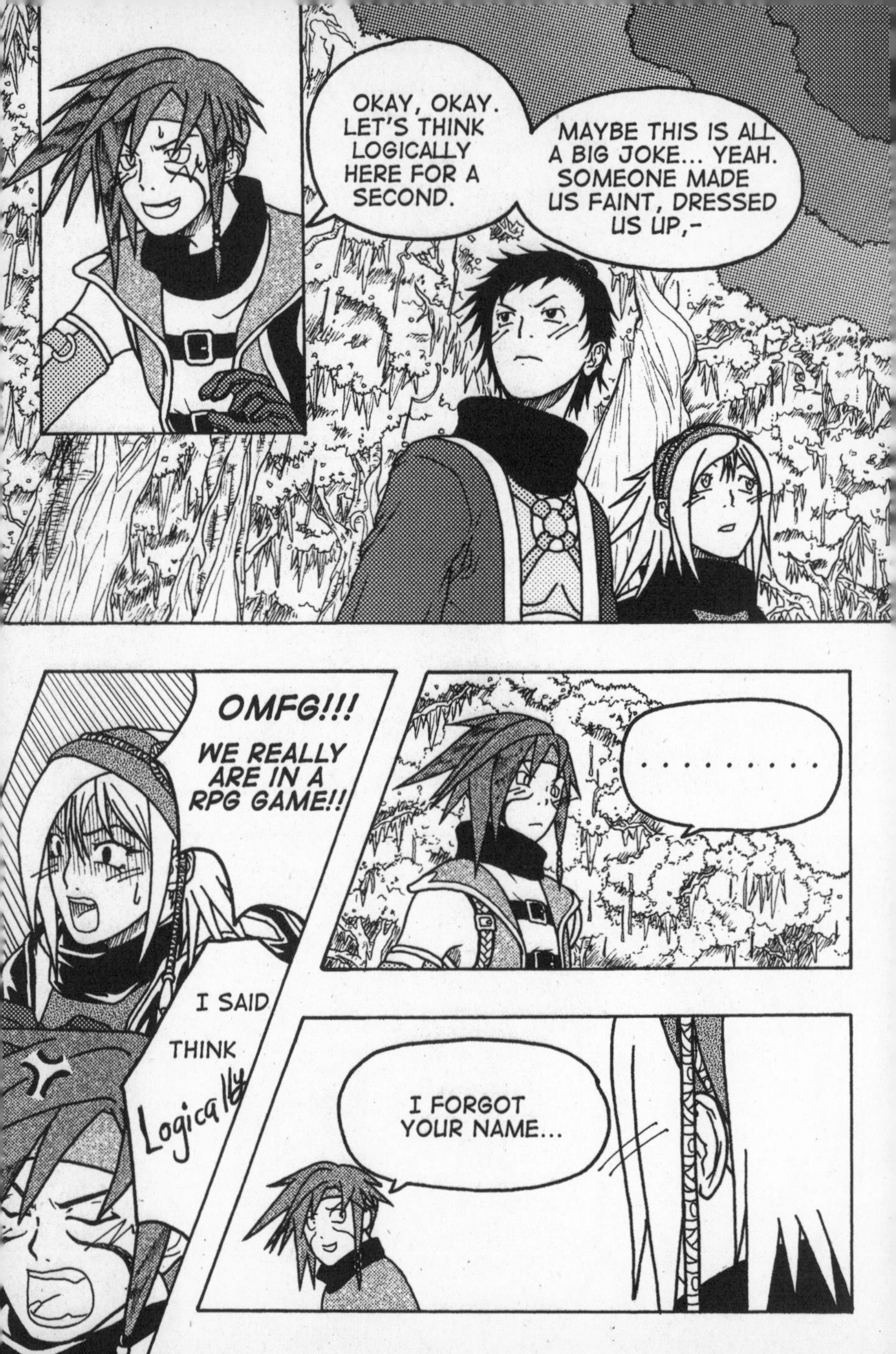
OKAY, OKAY. LET'S THINK LOGICALLY HERE FOR A SECOND.
MAYBE THIS IS ALL A BIG JOKE... YEAH. SOMEONE MADE US FAINT, DRESSED US UP,-
OMFG!!!
WE REALLY ARE IN A RPG GAME!!
I SAID
THINK
Logically
....
I FORGOT YOUR NAME...

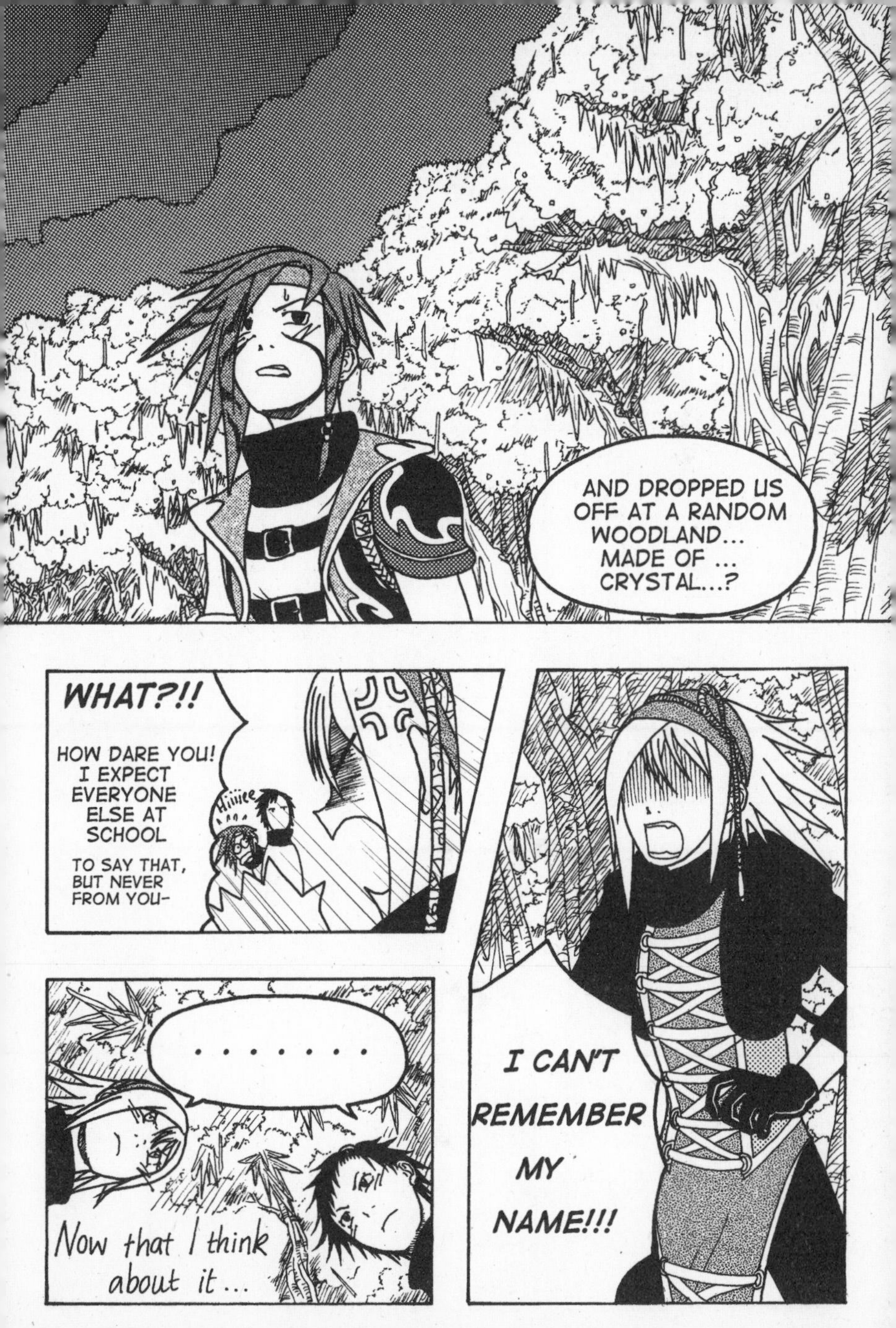
AND DROPPED US OFF AT A RANDOM WOODLAND... MADE OF ... CRYSTAL...?
WHAT?!!
HOW DARE YOU! I EXPECT EVERYONE ELSE AT SCHOOL TO SAY THAT, BUT NEVER FROM YOU-
Hiiiiee
I CAN'T REMEMBER MY NAME!!!
. . . .
Now that I think about it...

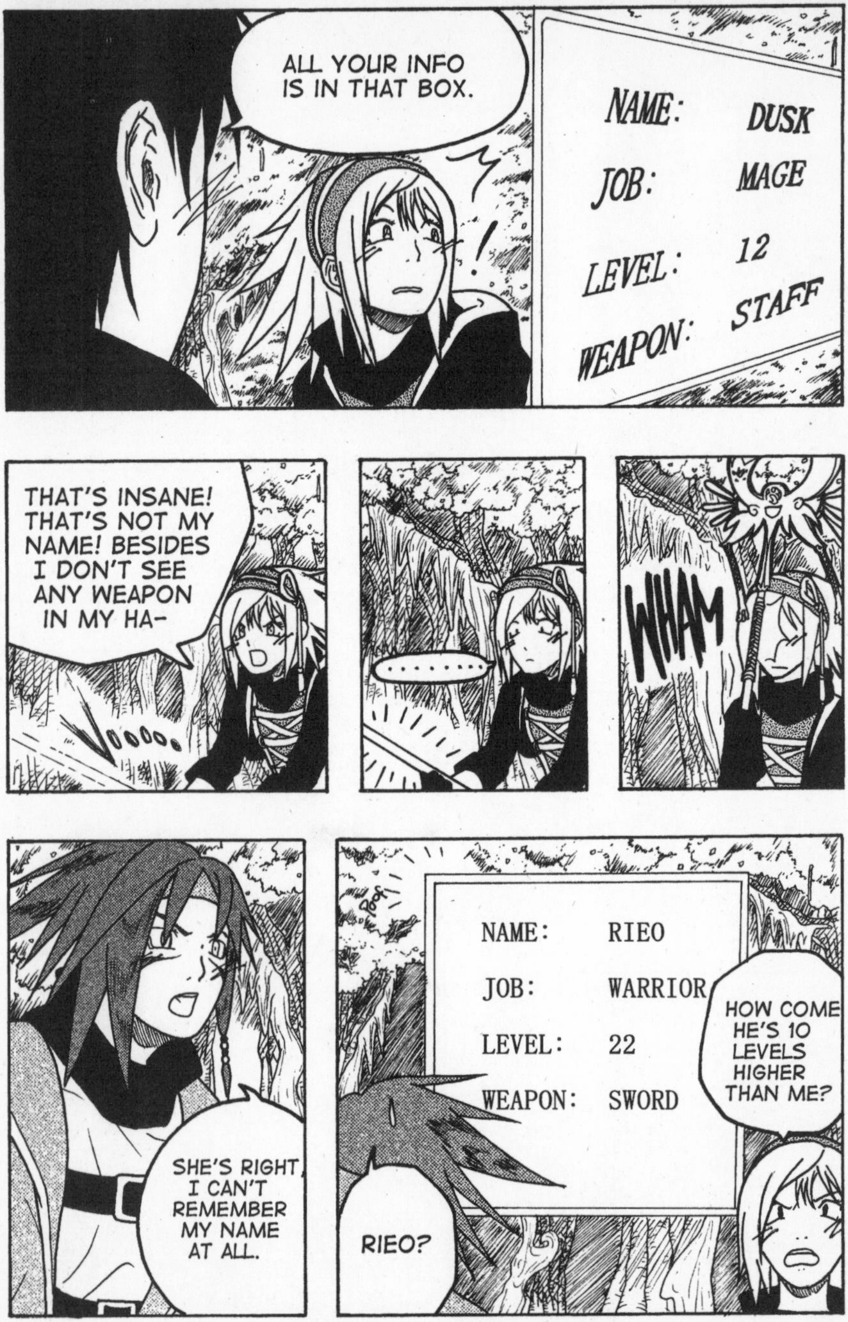
ALL YOUR INFO IS IN THAT BOX.
NAME: DUSK
JOB: MAGE
LEVEL: 12
WEAPON: STAFF
!
THAT'S INSANE! THAT'S NOT MY NAME! BESIDES I DON'T SEE ANY WEAPON IN MY HA-
Vooooo
....
WHAM
SHE'S RIGHT, I CAN'T REMEMBER MY NAME AT ALL.
NAME: RIEO
JOB: WARRIOR
LEVEL: 22
WEAPON: SWORD
RIEO?
HOW COME HE'S 10 LEVELS HIGHER THAN ME?

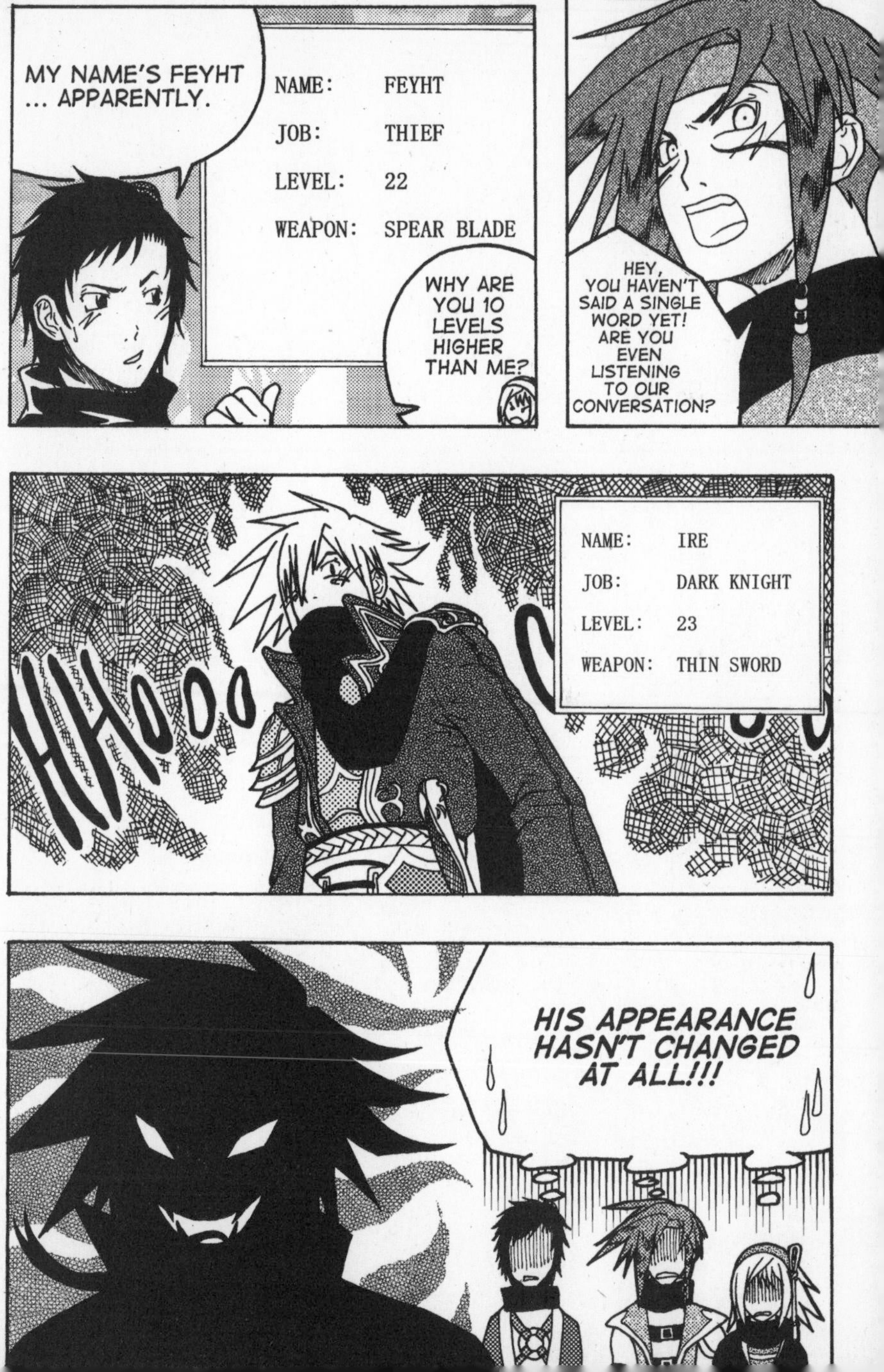
MY NAME'S FEYHT ... APPARENTLY.
NAME: FEYHT
JOB: THIEF
LEVEL: 22
WEAPON: SPEAR BLADE
WHY ARE YOU 10 LEVELS HIGHER THAN ME?
HEY, YOU HAVEN'T SAID A SINGLE WORD YET! ARE YOU EVEN LISTENING TO OUR CONVERSATION?
NAME: IRE
JOB: DARK KNIGHT
LEVEL: 23
WEAPON: THIN SWORD
HIS APPEARANCE HASN'T CHANGED AT ALL!!!

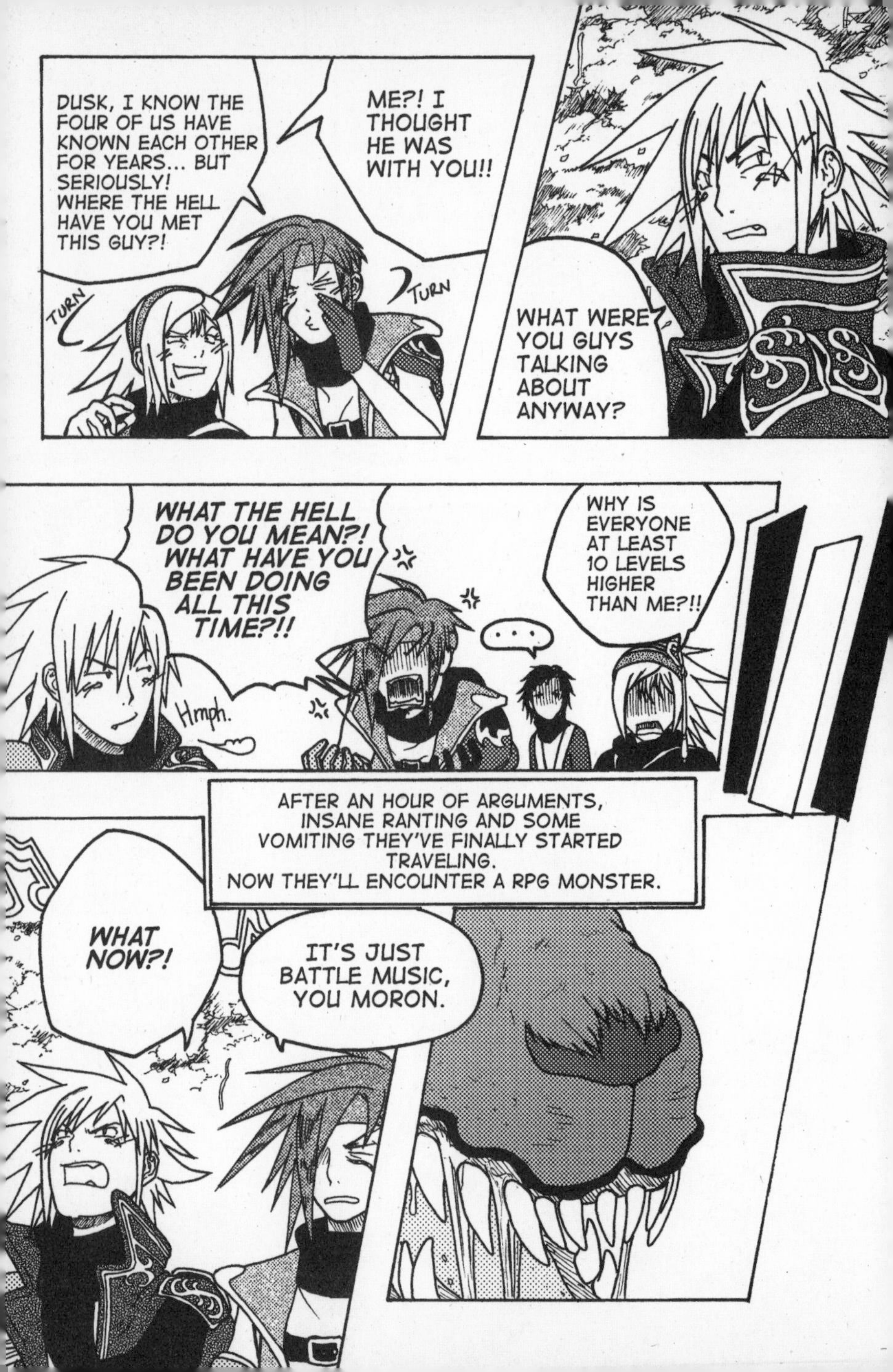
DUSK, I KNOW THE FOUR OF US HAVE KNOWN EACH OTHER FOR YEARS... BUT SERIOUSLY! WHERE THE HELL HAVE YOU MET THIS GUY?!
ME?! I THOUGHT HE WAS WITH YOU!!
TURN
TURN
WHAT WERE YOU GUYS TALKING ABOUT ANYWAY?
WHAT THE HELL DO YOU MEAN?! WHAT HAVE YOU BEEN DOING ALL THIS TIME?!!
Hmph.
...
WHY IS EVERYONE AT LEAST 10 LEVELS HIGHER THAN ME?!!
AFTER AN HOUR OF ARGUMENTS, INSANE RANTING AND SOME VOMITING THEY'VE FINALLY STARTED TRAVELING. NOW THEY'LL ENCOUNTER A RPG MONSTER.
WHAT NOW?!
IT'S JUST BATTLE MUSIC, YOU MORON.

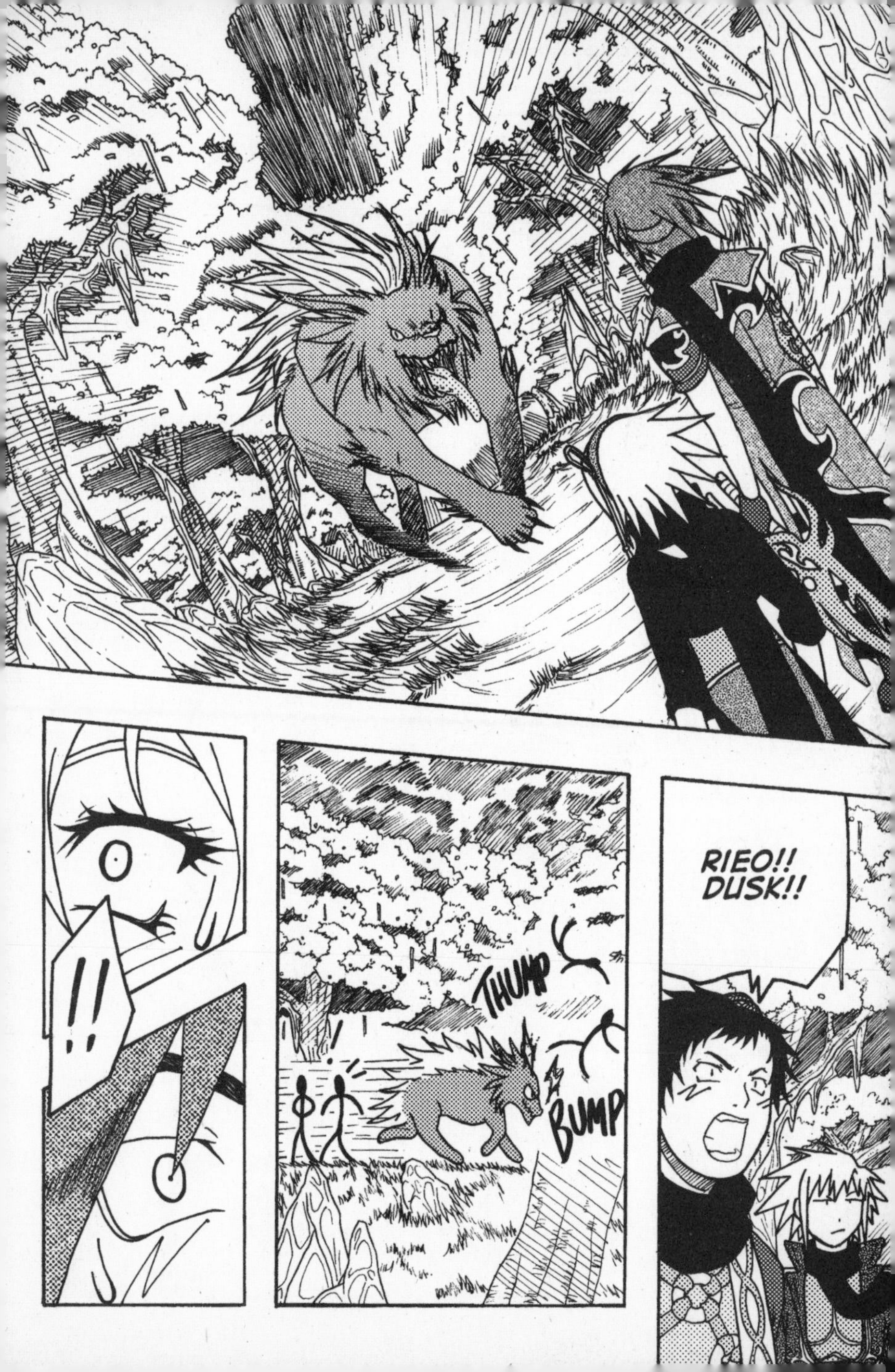
!!
THUMP
BUMP
RIEO!!
DUSK!!

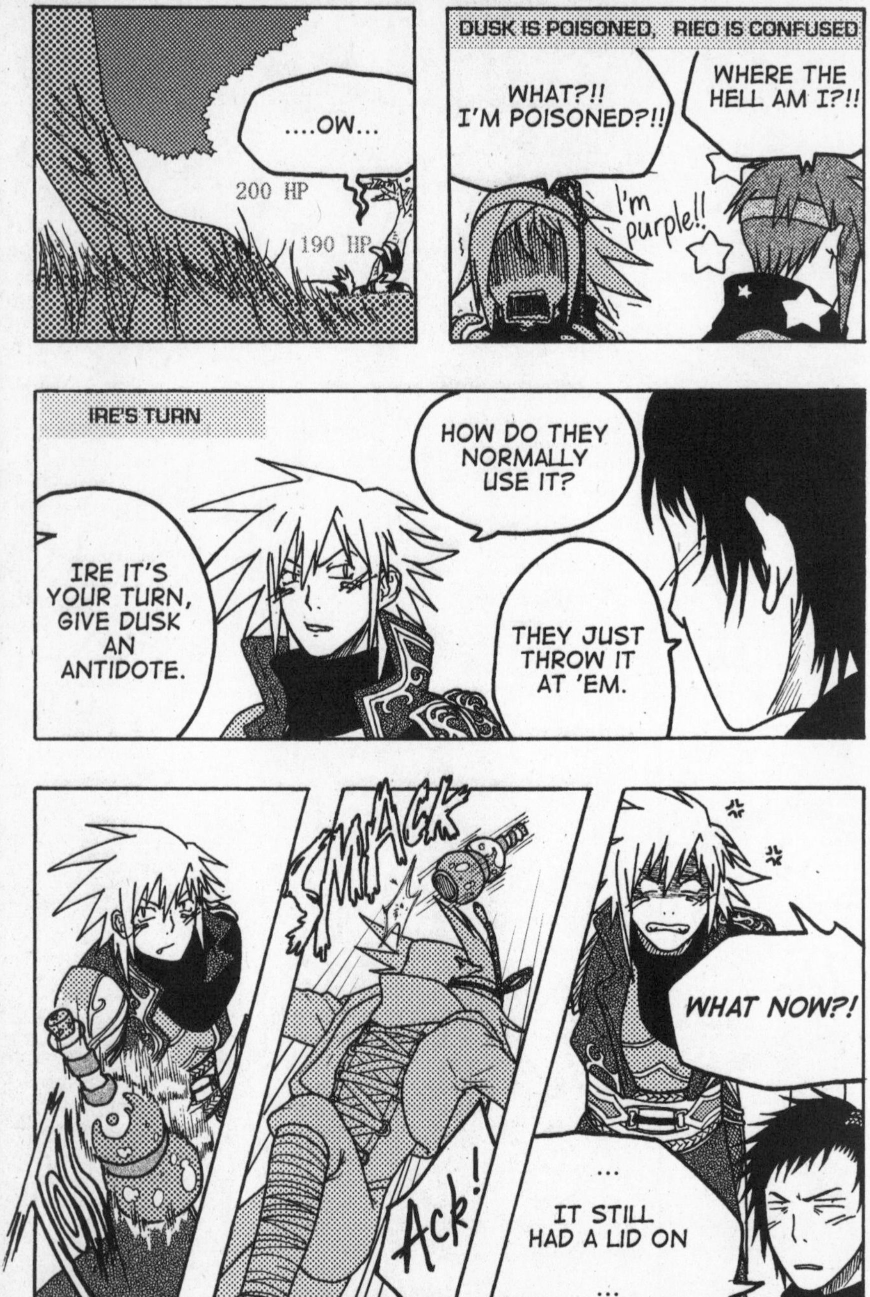
....OW...
200 HP
190 HP
DUSK IS POISONED, RIEO IS CONFUSED
WHAT?!! I'M POISONED?!!
WHERE THE HELL AM I?!!
I'm purple!!
IRE'S TURN
IRE IT'S YOUR TURN, GIVE DUSK AN ANTIDOTE.
HOW DO THEY NORMALLY USE IT?
THEY JUST THROW IT AT 'EM.
SMACK
Ack!
WHAT NOW?!
... IT STILL HAD A LID ON ...

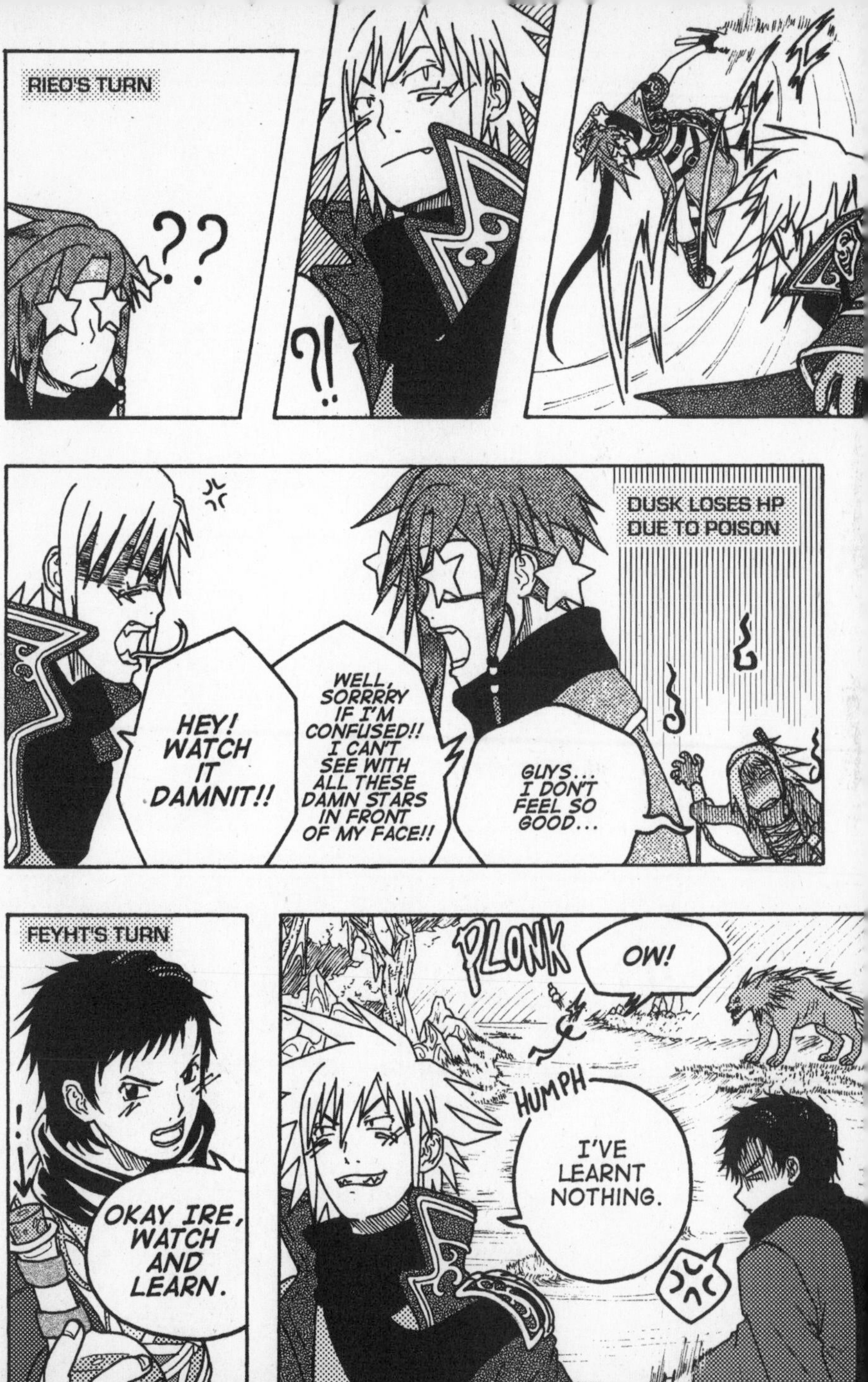
RIEO'S TURN
??
?!!
HEY! WATCH IT DAMNIT!!
WELL, SORRRRY IF I'M CONFUSED!! I CAN'T SEE WITH ALL THESE DAMN STARS IN FRONT OF MY FACE!!
DUSK LOSES HP DUE TO POISON
GUYS... I DON'T FEEL SO GOOD...
FEYHT'S TURN
OKAY IRE, WATCH AND LEARN.
PLONK
OW!
HUMPH
I'VE LEARNT NOTHING.

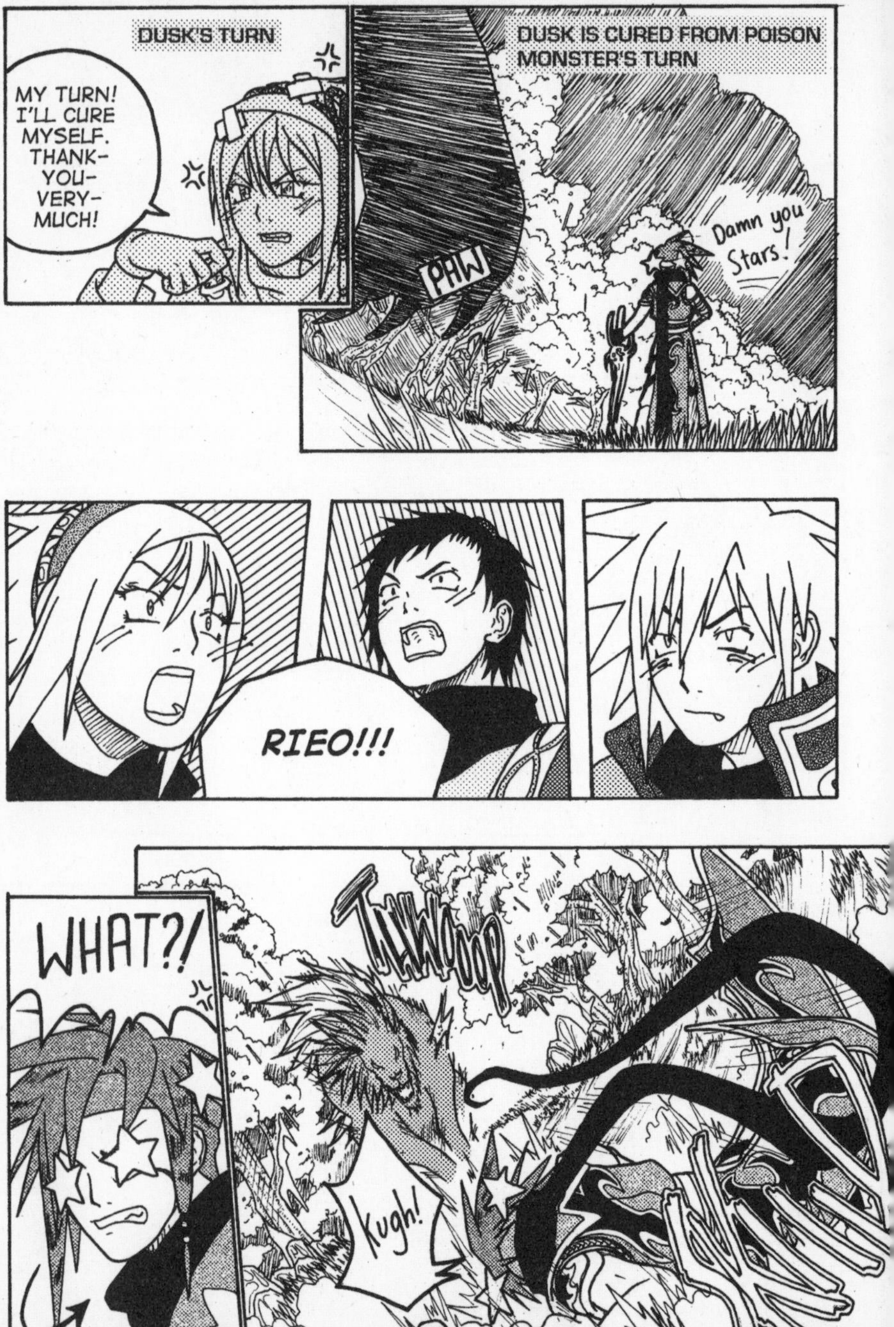
DUSK'S TURN
MY TURN! I'LL CURE MYSELF. THANK-YOU-VERY-MUCH!
DUSK IS CURED FROM POISON
MONSTER'S TURN
PAW
Damn you Stars!
RIEO!!!
TWWOOOP
WHAT?!
Kugh!

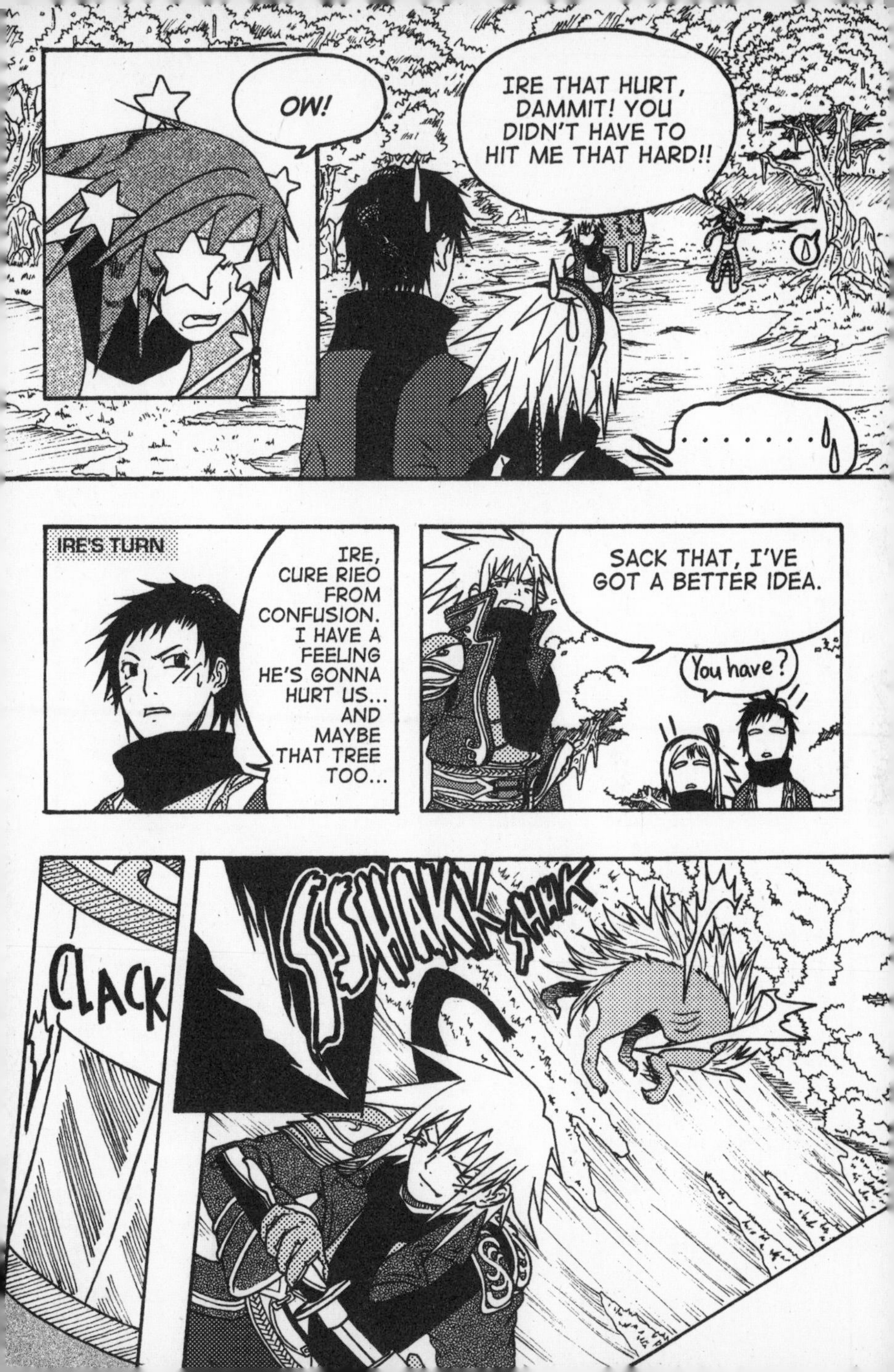
OW!
IRE THAT HURT, DAMMIT! YOU DIDN'T HAVE TO HIT ME THAT HARD!!
....
IRE'S TURN
IRE, CURE RIEO FROM CONFUSION. I HAVE A FEELING HE'S GONNA HURT US... AND MAYBE THAT TREE TOO...
SACK THAT, I'VE GOT A BETTER IDEA.
You have?
CLACK
SHAKK-SHAK

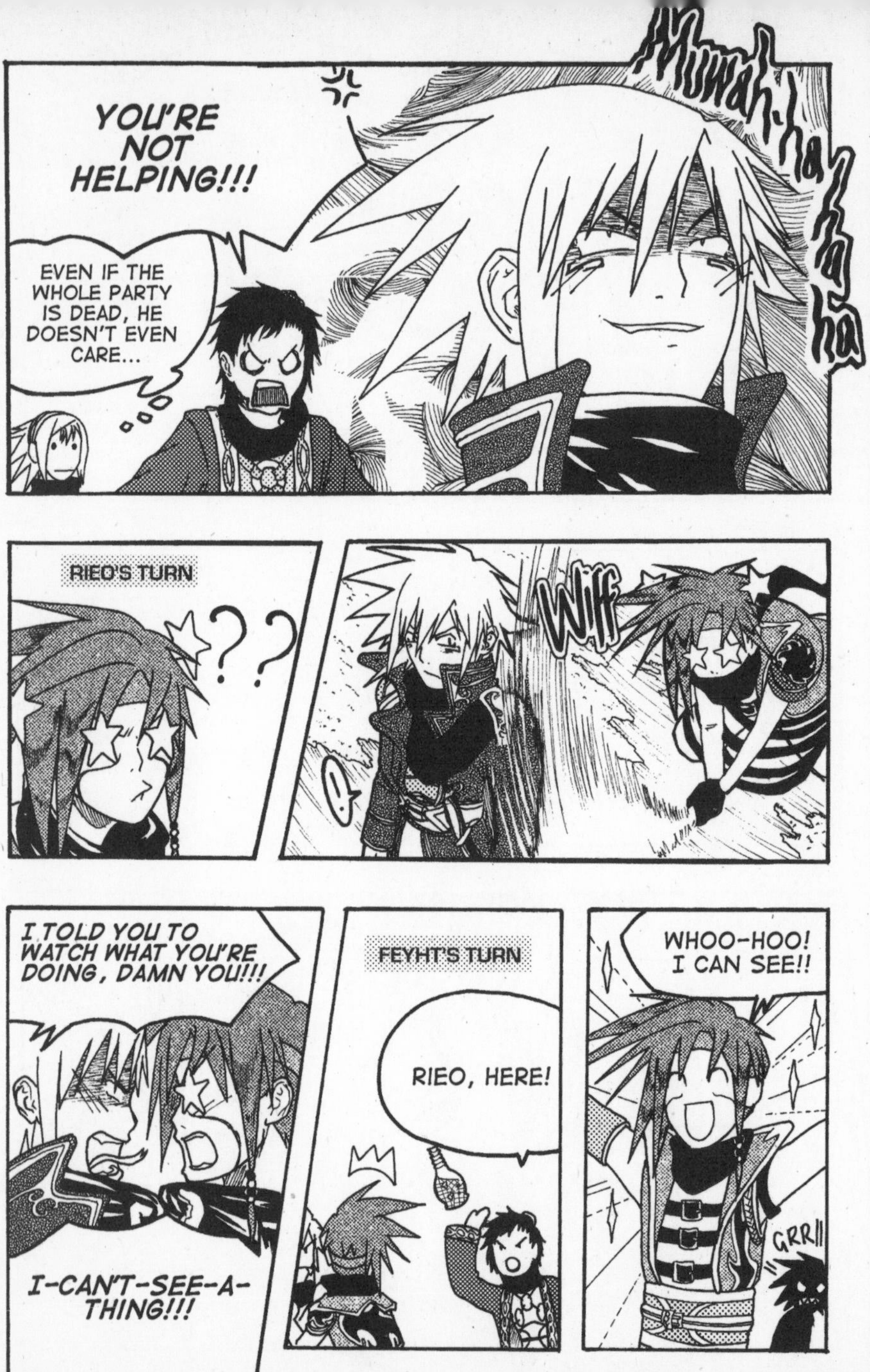
YOU'RE NOT HELPING!!!
EVEN IF THE WHOLE PARTY IS DEAD, HE DOESN'T EVEN CARE...
Muwah-ha-ha-ha-ha
RIEO'S TURN
Wiff
I TOLD YOU TO WATCH WHAT YOU'RE DOING, DAMN YOU!!!
I-CAN'T-SEE-A-THING!!!
FEYHT'S TURN
RIEO, HERE!
WHOO-HOO! I CAN SEE!!
GRR!!

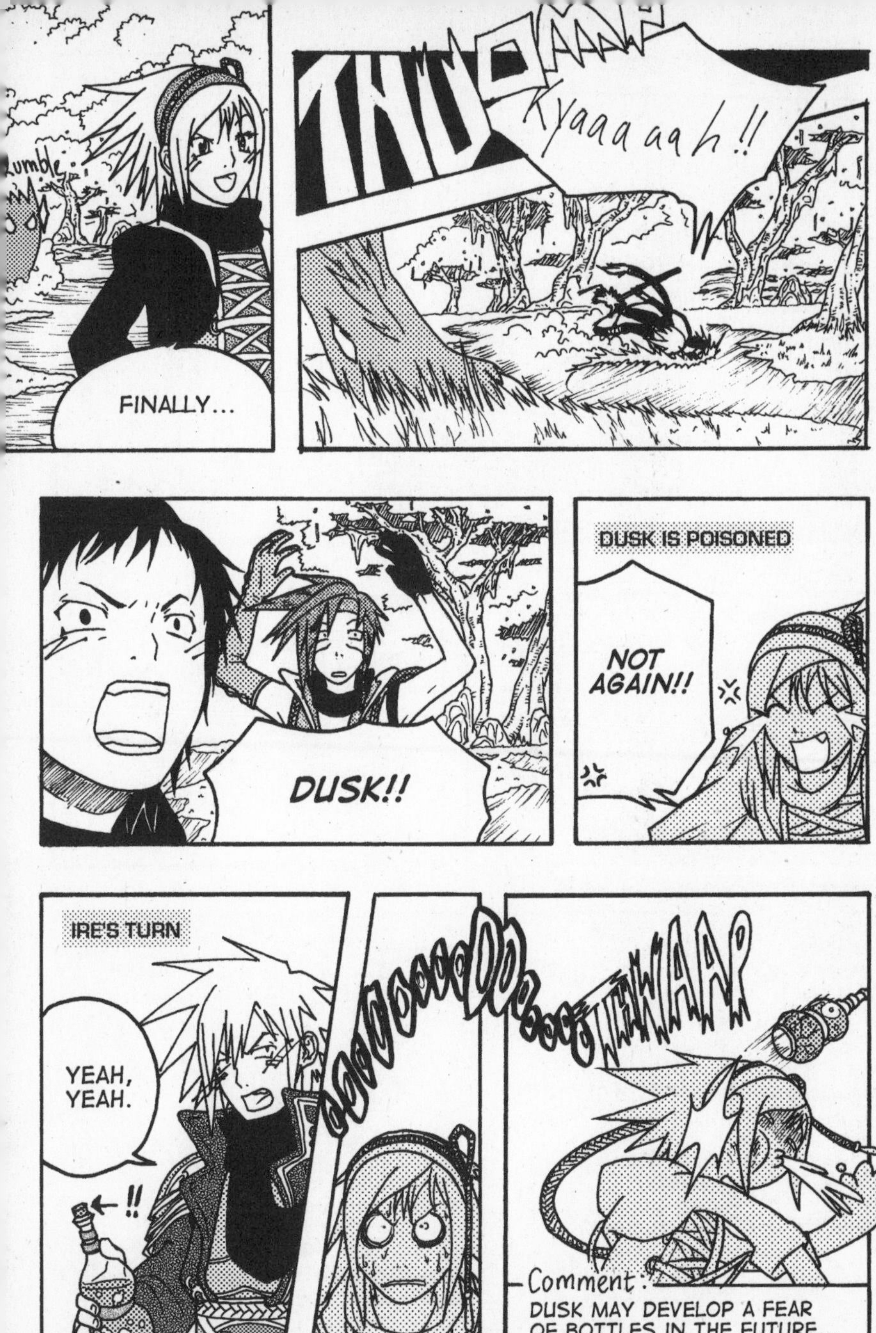
Rumble
FINALLY...
Kyaaaaaah!!
DUSK!!
DUSK IS POISONED
NOT AGAIN!!
IRE'S TURN
YEAH, YEAH.
!!
Comment:
DUSK MAY DEVELOP A FEAR OF BOTTLES IN THE FUTURE...

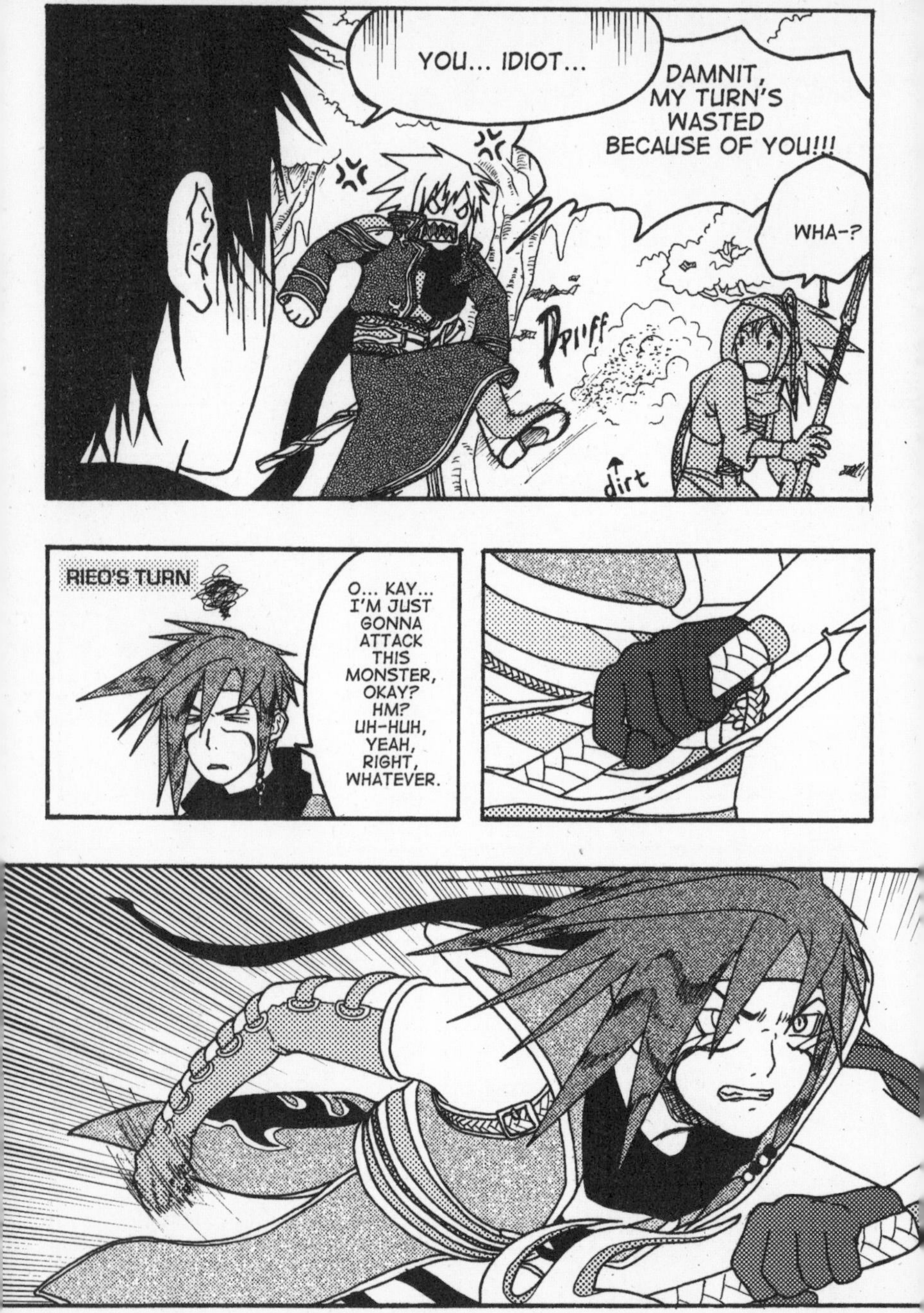
YOU... IDIOT...
DAMNIT, MY TURN'S WASTED BECAUSE OF YOU!!!
WHA-?
Ppfff
dirt
RIEO'S TURN
O... KAY... I'M JUST GONNA ATTACK THIS MONSTER, OKAY? HM? UH-HUH, YEAH, RIGHT, WHATEVER.

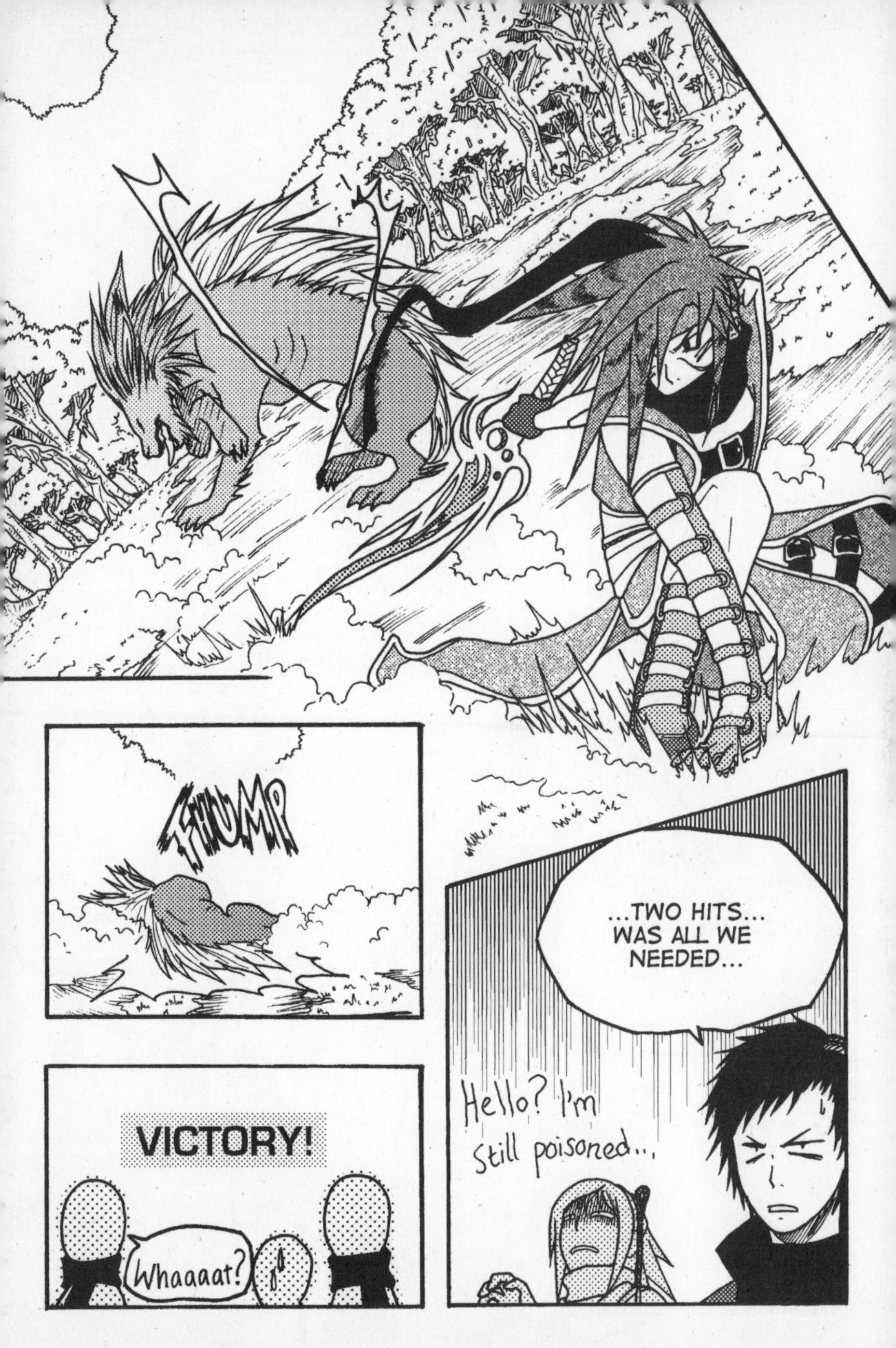
FHUMP
VICTORY!
Whaaaat?
...TWO HITS... WAS ALL WE NEEDED...
Hello? I'm still poisoned...

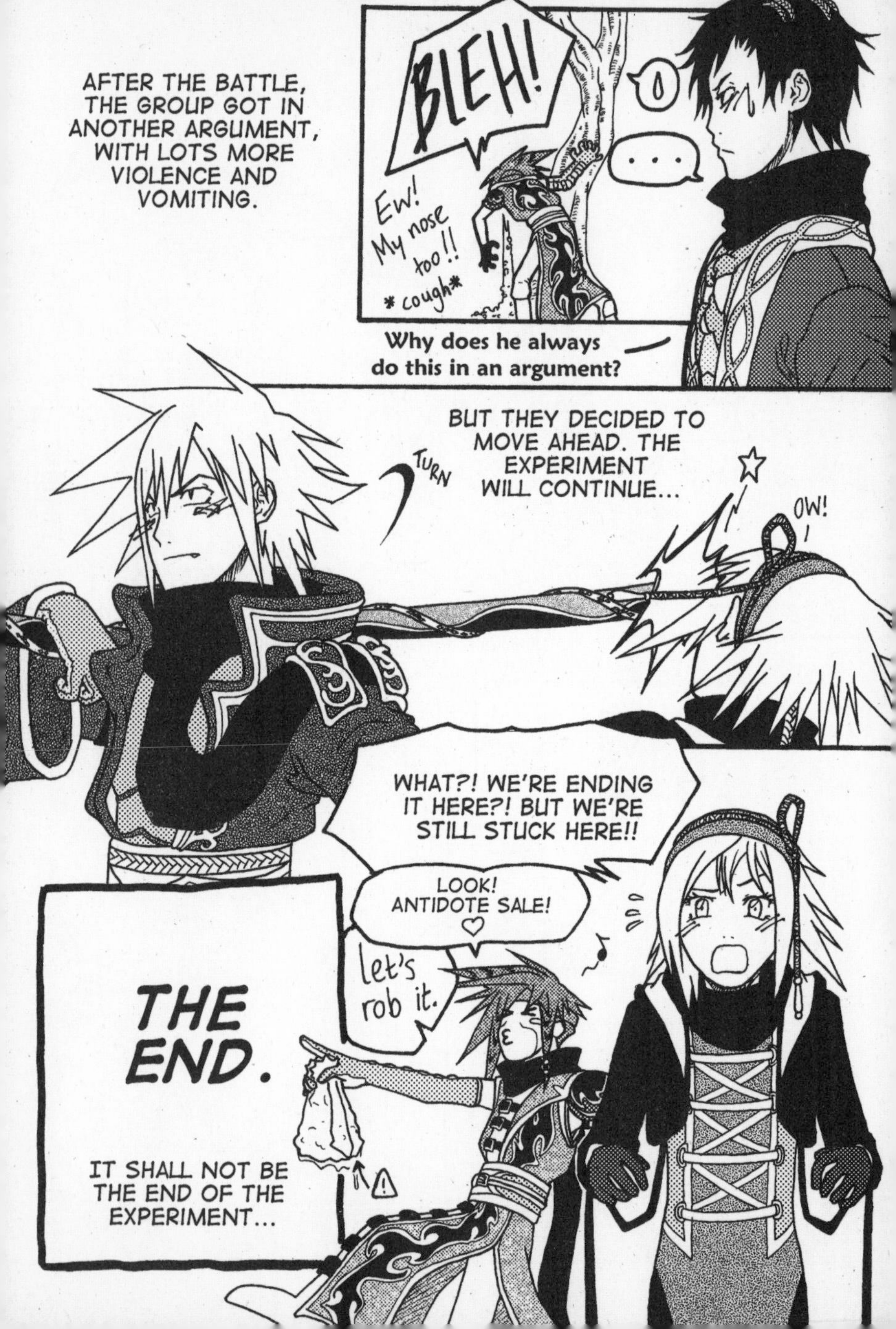
AFTER THE BATTLE, THE GROUP GOT IN ANOTHER ARGUMENT, WITH LOTS MORE VIOLENCE AND VOMITING.
BLEH!
Ew! My nose too!! *cough*
...
Why does he always do this in an argument?
TURN
BUT THEY DECIDED TO MOVE AHEAD. THE EXPERIMENT WILL CONTINUE...
OW!
THE END.
IT SHALL NOT BE THE END OF THE EXPERIMENT...
WHAT?! WE'RE ENDING IT HERE?! BUT WE'RE STILL STUCK HERE!!
LOOK! ANTIDOTE SALE! ♡
let's rob it.

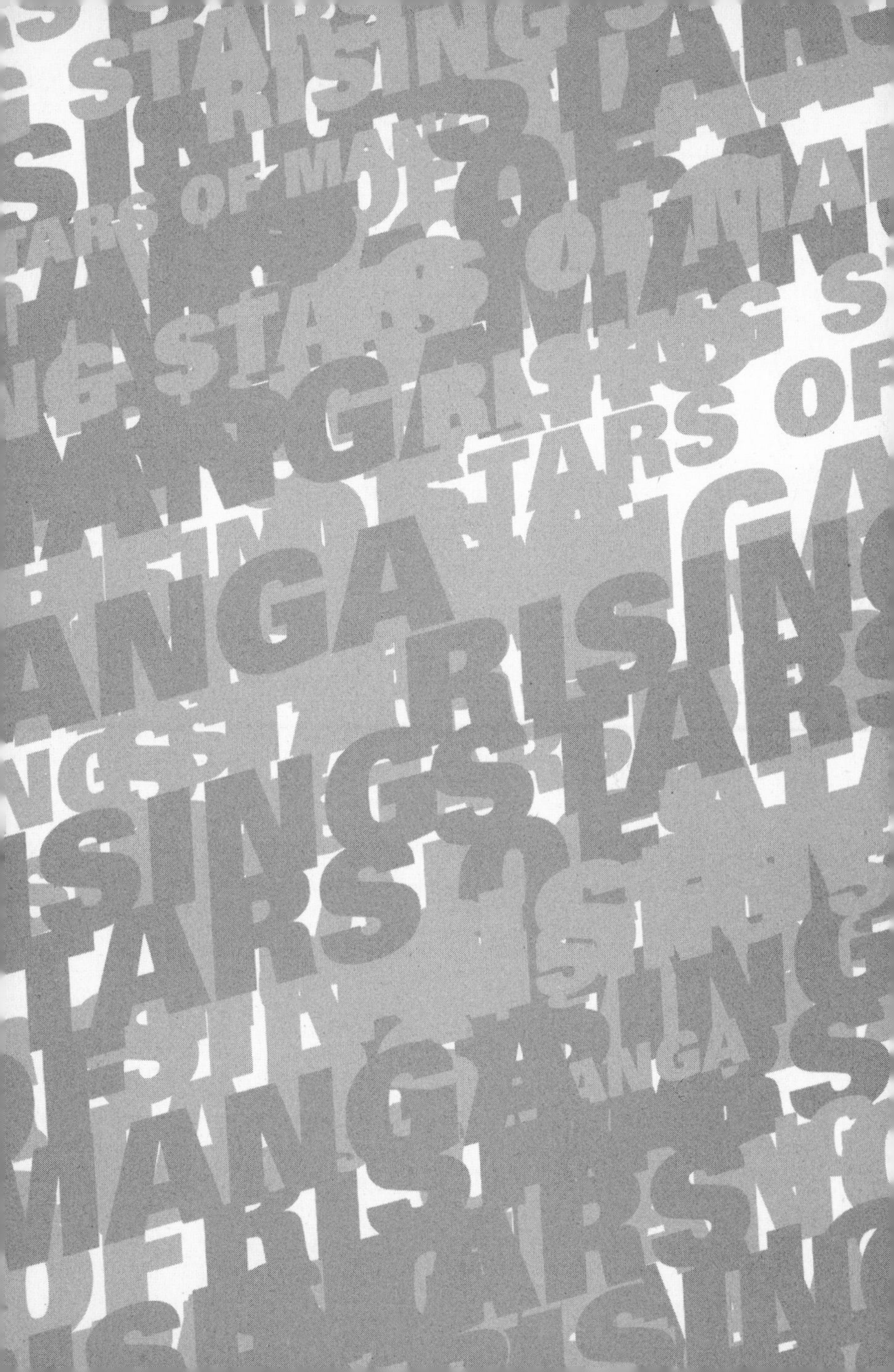

the RISING STARS of MANGA
United Kingdom and Ireland

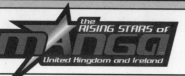

:WHERE ARE THEY NOW

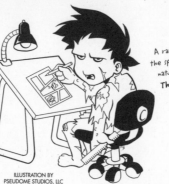

A rare image of the specimen in his natural habitat:
The RSoMbie.

ILLUSTRATION BY
PSEUDOME STUDIOS, LLC

"Want to be a manga artist? No one makes it easier than TOKYOPOP!"
-*WIZARD*

The grind of producing a complete 20-page manga is no small matter. Sleep deprivation, intense focus, and the absence of sunlight and outdoor air has contributed on numerous occasions to the RSoMbification of many fresh-faced manga-ka. Those that do not expire in the endeavor, however, face even greater challenges as they move onto professional projects with TOKYOPOP and other publishers. We are constantly seeking talented new manga-ka to both create and collaborate on original graphic novels. *Rising Stars of Manga* has not only exposed the talents of its finalists to the world, but has also been the proving-ground where we discover the best and brightest creative talent.

We thought it would be fun to catch up with these past winners, and preview some of their upcoming projects. These names are only the beginning. There are other finalists with whom we are working that cannot be announced at this time, and we trust that this success will continue with the winners from the volume you hold now in your hands. Hopefully these manga-ka will prove to be an inspiration to all the RSoMbies of future contests.
—*Brandon Montclare*

the RISING STARS of MANGA
United Kingdom and Ireland

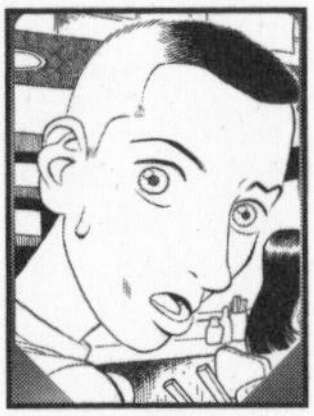

::
Wes Abbott
RSoM 2: "Dogby Walks Alone"
It's been a long, lonely walk for the fan favorite Happy Place mascot. At long last we are proud to announce that the *Dogby Walks Alone* Original Manga series is **available now!**
::

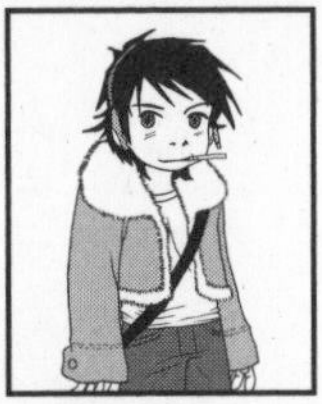

::
George Alexopoulus
RSoM 5: "Can I Sit Here?"
George can be seen applying his artistic skills to the Original Manga *Go With Grace*. **Available Now!**
::

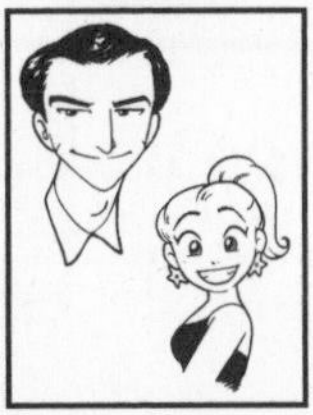

::
T Campbell & Amy Mebberson
RSoM 5: "Pop Star"
T and Amy have created an original expanded story based on their winning "Pop Star" entry. This series, now called *Divalicous!*, is spreading the fame of Tina Young worldwide. **Available Now!**
::

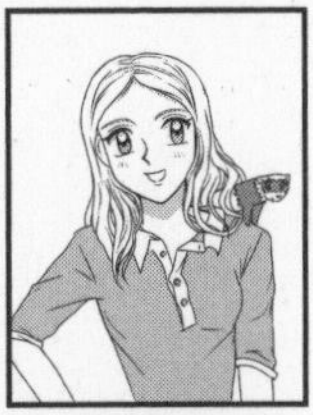

::
Lindsay Cibos
RSoM 2: "Peach Fuzz"
RSoM 2 Grand Prize entry "Peach Fuzz" is now an Original Manga series. Fun for all ages continues as we explore further the epic struggle inherent in the relationship between man (well, a girl) and beast (here, a ferret). *Peach Fuzz* was also serialized in many U.S. and Canadian newspapers. **Available Now!**
::

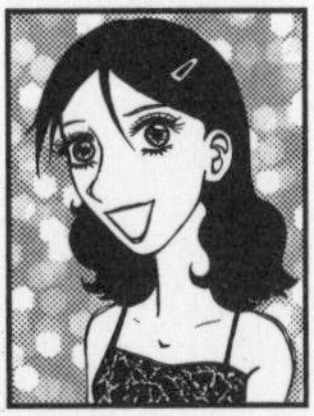

::
Tania Del Rio
RSoM 2: "Love Sketch"
We all loved her *RSoM* entry, and so did the editors at Archie Comics. Tania has picked up both the writing and art duties during her critically-acclaimed run on *Sabrina*. She's also working on an upcoming manga about quinceañeras for TOKYOPOP.
::

the RISING STARS of MANGA
United Kingdom and Ireland

::

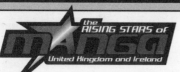

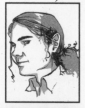

Paul Duffield
RSoM UK & Ireland 1: "Falling Star"
Congratulations to Grand Prize Winner Paul Duffield for being awarded "Overall Festival Winner" for a short animated film of his original project "Rolighed" at London's International Manga and Anime Festival November 2006.

::

::

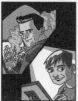

Joshua Elder & Erich Owen
RSoM 5: "Mail Order Ninja"
Top prize winners in RsoM 5, Erich and Josh have expanded the *Mail Order Ninja* mythos with a new ongoing series for TOKYOPOP. You can also see the adventures of boy and ninja unfold in the funny pages starting 2007.
Available Now!

::

::

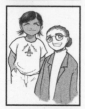

Irene Flores & Ashly Raiti
RSoM 3: "Life Remains"
Irene and Ashly wowed us with their touching relationship story in *RSoM 3*. The creators evidence a broad artistic range as they delve into the gothic genre with the Original Manga series *Mark of the Succubus*. **Available Now!**

::

::

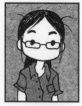

Amy Kim Ganter
RSoM 4: "The Hopeless Romantic and The Hapless Girl"
Amy proved she could handle the ups and downs of love in her *RSoM 4* Third Place entry. Fans can read about new misadventures in romance in the full-length Original Manga series *Sorcerers & Secretaries*. **Available Now!**

::

::

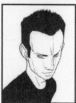

Shane Granger
RSoM 2: "Possessions"
The reader immediately feels the impact of Shane's pencils in his RSoM entry. His skill and creativity in penciling have been applied to the ongoing Original Manga series *Psy-Comm*.
Available Now!

::

the RISING STARS of MANGA
United Kingdom and Ireland

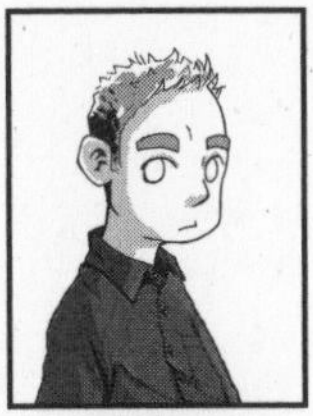

::
Andy Helms
RSoM 4: "Bombos versus Everything"
It turns out that everything is—well—a lot, so be on the lookout for more bat-smacking action in the full-length Original Manga series *Bombos versus Everything;* based on Andy's Grand Prize entry.
::

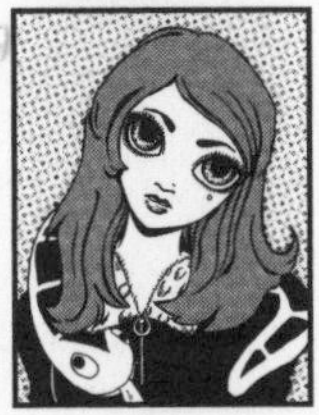

::
Marty LeGrow
RSoM 2: "Nikolai"
Marty's vision of manga impressed us with its innovative style and uncompromising attitude. Her unique flair is being applied to the new Original Manga series *Bizenghast*. **Available Now!**
::

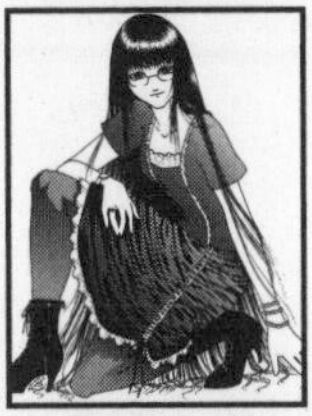

::
Sonia Leong
RSoM UK & Ireland 1: "Fatal Connection"
Her entry took us to ancient Japan, and now she's gone to Renaissance Italy to update classic Shakespeare in her full-length manga *Romeo and Juliet,* through Metromedia.
::

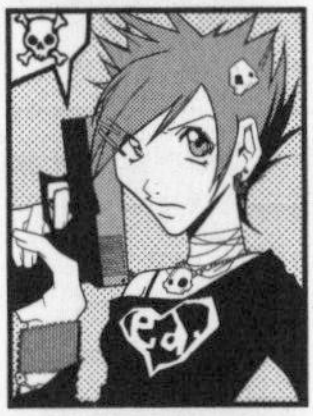

::
Christy Lijewski
RSoM 3: "Doors"
After her *RSoM* entry helped her land a gig at Slave Labor Graphics on the creator-owned *Next Exit* series, Christy returned to the TOKYOPOP fold with the full-length Original Manga *Re:Play.* **Available Now!**
::

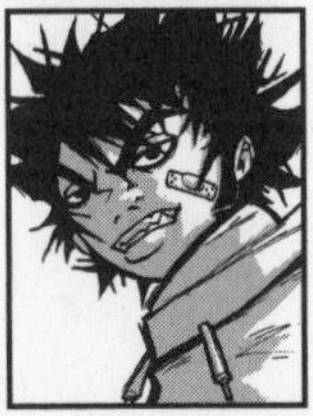

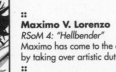

::
Maximo V. Lorenzo
RSoM 4: "Hellbender"
Maximo has come to the aid of fellow *RSoM 4* winner Andy Helms by taking over artistic duties on *Bombos versus Everything.*
::

the RISING STARS of MANGA
United Kingdom and Ireland

::
Morgan Luthi
RSoM 5: "Seed"
Morgan has taken on the challenge of creating a whole new series for TOKYOPOP called *Snow*. **Available Now!**
::

::
Nathan Maurer
RSoM 3: "Atomic King Daidogan"
A mix of wild hilarity, over-the-top action, and lovable characters made "Atomic King Daidogan" the top entry in *RSoM 3*. His Grand Prize entry is now a full-length Original Manga.
Available Now!
::

::
Karen Remsen
RSoM 4: "Le Masque"
Look for her original "Chronicles of Koryo" back-up feature in *Threads of Time 7*.
::

::
Michael Schwark & Ron Kaulfersch
RSoM 1: "Van Von Hunter"
Elder statesmen to RSoMbies everywhere, Mike and Ron continue to sponsor *RSoM* hopefuls on the forums at www.pseudome.net. And keeping up the street cred, their Second Place entry from *RSoM 1* is now the Original Manga series *Van Von Hunter* and has been serialized in newspapers, too. **Available Now!**
::

::
Michael Shelfer
RSoM 5: "Blue Phoenix: No Quarter"
RSoM 5's online People's Choice winner has taken on the artist duties for an original story in TOKYOPOP's new *Star Trek* manga anthology. **Available Now!**
::

the RISING STARS of MANGA United Kingdom and Ireland

::

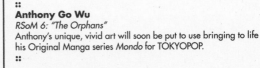

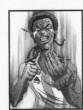

Felipe Smith

RSoM 3: "Manga"

The Second Place entry in *RSoM 3* made every editor fear slightly for our lives. Luckily, it turns out that Felipe is really a nice guy. Check out his latest manga creation: *MBQ*. **Available Now!**

::

::

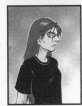

Jess Stoncius

RSoM 4: "Work Bites"

Work still bites. Catch up with the dark tribulations of the wannabe-lord-of-the-night-yet-stuck-in-my-crappy-job-at-the-mall vampire Lars in the forthcoming full-length Original Manga series *Work Bites*.

::

::

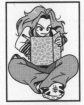

Emma Vieceli

RSoM UK & Ireland 1: "Between the Lines"

Emma has taken her flair for drama to a graphic novel adaptation of *Hamlet* for Metromedia. She has also contributed to a number of manga tutorials and has published a short story in Sweatdrop Studios' *Pink is For Girls*.

::

::

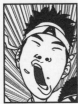

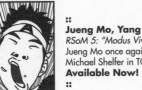

Jueng Mo, Yang

RSoM 5: "Modus Vivendi"

Jueng Mo once again finds himself alongside fellow *RSoM 5* alumni Michael Shelfer in TOKYOPOP's *Star Trek* anthology.

Available Now!

::

::

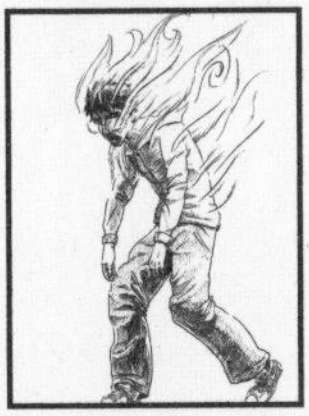

Anthony Go Wu

RSoM 6: "The Orphans"

Anthony's unique, vivid art will soon be put to use bringing to life his Original Manga series *Mondo* for TOKYOPOP.

::

::

TIPS FOR MANGA-KA

Maybe this volume of *Rising Stars of Manga* has inspired you to take a hands-on approach in the manga revolution. Or perhaps you are one of the thousands of aspiring creators who have already entered one of our previous competitions. Either way, if you want your own manga star to rise, it's best that you review the following tips provided by our editors.

LAYOUT:

Before you begin your pencilling, you should map out each page in very rough thumbnails. Plan ahead as to how you want to establish the panels, and where you will place the objects and characters within the panels. Also remember to leave enough room for appropriately-sized word balloons. Having a solid plan of attack ensures that your manga will not get out of control. More importantly, it forces you to think about your storytelling—make sure every panel has an individual attitude as well as a direct purpose to the story as a whole.

Advanced Layout Tips:

★ Be sure to vary the reader's viewpoint from panel-to-panel. Zoom in or out with panel depth; and employ worm's eye and bird's eye perspectives. Maintaining a steady, unmoving camera throughout will make your manga appear stagnant and slow, so have fun and be creative!

★ Keep the pacing of each individual page moving forward. More so than in other sequential art mediums, manga is meant to have a fast and even pace. Generally, you want your manga to be a "page-turner" where the reader's eye never stops.

SCRIPT:

It has been our experience that most *RSoM* creators are artists first and writers second. Therefore, recognize your limitations and work within them. Try to tell uncomplicated stories that do not depend on excessive amounts of exposition or development. Also be sure that your story is complete, with a begining, a middle, and an end. Yes, there have been winning entries in *RSoM* without a satisfying ending. But nothing infuriates a judge more than a "to be continued" tagged onto the last page, or a story that has no ending at all. Your manga stands a much better chance of being published if it is definitive and understandable; rarely will you lose points for being too simple. Also, add the dialogue and narration to your thumbnail layout. You can always go back and tweak the script after your artwork is finished, but it is good to nail down a narrative pace early in the creative process.

Advanced Scripting Tips:

★ Write what you know. This axiom of creative writing survives because it is efficient more often than not.

★ Consider collaborating with a writer. Find someone who shares your passion with manga storytelling and with whom you can work comfortably. Work together and pool your strengths toward creating the very best entry.

:RSoM TIPS

PENCILS:

Here your raw talent will carry you. The best thing you can do to improve your rendering is repeated practice. As you draw, be mindful of the nuances particular to manga aesthetics. More so than other sequential art mediums, manga favors simplicity in art. You should not include meticulous, minute detail as it tends to slow down the pace of your manga. For the same reason, your art should fit into fewer panels per page. While the visual pace is often faster, manga artists usually need to concentrate more on character rendering—including body language and character expression—than other sequential art mediums. Also, remember to keep your manga consistent between panels. Make sure anatomy, clothing, and objects remain visually constant throughout.

Advanced Pencilling Tips:

★ Study Life Drawing. Most communities will have affordable Life Drawing classes available for every level of student. These classes will help refine all of your pencilling skills, especially in perspective and anatomy.

★ Learn to draw backgrounds and show us your ability to have characters interact with their environment. You are not fooling anyone when you set all your scenes in a room with four blank walls, an inter-dimensional void, or at night.

FINISHES:

Finishes refer to the inking and toning of your manga. Both of these are done to embellish your pencils, as well as to add depth and texture to the pages. As with layout and pencilling, your finished art should be informed by traditional manga aesthetics. Manga inking is primarily a technique for defining your line-work. Manga inkers should avoid cross-hatching or other shading methods. Don't think of your manga as black-and-white. Rather, you should approach finishes as coloring in grayscale. As in inking, tones add to the depth and definition of your art. The infinite patterns and shades can also be used to facilitate storytelling by setting moods, establishing contrasts and contributing purely to the beauty of the work.

Advanced Finishing Tips:

★ Vary your line-weight when inking. Varying the width of your lines will add dimension and depth to finished pencils. Invariable line-weight tends to flatten your rendering and stall any sense of the object's or character's motion.

★ Use digital tones. While the use of zipotone is a noble profession, it is a difficult and often heartbreaking endeavor that is being replaced, even in Japan, by digital tones. Digital tones are easier to manipulate, allow for greater experimentation, and are more cost effective. Be sure to tone your art at final size and save your pages as layered files.

LETTERING:

Just remember that it counts! Interesting fonts are great, but make sure they are crisp and clear. You can use different fonts for different characters or narrative situations, but don't go overboard with variation. Don't use fonts with serifs, as they are often unclear and do not reproduce well inside word balloons. Remember not to crowd panels with script, and be certain not to cover up important areas of your art with word balloons. Don't forget to incorporate your word balloons and lettering into the thumbnail layout. And, please, **remember to proofread your manga.**

INSIDER INFO:

So, you have your entry for the next *Rising Stars of Manga* and you are sure it will blow our mind. To reward those who make it this far, the judges want to offer a few helpful hints.

★ Shoot for 17 pages. One of the most common problems is poorly paced manga (sometimes even appearing unfinished after 20 pages). When you plan your manga, pace it for 17 pages. This allows you room to either add or remove pages as it develops on the drawing board.

★ Send it in early. As soon as we receive a qualified entry it goes into a pile that can be read by our editors. While every entry is reviewed by at least one judge, entries that are around longer naturally have an increased chance of being read by several editors (and the more people who read it, the greater the chance that someone will recognize your genius). Also, if you plan to send it in early, you allow yourself more time to correct any last minute mistakes that may arise.

★ Less story is more. Another common problem is entries with so much story squeezed into them that the final product is convoluted and indecipherable. Save your complex tales for a multi-volume project down the road, and don't use *RSoM* to pitch your personal magnum opus. Focus instead on a short, easy-to-tell manga where you can exhibit your skills as a visual storyteller.

★ Enter *Rising Stars of Manga*. This is really not as dumb as it sounds. Even if you aren't a finalist, you should approach every competition as preparation for a future in manga. You will notice that each entry will improve upon the last, and that you are progressing toward a level of professional talent. And you know who else notices? We do. With six US and two UK competitions now on the books, our editors often notice new manga from previous entrants. While we can't offer personal feedback to every *RSoM* manga-ka, there are creators for whom we are silently rooting, and we look forward to their entries in each competition.

Also, use the resources available on the TOKYOPOP website. Besides the mechanical specifications on the *RSoM* webpage, the *RSoM* webpage contains hints and tips similar to the ones listed here. Most importantly, the webpage has the definitive contest rules, a must-have if you want to avoid disqualification. The TOKYOPOP website is also a great source of info and support. Whether you read the message boards or shuffle through the art posted by other aspiring manga-ka, there's a lot to learn, and a lot of community to participate in. Wherever you find your support and inspiration, we can't wait to see what you can do! Good luck, and see you in the next *RSoM!*

—*Brandon Montclare & Hope Donovan*

::

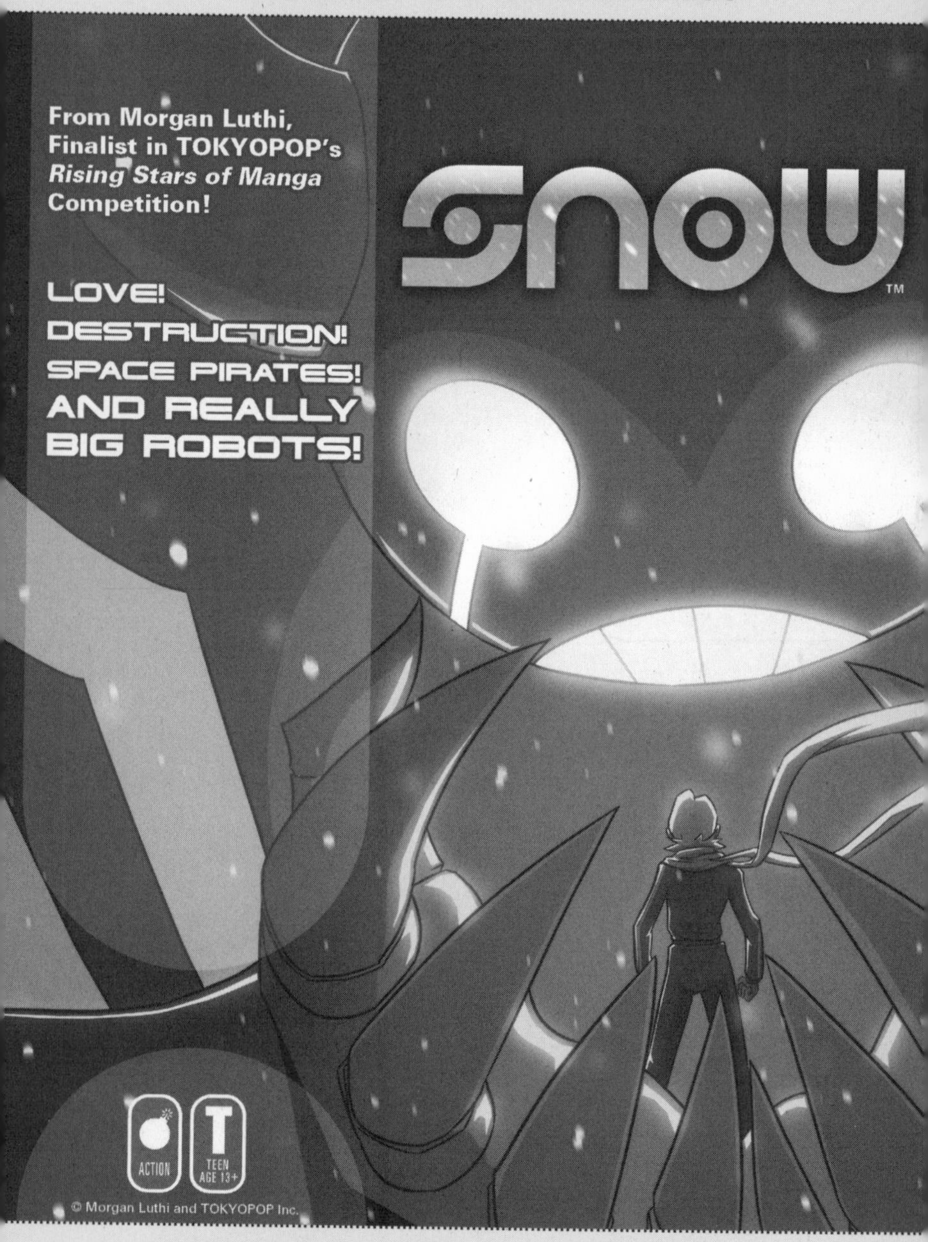
From Morgan Luthi,
Finalist in TOKYOPOP's
Rising Stars of Manga
Competition!
SNOW™
LOVE!
DESTRUCTION!
SPACE PIRATES!
AND REALLY
BIG ROBOTS!
ACTION
T
TEEN
AGE 13+
© Morgan Luthi and TOKYOPOP Inc.